# A Practical Approach to Costume Design and Construction

## VOLUME II

# A Practical Approach to Costume Design and Construction

## VOLUME II

# *Construction*

## Beverly Jane Thomas

*Florida Atlantic University*

ALLYN AND BACON, INC.

Boston   London   Sydney   Toronto

*Frontispiece:* Historical source, the Duc du Berry's *Book Of The Hours* (left), and the finished costume as used in Shaw's *St. Joan* (right).

*Illustrations in this book were drawn by the author.*

Copyright © 1982 by Allyn and Bacon, Inc., 470 Atlantic Avenue, Boston, Massachusetts 02210. All rights reserved. No part of the material protected by this copyright notice may be reproduced or utilized in any form or by any means, electronic or mechanical, including photocopying, recording, or by any information storage and retrieval system, without written permission from the copyright owner.

**Library of Congress Cataloging in Publication Data**

Thomas, Beverly Jane.
  A practical approach to costume design and construction.

  Bibliography: v. 1, p.  v. 2, p.
  Includes indexes.
  Contents: v. 1. Fundamentals and design—v. 2. Construction.
  1. Costume design.  2. Costume.  I. Title.
TT507.T466      792'.026      81-7950
ISBN 0-205-07273-9 (v. 1)      AACR2
ISBN 0-205-07367-0 (v. 2)

*Managing Editor:* Robert Roen

Printed in the United States of America.

Printing number and year (last digits):
10 9 8 7 6 5 4 3 2 1    86 85 84 83 82 81

# Contents

# Introduction

You have mastered the hypothetical design and are standing in an empty costume room. You now reach that well-known question, "Okay, now what do I do?" Perhaps you remember those collegiate posters that said, "Tomorrow I've got to get organized." Well, tomorrow has come at last.

Organization is the key factor in going from the idea to the production. Of course, you may be one of the fortunate few who can turn their designs over to a commercial construction house and never touch a pair of scissors or a needle. If you are, you don't need this book. That, however, is a position that is more frequently earned after many years of hard work, long hours, and bloody fingers.

As with *A Practical Approach to Costume Design, Volume I*, I should like to keep to a conversational format. I should also like to reiterate a few basics that apply to this book as well. Circumstances vary, not only between the commercial and non-commercial theater, but within types of theater organizations.

An empty costume room may be just what is needed in a community theater situation, in which the actual sewing is not done on the premises but is farmed out and done in many homes, or most of the costumes are rented. Then that room may be used strictly for storage.

In Chapter 1, when I speak of setting up a costume shop, I am basically referring to a university and/or resident theater situation, even perhaps a potentially commercial construction house of your own. The requirements for a stock company or touring company would be limited considerably from those mentioned in Chapter 1 to those of strictly a wardrobe person's requirements. Stock of one- or two-week turn-arounds requires little more than washing, drying, and light repair facilities. Touring companies carry light repair facilities with them and depend more often than not on commercial laundry and dry cleaning establishments.

I once worked in a stock company that got kicked out of its theater and moved into a barn. We literally cleared out the animals one day, disinfected the next, and on the third day I set up a costume shop in what had been the stall of a Brahma bull. I certainly don't wish those circumstances on anyone, but it was indeed a "varied situation." You have to be prepared to meet all kinds of them.

This book is oriented toward the "how-to" of construction. Have you noticed that costumers always "build" or "construct" a costume, while dressmakers "make" a dress? I think there is an important distinction here which needs an explanation. In Part 5 (miscellaneous tricks of the trade) I discuss this difference in literal technique terms, but a word or two should be said in figurative ones as well. Practically speaking, a costume gets far more wear (and tear, if one isn't careful) than the everyday garment. I know you're saying to yourself, "But it's only worn for four hours a night, for X number of nights." True, but look what happens to it during those few hours.

First of all, the theatrical situation in which a costume finds itself is always one of exaggeration and/or conflict, two of the basic ingredients of all plays. The energy level of the character is heightened, to say nothing of the energy level of the actor portraying it. The everyday garment does not get stabbed every night, a pie in the eye, duel broadsword, fall off the top of buildings, or sail through the air. It is therefore necessary to fortify the costume to make it stronger than the ordinary garment.

On the other hand, in the normal theatrical situation the costume does not get the close scrutiny that the everyday garment receives. Remember the costumer's byword: "Don't worry about it if you can't see it from three feet away" or "on a flying horse." This predisposes the normal situation to a proscenium stage. If you are working in a small house or an arena situation, this obviously doesn't hold water. So some of the lack of finishing touches which you can eliminate in the proscenium house have to be done for the arena situation.

There are many ways to design a costume. There are many techniques used to construct them. Some are old, tried, and true. This book is not devoted to sewing techniques, except where specifically oriented to the costume craft. You should already know how to sew. If not, I suggest you learn. You may wish to enroll in some home economics courses or a basic construction course in your theater department. If you are not in a formalized schooling situation, you may want to take a sewing course offered by any number of places—community adult education classes, local department stores, or sewing centers. Places that sell sewing machines have a vested interest in teaching you.

If self-taught, you might want to add a good sewing techniques book to your library. I personally am partial to *The Vogue Sewing Book* published by Vogue Patterns, New York, 1975. My partiality is due to its completeness right down to directions on how to make Chinese frog closures.

The varied techniques discussed in this book work for me (some more than others). Several I have "re-invented" by taking an idea and adapting it to my own needs. Some of these processes are in general use, but are found scattered through many books. I have attempted to collect these and clarify them for the progression used in costume manufacture.

My system of pattern drafting is one I have devised through adaptation, invention, and compilation over a twenty-year period. It works and is easily explainable, but there is absolutely no system that will account for all the variations possible with the human form. Therefore, there are no substitutions for fittings. Also, I am constantly learning new techniques.

To do any pattern drafting, you must work from measurements. At the end of this introduction are male and female measurement charts for the "ideal" male and female figures, according to manufacturer's standard sizes. These are for the scaled patterns you will find throughout this book *and so marked.* The female is 5'6" tall (without shoes) and wears a

size 12 dress. The male is 5'10" and wears a 38 regular suit. All patterns are scaled $\frac{1}{8}$" = 1" unless it is a particularly large piece. In that case $\frac{1}{16}$" = 1" will be used; *all are marked.* Unscaled pattern ideas are so marked. In the $\frac{1}{8}$" to 1" patterns the seam allowance is marked except for those patterns that use stretch fabrics. When the scale is reduced to $\frac{1}{16}$" to 1", it is impossible to mark the seam allowance. You will need to do this after you have increased the scale.

For historical accuracy I have tried to use actual garments when available, paintings contemporary with the various periods, and in some cases even contemporary cartoons. There are times of course when these methods are slightly faulty, in which case I, like all of my fellow designers, adapt to what we interpret to be correct because it achieves the period line.

This is particularly true for certain undergarments (Chapter 3). It was not until the Baroque period that painters paid much attention to the everyday person. Thank heavens for those few who did—such as the Brueghels and the Limouge brothers who illustrated the Duc du Berry's *Book Of The Hours.*

At this time I should like to thank all those at the various museums all over the world that helped me dig through backlogs and trunks and allowed me close perusal of their displays: The Brooklyn Museum, U.S.A.; The Victoria and Albert Museum and the Assembly Room Museum of Costume at Bath, England; the Museum of Childhood, Scotland; The Viking Museum, Norway; The Louvre, Le Musee Des Arts Decorative, The Jeu de Paume, The Montmartre Musee des Les Enfants, France; and The Museum of Fine Arts in Tokyo, Japan. You may be asking yourself why I should dig into toy museums. Dolls are an excellent source of clothing construction. Before the days of fashion plates, dolls were used by dressmakers as illustrations of their craft. These are known to doll collectors as fashion dolls. Their clothing is often an exact miniature of the life-size models.

I should also like to thank the countless people who donated their antique and period clothing to me over the last 25 years. They proved to be an invaluable source of patterns and techniques.

# A Practical Approach to Costume Design and Construction

## VOLUME II

# ONE

# Preparation for Construction

You are almost ready to begin actual construction but first you must do some special preparation. You will need to find a shop or at least organize one if you are starting fresh. If the job is new, you will have to familiarize yourself with existing stock and costume equity. In most cases you will probably wish to reorganize it to suit your preferences. You may need to order certain equipment and basic supplies. You will have to prepare measurement charts and take measurements. You might have to find or construct certain underpinnings before you can construct the exterior garments.

I made an appointment with a budding young actor for a measurement call in early June. The first dress rehearsal was four weeks away. He failed to keep his appointment and when questioned by the stage manager, he said, "Is my costume done already?" I asked the stage manager if he thought we were leprechauns. Remember, it is not done by magic but by careful preparation and long hours of hard work.

# 1

# Setting Up a Costume Shop

I would love to be able to set down the ideal shop so that all you would have to do is copy it. I've worked in countless theaters, have visited friends in countless others, and, frankly, have yet to find an ideal shop.

### How Much Construction Is Required

The first thing you must decide is how much actual construction you wish to do. If you are only going to build for three or four plays a year, your requirements would be very simple compared to those who do eight and twelve productions during that same time span. If you decide to build only the ladies' garments and rent the gentlemen's, or have them tailored elsewhere, you would not need the same equipment as those who build both, plus jewelry, hats, wigs, shoes, and hand props (fans, parasols, armor, swords, etc.). Do you also do the drapes and upholstery on your machines? These criteria must be decided upon.

### How Much Personnel Is Required

The next question is how big a staff do you need? Is this a one-person operation with occasional outside free labor? Are you completely staffed with cutters, fitters, tailors, seamstresses, milliners, pressers, and finishers? Most of us fall somewhere between these two extremes.

### Special Requirements

The next problem is space. You need space for cutting tables, ironing boards, sewing machines, dyeing and laundry tubs, washing machines, dryers, and storage for fabric to be constructed, to say nothing of the countless notions required in the sewing

process. You also need racks and shelves for hanging and stacking newly constructed items. You will need space for storing your backlog of previously constructed items. This should include drawer space, shelves, and hanging space.

It is very convenient to have all this space in one connected area, but not absolutely necessary. I know of one university that for many years had a room approximately 12' × 24' with long built-in drawers, floor to ceiling on all four walls. It was appropriately nicknamed the "coffin" room. A permanent ladder on ceiling tracks moved up and down the middle. It was a wonderful storage area for a thousand different items. Each drawer was labeled as to what it carried and what period (correct and up-to-date labeling saves hours).

Outer garments should be hung. Underwear and all types of knitted garments can be stored in boxes. Hats, shoes, and wigs may be stored on shelves.

Your storage area should be dry, and the temperature should remain between 48°F and 80°F. Costumes must be stored clean. If you use fiberglass, felt stiffener, spray paint, or carbon tetrachloride (dry cleaning fluid) in any quantity, your work area needs to be well ventilated.

It is often advisable to keep your wet work areas separated from dry. Wet work areas include the laundry items. By all means keep all small electrical appliances away from wet areas.

### Equipment Requirements for Basic Construction

A good rule of thumb for adequate production might be the following:

1. *2 ironing boards*
2. *2 professional steam irons that work on distilled water and have a fine shot of steam available with the press of a lever*

3. 2 cutting tables 45" wide by 72" long by at least 48" high, so you don't break your back constantly leaning down. An excellent substitute for the 2 cutting tables (if you have the space) is an enormous pingpong table raised to 48" in height.
4. A series of unpainted furniture chests to fit under the cutting tables for drawer storage without wasted space
5. 5 sewing machines
   a. 2 dressmakers in cabinets that do straight stitch, zigzag, have drop arms, buttonholes, and blind hem stitch
   b. 1 dressmaker in a cabinet that does everything, as many fancy stitches as possible, smocking, stretch stitch and 2 needle embroidery without pressure foot or feeder teeth
   c. One heavy duty commercial straight stitch machine (particularly necessary for drops, drapes and upholstery)
   d. One very light portable that will run anywhere on any current and can be taken with you practically on stage
6. Double, big, old-fashioned laundry tubs
7. A washing machine
8. A dryer
9. A powerful blowgun hairdryer
10. Equipment cabinets that can be locked
11. For pattern storage, file cabinets that can be locked
12. Manufacturers sized dummies
    a. Female sizes 8, 12, 16, 20
    b. Male sizes 30, 34, 38, 40, 42
       These sizes can be added to by judicious padding or cutting methods. It is not necessary to have one in every size.
13. An assortment of canvas headblocks, sizes 21" to 25"
14. An assortment of hat blocks in various shapes and sizes
15. 2 sleeve boards ⎫
16. 2 tailor's hams ⎬ one for each
17. 2 tailor's rolls ⎪ ironing board facility
18. 2 velvet boards ⎭
19. A large cork or pin board on one wall to hang sketches, notes, bills, swatches, and all the other items one must find quickly
20. At least 1 full-length mirror (a triple one is great if you have the room)
21. A fitter's platform
22. An electric curling iron, preferably one that shoots steam
23. An awl
24. A leather punch
25. A sailor's leather palm
26. Scissors and shears for various purposes
27. Seam rippers
28. Tracing wheels
29. Tracing paper of different colors
30. A grommeter
31. Wire cutters
32. Hammer
33. Pliers
34. Staple gun
35. Hot glue gun
36. A regular and a phillips screwdriver
37. Several clothes brushes
38. Shoe shine kit
39. A boot jack
40. A feather duster
41. A small drill
42. Machine oil
43. A small screwdriver (short-handled)
44. 5 sewing machine brushes
45. First aid kit
46. Fire extinguisher
47. Paint spray gun or Hudson compressed air sprayer
48. A supply of paint brushes and paints (see Chapter 18)
49. Tailors chalk in various colors
50. Marking pencils
51. Laundry marking pens and iron on name tape
52. A hot plate and some way to boil water, at least a gallon at a time

## Notion Requirements

You will also require hundreds of notions; you can make out your own list of needs, but you should have at least the following:

1. Pins by the gross
   a. Steel straight pins, the longer the better
   b. Push pins to hold up sketches and notes to the cork board
   c. T-pins for hat and wig making
   d. Safety pins in every conceivable size
2. Sewing machine needles
   a. Sizes 9 through 18 sharps
   b. Sizes 9 through 16 ball points
   c. Sizes 16 and 18 leather points
3. Hand sewing needles, all sizes. Be sure to include both embroidery and curved needles.
4. Thread in white, black, and gray
   a. Dual duty
   b. Buttonhole thread

c. *Carpet thread*
   *It is only an affectation to use colored thread. Black, white, and gray are all that are needed for most stages. This allows you to buy in bulk and saves time on all that bobbin winding. You can't see it from most stages anyway, even the smallest.*
5. *Knitting needles of various sizes*
6. *Crochet hooks of various sizes, including an extra large hook (great for fast hats, shawls, bags, and chain mail)*
7. *Various closings in all available sizes and colors*
   a. *Hooks and eyes*
   b. *Snaps*
   c. *Zippers*
   d. *Grippers*
   e. *Grommets*
   f. *Lacings*
8. *Pattern drafting equipment*
   a. *Pattern maker's compass*
   b. *Pattern maker's protractor*
   c. *Large French curve*
   d. *Large right angle*
   e. *48"-long steel T-square*
   f. *48"-long "yard" stick*
   g. *2 regular 36"-long yardsticks, one of which should be nailed along one edge of the cutting table*
   h. *5 measurement tapes (or 1 for each machine)*
9. *Several gallons of Elmer's glue*
10. *Bolts of muslin*
11. *Buckram*
12. *Hat wire*
13. *Florist wire*
14. *Electrician's color wrapped wire*
15. *Putty*
16. *Cardboard*
17. *Masking tape*
18. *Scotch tape*
19. *Twill tape*
20. *A good quantity of bobbins, steel if possible*

Therefore, your spatial requirements are those dimensions necessary to hold the previously mentioned items and equipment.

## Nice Little Extras

There are some nice little extras that make life a lot more pleasant, but are not absolutely necessary. A regular four-burner stove-oven combination is very helpful. The second is a merrowing machine, sometimes called in the trade a "baby lock." This machine overcasts a seam and cuts off the excess at one time. It is wonderful for chiffons and fabrics that ravel as fast as you cut them.

It's also nice to have a mangle. It roll irons large flat surfaces quickly (fabric that wrinkles in shipment, for example). Small drycleaning machines pay for themselves in no time. It's also nice to have a professional hood hair dryer for doing your own wigs. If you make many shoes, a shoemaker's sewing machine becomes a necessity. Pinking shears are nice, but no longer as necessary as they once were.

It helps save a lot of crises if you can rig up two baby fresnels at cross angles for a good look at the fabric under lights before it hits the stage. This is particularly vital when distressing garments. One fresnel needs whatever warm gel will be used; the other is for the cool gel.

My next acquirement for the storage area will be an electronic track for the hanging items, much like your local drycleaner has. Each hanger hole is numbered. One pushes a button until the desired number comes up, and plucks off the right item. This does demand constant inventory records, but think of the time one saves.

## The Arrangement of the Shop

As for the actual arrangement of your shop, each designer has his or her own way of doing things. There is no specific right or wrong; there is only what works for you. I would give you one rule of thumb, however; wherever you place things, two people should be able to get by one another with ease. Also, your doors should be wide enough and high enough to accommodate a lady in hoop skirts or panniers and high wig.

Now that you've got your shop going, you're ready to begin construction.

# 2

# The Proper Taking of Measurements

Before you can draft a pattern, you must have accurate measurements. A notebook for male measurements and a separate one for females should be kept. The measurements should be taken as soon as possible. It's wonderful to have these even before you design the garment, but not always possible. It is possible the minute the cast list is posted. In many cases a measurement call should be posted right beside the cast list with appropriately scheduled appointments.

## Requirements for the Initial Measurement Call

On the measurement call you should inform the players how they should dress, what type of shoes are required, etc. Some designers/fitters prefer to measure over leotards; some prefer to measure the body over basic underwear. It is *not* advisable to measure a nude body. This is not because of prudishness, but simply because there are few facilities for taking measurements conveniently in privacy. In this era of "let it all hang out," I must constantly remind players to wear underwear.

If you are doing a period show that requires certain figure distortions, you should have your corsets, hoops, bum rolls, panniers, or bustles at the measurement taking session. Hopefully, you will have these things in stock. If not, you must plan ahead and make at least one of these items that adjusts in size. It is very important to measure the body *with and without* these items.

It is also important at that first session to try on any stock items that you may wish to use, fitting them at that time for alteration. These should be previously located to facilitate time.

### Second Measurement Call

If the actor requires padding, two measurement sessions would be required—the first to measure his present body in order to construct the padding (see Chapter 3); then he should return for a second measurement session wearing his padding.

## Sample Measurement Charts

In this section you will find a male measurement chart (Table 2–1) and diagram (Fig. 2–1) for taking male measurements; and a female chart (Table 2–2) and diagram (Fig. 2–2) for taking female measurements. On the charts you will find letters and numbers in parentheses. These correspond to the letters and numbers on the sexually corresponding diagrams. As we now discuss the measurement charts, you may wish to refer to these four pages.

## General Information Requirements

Obviously, it is necessary to have the name of the actor, his address, and phone (phones) where he can be reached. His business phone may be his answering service or his agent in a professional situation. In a university situation this may simply be the department number of his major. In the community situation it is generally just what it says, a business number.

You also need to know the play and character. In a professional situation actors are cast fairly well to type, particularly as far as age goes. In the university situation sometimes it is necessary to put down how old the actor is and the age of the character to plan special wig or padding problems. This is not on the charts that follow, but you may wish to place it on yours.

Height and weight are self-explanatory, but a word of caution should be stated about these two. Everyone wants to be as tall and thin as possible. A lot of outright lying goes on. This, of course, is ridiculous. After you've been in the business long enough, you can make some very accurate guesstimates. Be polite. Write down what they tell you (in pencil) and then change it later if the point is crucial. The measurements will speak for themselves. If height is absolutely vital and you doubt the actor, line him up to the wall and measure his height. This is always necessary with growing children anyway. The exact poundage usually is not necessary, unless it is a matter of poundage to area of stress, such as an actress portraying Peter Pan who will need a harness with which to fly.

As for hair color and eye color, this is for identification purposes, so that you put the right face to the right body. It also helps if you have to choose colors for them. As an example, I recently designed *Little Mary Sunshine*, which has a chorus of six girls. I put them all in evening dresses of exactly the same design, but each had a different pastel color. By using their eye and hair colors, I tried to flatter them as much as possible.

*Manufacturers' Sizes*

It is always helpful to know manufacturers' sizes for suits (men's), dresses, shoes, shirts or blouses. Often many items are simply bought off the rack. For shoes you need both length (the number) and width (the letter or letters). The smaller the number, the smaller the foot. Women's sizes usually go from 4 through 12; men's 6 through 14. Both graduate by half sizes (7, 7½, 8, 8½, etc.). A woman's size 10 shoe is approximately as long as a man's 8 to 8½. Widths run from the narrowest of AAAAA to the widest of EEE. It goes AAAAA, four As, three As, two As, A, B, C, D, E, two Es, three Es. In manufacturer's parlance, five As are called "quins," four = "quads," three = "triples," two = "doubles."

Men's suit sizes are determined by the chest measurement and height. A regular size 40 means a man who has a 40″ chest and is between 5′ 8″ to 6′. A 40 short is a 40″ chest, but this man is between 5′ 4″ and 5′ 8″. A 40 long indicates a man between 6′ and 6′ 3″, and an x-long (extra long) is a man who is 6′ 4″ or over.

Shirts are determined by the neck size and sleeve length, so a shirt is bought according to two sets of numbers. The neck size is generally first. An average size is a 15½/33. The neck measurement is taken at the base of the neck; #13 on Fig. 2–1. The sleeve is measured from the spine around a *bent* elbow to the wristbone; #16 on Fig. 2–1.

Dress sizes are coded to mean certain things. The average female wears a dress of even numbers, 2 through 22. The thin but short-bodied female wears what is euphemistically called a "junior" size, which is always an odd number, 1 through 19. For the very tall woman (5′ 9″ and over) there are tall shops, which use both the even and odd numbers.

The more mature figure is given half numbers, 10½ through 22½. There is more allowance in the bust and waist. For the ample and more than ample figure, there are both even and half-numbered sizes, but no standardization (more the pity), so size actually means nothing and you must shop with a tape measure. Actually that is an excellent policy when doing any clothes shopping. Blouses are sold by chest measurement, 30 through 56.

**The Actual Taking of Measurements**

Now for the taking of measurements from the body itself. Let's start at the top and work down.

1. The Head: *Measure around the fullest part of the cranium (#17—Fig. 2–2; #18—Fig. 2–1; #1 in Fig. 2–3, later in chapter). Please note that women's hats are sold by this measurement. Men's hats have sizes corresponding to these measurements. A man with a 21″ head wears a size 6 hat. Heads come in only two shapes—very round or slightly oval. Check the appropriate box. Here is a chart (Table 2–1) for your reference.*

**Table 2–1.** Hat Size Equivalents for Men's Hats

| Head In Inches | Hat Sizes |
| --- | --- |
| 21″ | 6⅝ |
| 21½″ | 6⅞ |
| 22″ | 7 |
| 22½″ | 7⅛ |
| 23″ | 7¼ |
| 23½″ | 7½ |
| 24″ | 7⅝ |
| 24½″ | 7¾ (or ⅞) |
| 25″ | 7⅞ |
| 25½″ | 8 |

There may be ¼″ to ½″ variable according to the manufacturer.

2. The Neck: *Here you will need two measurements:*
   a. *The base of the neck.*
   b. *The throat (ladies) or around the Adam's apple for the men. This is for stand-up collars (#19, 20—Fig. 2–2; #13, 14—Fig. 2–1).*
3. The Shoulders: *This measurement is taken across the back from outside edge of shoulder bone to the same on the opposite shoulder (#11—Fig. 2–2; #15—Fig. 2–1).*
4. The Arm: *On the chart you will see "sh to elbow" and "to wrist". This translates into shoulder to elbow and to wrist.*

a.  *Place tape measure where you ended your shoulder measurement and measure to a bent elbow (sh to elbow) then continue on to wrist bone (to wrist) (letters D and E—Fig. 2–2; J and K—Fig. 2–1).*
    *Note: This should read something like 15" for shoulder to elbow and 25" to wrist; not 15" and 10".*

b.  *Upper arm (#8—Fig. 2–2; #10—Fig. 2–1). This measurement is taken around the bicep muscle flexed.*

c.  *Armseye (#37—Fig. 2–2; #9—Fig. 2–1). This measures the cap of the upper arm. The arm should hang down and you measure around it, as if there were a seam joining the arm to the shoulder. You would measure from the front seam to the back.*

d.  *Elbow (#9—female diagram; #11—male) This measured around a bent elbow.*

e.  *Wrist (#10—female diagram; #12—male). Measure wrist around wrist bone.*

5.  The Hand *(#18—female diagram; #17—male): The hand is measured around the palm, excluding thumb. Glove sizes for both men and women go by this number.*

6.  The Torso: *On the charts you will see "shoulders to W.F.". "R" and "L". This translates to shoulder to waist front, right side (R) and left side (L).*

a.  *Shoulder to W.F. is taken from the middle of the shoulder area between neck and outer edge of shoulder bone down to waist over nipple (Letter A on both diagrams).*

b.  *"Sh to W.B." (shoulder to waist back) is taken from the same spot on shoulder as the shoulder to waist front measurement, down to the waist over the back shoulder blade (Letter J—female diagram; B—male).*

c.  *"Sh to waist C.B." translates to shoulder to waist center back. (Letter F on both diagrams.) The measurement is taken down the spine from the neck radial joint (the first bump at the base of the neck often called the dowager hump) to the waist.*

d.  *Armseye to armseye F (front) and B (back). This is the measurement across the upper chest and across the back to that hypothetical seam where the sleeve joins the shoulder. It is where the curve of the armhole begins on a pattern with set-in sleeves. On both the female and male diagram the front is #1; the back is #12 on the female and #19 on the male.*

e.  *Shoulder to armseye (letter K—female diagram; letter I—male) is the same point at the front of the above measurement over the shoulder to the corresponding point at the back.*

f.  *Waist (#4—female diagram; #3—male) is the measurement taken around the center of the torso at the point where the body bends normally. Please be aware that today's men do not always wear their trouser waist on their actual waist, but often on their upper hips. Have them bend if necessary. Generally speaking, the male sh to W.F. measurement should be the same as the sh to W.B. measurement. Anatomically speaking, women require several more torso measurements than men.*

g.  *"Sh to point" translates to shoulder to nipple and along with its companion "point to point" measurement, is strictly a female one. I have named these AA and 2+ as extensions of the #2 line and the letter A line.*

h.  *Chest "exp" (expanded) and "rel" (relaxed) is that measurement taken around the upper torso across the nipples. Since garments must allow breathing room, always ask your actors to fill their lungs and expand their chest (#2 on both diagrams).*

i.  *Ribcage is another strictly female measurement. It is taken around the torso just under the breasts.*

j.  *Clavicle to waist center front is a measurement that men also occasionally need, but not always, so I did not include it on the male chart. It can be listed under "other if/as necessary." It is taken down the center front from the base of the clavicle (that little V-shaped bone) to the waist (Letter B—female diagram).*

k.  *Again, because of anatomical differences men only need one hip measurement, as a general rule. That is taken around the largest part of the buttocks; #4 on the male diagram. The corresponding line on a woman is the lower hip line; #6 on the female diagram. Generally speaking, this is approximately nine inches below the waist. Women also have an upper hip measurement; #5 on the female diagram. This is generally four inches below the waist or around the upper edge of the pelvic bone.*

l.  *"W.F. to W.B. thru crotch" translates to waist front to waist back thru crotch (letter M—female diagram; L—male). This is taken from the center front of the waist, between the legs and up the buttocks to the center back of the waist.*

7.  Legs: *All leg measurements are taken upright, but if a garment is very form fitting auxiliary measurements on a bent leg may be necessary.*

a.  *The inseam (letter H—female diagram; E—male) is taken from the center crotch down* the inside of the leg to just below the ankle bone.

b. *The outseam (letter I—female diagram; D—male) is taken on the side of the figure from waist to just below the ankle bone.*

c. *The thigh measurement (#13—female diagram; #5—male) is taken around the fullest part of the thigh.*

d. *The knee (#14—female diagram; #6—male) measurement is taken around the middle of the kneecap.*

   *Note: When making breeches that require a kneeband you will need another measurement, which is one inch below the kneecap. This, again, can be listed under "other as/if necessary."*

E. *The calf (#15—female diagram; #7—male) is taken around the fullest part of the lower leg.*

f. *The ankle (#16—female diagram; #8—male) is taken around the anklebone.*

g. *The waist to knee measurement (L—female diagram; C—male) is taken like the outseam, only to one inch below the kneecap.*

h. *Waist to floor "W.S." (with shoes) and "N.S." (no shoes) is taken on the side from waist to hip and plumb lined to floor.*

8. The Body Length: *"Sh to floor" equates into shoulder to floor and should be an extension of the sh to W.B. line to the floor, but without indentation to the waist.*

This should take care of all the basic needs. For some specific detail on a particular sketch, a space is marked "other measurements if/as necessary". There is also a place for notes and swatches.

The empty box under the "other measurements if/as necessary" can be used for a photo of the actor or actress. This is particularly useful when doing large musicals, operas, or extravaganzas. It helps to keep straight who is who.

### The Hat and Wig Chart

The head measurement on the costume chart will allow you to buy hats or hat frames. If you are making your own, you should fill out a hat and wig chart, as shown in Figure 2–3. (The same chart works for both sexes, but in case the actors' or characters' names leave doubt, one of the two center boxes can be marked.)

A chart like this, minus the line on the heads,

can be used to order wigs, as well. A picture can be drawn to show how the wigs should be styled. Use a box for swatches to send a hair clipping if you need a piece made to match a particular actor's own hair color. If the actor dyes his hair, have him put down exactly what he uses in the box marked "notes." Under "sketch" I sometimes send a slide of my costume sketch to the wig makers or to the firm from whom I am renting. These are often-used forms.

The first four lines are exact duplicates of the costume chart and for the same reasons. Even the head-around measurement is the same as the head measurement on those charts. The others are taken in the following ways:

1. Front Hair Line to Nape: *This is taken from where the hair begins in the center front of the forehead (directly in line with the nose) to where it ends on the nape of the neck. Lift long hair up, if necessary.*

2. Ear to Ear Across the Top of the Head: *This is taken from the hairline beside the top of the ear (excluding male sideburns), to the same place on the opposite ear.*

3. Ear to Ear under Chin: *From the same spot as #2 to the same spot on the other ear, but going under the chin with the mouth slightly open.*

4. Ear to Ear around Back of Head: *From and to same spots as #2, but around largest part of the cranium.*

5. Head around Hairline: *Is just that, but all the way around. If you are having wigs made, a tracing of the actual hairline should be sent. This can be done by opening one side of a small plastic bag, scotch taping it like a skullcap to conform to the head, and marking the hairline on it with an eyebrow pencil or butchers wax marker or crayon.*

6. Hairline at Nape: *This is taken just like #4, only from side to side at the very bottom of the hairline on the back of the neck.*

7. Around Head including Nose: *This is only necessary when making animal heads and helmets that cover the face.*

You are almost ready to begin construction. There is just one more detail and that is the area of hand props. If an actor must wear a sword, it should be available at measurement time. It may need a baldrick, or the costume may need to have a sheath. This also applies to all items that need to go into pockets. These must be measured as well. You and the actor together can then work out the whys and hows from this very first meeting.

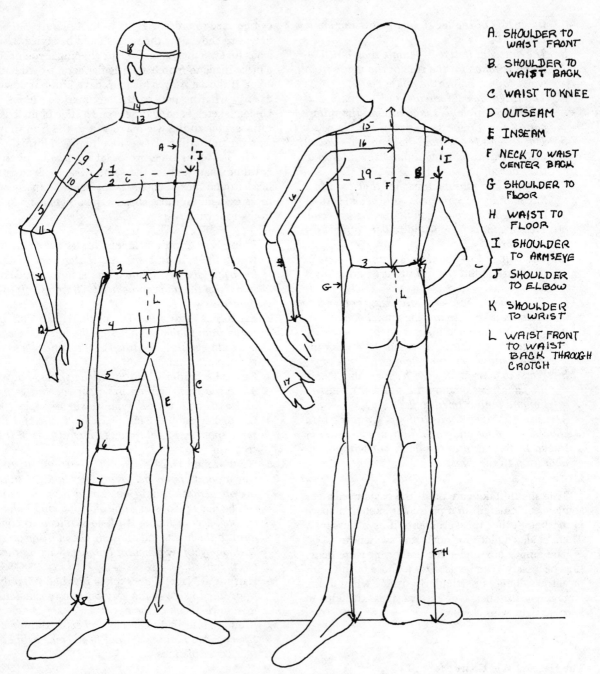

ALL HORIZONTAL LINES ARE NUMBERED: ALL VERTICAL ARE LETTERED

| | | | | |
|---|---|---|---|---|
| 1. ARMSEYE TO ARMSEYE FRONT | 5 THIGH | 9. ARMSEYE | 13. NECK-BASE | 17. HAND |
| 2. CHEST | 6 KNEE | 10. UPPER ARM | 14. ADAMS APPLE | 18 HEAD |
| 3. WAIST | 7. CALF | 11. ELBOW | 15. SHOULDERS | 19 ARMSEYE TO ARMSEYE BACK |
| 4. HIPS | 8 ANKLE | 12. WRIST | 16 SHIRT SLEEVE | |

On the right side of the figure:

A. SHOULDER TO WAIST FRONT
B. SHOULDER TO WAIST BACK
C WAIST TO KNEE
D OUTSEAM
E INSEAM
F NECK TO WAIST CENTER BACK
G SHOULDER TO FLOOR
H WAIST TO FLOOR
I SHOULDER TO ARMSEYE
J SHOULDER TO ELBOW
K SHOULDER TO WRIST
L WAIST FRONT TO WAIST BACK THROUGH CROTCH

**Figure 2–1.** *Diagram for Taking Male Measurements*

COSTUME MEASUREMENT CHART — MALE

| | | | |
|---|---|---|---|
| NAME: | | PLAY: | |
| ADDRESS: | | CHARACTER: | |
| PHONE: HOME | | BUSINESS: | |
| HEIGHT: | WEIGHT: | HAIR: | EYES: |
| SUIT SIZE: | SHOE SIZE: | SHIRT: SL. (16) | NECK: |
| SHOULDERS: (15) | | SH. TO FLOOR: (G) | |
| SH. TO ELBOW: (J) | TO WRIST: (K) | WAIST TO FLOOR: (H) | |
| UPPER ARM: (10) | ARMSEYE: (9) | WAIST TO KNEE: (C) | |
| ELBOW: (11) | WRIST: (12) | KNEE: (6) | ANKLE: (8) |
| SHOULDER TO W.F. R. (A) L. | | CALF: (7) | THIGH: (5) |
| SH. TO W.B. R. (B) L. | | INSEAM: (E) | |
| SH. TO WAIST C.B. (F) | | OUTSEAM: (D) | |
| ARMSEYE TO ARMSEYE F. (1) (19) | | W.F. TO W.B. THRU CROTCH: (L) | |
| SH. TO ARMSEYE F. (I) B. (I) | | | |
| NECK - BASE: (13) | AD'S. AP. (14) | HAND: (17) | |
| CHEST - EXP. (2) | REL. | HEAD: (18) | ROUND / OVAL |
| WAIST: (3) | | OTHER MEASUREMENTS IF/AS | |
| HIPS: (4) | | NECESSARY: | |
| NOTES: ↓ | SWATCHES: ↓ | | |

**Table 2–2.** Costume Measurement Chart—Male

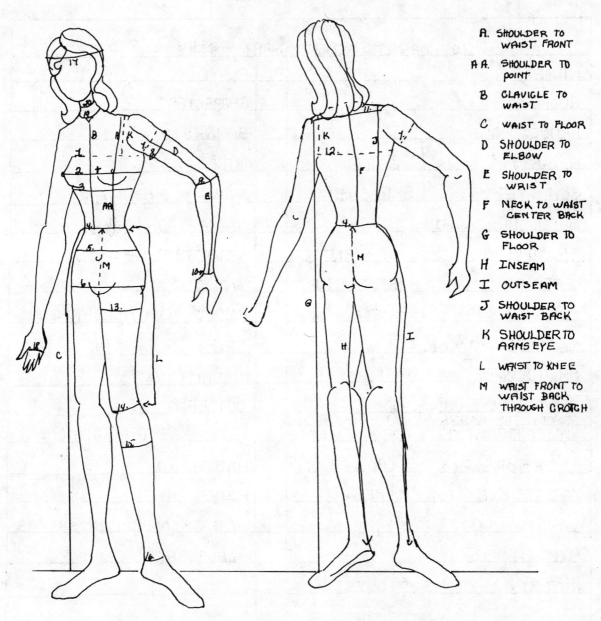

A. SHOULDER TO WAIST FRONT

A A. SHOULDER TO POINT

B. CLAVICLE TO WAIST

C. WAIST TO FLOOR

D. SHOULDER TO ELBOW

E. SHOULDER TO WRIST

F. NECK TO WAIST CENTER BACK

G. SHOULDER TO FLOOR

H. INSEAM

I. OUTSEAM

J. SHOULDER TO WAIST BACK

K. SHOULDER TO ARMSEYE

L. WAIST TO KNEE

M. WAIST FRONT TO WAIST BACK THROUGH CROTCH

## ALL HORIZONTAL LINES ARE NUMBERED: ALL VERTICAL ARE LETTERED

1. ARMSEYE TO ARMSEYE FRONT
2. CHEST ★ 2+ POINT TO POINT
3. RIBCAGE
4. WAIST
5. UPPER HIP
6. LOWER HIP

7. ARMSEYE
8. UPPER ARM
9. ELBOW
10. WRIST
11. SHOULDERS
12. ARMSEYE TO ARMSEYE BACK

13. THIGH
14. KNEE
15. CALF
16. ANKLE
17. HEAD
18. HAND

19. THROAT BASE
20. UPPER NECK
★ DENOTES SAME LINE FOR EXPANDED AND RELAXED

**Figure 2–2.** *Diagram for Taking Female Measurements*

## COSTUME MEASUREMENT CHART—FEMALE

| | | | |
|---|---|---|---|
| NAME: | | PLAY: | |
| ADDRESS: | | CHARACTER: | |
| PHONE: HOME | | BUSINESS: | |
| HEIGHT: | WEIGHT: | HAIR: | EYES: |
| DRESS SIZE: | SHOE SIZE: | BLOUSE SIZE: | |
| SHOULDERS: (11) | | WAIST: (4) | |
| SH. TO ELBOW: (D) | TO WRIST: (E) | HIPS: UPPER (5) | LOWER (6) |
| UPPER ARM: (8) | ARMSEYE: (7) | SH. TO FLOOR: (G) | |
| ELBOW: (9) | WRIST: (10) | WAIST TO FLOOR: (W.S)(C)(N.S) | |
| SHOULDER TO W.F. R. (A) L. | | WAIST TO KNEE: (L) | |
| SH. TO W.B. R. (J) L. | | KNEE: (14) | ANKLE: (16) |
| SH. TO WAIST: C.B (F) | | CALF: (15) | THIGH: (13) |
| ARMSEYE TO ARMSEYE F. (1) B. (12) | | | |
| SH. TO ARMSEYE: F. (K) B. (K) | | INSEAM: (H) | |
| SH. TO POINT: R.(AA) L. | | OUTSEAM: (I) | |
| POINT TO POINT: (2+) | | W.F. TO W.B. THRU CROTCH: (M) | |
| CLAVICLE TO WAIST: C.F. (B) | | HAND: (18) | |
| | | | ROUND / OVAL |
| NECK: BASE (19) | THROAT (20) | HEAD: (17) | |
| CHEST:EXP. (2) | REL. (2) | OTHER MEASUREMENTS IF/AS | |
| RIBCAGE: (3) | | NECESSARY: | |
| NOTES: ↓ | SWATCHES: ↓ | | |
| | | | |

**Table 2–3.** Costume Measurement Chart—Female

HAT & WIG MEASUREMENT CHART — MALE OR FEMALE

| | | | |
|---|---|---|---|
| NAME: | M. | PLAY: | |
| ADDRESS: | F. | CHARACTER | |
| PHONE: HOME | | BUSINESS: | |
| HEIGHT: | WEIGHT: | HAIR: | EYES: |
| HEAD AROUND (1) | | ROUND: | OVAL |
| FRONT HAIRLINE TO NAPE: (2) | | EAR TO EAR AROUND BACK: (4) | |
| EAR TO EAR ACROSS TOP: (3) | | EAR TO EAR UNDER CHIN: (5) | |
| HEAD AROUND HAIRLINE: (6) | | AROUND HEAD INCLUDING NOSE: (7) | |
| HAIRLINE AT NAPE: (8) | | OTHER MEASUREMENTS AS | |
| NOTES:↓ | SWATCHES: ↓ | NECESSARY: ↓ | SKETCH:↓ |
| | | | |

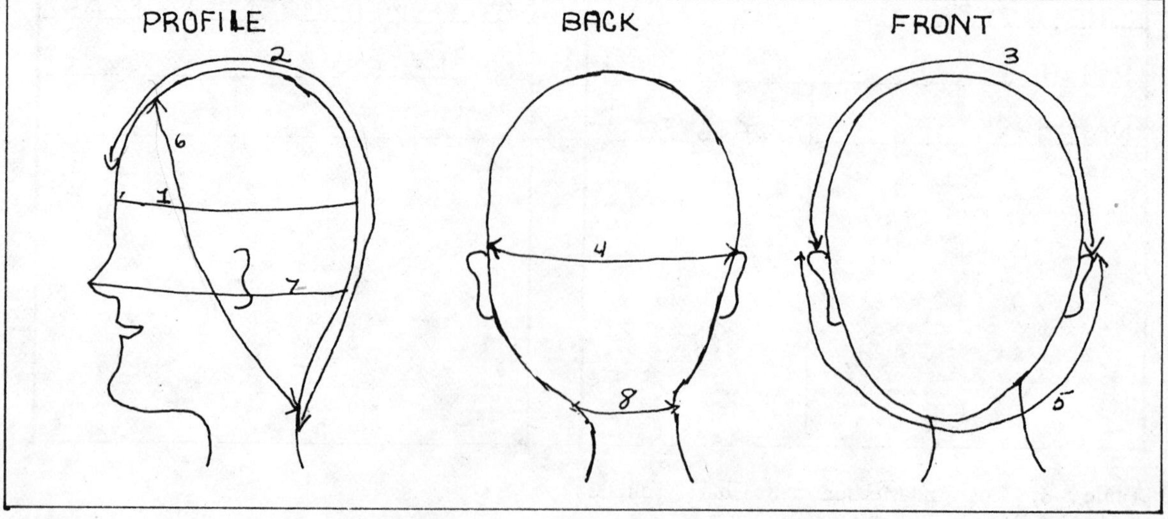

PROFILE  BACK  FRONT

**Figure 2–3.** *Hat and Wig Measurement Chart—Male or Female*

# 3

# Construction of Under Supports

If a bridge is to stand, it must have proper support from somewhere, either pilings or a cantilever, or both. So it is with the exterior costume. In this case, what you see may not be what you get. What you get may be considerably more.

**Figure Distortions**

If there needs to be any sort of figure distortion because of character or period requirements, that obviously must be done first, for that is the "piling" upon which the exterior (the superstructure) is built.

*Period Distortions*   The most common devices of period distortion are corsets, hoops (including panniers) and farthingales, bustles and bum rolls. Some period distortions are not truly figure or silhouette in nature, but that of style or mannerism. These include heeled shoes for Cavalier and Baroque gentlemen, plumed hats, ruffs, hobble skirts, trains, etc. These can often be taken care of by rehearsal clothes.

*Character Distortion*   The most common device of character distortion is padding.

*Rehearsal Clothes*

What are rehearsal clothes? Just exactly that; clothing worn by the players during the rehearsal period to enable them to become used to differences in the feel and use of clothing of another era. It is a temporary substitute for the costume.

Actors should be able to supply many items, as a dancer supplies her rehearsal leotards, tights, and shoes. All actresses should have a simple, floor-length skirt in their wardrobe and shoes with various heel heights ranging from flats to "character" shoes to spikes. Actors also should have a variety of shoes. The hobble skirt effect can be achieved by

slipping an elastic cord over a long skirt to the knees and making sure the elastic only stretches to the desired knee width of the planned costume.

Trains and their adjacent problems can be simulated simply by gathering a rectangle of the desired length to a waistband or on a draw string and worn over an actress's rehearsal skirt. Robes with trains can be simulated by an attachment of fabric to the shoulder.

If, however, the problem is compounded—e.g., a gown with train and houppelande sleeves or a dress with train, huge sleeves and high collar—a complete substitute should be used. This can be an old costume from stock that may be on its last leg of wear and tear or, perhaps, a mock-up of the actual costume, time permitting.

*Padding*

Padding requires immediate construction and regardless of problem, follows one general rule. A form-fitting garment must be constructed upon which the padding is built. There are several ways to do this.

*T-Shirt Method*   One of the quickest is what I call the T-shirt method. You have the actor wear a snug T-shirt. Over this you slip a larger T-shirt. You pad the required area between the two layers, much like a sandwich, tacking as you go (see Fig. 3–1). You then add a crotch strap that will hold the padding down. It will move with the actor comfortably and naturally. I often remove the T-shirt sleeves and use that fabric to make the crotch strap, giving it the same weight and stretchable quality as the rest of the garment. It is triangular in shape for the front to the center crotch, tapering to a strap about one inch wide, finished, that extends from center crotch to the center back waist. If a zipper is put down the back, this top can be attached to either a male dance belt or female dance briefs (or underpants).

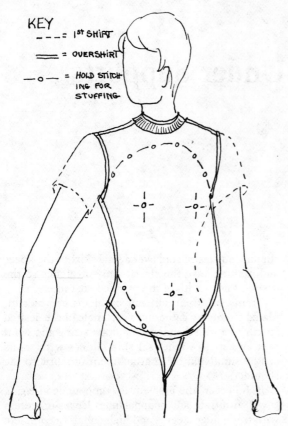

**Figure 3–1.**   *T-Shirt Method of Padding*

traying Stella to go from about two-and-a-half months of pregnancy to full term. I used the basic method above, but constructed it out of a very fine cotton lawn (non-stretch) with zipper compartments for added padding as the play progressed. This was attached to an old brassiere the actress owned which was a bit large for her. This allowed for additional underpadding of the breasts and still allowed her to wear a low-necked maternity top and look perfectly natural (See Fig. 3–2). I once found a Victorian advertisement for "gay deceivers" that read, "What God has forgotten, stuff with cotton." This brings up the illusion of making the breast seem larger.

*Leotard Method*   A pregnant padding can be worked in much the same manner, using a leotard or nude body stocking. Employing the same basic principle, enlargement of the breasts and buttocks can also be achieved. Instead of one leotard on top of another, build onto the leotard with various *washable* and *four-way stretch* fabrics or cut up pieces of an old leotard.

*Stuffing*   Various stuffings may be used, including foam rubber (pieces or chips), cotton batting, or polyester fiberfill. The last is my favorite, because it does not seem to bunch up in washing, as the cotton does, nor does it tend to mildew as some of the foam rubber does.

### Padding Tricks

A few plays require padding tricks; the character either grows or diminishes before your very eyes. *A Streetcar Named Desire* requires the actress por-

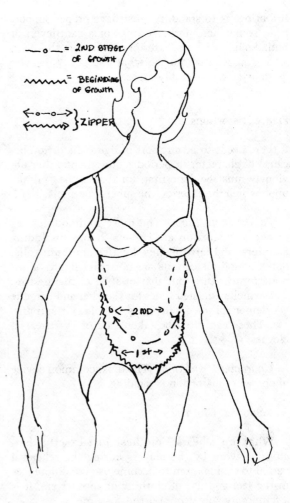

**NOTE:** THE SECOND PADDING IS SNAPPED TO UNDER POCKET

**Figure 3–2.**   *"Add-As-You-Grow" Pregnant Padding*

The basic principle over many centuries is pull in the lower section (waist to ribcage) to push up and out the breasts (and hips). One of the easiest and quickest ways of increasing the look of the breast is by wearing a French cut bra and putting a semi-circularly shaped foam wedge under the existing breast (see Figures 3–3 and 3–4).

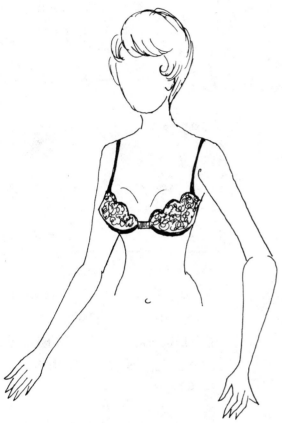

**Figure 3–3.** *Modern "French" Cut Bra*

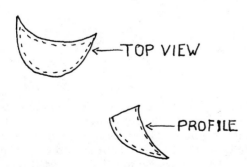

**Figure 3–4.** *Underpadding for Bra*

### The Bean Bag Sag

Before leaving this subject, I should like to share the "bean-bag method of sag" process (my private term) for giving a look of sagging flesh, be it breasts, buttocks, upper arms, etc. In some circumstances this process could be classified as padding but it really comes under a more general category. Make the properly shaped bag for the particular area, fill it with bird seed, and attach it to the appropriate undergarment. It may also be built into the exterior costume. It moves realistically and has the proper weight.

### The Corset

The next alternative is wearing a corset. During the 1950s and early 1960s when strapless evening gowns were very popular, there was a garment called a "merry widow," which acted as a combination waist cincher, strapless bra, and garter belt. Sometimes thrift shops will have them. Department stores still carry similar garments. Frederick's of Hollywood (6608 Hollywood Blvd., Hollywood, Calif. 90028, Phone: (213) 466-5151) also carries them, as well as an array of modern "gay deceivers." You might write for the catalogue.

*The Late Victorian Corset* The "merry widow" is great for the hourglass and/or wasp waist, but Figure 3–5 shows an example of a late Victorian corset including a scaled pattern. This pattern was adapted from Manet's painting *Nana* and a donated corset.

*Renaissance Corset* Figure 3–6 is a scaled pattern for a corset that gives the flattened Renaissance silhouette.

*Rococo Corset and Waist Cincher* Figure 3–7 illustrates the Rococo corset and its flat pattern pieces. My source for this was Hogarth illustrations, including *Marriage a la Mode* and *Scene in Newgate Prison*. The Rococo corset and waist cinchers are made the same way as shown in Figure 3–8. With the waist cincher I generally interface the outside fabric with muslin, and put the iron-on interfacing on the lining fabric. Because featherboning or steel is difficult for the dressmaker sewing machines to sew through, most external decoration has to be sewn on by hand. An industrial machine with a #18 sharp or #16 leather needle should zip right through featherboning.

The materials needed for the above are muslin or cotton square-woven fabric of fairly sturdy weight (80-80 muslin is fine), feather boning, and "stitch-witchery" or an iron-on interfacing of some sort.

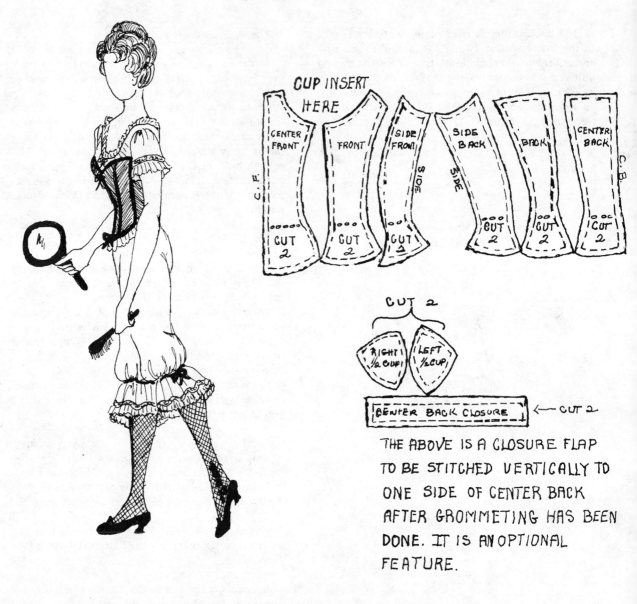

CUP INSERT HERE

CENTER FRONT

FRONT

SIDE FRONT

SIDE BACK

BACK

CENTER BACK

C.F.

SIDE

SIDE

C.B.

CUT 2    CUT 2    CUT 2    CUT 2    CUT 2    CUT 2

CUT 2

RIGHT ½ CUP    LEFT ½ CUP

CENTER BACK CLOSURE ← CUT 2

THE ABOVE IS A CLOSURE FLAP TO BE STITCHED VERTICALLY TO ONE SIDE OF CENTER BACK AFTER GROMMETING HAS BEEN DONE. IT IS AN OPTIONAL FEATURE.

NOTE: 1. CAMISOLE CUT ON THE SHOULDER
2. CORSET WORN OVER BOTH CAMISOLE AND BLOOMERS

SCALE: ⅛" = 1"

**Figure 3–5.** *Late Victorian Corset and Its Layout*

*Procedure for Corset Construction*

1. *Cut a double set of all pieces out of the muslin, as if you are to construct two garments.*
2. *Cut one set out of stitch-witchery or the iron-on interfacing.*
3. *Stay-stitch the interfacing ⅛" in from the edge of each piece so that the non-glue side is down and the glue side is up (or free). You can tell the glue side because the little drops of glue have a shine. (It doesn't matter with stitch-witchery.)*

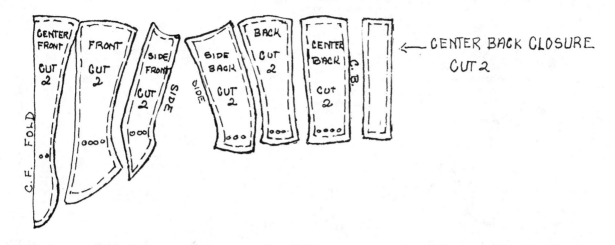

SCALE ⅛" = 1"

FOR AN ASSEMBLED VIEW SEE FIGURE 3-13

NOTE: CIRCLE LINE INDICATES NATURAL WAISTLINE

**Figure 3–6.** *Scaled Pattern for a Renaissance Corset*

4. Now the glue side becomes the "wrong" side of those pieces. With this in mind, construct two garments.
5. Tailor tack open all seams on the interfaced garment, clipping where necessary. DO NOT PRESS WITH IRON YET!
6. Press open all seams on muslin garment, clipping where necessary.
7. Bag the two garments together by putting right side to right side and sewing up center back and across the top, leaving the bottom open.
8. Clip any underarm curves and corners.
9. Turn right side out.
10. Clip bottom curve about ⅜" and turn up ⅝". Baste each edge still leaving it open.
11. Machine stitch channels for feather boning (usually ¾" wide), as shown in Figure 3–5.
12. Insert feather boning, which should be cut ⅜" short of finished length, so that bottom may be machine stitch closed.
13. Remove bastings.
14. Now press with the steam iron, so that the glued interfacing or stitch-witchery does its bonding best.
15. Grommet for lacings.

*Alternative Corset Construction*

For those times when an even sturdier corset is required, there is the twill tape and flexisteel stays method, as illustrated in Figure 3–9. This follows the above process steps #1 through #6. For step #7 on the muslin garment, machine stitch the twill tape to make channels. Do not forget to leave ⅝" seam allowance down either side of your center back opening.

8. Insert flexisteel stays, cut to allow ⅝" seam allowance at top and bottom. Cap ends.
9. Now bag the two garments, right side to right side, leaving opening for turning along one straight edge.
10. Clip all curves.
11. Turn right side out.
12. Press with steam iron to allow fusible material to do its job.
13. Top stitch around edges.
14. Grommet for lacings.

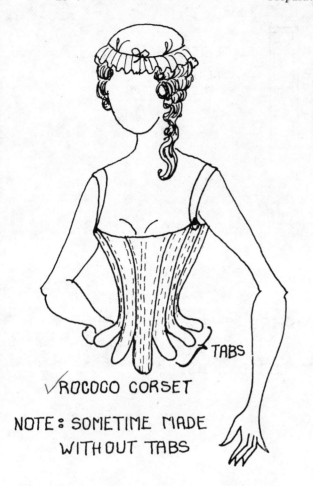

NOTE: WHEN ASSEMBLING THE VERTI-
CAL SEAMS (CENTER FRONT TO
SIDE FRONT, ETC.) ONLY SEW
FROM THE TOP TO THE WAIST.
LEAVE THE TABS FREE. THE
BONING CHANNELS (NOT MARK-
ED) MUST ALSO FOLLOW THIS
PRINCIPLE.

✓ROCOCO CORSET

NOTE: SOMETIME MADE
WITHOUT TABS

TABS

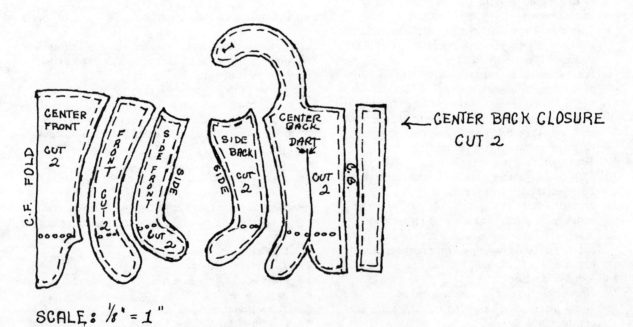

CENTER BACK CLOSURE
CUT 2

SCALE: ⅛" = 1"

**Figure 3–7.** *Rococo Corset and Scaled Pattern*

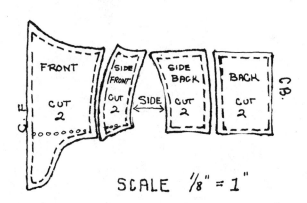

SCALE ⅛" = 1"

NOTE: DEPENDING ON THE DESIRED
PLACE FOR LACINGS, EITHER
THE CENTER FRONT OR THE
CENTER BACK MAY BE CUT
ON THE FOLD

**Figure 3–8.** *Scaled Pattern Waist Cincher*

(THE ABOVE ACTUAL WIDTH OF ¼")

**Figure 3–9.** *Flexisteel Stays*

### The Binder

Before leaving the subject of corsets completely, something should be said about the binder. This was an item popular only two times in fashion history; in the Empire-Regency era, when it more accurately resembled the present day brassiere shown in Figure 3–10; and in the 1920s, when the no-bust "little boy" look was the rage. This was a garment that literally flattened the breasts and was made of an elasticized fabric. Large-breasted women who wished to be fashionable bound themselves with wide strips of non-stretchable fabric, to their own

injury. The same method can be used today, but I personally prefer to design the outer garment to give the illusion of a no-breast look, rather than require that kind of torture of an actress.

### The Hoop

The next undersupport of importance to the period silhouette is the hoop in all its various names and forms. There is the bell farthingale (also called the Spanish farthingale), the cartwheel farthingale, the Spanish pannier, the Rococo pannier, the Victorian hoop of 1855, and the Victorian hoop of 1860 and 1865.

*Construction of the Bell Farthingale*   Let us consider the construction of the bell farthingale (see illustration and scaled pattern in Figures 3–11 and 3–12). The pieces should be cut from a sturdy cotton or 80-80 muslin, as shown. Also needed is twill or bias tape 1" wide, steel banding, the same type that is used to support large packages or by moving and storage companies, who are usually happy to sell it to you. You need masking tape and tin snips (or wire cutters, but that's the hard way).

Construction procedures are as follows:

1. *Cut pieces, as illustrated in Figure 3–12.*
2. *Sew pieces together, leaving center back seam open, so that garment can be laid out on table.*
3. *Sew twill or bias tape on for channel to "wrong" side, as indicated in Figure 3–11.*
4. *Sew up center back seam, leaving a seven-inch opening at top. DO NOT SEW OVER TWILL TAPES. Lock machine stitch at each end of twill tape channels, but leave channels free for their respective hoops.*
5. *Put on waistband like any waistband. A few gathers or pleats can adjust for a slightly smaller waist without difficulty.*
6. *Cut steel banding one inch longer than each channel. This banding is usually ½" to ⅝" wide.*
7. *Wrap steel banding with masking tape, so that the steel edge will not cut through stitches with normal wear and tear.*
8. *Starting with the top channel, feed banding through until you come out the other side.*
9. *Make one-inch overlap and bind together with masking tape.*
10. *Turn up a 1½" hem. Stitch, leaving a one-inch opening.*
11. *Last band should be threaded into hem.*

**Figure 3–10.**  *Regency Binder*

*Construction of Cartwheel Farthingale*  For the cartwheel farthingale, illustrated and scaled in Figure 3–13, the materials needed are sturdy cotton (80-80 muslin), feather boning, twill tape, masking tape, wire cutters, several coat hangers, which have been straightened out and the hooks cut off, florists wire, and a hot glue gun. The procedure is as follows:

1. *Cut pieces as illustrated.*
2. *Sew twill tape channels, as shown in Figure 3–14, leaving a four-inch opening on the center front seam to the waist.*
3. *Put on the waistband in the same way as described in step #5 of the bell shaped farthingale.*
4. *Now cut feather boning two inches short of channel length.*
5. *Feed feather boning into channels.*
6. *Tack at bottom end.*
7. *Turn up a 1½" hem and machine sew, leaving a channel opening of 1½" to 2".*
8. *Put hangers together to achieve desired circumference. They can be fastened together by a combination of florist wire and hot glue, but try not to leave a big bump. (If your scene shop is equipped to handle welding, these can be welded together quite smoothly, but then it must be placed in the hem and the hem sewn by hand.)*

9. *Wrap with masking tape.*
10. *Feed through hem channel.*
11. *A ruffle or the whole bottom half of a petticoat may be added to this circle. (In that case, should be added before hanger-hoop is fed into hem channel.) For this "skirt" you must cut a rectangle 178" wide by 45⅝" long. You then sew your center back seam leaving 176½ inches, which are gathered to the circumference of the outer rim of the hoop. The 45⅝ inches allows for Jane Doe's waist-to-floor measure plus 2⅝ inches for hem and turn under.*

Please note that the farthingale in Figure 3–14 is my solution to the problem and does give the proper silhouette, but it is an adaptation of the period silhouette and not taken from an actual garment.

*Construction of Spanish Panniers*  I devised the pattern and illustration for the Spanish pannier in Figure 3–15 strictly to achieve the visual effect. I have yet to see an actual one, but the Spanish Baroque painting of Marianna of Austria (a Spanish princess) by Velasquez shows the exterior line. By definition, panniers are hoops that extend the width of the silhouette and thereby minimize the thickness of the body when in profile.

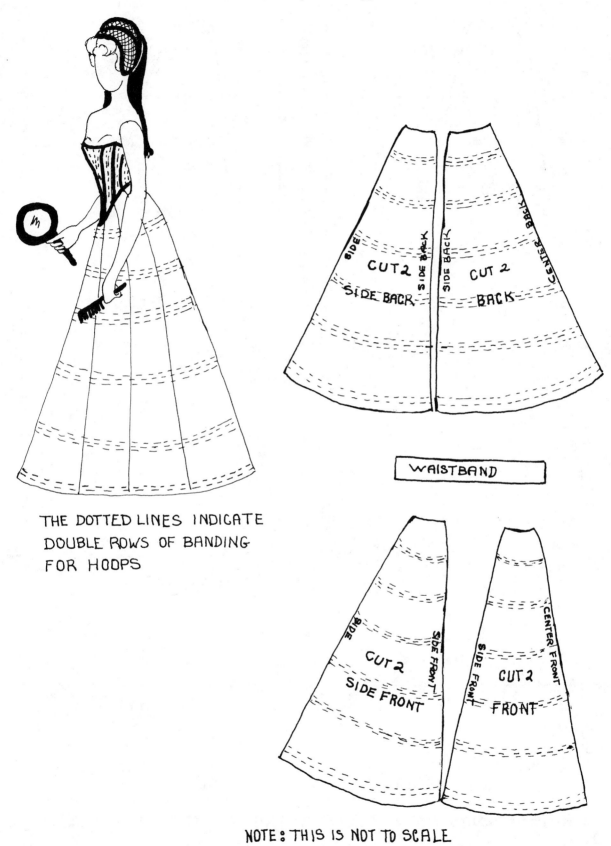

THE DOTTED LINES INDICATE
DOUBLE ROWS OF BANDING
FOR HOODS

WAISTBAND

NOTE: THIS IS NOT TO SCALE

**Figure 3–11.** *Bell (Spanish) Farthingale*

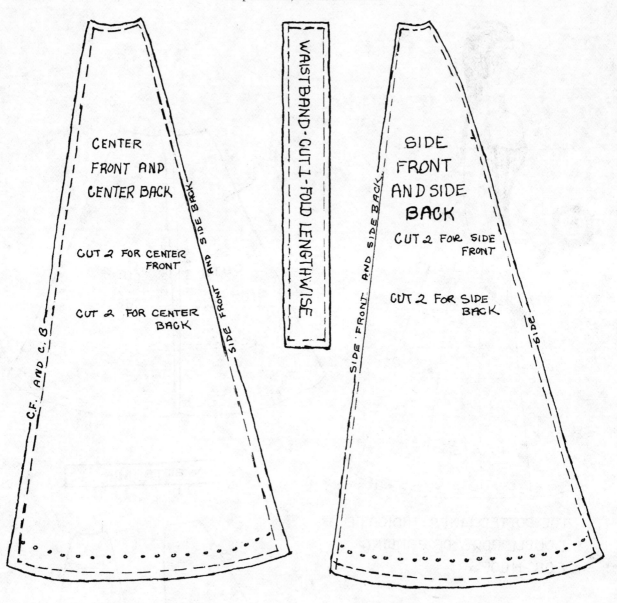

SCALE: ⅛" = 1"

NOTE: CIRCLED LINE INDICATES 2" HEM ALLOWANCE

(FOR ASSEMBLED VIEW SEE ILLUSTRATION IN FIGURE 3-11)

**Figure 3–12.** *Scaled Pattern for Bell Farthingale*

SCALE: ⅛" = 1"    CUT 1

FOR SKIRT: CUT 1 REC-
TANGLE 178" WIDE BY
45 ⅝" LONG (FOR JANE DOE.)

THE 178" ARE GATHERED
TO THE CIRCUMFERENCE
OF THE CIRCLE

THE 45 ⅝" ALLOWS FOR
JANE'S WAIST TO FLOOR
MEASUREMENT, PLUS 2"
FOR THE HEM. THE ⅝" IS
SEAM ALLOWANCE

NOTE: 1 THE DOTTED LINES SHOW BONING CHANNELS
(THE HEM CHANNELS MAY NOT BE NECESSARY)
2 THE CORSET IS A SEPARATE GARMENT

(FOR SCALED PATTERN OF CORSET SEE FIGURE 3-6)

**Figure 3–13.** *Cartwheel Farthingale with Scaled Pattern*

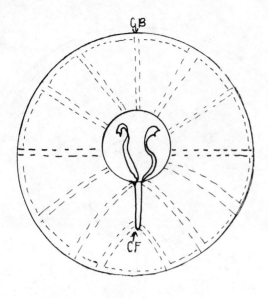

TOP VIEW CARTWHEEL FARTHINGALE

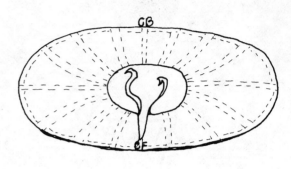

TOP VIEW OF SPANISH PANNIER

NOTE: THIS IS NOT TO SCALE

**Figure 3–14.** *Layout for Twill Tape Channels on Cartwheel Farthingale and Spanish Panniers*

The materials needed are essentially those needed for the bell farthingale, and the process is almost the same. The only difference is that because of the severity of the side curves, bias tape must be substituted for the twill tape on the channels.

*Construction of Rococo Panniers*  The Rococo pannier illustrated in Figure 3–16 is a complicated thing of tubular steel and hinges. This can be copied by a good shop welder. It can also be achieved by the bent wood process—the soaking of wooden strips until they are pliable. In Florida a rattan manufacturer showed me how to soak and bend tube bamboo, but split bamboo works much more easily and without the soaking. Both methods are time consuming and expensive.

Therefore, an illustration for an adaptation, which uses the same process as the cartwheel farthingale, is quicker and simpler to do, and gives a very accurate silhouette, is shown in Figure 3–17. Cut and sew as illustrated and place channels with bias tape along seams. Use masking tape wrapped flat bandings for circumference hoops and featherboning for flat supports. An even quicker method is to adapt an already existing circular hoop to the side oval shape by means of ribbons tied on the inside to form the proper shape, as illustrated in Figure 3–18.

*Construction of Hooped Crinoline*  The difference between the Victorian hoop of 1855 and that of 1865 is strictly in the width of the bottom circumference and the "fishtail" shape of the 1865 hoop. This is really more of an egg shape with the small end at the center back. The period just preceding this was called "crinoline" because of the use of multiple starched petticoats. The first hoops were channeled into the petticoats with at least one more petticoat worn on top, so that the ridges of the hoops would not show. These hooped petticoats were generally built in three to five tiers with a banded hoop at the bottom of each tier and then a ruffle covering the hooped hem. This is shown in scale and illustration in Figure 3–19. The process is consistent with those already described.

*Construction of Belled Hoop*  After 1865 the belled birdcage became popular. It was strictly a hoop over which several petticoats had to be worn and under which a respectable woman wore pantalettes, a straight legged forerunner of the bloomer. This is illustrated in Figure 3–20. Its 1865 fishtail cousin is illustrated in Figure 3–21. Figure 3–22 shows patterns for both.

The materials needed for it are steel banding, tin snips, twill tape, masking tape, a cotton waist band

NOTE: THIS CORSET IS MERELY AN ADAPTATION OF THE RENAISSANCE CORSETS IN FIGURES 3-6 AND 3-13

EITHER BONING, HORSEHAIR OR BUCKRAM MAY BE USED TO STIFFEN THE HEM.

FOR SKIRT: CUT 1 RECTANGLE 194" WIDE BY 43" LONG FOR JANE DOE. THE PRINCIPLE OF ASSEMBLY IS THE SAME AS THAT FOR THE CARTWHEEL FARTHINGALE.

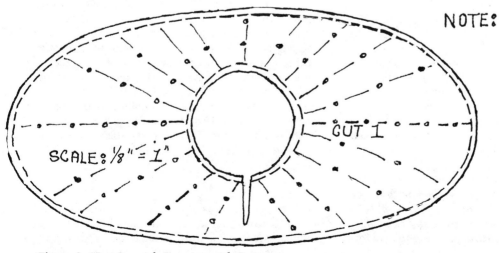

SCALE: ⅛" = 1"

CUT 1

NOTE: THE DOT-DASH LINE (—○—) IS TO SHOW THE PLACEMENT FOR THE BONING CHANNELS

**Figure 3–15.** *Spanish Pannier with Pattern*

NOTE: LITTLE IS KNOWN ABOUT THE UNDER GARMENTS FOR THE LOWER HALF OF THE ROCOCO LADY. (SHE DID WEAR STOCKINGS) THEREFORE THE ABOVE "FISHNETS" AND DANCE BRIEFS ARE MY OWN IDEA.

**Figure 3–16.** *Rococo Panniers—Factual Representation*

and cotton bands to cover the steel banding. The procedure is as follows:

1. *Cut the steel banding one inch longer than the desired circumference for each hoop of the seven, starting with the bottom and largest.*
2. *Close and wrap with masking tape.*
3. *Encase in cotton bands cut 1¼" longer than steel banding and twice the width of the wrapped banding, plus 1½ inches.*
4. *Make waist band.*
5. *Attach eight strips of twill tape evenly spaced around waistband and cut to the length of the waist-to-floor measurement (with shoes) plus 14 inches, which allow for the gradually expanding circumferences (two inches per hoop in each direction).*

6. *Mark each tape where each hoop will be attached. Note: The top hoop should be approximately eight to nine inches below the waist and the rest evenly spaced to the floor.*
7. *Now divide your hoops into eight equal sections.*
8. *Attach to twill tapes as marked.*

It should go without saying that a short woman might not need seven hoops, and a tall woman might need eight or nine. Also, the larger the circumferences, the more length that is needed for the twill tape.

For the egg-shaped hoop of 1865, obviously your two center back tapes will need the longest extension, and the two side backs will also need some extension beyond the above 14 inches extra required for the equidistant belled hoop.

### The Bustle

There are two silhouette extensions that cannot strictly be termed as hoops. The first is the bustle, which grew out of a necessary addition to the fishtail hoop. The added weight of that hoop in itself required a little support, so a crescent pad (in some cases, a double pad) was worn under the hoop to prevent it from dragging (see Fig. 3–23). It was supported by being worn around the waist.

The bustle was shaped somewhat differently between the 1870s, when it greatly resembled the bell farthingale with added rear padding, and the 1880s. The simplest way to achieve the look popular in the '70s is to use your moderate bell farthingale and add to it the pad mentioned above. In the late 1880s, it was all back froufrou and vestiges of the early '80s sheath in the front. The 1880's bustle is shown in Figure 3–24. This may be constructed from either coat hanger wire, bent to shape and wrapped in masking tape, or steel banding. These are then covered with thin aluminum screening. All screen edges must be taped, as well, and hot glued on. Then the whole bustle is sewn to a waistband. A bustle of this type was worn over the petticoat and directly under the exterior garment. It therefore required a bustle cover (Fig. 3–25). The "ins and outs" of the bustle can be clarified to this extent: It originally came "in" around 1870, when it was "very big," so to speak. By 1878 it had declined to the sheath, only to return more modestly from 1885 to 1890.

### The Bum Roll

The bum roll was also called a bolster and was nothing more than a garment that looked like a stuffed sausage and worn around the upper hip in Renaissance Europe. These can be seen in Adriaen

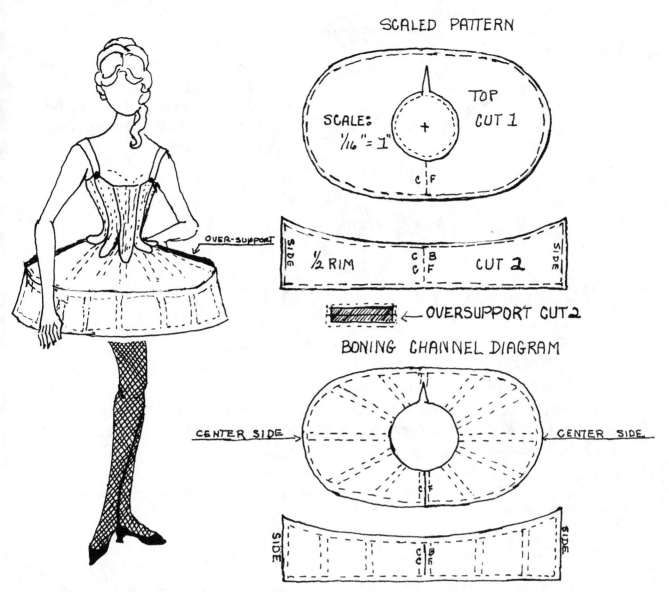

**SCALED PATTERN**

SCALE: 1/16" = 1"

TOP CUT 1

C F

SIDE 1/2 RIM CUT 2 SIDE

C C / B F

← OVERSUPPORT CUT 2

**BONING CHANNEL DIAGRAM**

CENTER SIDE → ← CENTER SIDE

C F

SIDE SIDE

C C / B F

OVER-SUPPORT

NOTE: THIS IS MADE ON THE SAME PRINCIPLE AS THE CARTWHEEL AND SPANISH FARTHINGALE. WHAT RAISES THE SIDE FOR THE SLIGHT UPWARDNESS OF THE ROCOCO LOOK IS THE OVER-SUPPORT. THE LENGTH OF THIS PANNIER FROM WAIST TO CENTER SIDE IS 12". THE OVER-SUPPORT IS 10", 2" SHORTER. THIS WILL PULL UP SIDE JUST ENOUGH. THEREFORE THE RIM IS CUT TO COMPENSATE. THE OVER-SUPPORT IS ATTACHED AT RIM EDGE AND AT WAIST. YOU MAY WANT AN EVEN WIDER PANNIER FOR A COURT DRESS. LENGTHEN AT CENTER SIDE AND LENGTHEN OVER-SUPPORT ACCORDINGLY.

IN THE EARLY TO MIDDLE ROCOCO (AND IN COUNTRIES SUCH AS ITALY AND ENGLAND) THE ABOVE UPWARD LOOK WAS NOT IN VOGUE. IN THESE CASES THE OVER-SUPPORT MAY BE ELIMINATED.

**Figure 3–17.** *Adaptation of Rococo Pannier*

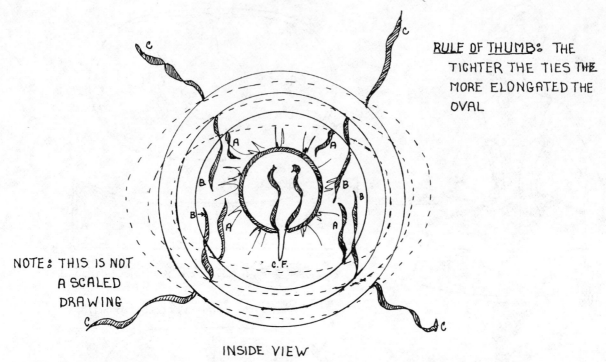

RULE OF THUMB: THE TIGHTER THE TIES THE MORE ELONGATED THE OVAL

NOTE: THIS IS NOT A SCALED DRAWING

INSIDE VIEW

TO CONVERT A CIRCULAR HOOP TO OVAL PANNIERS ADD TIE AND TIE TOGETHER #A TO A; B TO B; C TO C (AND SO ON IF THERE A MORE HOOPS)

**Figure 3–18.** *Adaptation of Circular Hoop to Oval*

Pietersz Van de Jenne's illustrations *Emblemata of Johan de Brune.* A pattern for one of these is scaled in Figure 3–26.

The materials needed are sturdy cotton and twill tape for ties. The procedure is as follows:

1. *Cut and sew as pictured in Figure 3–26, leaving a two-inch opening for turning.*
2. *Clip curves.*
3. *Turn rightside out.*
4. *Attach ties.*

### Petticoats

Petticoats are generally cut on the same pattern as the skirt that is worn over it (Chapters 6 and 7). There are decorative petticoats, which are seen, and utilitarian ones that are not seen. They may be lace-trimmed, trimmed with ruffles, or have a horsehair border for stiffening. One exception is the 1880s petticoat that supports the sheath silhouette with back detail (Fig. 3–27). Figure 3–28 is a pattern for one with an optional train. Both take a series of ruffles up the center back from hem to waist; when sewing, it is easiest to start at the bottom and work up. Each ruffle should be cut six inches deep. This allows ⅝" seam for attachment, a one-inch overlay, and one inch for a rolled hem. The length is figured by mea-

surement of the width of each tier "times three" for fullness. The top tier is the one exception, it is eight inches deep.

### 1920s Slip and Teddy

Figure 3–29 shows a 1920s "slip." This garment was suspended from shoulder straps, and its length depended on the skirt height of any given year; 1920 being very nearly mid-calf, to 1929 being about two inches above the knee.

Also in Figure 3–29 you will see a pattern for a 1920s "teddy." This was an all-in-one undergarment with legs. It was worn in place of the slip and was considered more modest by the conservative flapper.

### Pantalettes and Bloomers

Both pantalettes and bloomers can be cut on any commercial straight-leg pyjama pant pattern. Pantalettes generally came to the anklebone and were trimmed about twelve inches around the bottom and up the leg with multi-rows of lace.

Bloomers are gathered to just below the kneecap and are usually cut seven inches longer than the waist-to-knee measurement, leaving a four-inch hem into which is stitched a ⅝" to ¾" channel for

SCALE FOR HOOPS: 1/16" = 1"

FOR WAIST BAND CUT
RECTANGLE 5" X 27½"

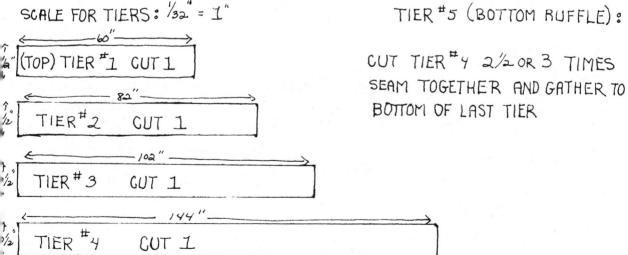

SCALE FOR TIERS: 1/32" = 1"

60"
1/4" (TOP) TIER #1 CUT 1

82"
1/2" TIER #2 CUT 1

102"
1/2" TIER #3 CUT 1

144"
1/2" TIER #4 CUT 1

TIER #5 (BOTTOM RUFFLE):

CUT TIER #4 2½ OR 3 TIMES
SEAM TOGETHER AND GATHER TO
BOTTOM OF LAST TIER

**Figure 3–19.** *Victorian Hooped Petticoat (1850s) with Scaled Pattern*

NOTE: 1 THE OFF-THE-SHOULDER CAMISOLE
      2 THE PANTALETTES

**Figure 3–20.** *Victorian Birdcage Hoop (1855)*

NOTE: PAD OR HORSEHAIR
      SUPPORT

**Figure 3–21.** *Fishtail Hoop (1865)*

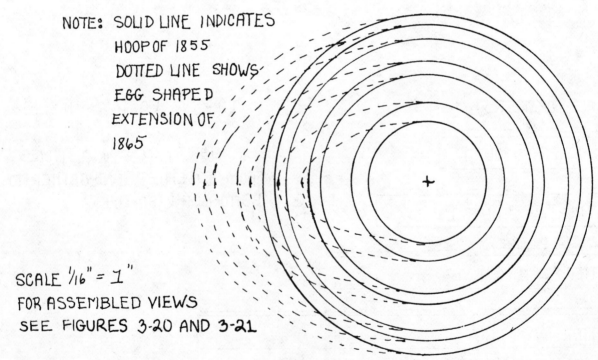

NOTE: SOLID LINE INDICATES
      HOOP OF 1855
      DOTTED LINE SHOWS
      EGG SHAPED
      EXTENSION OF
      1865

SCALE 1/16" = 1"
FOR ASSEMBLED VIEWS
SEE FIGURES 3-20 AND 3-21

**Figure 3–22.** *Scaled Pattern for Birdcage and Fishtail Hoops*

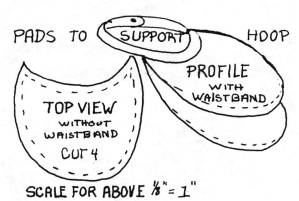

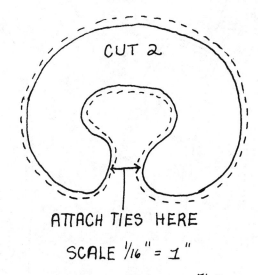

**SCALE FOR ABOVE ⅛" = 1"**

**Figure 3–23.** *Crescent Pad Worn under Hoop*

**ATTACH TIES HERE**

**SCALE ¹⁄₁₆" = 1"**

**SEAM ALLOWANCE ⅝"**

**Figure 3–26.** *Pattern for Bum Roll (Bolster)*

**Figure 3–24.** *Wire Cage Bustle—Late 1880*

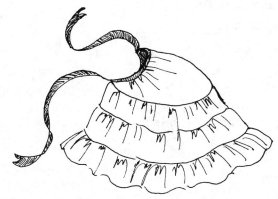

**Figure 3–25.** *Bustle Cover*

**BACK VIEW**

**Figure 3–27.** *Sheath Petticoat—1880 to 1885*

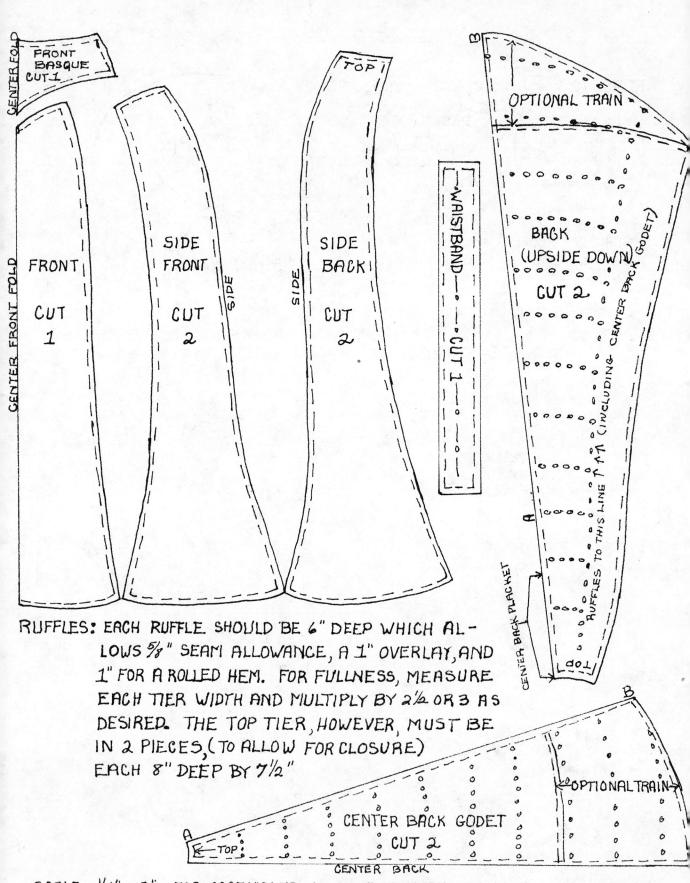

RUFFLES: EACH RUFFLE SHOULD BE 6" DEEP WHICH AL-
LOWS ⅝" SEAM ALLOWANCE, A 1" OVERLAY, AND
1" FOR A ROLLED HEM. FOR FULLNESS, MEASURE
EACH TIER WIDTH AND MULTIPLY BY 2½ OR 3 AS
DESIRED. THE TOP TIER, HOWEVER, MUST BE
IN 2 PIECES, (TO ALLOW FOR CLOSURE)
EACH 8" DEEP BY 7½"

SCALE ⅛" = 1" FOR ASSEMBLED VIEW SEE FIGURE 3-27

**Figure 3–28.** *Scaled Pattern for 1880s Sheath Petticoat with Optional Train*

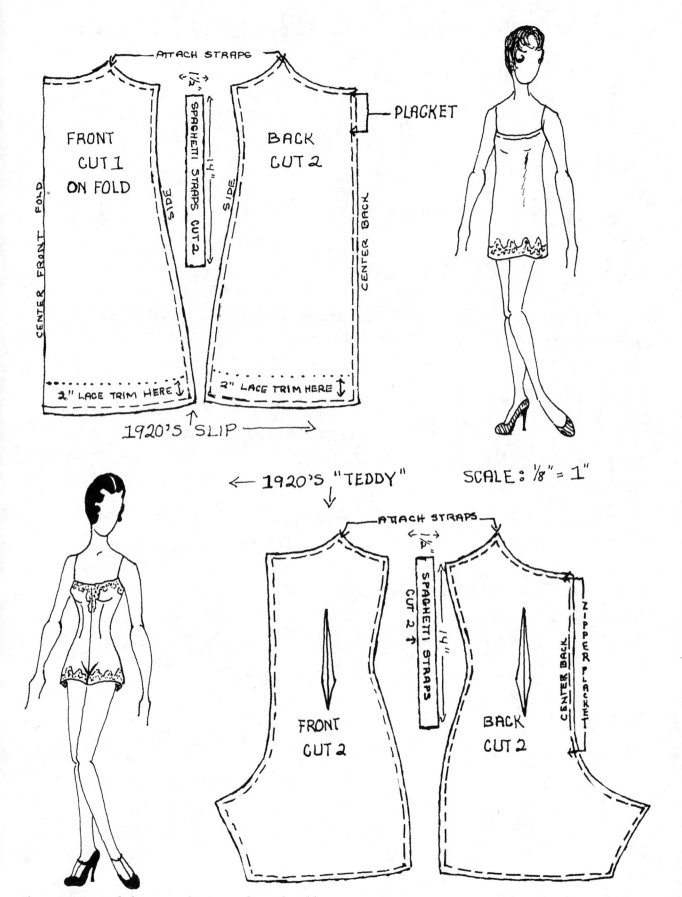

**Figure 3–29.** *Scaled Patterns for 1920s Slip and Teddy*

A. & B. PATTERN FOR AN OFF-THE-SHOULDER CAMISOLE + ALTERNATE

A.

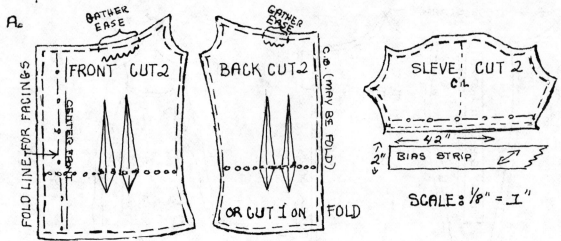

GATHER EASE

FOLD LINE FOR FACINGS

CENTER FRONT

FRONT CUT 2

GATHER EASE

BACK CUT 2

C.B. (MAY BE FOLD)

OR CUT 1 ON FOLD

SLEVE CUT 2
C.L.

←— 42" —→

↑2"↓ BIAS STRIP

SCALE: 1/8" = 1"

B.

FOLD LINE FOR FACING

PLEATS 3-1"    LACE INSERT    PLEATS 3-1"

CENTER FRONT

CUT 2

ALTERNATE FRONT

A. FOR AN ASSEMBLED VIEW SEE FIGURE 3-21

B. FOR AN ASSEMBLED VIEW WITH ALTERNATE
FRONT SEE FIGURE 3-20

NOTE: ALL NECKLINES ARE FINISHED IN A BIAS
STRIP. A FACING CHANNEL CAN BE
USED WITH EITHER A DRAW STRING OR
ELASTIC AS AN ALTERNATE METHOD ON "A".
THIS APPLIES TO "C", AS WELL

KEY: CIRCLE LINE (∘∘∘) INDICATES NATURAL
WAIST; THE DOT AND DASH (—∘—) = FOLD
BACK FACING LINE

C. PATTERN FOR AN ON-THE-SHOULDER CAMISOLE
SCALE 1/8" = 1"

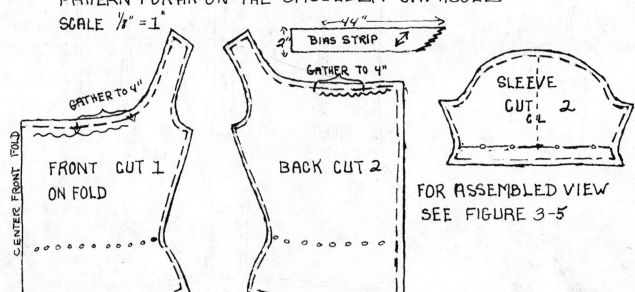

←— 44" —→

↑2"↓ BIAS STRIP

GATHER TO 4"

GATHER TO 4"

CENTER FRONT FOLD

FRONT CUT 1
ON FOLD

BACK CUT 2

SLEEVE
CUT 2
C.L.

FOR ASSEMBLED VIEW
SEE FIGURE 3-5

**Figure 3-30.** *Scaled Patterns for Camisoles*

either elastic or a drawstring. Lace can be added if desired. A pretty and fancy way of gathering them to the knee is eyelet trim through which ribbon may be threaded. This, of course, is done on the outside of the garment.

For bloomers to be worn by dancers, I usually pick a knitted fabric. In those cases in which a woven fabric must be used, I insert a diamond gusset at the center where the crotch seams meet. Remember to cut this gusset on the bias. I also flare the legs to a slight A-line from the side waist. It just gives a little more stretching room.

### Camisoles

Victorian women also wore "corset covers," a garment also known as a "camisole." It was a dainty low-cut blouse-like undergarment that was worn over the corset, but tucked into hoop and petticoats. By the late 1880s and '90s this same garment was worn under the corset. Examples of these can be seen in Figures 3–5, 3–19, 3–20, and 3–21. Figure 3–30 shows patterns for these.

One of my colleagues and I were asked to judge a theater conference several years ago. An extremely well-endowed young woman was anxiously braless in a very physically demanding part. It was evident that there was more life to her breasts than to her character.

"Well, what do you think?" I asked.

"Clothes may make the man," said my colleague, drawing on his pipe. "But it is underclothes that make or break a woman."

# TWO

# Pattern Drafting

Pattern drafting has been compared to a jigsaw puzzle designed by Fu Manchu. It seems to have all the mysteries of the East attached to it. There are many ways of doing the same thing and you will probably prefer one to the others. Some of us like to drape and cut from the draped form. What you see is what you get. This technique has its distinct advantages. The disadvantage is its consumption of time. Some people prefer flat pattern drafting, but you have to develop a knack for fitting puzzles together.

Are you one of those people who religiously cut out every notch on a commercial pattern and sew exactly by the instruction sheet? If so, you have a little homework to do before tackling pattern drafting.

Try laying out your pattern and studying the shapes of the pieces. Visualize how they fit together. Now cut, only marking the vital details (darts, gathers or drapings, etc.), but no notches. Put the directions away. Now put the garment together. Did you really need that notch to tell you what was the front of the dress? It has the bust dart and usually a lower curve to the neckline.

In this section we will discuss draping techniques, the adaptations of various existing patterns, and flat pattern drafting from measurements. Flat pattern drafting at best is still an inexact science. The reason lies not in the method but in the variables within the human form. Therein lies the endless fascination of the craft, the element that raises

it above the craft level to an art. It also requires many fittings and we shall discuss that in this section as well.

My intention is to show you the way to drafting all that your imagination can conceive. This is not a specific source for period patterns per se, although period adaptations will be discussed, but only in that light. Recently several excellent books on period patterns have come out, but your best sources are the garments themselves.

In these eight chapters the patterns include approximately ⅝" seam allowance all the way around, and like those in Chapter 3, they are scaled to fit the measurements of John and Jane Doe, described in the introduction.

All muslin used for any technique of pattern making should be preshrunk. The most convenient width of muslin for pattern drafting is 45 inches, but 36 inches is adequate for all but the most circular of designs.

Again, as in Chapter 3, the patterns include seam allowance, but that becomes a variable in Chapter 6, wherein we discuss how to draft, not specific patterns.

There really is nothing mysterious about drafting patterns. In my shop I have a sign that says, "Construction is a logical process going from A to D. Just remember to stop by B and C on the way." That sums up pattern drafting as well.

# 4

# Draping

Draping is the art of pinning the fabric directly onto the form (or the actor) and creating the costume in what may seem a one-step process. It involves considerably more than that, but its main advantages are that you can sometimes save on the number of fittings, and you can see in the third dimension exactly what you will get.

It works better if you are draping the actor himself, because it immediately allows for the adjustment of his particular figure peculiarities. If you are doing this, remember to work from the right side of the fabric, because if you work it "inside-out" you have reversed the garment and the actor may not be (and probably is not) perfectly even on both sides.

## Draping Directly on the Actor

Figures 4–1 through 4–3 show the process of draping directly on the actress. This particular pattern is a mock-up for a dolman-sleeved evening dress to be made out of a garnet "silesta" knit with a garnet velvet belt. It is easiest if you have the actress wear a leotard and tights. They tend to smooth the figure and give a surface to which pieces may be pinned.

Figure 4–1 shows the right side being pinned. The back and front are exactly the same, except for a zipper up the center back. Figure 4–2 shows the addition of the left side. Figure 4–3 shows the addition of the skirt (before hem markings) and a piece of fabric around the waist to simulate the look of the belt. Lower sleeves will be added and more fullness to the skirt.

### Mock-ups

Professional cutters often drape a mock-up of a costume if there is any question about how something is to be made. I usually drape a mock-up of an item I am making for the first time, because it allows me to play around until I get just the right line for which I am looking. A case in point is the woman's Cavalier jacket and stomacher shown in Figures 4–4 through 4–9.

Figure 4–4 shows the pinning of the back fabric, which will become two pieces, the center back and the side back. The seam lines are marked with dotted lines in magic marker or something equally permanent. The same process is used for the front, but in this instance I used two pieces of scrap muslin. It can be done with one piece of muslin, as was the back. These pieces are then removed, cut (allowing seam allowances of five-eights of an inch all the way around), and repinned onto the form as shown in Figure 4–5.

Figure 4–6 shows these pieces cut, repinned, and a stomacher added, which has been cut on the fold. This figure also shows the addition of a bias cut piece of fabric from which the collar will be cut. Figure 4-7 shows the collar cut and repinned. The same rule of thumb that applies to cutting flat patterns obviously applies to draping as well. The only way a straight edge will curve is to cut it on the bias.

In Figure 4–8 we see the pieces with adjustments marked on them and labeled for cutting. The muslin mock-up is cut from this with any and all additions and corrections. Please note the addition in the case of the sleeves shown in the assembled mock-up of Figure 4–9.

### Construction Lining

Often the muslin mock-up is used as a construction lining in the actual costume. A construcion lining is an interfacing that is stay-stitched directly to the "wrong" side of the fabric which serves to give added body and durability to the finished garment.

**Figure 4–1.** *Pinning the Right Side*

**Figure 4–2.** *Addition of Left Side*

**Figure 4–3.** *Addition of Skirt and Belt*

**Figure 4–4.** *Pinning the Back Fabric*

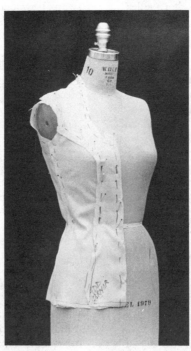

**Figure 4–5.** *Pinning the Front*

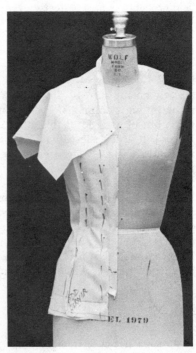

**Figure 4–6.** *Addition of Stomacher and Collar*

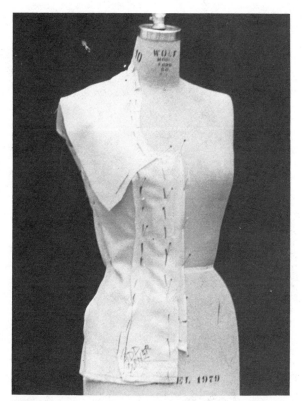

**Figure 4–7.**   *Collar Cut and Repinned*

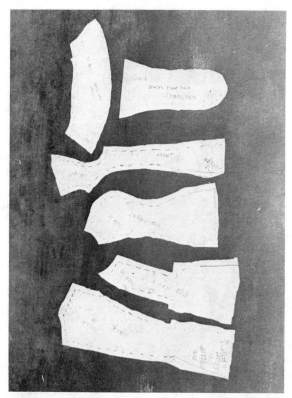

**Figure 4–8.**   *Pieces with Adjustments Marked and Labeled*

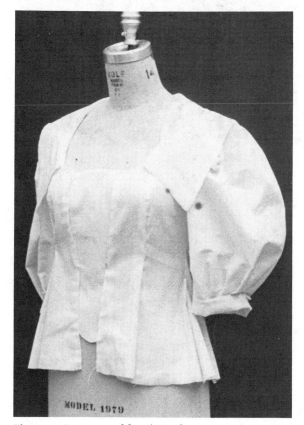

**Figure 4–9.**   *Assembly of Mock-up*

**Figure 4–10.**   *Completed Outfit for* The Miser

**Figure 4–11.**  *Draping in Conjunction with Flat Pattern Process*

**Figure 4–12.**  *Hedda Gabler's Dress, Act Three*

Figures 4–4 through 4–9 show the draping and pattern cutting of a Cavalier jacket-bodice to be used in Florida Atlantic University's production of *The Miser*. The pattern was drafted on a size 10 dress form. The show was then cast but the actress requiring that costume wore a size 12. To achieve the proper period silhouette, the waist needed to be raised one inch. These adjustments were made at the first fitting. A new pattern was cut that was then used as a construction lining. The final results can be seen in Figure 4–10.

Construction linings are often the secret ingredient in making cheap fabrics look more expensive and heavier. It allows you to use a knitted velour for velvet and still have the look of a woven fabric, because it cuts down or prevents stretching. (This does not always work, but it can. The way to test it is to stay stitch a twelve-inch square of muslin to one of the velour, wash it, and dry it to see if the stretch fabric bags out. If it does, *don't* use it.) There are many uses for construction linings which you will see as we go along.

Since we are discussing muslin in this context, please remember to preshrink your muslin (wash it, dry it, and press it out) before you cut patterns, exterior garments, or construction linings. Muslin has a 3 percent to 10 percent shrinkage factor; the looser the weave, the higher the percentage of shrinkage.

## Disadvantages to the Draping Process

There are a few disadvantages to the draping process that should be considered. It is a one-at-a-time process and not very helpful for mass production of the same garment. Then, too, it tends to waste fabric more than laying out the flat pattern.

It probably works best in conjunction with the flat pattern process. In Figures 4–11 and 4–12 we see such a situation. I had already done the skirt for *Hedda Gabler's* third-act dress (a dress for dying in!) by flat pattern drafting, but I needed to see the over drape in the third dimension. I dressed the dummy in the proper undergarments and draped a similar fabric, using it as my pattern (Fig. 4–11). You can see the final result in Figure 4–12.

## Periods that Require Draping Techniques

The art of draping is exceedingly important for those periods that primarily employ fold upon fold— e.g., Roman, Greek, and Empire. The ancients daily draped their bodies from basic geometric shapes, the circle, rectangle, and semi-circle. This can be done today, but it has several disadvantages.

First of all, you must teach the actor not only how to drape it, but how to move so that it stays draped. The folds will not necessarily stay where both you and the actor may want them, and the care it takes to keep properly draped may impede either his movement or characterization (or both). Of course, if authenticity is the primary value, you have no alternative. If, however, you wish to make a visual statement with a particular line or fold, then the costume is created by draping the actor (or form), and is constructed so that the folds are stitched to stay where you want them. The actor is thereby relieved of having to constantly worry about his appearance.

There is only one truly effective way to learn how to drape. Jump in with both hands, several spare yards of fabric, scissors, and pins, and do it.

# 5

# The Adaptation of Existing Patterns

The invention of the sewing machine in the middle of the 19th century changed the garment business. The dressmaker, who had previously gone from home to home, could stay in her shop. The homemaker became her own dressmaker and fashion was more easily accessible to the rural communities, where previously it had been dictated by the whims of the city inhabitants. Out of all this grew the fashion magazine and today's commercial pattern business. Since nothing about the human form has basically changed in several thousand years, many of these commercial patterns can be adapted to costume use. It is also a matter of record that fashion, like history, constantly repeats itself. Therefore, the full-skirted evening gown of the 1950s is basically the same line as the crinoline skirt of the 1850s. A fitted bodice may have three, five, seven, or nine pieces but it still conforms to the basic female shape. The look of the Empire waist returned in the 1960s, the shift and the smock in the '70s, but those have been around for years. It only takes a good eye and a little judicious piecing to adapt men's current patterns to period styles.

You may wish to take a pattern from a dress you found in Aunt Minnie's trunk. You may have found a pattern scaled down from a museum garment. Merely by enlarging the scale you could use this. These are all avenues to explore before worrying about completely drafting your own pattern from scratch.

## Helpful Fads and Events

Every now and then a particular fad helps. Right now we seem to be in "the rhinestone cowboy" stage. Western gear is being worn everywhere and for any occasion. Those patterns haven't changed in 100 years. Stock up!

Speaking of the West brings to mind the fine old tradition of square dancing which still flourishes, mostly west of the Mississippi. Commercial patterns cater to this need of square dance clothing, which can easily be adapted to period styles.

The Bicentennial of 1976 was a great help for Rococo patterns. I stocked in every even vaguely (and several were indeed "vaguely") commercial pattern in every size, cut them all in muslin, and have them stored away. Always use muslin for permanent patterns; tissue paper deteriorates quickly.

Heaven bless Halloween! It makes the pattern companies put out a few basic costume patterns, mostly in children's sizes, but you can always enlarge.

Weddings are another boon to the costumiere. For some reason, wedding gowns seem to have basic period lines. Perhaps this is because a wedding is an understandably romantic occasion and we tend to confuse the occasion with the style, thinking that because something is "old-fashioned" it is romantic. Whatever the reason, the patterns are most helpful.

## Adaptations of Commercial Patterns

You need not be confined to just those patterns that look like what you want. You can take a basic pattern and by changing a neckline here and a sleeve there, you have a new creation. *Vogue*, *Butterick*, and *McCall's* all have what they term "basic" patterns, generally a three-piece bodice, simple straight sleeves, and a straight A line skirt, as illustrated in Figure 5–1. Let's play around with that, add a leg-o-mutton sleeve, a stand-up collar, and a simple gored skirt as in Figure 5–2. Presto Change-o! A gay-nineties creation!

Now play around a little more. Drop the shoulder line, add a pagoda sleeve with false inner sleeves,

BASIC PATTERN PIECES INCLUDE THE BODICE FRONT
AND BACK, THE SLEEVE, 2 FRONT SKIRT PIECES, AND
2 BACK SKIRT PIECES

**Figure 5–1.** *A Female Garment from Basic Pattern*

ADDITIONS INCLUDE A STAND-UP COLLAR, BELT, A LACE
RUFFLE, PUFFED UPPER SLEEVES, AND TRIM OF LACE
AND VELVET

**Figure 5–2.** *Adaptation of Basic Pattern into a Dress of the 1890s*

point the waist, change the collar a bit or a neckline that has been made bigger, and add a full gathered skirt. In Figure 5–3 we see a result that looks remarkably like an 1850s dress.

Because men's fashion changes have been less drastic during the better part of the last two centuries, adaptation of their styles is even easier. Figure 5–4 shows a modern suit with the wide lapels, nipped waist, and slightly flared pant leg. With very little adjusting this can be altered into the pre-Raphaelite style of the 1880s and '90s (see Fig. 5–5).

Figure 5–6 shows a modern duffle coat and its adaptation into a Norfolk jacket. The knickers illustrated can be made by cutting off any pair of trousers and using the cut-off part to make the knee-band.

Figure 5–7 shows the adaptation of a modern sports coat into a turn-of-the-century man's sack coat. In this case, the center opening was merely rounded at a sharper angle and the coat buttoned higher. This can be done directly to the garment as well as to the pattern. This type of commercial adaptation can get you back to the late 19th century for men and the mid-19th century for women, as draping can get you from biblical to Byzantine. But what are you going to do with the almost 1000 intervening years?

## Cut from Antique Garments

You may have found some antique clothes full of moth holes and purple with age, but before you throw them out, carefully cut them apart, avoiding the seams. Lay them on muslin and draw around them. Now add a uniform ⅝" seam allowance on all sides of each piece. Be sure that you mark all darts, gathers, pleats, folds, etc., and label each piece as to what it is. You might make a sketch of it as well. Now you may throw out the moth-eaten original.

Museums are often helpful in allowing you to take patterns off some of their costumes if you write ahead and make all necessary arrangements. They will want time to check up on you to make sure you will handle their items with care. (Always wear gloves when handling any such items.) Of course, they will not let you take the garment apart, but you don't have to do this to derive the pattern. However, tell them you need to pin the garment onto a dress form.

Once the item is on the form, lay a piece of muslin on top of the particular section you are working. Pin outline the shape of the piece. With a pencil, draw a dotted line between the pins. Remove and lay this flat. Now add a uniform ⅝" seam allowance around all sides and go on to the next piece. Skirts

ADDITIONS INCLUDE A "PETER PAN" COLLAR, PAGODA
SLEEVES, BELT, AND FULL UNDER SLEEVES

ALTERATIONS INCLUDE CHANGING THE BODICE TO A
FRONT BUTTONED OPENING, AND THE SKIRT CUT TWICE
AND GATHERED TO WAISTLINE

**Figure 5–3.** *Adaptation of Basic Pattern into an
1850s Dress*

**Figure 5–4.** *A Modern Three-Piece Suit*

ALTERATIONS INCLUDE WIDER LAPELS, CUFFS TO THE
SLEEVES, INSET POCKETS WITH FLAPS, AND SLIGHTLY
FLARED TROUSERS. THE WAISTCOAT WAIST LINE WAS
ROUNDED.

**Figure 5–5.** *Three-Piece Suit Adapted to Pre-
Raphaelite Style*

NORFOLK JACKET

DUFFLE COAT

ADDITIONS INCLUDE OVER-THE-SHOULDER WELTS, LOWER POCKET FLAPS, CUFFS, AND ELBOW PATCHES

DELETIONS INCLUDE SLEEVE BELTS AND YOKE POCKETS

ALTERATIONS INCLUDE A SHORTER COAT LENGTH AND NARROWED LAPELS

**Figure 5–6.** *Duffle Coat Adapted to Norfolk Jacket*

SPORTS COAT

SAC COAT

ADDITIONS INCLUDE A THIRD,TOP, BUTTON
AND BUTTONHOLE AND BIAS TRIM AROUND
EDGES

ALTERATIONS INCLUDE THE CUT-AWAY CURVE
TO FRONT AND REAPPORTIONMENT OF COLLAR
FOLD

DELETION IS THE PATCH POCKET IN EXCHANGE FOR INSET POCKETS WITH WELTS

**Figure 5–7.** *Sports Coat Altered to Early 20th Century Sac Coat*

can be done by laying the garment on the table so that one section at a time is flat. In this case one can often work from the inside for detail clarification. If you are taking the pattern of a full sleeve, stuff it with tissue paper to get its true shape. This process, illustrated in Figure 5–8, is time consuming but is often worth it.

Some of this work has been done for you and put into book form; cf. Janet Arnold's two-volume set *Patterns Of Fashion: English Woman's Dress and Their Construction*, (Volume I, 1660–1860; Volume II, 1860–1940); Hill and Bucknell's *The Evolution of Fashion: Pattern and Cut from 1066 to 1930*; Blanche Payne's *History of Costume*; and Norah Waugh's two works *The Cut of Women's Clothes, 1600 to 1930* and *The Cut of Men's Clothes, 1600 to 1900*. They have reduced these patterns to scale drawings (as I have for much of this book).

### Scaling up from Museum Garments

Many of these patterns have been scaled to fit the figure of an average man and woman. In some cases

**Figure 5–8.** *Cutting from an Actual Period Garment Without Taking It Apart*

they are scaled down from the measurements of the original owner of the garments. Each book tells how their particular scaling was done.

*Scaled for the Average Male and Female* If the patterns have been scaled for the average male and female, you will find them proportioned for today's average. Just scale up and try it on your average-sized dummy and you can make any corrections or alterations as your particular design may dictate.

*Scaled Directly from the Garment* If the pattern has been scaled directly from the garment, you will probably find the shoulder a bit small and the overall shorter than you desire. In this case you will have to adjust the pattern to a better proportion before you make any design corrections. This is just an added step.

Regardless of the above situation, you must first increase the pattern from its "doll clothes" size to people proportions. This can be done in two ways; the direct scale method (by counting inches) or what I have termed "the point system".

*The Direct Scale Method* The direct scale method is really very simple. For an example let's take the bodice back piece. If the ⅛" scale shows seventeen inches from center back neck to waist, you draw a line on your muslin seventeen inches long. Using your T-square, yardstick, and french curve, grid each successive measurement from that line.

*The Point System* Figure 5–9 illustrates the point system which you might find quicker and, if you are not the best of mathematicians, it is often more accurate. The procedure is as follows.

1. *Trace the pattern accurately from the book onto a piece of tablet paper.*
2. *Cut this out.*
3. *Now place the straight edge of the paper pattern onto a straight line that you have marked on your muslin. You may use the selvedge edge as a guide, but leave seam allowance if necessary. Note: For bias pieces it is best to cut the pattern piece on the straight for accurate, unwarped measurement. It then should be recut on the bias.*
4. *Using a yardstick from the pivotal point of the bottom left corner, increase each measurement to scale and make a dot (point).*
5. *Repeat until all the edges are increased.*
6. *Connect all the dots.*
7. *Add seam allowance if and where necessary.*

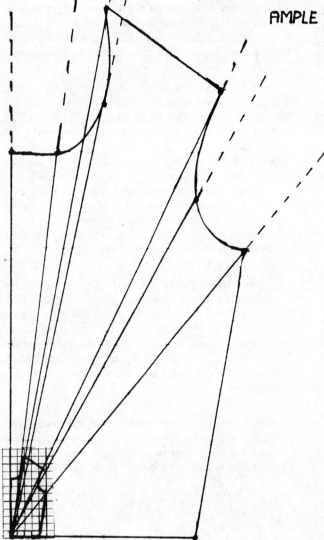

THE SCALE OF THE SMALL BODICE IS THAT EACH
SQUARE EQUALS 2". THIS WAS INCREASED
TO A SCALE OF 1/4" = 1".

NOTE: THIS IS STRICTLY A HYPOTHETICAL EX-
AMPLE AND WAS NOT DRAFTED TO SIZE.

**Figure 5–9.** *The Point Method for Increase or Decrease of Scale*

As a word of caution, be very careful when tracing your "doll clothes" pattern. The width of a pen line in 1/8" or 1/16" scale can make as much as an inch difference in the overall increased pattern.

*Reverse Scale* Remember that old saying, "What goes up must come down"? Let's amend that to "What goes up *can* come down." If you have a lack of storage space for your patterns, you might wish to reduce certain garments to "doll clothes" size for easy storage. Both the direct scale method

and point system work in reverse for just such a purpose.

These methods will certainly increase your flexibility, but you may still need to have at your fingertips the means of expressing your own ideas that the aforementioned cannot provide. How do you create an Oberon or an Ariel, the Wicked Witch of the West or the Queen of the Night? These questions have only one answer, flat pattern drafting from measurements.

# 6

# Flat Pattern Drafting
## from Measurements

No matter how detailed the following explanations may be, flat pattern drafting will be difficult for the novice. Please keep in mind that this is a general technique, one that works in most cases, but not everyone fits the rule. Rules of thumb are truisms that have been discovered and used over many years because they work about 85 percent of the time. Why they work may remain unknown, but that does not matter. The fact that they work so frequently is sufficient.

In this chapter we will discuss the drafting of general items; a bodice, a sleeve, facings, a skirt, a pair of pants, and a sloper. What is a sloper? A sloper is a configuration of one-quarter of the body, usually further divided into the upper half (shoulder to waist) and lower half (waist to ankle or floor). Therefore, you would have a sloper for a bodice front, bodice back, sleeve, skirt or pants front, and skirt or pants back. Manufacturers have slopers in specific sizes that are used as tools from which specific patterns are drafted. They take as much time to draft as a specific pattern, but if you draft one for each size, you can save time at a later stage, particularly in mass production techniques. Figure 6–1 shows a female sloper for our friend Jane, and Figure 6–2 is a sloper for her brother John. They are made to scale and you may increase them and use the sloper method if you wish.

## Equipment Needed

Before we begin, let us briefly review some special equipment you will need for pattern drafting: A T-square to get proper 90° right angles and perpendicular lines; a protractor; a compass (one of those big ones used for school blackboards is great); and, if

necessary, a high school text book on plane geometry or at least a handy reference to axioms, postulates, and geometric formulae.

## The Sloper Method

The slopers should be made of either muslin or brown wrapping paper, and all pieces must be properly labeled. (I personally prefer to work with muslin as it is a fabric and molds like one, a quality non-existent in the brown paper.) A good idea is to punch-hole the cross section lines so that they can be marked easily with chalk when you make your final patterns.

### The Female Sloper

Since each section varies slightly let us take Jane's sloper, piece by piece. As shown in Figure 6–1, the female sloper has a bodice front, a bodice back, a skirt front, a skirt back, and a sleeve.

*Use of Sloper for a Three-Piece Bodice*  Let us use the chest sloper to make a conventional three-piece bodice pattern. The steps are as follows:

1. *Lay the sloper front on the straight grain of the muslin.*
2. *Draw around it and chalk mark all dots.*
3. *At this point you have a choice:*
   a. *You may cut up your original sloper, or*
   b. *You may cut out a muslin sloper and slash it, redrawing a second sloper to be stored for the next time. (I prefer alternate b.) Whichever way you choose, you must slash the sloper from one-half inch to the right of*

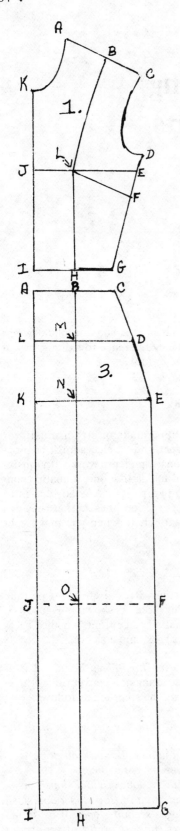

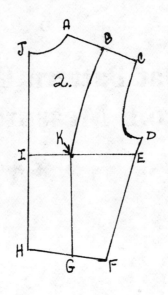

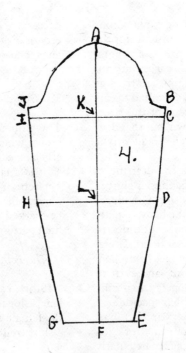

1. BODICE FRONT SLOPER
2. BODICE BACK SLOPER
3. SKIRT SLOPER
4. SLEEVE SLOPER

NOTE: DOTTED LINE INDICATES KNEE LINE

SCALE 1/8" = 1"

**Figure 6–1.**  *Basic Sloper for Jane Doe*

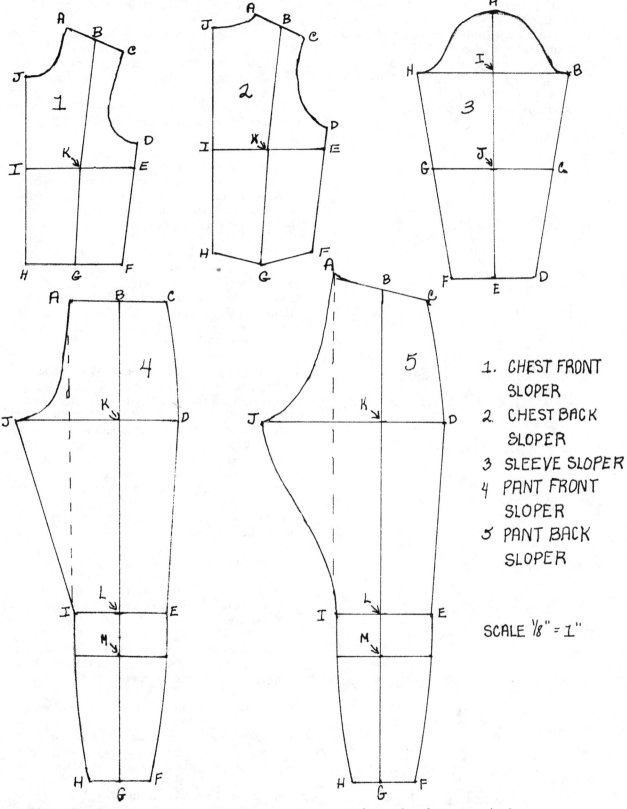

1. CHEST FRONT SLOPER
2. CHEST BACK SLOPER
3. SLEEVE SLOPER
4. PANT FRONT SLOPER
5. PANT BACK SLOPER

SCALE ⅛" = 1"

NOTE: DOTTED LINE IS MERELY AN ADDITIONAL GUIDE LINE

**Figure 6–2.** *Basic Sloper for John Doe*

point L to F and from one-half inch to the bottom of point L to H, as shown in Figure 6–3. **Do not entirely disconnect the wedge.**

4. *Separate at F to allow one inch.*
5. *Separate at H to allow one-and-a-half inch.*
6. *Draw your desired neckline. (This is also shown on Figure 6–3.)*
7. *Connect these spaces on lines I to G and D to G.*
8. *Now bisect these spaces, creating a new LH line*

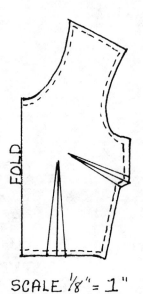

SCALE ⅛" = 1"

**Figure 6–3.** *Bodice Front Cut from Bodice Sloper*

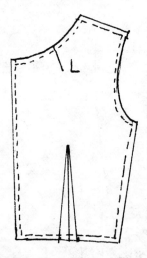

SCALE ⅛" = 1"

**Figure 6–4.** *Bodice Back Cut from Bodice Sloper*

*and an LF line. (This gives you the dart in Figure 6–3.)*
9. *Go around the entire piece marking a uniform ⅝" seam allowance, except for neck and armhole curves. (The ⅝" is subtracted from existing sloper curves on these two openings for greater ease.)*
10. *Now pin your darts together. This will give you a notch when you cut out the piece.*
11. *Cut out the pattern piece.*

Exactly the same process is repeated for the back bodice piece with this exception—there is no bust dart. Since this is a scooped neckline, you may wish to take a little back neck dart as indicated on Figure 6–4 by a little line marked L.

*Use of Sloper for Four-Gored Skirt Pattern* Let us now go onto the skirt sloper. The procedure is essentially the same. In this case, however, the skirt front and back patterns are exactly the same. You slash your sloper along line BG. Draw your desired gores, allowing for a little ease and seams. This is illustrated in Figure 6–5.

*Use of Sloper for Fitted Sleeve* As we can see in Figure 6–6, the same thing holds true for the sleeve. We must slash the sleeve vertically along line AF and move the sloper left-hand piece to the other side. This will give us the seam on the back elbow side of the garment, and allow us an edge for a conforming dart at L. This little dart is like the neckline dart. It should be marked on the person or form, but, as a rule of thumb, a total of one inch on the AF line at the elbow point is usually sufficient. That equates to a half-inch on each side of the line going to nothing at the elbow point.

*The Male Sloper*

Figure 6–2 shows the pieces of the male sloper—a front chest, a back chest, a front leg, a back leg, and a sleeve.

*Use of Sloper for Shirt Pattern* Let's make a simple open-necked shirt with a yoke from our chest slopers. The procedure is as follows:

1. *Do exactly as you did for steps #1 and #2 for the female bodice.*
2. *Mark where you wish your yoke line to be.*
3. *Slash along that line and draw the yoke piece, again adding uniform seam allowance on all sides, except for neck and armhole curves.*
4. *Now for the additional fullness that you may wish to gather onto this yoke, slash your bottom sloper piece on the BG line and separate to include this.*
5. *Repeat for the back.*

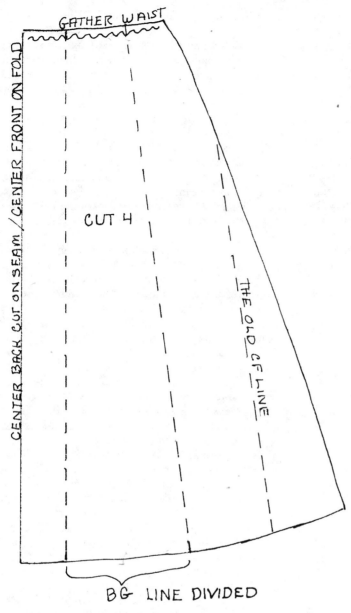

SCALE ⅛" = 1"

**Figure 6–5.** *Skirt Cut from the Skirt Sloper*

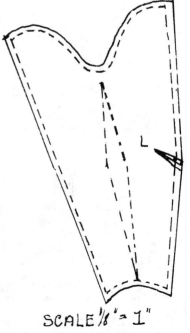

SCALE ⅛" = 1"

**Figure 6–6.** *Sleeve Pattern Cut from Sloper*

All of the above steps are illustrated in Figure 6–8. Figure 6–9 shows the use of the sleeve sloper to achieve a full sleeve that will be gathered to a wristband and into the armhole.

*Use of Sloper for a Full Sleeve*   As we did to the lower chest piece to achieve added fullness, so we must do to the basic sleeve sloper. We must slash it along the BE line and separate it.

*Use of Sloper for a Pair of Trousers*   Once again by repeating the same basic procedures, we can use the leg slopers (front and back) to create a pair of trousers. For ease you will need a dart or pleat along the BG line. Slash your sloper accordingly. Unless you are making those very form-fitting trousers of the 1820s, you will probably want to ease out the leg area a bit. These two items are illustrated in Figure 6–7.

There are hundreds of possible variations for spe-

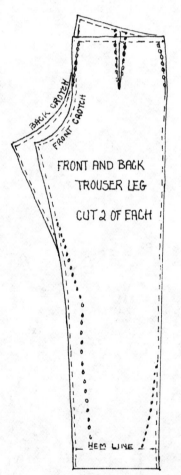

KEY: (o-o-o) CIRCLE LINE INDICATES SLOPER LINES
      (——) SOLID LINE IS CUTTING LINE
      (----) DOTTED LINE IS SEAM LINE

**Figure 6–7.**  *Using the Leg Sloper to Draft Trousers*

cific designs, some of which will be discussed in Chapters 7 through 10. The preceding should have shown you how slopers are used. Right now we need to understand how one drafts the sloper in the first place.

**Drafting the Original Sloper**

There is only one difference in drafting a sloper and drafting a garment. As we have seen, the sloper does not concern itself with either sewing or design details (darts, seams, etc.)

We will take each general section separately; the leg, the skirt, the chest, and the sleeve.

*Drafting the Leg Sloper*   The one important thing to remember when drafting the leg sloper is that from the waist to the crotch area it is one-quarter the *body*, but from the crotch to the ankle it is one-half the *leg*.

We will be using John Doe's measurements and following Fig. 6–2 for the explanation. The procedure is as follows:

1. *On the vertical grain of the muslin, draw a line that corresponds to John's waist-to-ankle measurement (40"). Be sure to leave plenty of room on either side of this line. Using Figure 6–2, this becomes the BG line.*
2. *Take John's waist measurement and divide it by four to equal one-quarter of his body (8"). Now divide that measurement by two (4") and put the resulting amount of inches on either side of your vertical line and perpendicular to it. In Figure 6–2 this becomes the AC line.*
3. *Now take John's waist-to-knee measurement (26") and on the BG line, starting at B, measure down and put a mark, letter L.*
4. *Take his knee measurement (15") and dividing by two (7½"), you have the length of the IE line. This length, of course, must be equally divided on either side of the BG line (3⅝") and the IE line must be perpendicular to BG.*
5. *At letter L, measure down the BG line the distance from knee to calf and make a mark, letter M.*
6. *To achieve the perpendicular calf line, divide the calf measurement (15") by two (7½"), placing half of this on each side of the BG line. (In this case it is exactly the same as the knee.)*
7. *To create the perpendicular ankle line, HF, divide the ankle measurement (10") by two (5"), placing it equally on either side of BG (2½" per side).*
8. *Measure down the BG line nine inches and make a mark, letter K. (Why nine inches? Here is a rule of thumb. The average person, when*

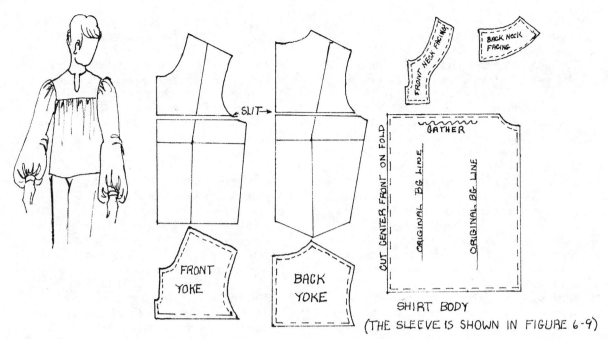

**Figure 6–8.** *Using the Chest Sloper to Create a Shirt Pattern*

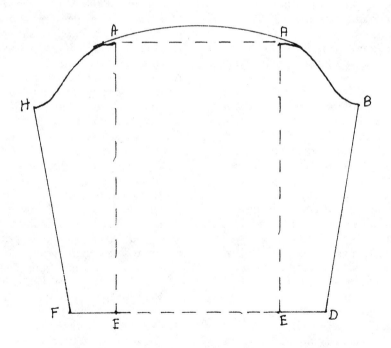

NOTE: SEAM ALLOWANCE AND EXTRA LENGTH
FOR PUFFING MUST NOW BE ADDED

SCALE ⅛" = 1"

**Figure 6–9.** *Use of Sleeve Sloper to Draft Full Sleeve*

*sitting in a straight chair with both feet on the ground measures nine inches from waist to seat.)*

9. Take John's hip measurement (38") and divide by four (9½"). Divide the result by two (4¾"), and on a perpendicular line at letter K, put that result equally on either side of the BG line.

10. Now draw a dotted line from A to KD. Extend your perpendicular KD bisecting line through point K beyond the AI line about four to six inches.

11. For the crotch curve, first take the waist-front to waist-back through crotch measurement (31") and divide by two (15½"). For the front crotch measurement subtract two inches (13½"). (When we get to the back we will add these two inches to that half crotch measurement. I don't know why this works, but it does—another rule of thumb!)

12. With your french curve, give yourself the resulting measurement of step #11 just to the KD line. This curve measurement gives you point J. This line may measure slightly more than the result of step #9.

13. Now connect all the vertical points; that completes the front leg sloper.

14. For the back leg sloper we use the front leg and all its markings, but the back crotch must be extended as shown in Figure 6–2.

*Drafting the Skirt Sloper* For this sloper we will use Jane's measurements and Figure 6–1 for reference:

1. On the vertical grain of the fabric, draw a line that corresponds to Jane's waist-to-floor measurement (waist-to-knee = 26" + knee-to-floor of 17" = 43"). Remember to leave plenty of room on either side of this line. In Fig. 6–1 this is the BH line.

2. Taking Jane's waist measurement (26") and dividing it by four (6½"), put equal amounts of that result on either side of the BH line. This forms the AC line.

3. From point A, make a vertical line also corresponding to Jane's waist-to-floor measurement (43") which runs directly parallel to the BH line. This becomes the AI line.

4. On this AI line, measure down four inches from point A and make a mark, letter L. (The four inches, like the previously mentioned nine inches is a rule of thumb.)

5. On this same line, again starting at point A, measure down nine inches and make a mark, letter K.

6. At point L, make a perpendicular line that is one-fourth of the upper hip measurement (35" ÷ 4 = 8⅜"). This is the LD line.

7. At point K make a perpendicular line that is one-fourth of the lower hip measurement (39½" ÷ 4 = 9¼"). This makes the KE line.

8. At point O, draw a perpendicular line. This equals the waist-to-knee measurement.

9. Now at point E, draw a vertical line to point G. This should be parallel to the BH line from its bisecting points of N and O at letters E and F.

10. Using your french curve, connect points C, D, and E.

*Drafting the Chest Sloper* This sloper continues using Jane's measurements and Figure 6–1.

1. As illustrated in Figure 6–10, draw a line down the vertical grain of the fabric and another line perpendicular to the first. (Be sure you leave working room on all sides, but you will need much more space to the right than the left.) This will form a right angle.

2. At the corner point of the right angle, draw a line 17° from the 90° perpendicular mark. This line should equal in length half of the shoulder measurement. (15" ÷ 2 = 7½") This becomes point C. You will need a protractor for this.

3. Now take one-fourth of Jane's neck measurement at the base of the neck. (14" ÷ 4 = 3½")

4. Starting at the corner point but following the 17° angle line, measure down the result of step #3 and put a mark. This becomes letter A.

5. Divide the AC line equally. This divisional point becomes letter B.

6. Draw a perpendicular line down from letter B, corresponding in length to the shoulder-to-point measurement. At the end of this line, draw a line perpendicular to the original line, of a length equal to one-fourth of the chest measurement, expanded (9⅛"). This becomes the JE line. The J is marked on the original vertical line of step #1.

7. At a point halfway between J and E, mark a point lettered L. With your french curve, connect B to L. Now mark letter L.

8. At point L, mark a line perpendicular to the JE line whose length corresponds to the distance from point to waist front (8¼"). This becomes point H, and creates the BH line.

9. Measure up one-and-a-half inches from point E, and this becomes point D.

10. At H make a line perpendicular to the BH line. The point of intersection with the original vertical line of step #1 becomes point I.

11. Now take one-fourth of Jane's waist measurement (26" ÷ 4 = 6½"), and starting at point I, measure this result on the IH line to arrive at point G.

12. You can now connect the DG line going through E.

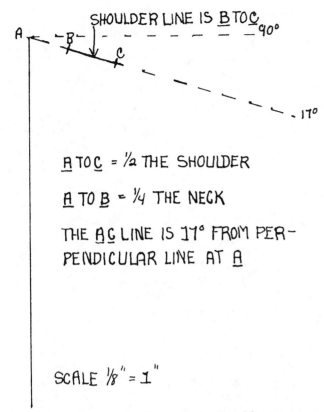

SHOULDER LINE IS <u>B</u> TO <u>C</u> 90°

A TO <u>C</u> = ½ THE SHOULDER

A TO <u>B</u> = ¼ THE NECK

THE <u>A</u><u>C</u> LINE IS 17° FROM PER-
PENDICULAR LINE AT <u>A</u>

SCALE ⅛" = 1"

**Figure 6–10.** *How to Compute the Shoulder Line*

For the back neck curve, the rule of thumb for the average female is three inches. This can be achieved by extending the KI line and using your french curve to get three inches from point A to a new point K. On the back sloper the KI line equals the JH line. Once you have the new J, use that and measure down the JH line to find a new H. This measurement must correspond to the shoulder-to-waist, center back measurement (for Jane 16½"). As you see in Jane's case it is not the same place. Therefore, a new HF line must be drawn.

*Drafting the Sleeve Sloper*　For the sleeve sloper let us stay with Jane's measurements and Figure 6–1.

1. *Draw your vertical line to correspond to Jane's shoulder-to-wrist measurement (22½"). This becomes the AF line.*
2. *Starting at A, measure down 6½ inches and make a mark lettered K. The 6½ inches is derived by dividing the shoulder-to-elbow measurement to find the place for the upper arm measurement (13" ÷ 2 = 6½" in Jane's case).*
3. *At K, draw a line perpendicular to it that extends equidistantly on either side of K to a measurement corresponding to the upper arm measurement (11" in total; 5½" on each side of K).*
4. *Once again starting at A, measure down the AF line a distance corresponding to the shoulder-to-elbow measurement (13") and mark point L.*
5. *At L, draw a line perpendicular to it that extends equidistantly on either side of L to a measurement corresponding to the elbow measurement (9¾" in total; 4⅞" on each side of L).*
6. *At F, repeat the process in steps #3 and #5 with the measurement corresponding to the wrist measurement (6" in total; 3" on each side of F).*
7. *Measure up from I and C, one inch for points J and B.*
8. *Now connect your JG line going through J and H and your BE line going through C and D.*
9. *Now you must plot a convex upper arm curve to ease into the concave curve of the armhole. As a rule of thumb, the armhole circumference for the average female is approximately 20 to 22 inches depending on the desired fullness. This should be equally divided on either side of the line.*

13. *Starting at point I, measure up 13¾ inches (Jane's clavical-to-waist measurement) along the IJ line to arrive at point K.*
14. *By using your french curve, you should be able to arrive at the neck and armhole curves but you will need to double-check these by means of Jane's measurements and one general rule of thumb.*
15. *The front neck curve should generally be five inches on the average female.*
16. *The beginning of the armhole curve should be a line parallel to the BL line for the distance of the armhole to armseye measurement (which in Jane's case is 6"). It should then curve outward to meet point D. At that shoulder to armseye point, the distance between it and the KI line should equal half of the armseye-to-armseye across the front measurement (16" ÷ 2 = 8").*

As with the front leg sloper, the front chest sloper is used to create the back with two differences—the back neck curve and the length of the center back line.

A word of caution should be mentioned here: This curve seems to be the biggest stumbling block that beginning pattern drafters face. Everyone wants to make too steep a curve. If an error is to be made, it is better to err on the generous side. Excess can always be removed. Fabric is not like your hair after a bad hair cut; it won't grow back.

## Drafting Directly per Garment

The method of drafting directly per garment is almost the same as that used in drafting the sloper, only we figure in the seam allowances, the darts, gathers, pleats, etc., as we go along. The biggest advantage to this is its saving of time.

After you have mastered this technique, you can use it directly on the wrong side of the fabric if you wish. That eliminates the muslin altogether unless the garment needs a construction lining. Then your muslin pattern may become your construction lining. For now, we will continue to use muslin to make our patterns.

Before we tackle a specific pattern, let us discuss how seam allowances are computed. The "given," to borrow a mathematical expression, is that all seam allowances are 5/8" wide. Therefore any pattern piece, unless cut on the fold, must have 1¼ inches added to its body measurement if it is to fit the body exactly. This does not allow for much "moving-around room." In costume parlance "moving-around room" is called "ease." As a general rule of thumb, an extra quarter-inch is added to the total of each pattern piece's measurement. This brings our additional 1¼ inch to a 1½ inch measurement.

### Drafting a Female Dress

Figure 5–1 illustrates the basic dress we shall now draft. We shall divide it into its component pieces—the skirt, the bodice, and the sleeve.

*The Skirt Front*   The skirt is an A-line, cut of four basic pieces because the center front is on the seam. It has two darts in the front and back. A zipper will be in the center back seam. Its pattern pieces are illustrated in Figure 6–11. The drafting procedure is as follows:

1. On your muslin, draw the vertical line for JE, its length corresponding to the waist-to-floor measurement. (Once again we shall use Jane Doe. Therefore this measurement would be 43".) To this you must add 5/8" for seam allowance, plus whatever hem you desire. A standard hem is usually two inches (43" + 2" = 45 + 5/8" = 45⅝").
2. As you did with the sloper, measure down the JE line 4⅝" to find K, and make your upper hip line. Using one-quarter the upper hip measurement (35"), add 5/8" for seam allowance plus ¼" for ease, giving an additional total of 7/8" (8¾" + 7/8" = 9⅝"). This measure is equally divided on either side of point K (4¾"). This then gives you the HB line.
3. At H, measure up in a direct perpendicular 4⅝ inches to find point I. Then measure down five

inches to find G, and continue down to F so that the entire IF line equals the length and runs parallel to the JE line.
4. At G, draw a direct perpendicular going through point L to the length of the lower hip measurement (39½") plus 1¼ inches seam allowance (40¾"), plus a little ease. This gives you point C.
5. At point I, make a perpendicular line equal to one-fourth the waist measurement (6½") plus 5/8" seam allowance and one inch for the dart (6½" + 5/8" = 7⅛" + 1" = 8⅛"). This gives you point I and the IA line.
6. Connect A to C through B with your french curve. Make your A-line flare as wide as desired. Continue this line the same length as both the GF and LE lines. This gives point D.
7. Connect E to D in a gentle curve. Connect E to F in a straight line. This gives you the FD line.
8. To plot the dart, measure a half-inch on each side of point J on the IA line and mark. Connect these marks to point K.
9. Cut out your pattern.

*The Skirt Back*   You may use your skirt front pattern to make your skirt back in one simple step. Lay out the skirt front, mark all darts, and add 5/8" to the center fold line (IF line), which now becomes the center back seam.

*The Bodice Front*   There is one note of caution you must always remember when drafting the bodice pieces! You can allow for seam allowance everywhere but the shoulder seam and, on occasion, the neck and armhole curves. There are specific reasons for this. The shoulder line is the line from which all else is plotted. Tampering with it throws everything off. It is easier to simply add on the 5/8" as a later step.

Beware of the concave curves of the neck and armhole. They are plotted exactly and sometimes need the extra ease that the sewing line of 5/8" will give them, but sometimes they do not. This should be plotted carefully with the individual measurement.

Figure 6–11 shows the basic pattern pieces for the bodice, the front, which is cut on the fold, and two back pieces. The front piece has four darts, the back pieces one each.

1. Plot the shoulder line exactly as you did for your sloper. (This is illustrated in Figure 6–11.) This becomes the AC line.
2. Divide it equally and you have point B.
3. At B, draw a vertical line running parallel to your original vertical line, corresponding to the shoulder-to-waist front measurement, plus 5/8" for the waist seam.
   (18¼" + 5/8" = 18⅞") This gives you point H.

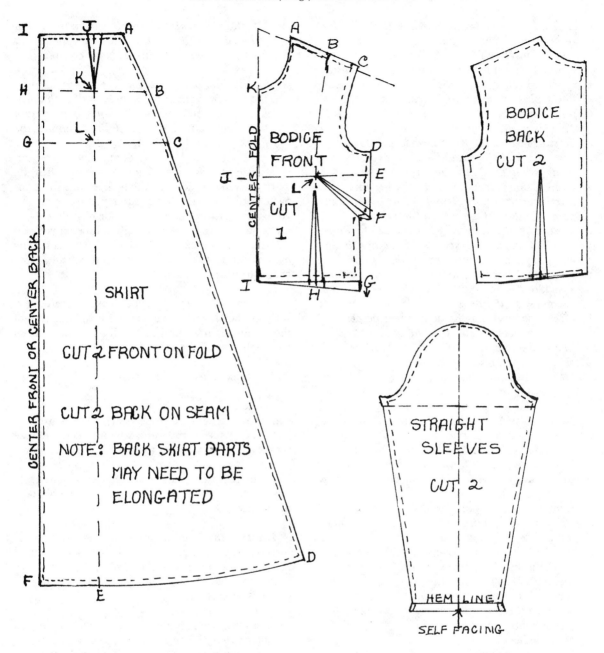

KEY: SOLID LINE IS CUTTING LINE
SMALL DOTTED LINE IS SEAM LINE
DASH LINES ARE DRAFTING AIDS

SCALE ⅛" = 1"

**Figure 6–11.** *Drafted Pattern for a Basic A-Line Dress (Figure 5–1)*

4. At H, draw a perpendicular line that also intersects with the original vertical line. This point of intersection becomes point I.

5. From point I, measure the waistline to correspond to one-quarter the waist measurement (6½"), plus ⅝" seam allowance, plus 1½ inches for waist dart (6½" + ⅝" = 7⅛" + 1½" = 8⅝"). This gives you point G.

6. Starting at B on the BH line, measure down the equivalent of the shoulder-to-point measurement and mark that point letter L.

7. Draw a line perpendicular to the BH line that intersects with the original vertical line. This point of intersection becomes letter J.

8. Starting at J, and passing L, continue this line until its length corresponds to one-fourth the chest expanded measurement (36½"), plus ⅝" for seam allowance, and one-quarter-inch for ease (36½" + ⅝" = 37⅛" + ¼" = 37⅜"). This becomes the JE line.

9. Measure two inches up on a direct perpendicular from point E, and you will get point D.

10. The armhole curve of CD is achieved exactly as it was on the sloper pattern.

11. Starting at I, measure up the original vertical line, past J, a length that corresponds to the clavical-to-waist, center front measurement (13¾"), plus 1¼ inches for seam allowances, and one quarter-inch for ease (13¾" + 1¼" = 15" + ¼" = 15¼"). This becomes letter K.

12. Now add ⅝" seam allowance to the AC line, as illustrated in Figure 6–11, and move up your letters accordingly.

13. Connect the new point A to your K exactly as you did the neckline curve on the sloper pattern.

14. For the bust dart, make a straight, downward, perpendicular line from point E. At point L make a 17° angle using the JE line as your 90° mark, as illustrated in Figure 6–10. The point at which this line intersects with the DE dotted line becomes letter F.

15. Now connect F to D.

16. With a dotted line, extend the vertical perpendicular of the FD line and do the same horizontally for the IG line until they intersect each other.

17. However big you make your bust dart, you must add an equal amount to this extended DF line below the point of the IH intersection. If your bust dart is one inch deep you must drop this mark one inch.

18. Now connect the H point to the new G point to create a new IG line. Connect the new G to F.

19. To plot the waist dart, simply mark ¾" on either side of the BH line and mark the apex a half-inch below point L. Now connect the marks.

20. To plot the bust dart, mark a half-inch up on the FD line from point F, and a half-inch down from F on the FG line. The apex is marked a half-inch below L on the LF line. Connect the marks.

*Drafting the Bodice Back:* As we did with the skirt, so we shall do with the bodice: Use the front pattern to make the back. After you have cut out your front pattern, baste shut your bust dart. Now lay it on another piece of muslin, allowing yourself ⅝" seam allowance for the center back seam. The back neckline curve is plotted exactly as the sloper back pattern.

*Drafting the Sleeve:* Your sleeve is drafted exactly as the sloper sleeve was, with the addition of the ⅝" for seam allowance on all four sides, plus a half-inch in each direction for ease.

*Drafting Basic Male Garments*

Figure 5–4 shows the basic male garments of a shirt, vest, jacket, and trousers. The vest, shirt, and jacket are made on the same principle as the female dress bodice but without the front bust dart. Sleeves are unisexual and are treated as such in Chapter 9. The one item that bears separate attention are trousers, although they are by no means exclusively male attire.

*Drafting the Front Trouser Leg* Figure 6–12 illustrates the basic pattern for the trousers pictured in Figure 5–4. It consists of four pieces, but only two pattern pieces, the front leg and the back. There is one dart in each piece.

1. As with the leg sloper, you must draw a line whose length corresponds to the waist-to-floor measurement (43") plus ⅝" for seam allowance at the waist. The trouser is seldom worn all the way to the floor so the measurement can be considered to include the two inches necessary for a hem. This line becomes the BF line.

2. At B, measure down approximately nine inches on the BF line and mark that spot with the letter I.

3. Draw a line perpendicular to the BF line at point I.

4. To complete the distance from I to D, take one-quarter the hip measurement (9½") plus 1½

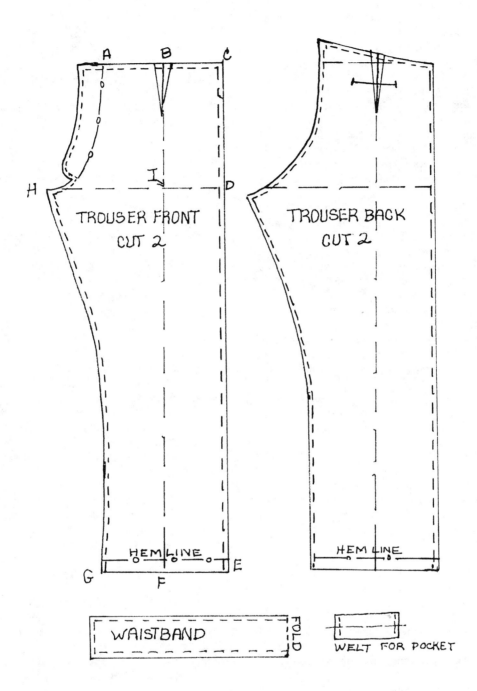

SCALE ⅛" = 1

**Figure 6–12.** *Trousers Drafted from Figure 5–4*

*inches for seam allowance and ease (11"), and divide this by half (5½"). The distance between I and D is this amount. Mark spot D.*

5. *To compute the AC line which intersects point B, take one-fourth the waist measurement (8") plus 1½ inches for seam allowance and ease (9½"), plus one inch for the dart (10½") and divide it equally on each side of point B (5¼" on each side).*

6. *Now connect C and D and continue in a parallel line for the outseam measurement (41") plus two inches for hem (43" just like the waist-to-floor measurement). The bottom of this line is point E.*

7. *At E, draw a perpendicular line to the CE line which also intersects point F and continues.*

8. *The front and back crotch curves are computed exactly the same as they were for the leg sloper, plus ⅝" for seam allowance at the top. (This leaves 14⅛" for the front curve and 18⅛" for the back curve.)*

9. *The point where the curve measurement meets the extended ID line becomes point H.*

10. *The HG line should equal the inseam measurement (32") plus two inches (= 34"). If it does not equate, you need to adjust your crotch curve.*

11. *To plot the dart, mark off one-half inch at either side of point B. Now, measuring down the BF line four inches, mark the apex. Now connect the dots.*

*Drafting the Back Trouser Leg   Et encore!* We once again use the front pattern to create the back, but with two differences. The dart "apexual" point should be lowered down the BF line six inches from B. The back crotch curve should be replotted for 18 inches.

## Drafting Facings

Facings are the easiest of all things to draft. Once you have your pattern pieces cut out, lay them down again and draw around the edge you wish faced; lift up and "eyeball" the inner edge of the facing (see Fig. 6–13). "Eyeballing," when used in a pattern drafting context, means to draw free hand, just by sight. If this process frightens you, you can measure 2½ inches inside your already drawn line and cut on this line.

## Sizing

Drafting the individual costume saves the sizing step because you have drafted it for a specific person, in a specific size; but in case you wish to save a

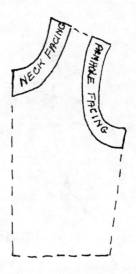

UNSCALED

**Figure 6–13.**   *How to Cut Facings from Pattern*

specific pattern that was a size 12 and at a later date make it again for a size 10, or use one pattern for several similar outfits in the same show (the Mounties, the Pirates, the Cowboys, or the Indians), there are a couple of short cuts to sizing with which you should be cognizant.

By adding ⅝" seam allowance you can increase any pattern one full size; a 12 to a 14, or a 9 to an 11. Likewise, by subtracting that ⅝" you can reduce it one size, but this should be done with specific measurements in mind. Two little maids from school may both be 5'6" tall, but one wears a 10 and the other a 14, yet both have the same shoulder width and center back length. Also remember to only add or subtract seam allowance, not curves or folds.

Recently American pattern companies have started to print patterns in the European manner. In Europe a printed pattern has three or four sizes included and you cut accordingly. To save storage room I have adopted this method particularly to drafting slopers, and mark one sloper for three sizes.

## Mass Production

The sloper drafted to three sizes can cut time greatly for mass production. You decide if you need three size 12 bodices, stack up three layers of muslin, draw your pattern from the sloper once, cut once, and you have three sets of patterns. The same can be done to three layers of exterior fabric if you desire.

Many wish they could save cutting time the way manufacturers do, by cutting a stack all at once but for a relatively small operation; this is, of course, impossible. However I can suggest a little bit of organization that might be helpful. Cut all of one type of garment at a time. Cut all the skirts, then move on to the bodices, suit coats, trousers, etc. It also saves instruction time if they are sewn this way as well.

We shall discuss more of these mass production techniques in reference to specific items in Chapters 7, 8, and 10.

### More Specifics on Rules of Thumb

A few more specifics about my rules of thumb might be helpful. I always keep a notebook on all my experiments, whether they are in drafting, cutting, formulas for salt plaster, certain dyes, etc. These notebooks are catch-alls for my successes and failures and have been an invaluable help in writing this book, teaching, and doing.

This habit of keeping notebooks came about in two ways. As a debater in both high school and college, I learned to glean facts and file them in a fairly organized fashion. Then too, during my freshman year of college, a graduate student suggested that if I thought of going to graduate school, I should keep all my class notes. (She was bemoaning the fact that she had not!) I took her advice. These two "elements" got me into the habit, and my notebooks now extend back twenty-some years. In such notebooks one begins to see certain things that recur so often that they became my rules of thumb. For instance:

*Width Equals Height*   It is usually true that the distance from the tip of the longest right finger to the tip of the longest left finger across the straight arms and back shoulder will equal the person's height.

*The 9" Waist-to-Seat Measurement*   When we discussed the drafting of John Doe's leg sloper, we talked about the nine inches usually required from waist to seat when the person is seated. This applies to both men and women. It usually equates to a general table: People 5'2" to 5'5" need about 8½ inches; 5'5" to 5'9" need nine inches; and 5'9" to 6' about 9½ inches. Nine inches is the average. If the person is over 6' use ten inches as your guide. If they are under 5'2" use eight inches.

*Adjusting Pants for Fat Fannies*   If a lady has a large fanny, you may want to extend the back crotch curve as shown in Figure 6–14.

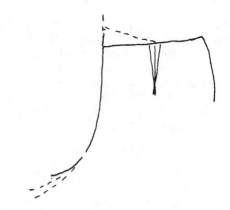

UNSCALED

**Figure 6–14.**   *Elongating Crotch Curve*

*Adjusting for Pot Bellies*   If a gentleman has a pot belly, you may wish to do a similar extension on the front crotch curve.

*The 4" to Upper Hip Measurement*   When we were discussing the skirt sloper, we used a general four inches to the upper hip measurement. This, like the previously discussed nine-inch measurement, is an average for women from 5'2" to about 6'. Because of anatomical differences, men do not need this measurement; their hip curve is much less pronounced. If a woman is shorter than 5'2" you may wish to go to three inches. If she is 6' or quite heavy, you may need to extend this to five inches.

*The 5" Front Neck Curve*   During our discussion of the front neck curve for the bodice sloper, we said that the average female neck curve at the front is five inches. To this I should add that the average back neck curve is three inches. The average female neck measurement is around 14 inches at the base. The total of these measurements (16") allows for seams and ease. This works for men as well as women.

If the base measurement is 15 inches, allow 3½ inches for the back neck. If 15½ inches, use 3½ inches for back neck and 5½ inches for the front. A 16-inch or 16½-inch base measurement requires 6 inches for the front and 3½ for the back. A 17-inch neck and an 18-inch neck take 6 inches for the front and 4 inches for the back.

*The 18" Armhole Curve*   We also discussed the 18-inch average armhole for the female. Most street clothes use less but I use 18 inches because this gives the actress more freedom. I use 20 inches for the average man.

If someone has a particularly heavy upper arm, 22 inches will usually suffice. Except for specific items, I generally cut both front and back armholes alike. This works and saves time. One exception is in tailoring a man's suit coat where less of a curve is needed in the back. Whatever armhole you use, add 2 inches for ease to the convex curve of the upper sleeve measurement.

These drafting principles should enable you to draft anything, but we need to discuss some specific techniques for certain garments which I have divided into male and female gender. Ladies use trousers and men sometimes wear skirts—the kilt for example. I simply divided them by their major use. Since it is only polite to let the ladies go first, let us move on to garments of the feminine gender.

# 7

# Drafting and Construction— Ladies' Garments

Ladies' garments can be divided into four main items: the shift, the skirt, the bodice, and the jacket. Shifts include the cyclas, houppelandes, bliauts, caftans, mu-mus, smocks, Dior's 1950 sac dress, and Mary Quant's 1960s tent dress. Skirts come gathered, pleated, circular, semi-circular, and gored. Bodices have no fewer than three pieces and can go up to as many as eleven, excluding sleeves, which we will discuss separately in Chapter 9. Jackets are nothing more than elongated bodices. A waistless dress is really a shift. A waisted dress is composed of the aforementioned bodice and skirt.

The one garment that acts as odd-man-out is the princess line dress. It is too form fitting to be a shift, yet it does not have a waist.

We shall discuss each of these specifics in terms of drafting them and adapting them to certain period lines, but not in terms of period clothing specifically.

## The Shift

### A Shift without a Yoke

The shift is a garment whose pivotal and support point is the same, the shoulders. There are two types of shifts, those with a yoke and those without. Figure 7–1 shows a basic shift scaled to Jane Doe's measurements. It may have either three or four pieces, depending on whether you cut the center front on the fold or not. It has a choice of hemlines, floor length, street dress length, or blouse length.

This shift can be used as is for any number of period robes and dresses. Figure 7–2 shows it adapted to a Chinese robe by narrowing the hem

width and adding straight sleeves, a mandarin collar, and side front closure.

Figure 7–3 shows its adaptation to a houppelande robe. A center back godet that helps to form a train and houppelande sleeves, fur collar, and a belt at the ribcage level have been added. By the way, the undergown is the same shift pattern with neckline lowered and tight over-wrist sleeves added (see Fig. 7–3).

The patterns in Figures 7–1 through 7–3 are to scale and may simply be enlarged. You can also draft them yourself using the procedures discussed in Chapter 6, either by using your bodice and skirt slopers or bodice and skirt drafting techniques.

### A Shift with a Yoke

Yokes come in three basic shapes: square, semi-circular, and U-shaped. The V-shaped yoke is merely a variation on the U-shaped theme. Often the square and semi-circular yokes require a sleeve variation but the U-shaped does not.

*The U-Shaped Yoke*  The U-shaped yoke is illustrated in Figure 7–4. By using the bodice front sloper of Chapter 6, your pattern drafting understanding can be simplified.

1. *Trace around the shoulder, neckline, and armhole curve of the sloper.*
2. *Lift the sloper up and draw your U-shaped yoke.*
3. *Cut the yoke. The outer edge of the yoke now becomes the outline of the curve, but you will need to redraw this line and add ⅝" seam allowance to it. (This is also illustrated in Figure 7–4.)*
4. *Now draft the remainder of your shift as you did the yokeless shift.*

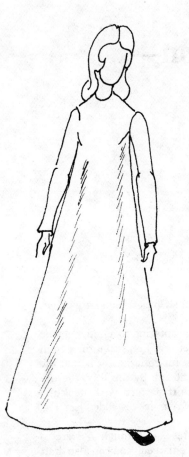

NOTE: THE SLEEVE PICTUR-
ED ABOVE IS THE
SAME AS THE ONE
DRAFTED IN FIGURE
6-11

KEY: ⓐ SOLID LINE = CUTTING
             LINE.
     ⓑ LONG DASH LINE =
         DRAFTING AIDS
     ⓒ SHORT DOTTED LINE =
         SEAM LINE

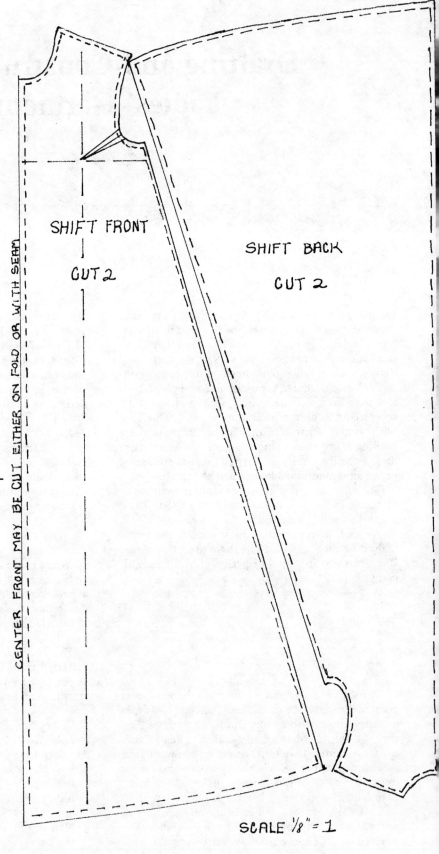

SHIFT FRONT

CUT 2

SHIFT BACK

CUT 2

CENTER FRONT MAY BE CUT EITHER ON FOLD OR WITH SEAM

SCALE ⅛" = 1

**Figure 7–1.**   *The Basic Shift*

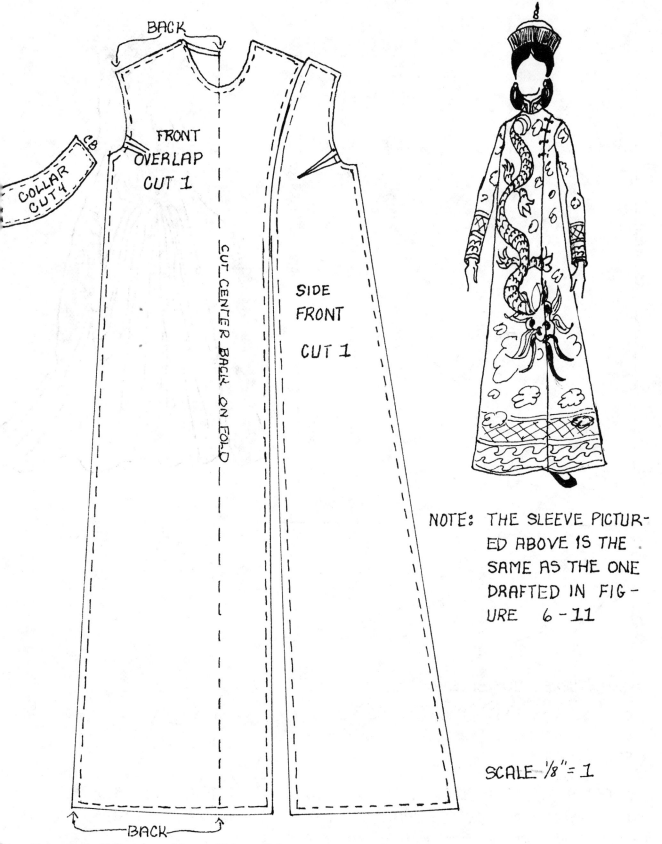

BACK

COLLAR
CUT 4

FRONT
OVERLAP
CUT 1

CUT CENTER BACK ON FOLD

SIDE
FRONT
CUT 1

BACK

NOTE: THE SLEEVE PICTUR-
ED ABOVE IS THE
SAME AS THE ONE
DRAFTED IN FIG-
URE 6-11

SCALE 1/8" = 1

**Figure 7–2.** *Basic Shift Adapted into a Chinese Robe*

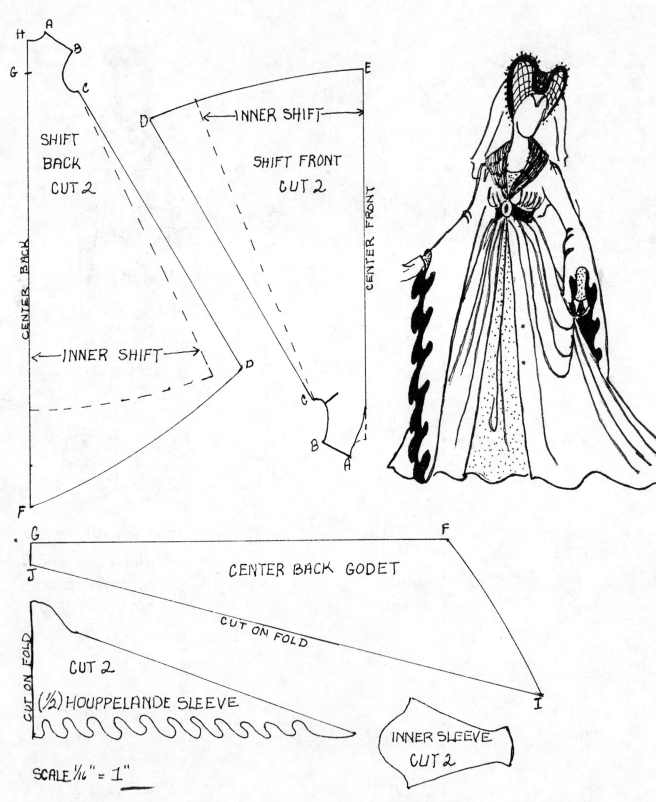

SCALE ⅟₁₆" = 1"

NOTE: AT ⅟₃₂", SEAM ALLOWANCE IS IMPOSSIBLE TO MARK. THEREFORE, YOU MUST ADD IT TO ANY PATTERNS WHICH ARE SCALED ⅟₁₆"= 1"

**Figure 7–3.** *Shift Adapted to Houppelande Gown (and Inner Shift)*

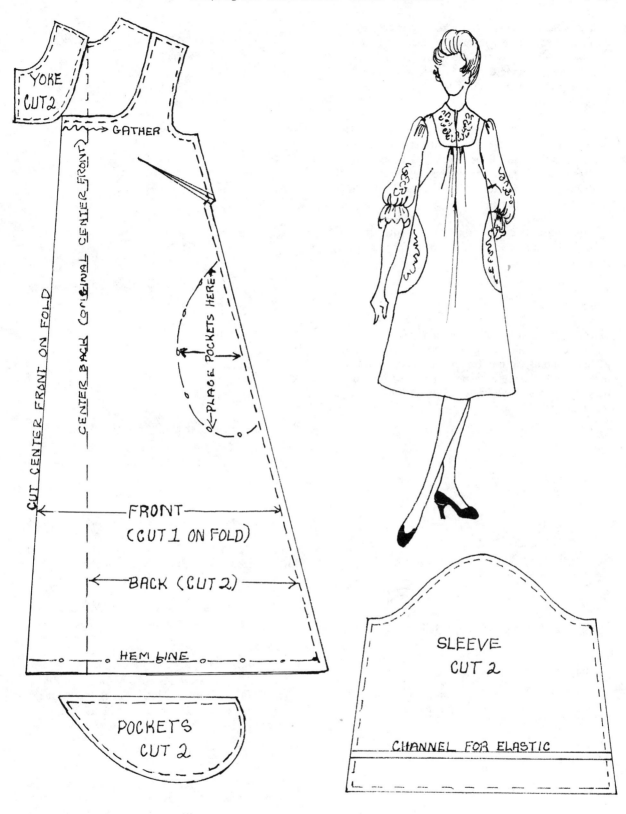

**YOKE CUT 2**

GATHER

CUT CENTER FRONT ON FOLD

CENTER BACK (ORIGINAL CENTER FRONT)

PLACE POCKETS HERE

FRONT
(CUT 1 ON FOLD)

BACK (CUT 2)

HEM LINE

POCKETS CUT 2

SLEEVE CUT 2

CHANNEL FOR ELASTIC

SCALE ⅛" = 1

**Figure 7–4.** *Drafting a Shift with a U-Shaped Yoke*

If you desire excess fullness to be gathered to the yoke, split the piece you first drafted in step #4 at the spot where you desire the fullness. If it is to be in the center, you merely need to add it to the center front as pictured by the dot and dash line on this piece in Figure 7–4.

*The Square Yoke* Figure 7–5 illustrates the square-yoked shift. The only difference that this causes is in the addition of a sleeve, bacause it forces the use of a semi-raglan one. (The raglan sleeve will be discussed in Chapter 9.) This is much the same as the shirt in Figure 6–7.

*The Semi-Circular Yoke* The semi-circular yoke is illustrated in Figure 7–6. It too, uses the semi-raglan sleeve.

## The Skirt

Skirts are garments whose pivotal and support point is the waist, or the ribcage if one is drafting certain periods such as Gothic, Italian Renaissance, or Empire. The skirt may be attached to a bodice, or it may be worn separately. If it is a separate item, it requires a waistband.

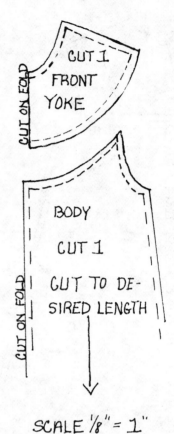

**Figure 7–6.** *Drafting a Semi-Circular Yoke*

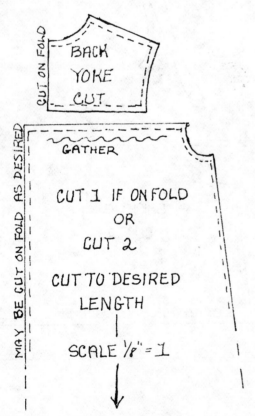

**Figure 7–5.** *Drafting a Square Yoke*

*The Waistband* Regardless of the skirt's style all waistbands are cut by the same formula. It doesn't even matter whether the wastbands are for skirts or trousers or Eisenhower jackets. Let's use Jane's measurements to work our formula.

1. *Take the waist measurement (26") plus two inches (1¼" for seam allowance and ¾" of overlap) for the length. In Jane's case this would be 28 inches.*
2. *The standard depth of the waistband is four inches. This allows 1¼ inches for seam allowance; the remainder is folded in half so that the finished band is 1⅜ inches deep. This is illustrated in Figure 7–7.*

*The Gathered Skirt*

The easiest of all skirts to make is the gathered skirt. It is essentially a rectangle that is pulled tight by means of a running stitch. This is computed easily without resorting to a pattern of any sort.

For adequate fullness the rule of thumb is that the rectangle should be at least three times the

**Figure 7–7.** *Drafting a Waistband*

width of the waist. For Jane this would equate to 3 × 26″ or 78 inches. To this you add 1¼ inches per seam. If you are "railroading" the fabric you would have only one seam (a total of 78¼″). "Railroading" is a costumer's term that means using the width of the fabric (from selvedge to selvedge) as the length of the garment.

If you are cutting your skirt in lengths, you would have at least two seams, possibly more, depending on the width of the fabric. You would have two lengths of 60-inch or 54-inch fabric and three lengths of 45-inch or 36-inch fabric. (You can always have more fullness than an exact three times the waist measurement, but it looks skimpy to have less.)

The length depends on the style desired. If it is floor-length, you would take the waist-to-floor measurement (43″) plus two inches for a hem (45″) and ⅝″ for the waist seam allowance (a total of 45⅝″). You would therefore have a rectangle that would be 45⅝ inches long by at least 99¼ inches wide.

To construct this, sew up your seam (or seams), making sure that you leave a seven-inch opening at the top of one of them. Run two rows of gathering stitches around the top and pull to the desired circumference. Then attach this either to a bodice or a waistband. Add your zipper or closure items and hem it up two inches. This skirt is illustrated in Figure 7–8A.

*The Pleated Skirt*

The pleated skirt is either unpressed (as in skirt B of Figure 7–8) or pressed and/or sewn down as in a kilt (skirt C in Figure 7–8).

*The Skirt with Unpressed Pleats* It takes three inches of fabric for a one-inch pleat; therefore, the original formula for cutting a gathered skirt applies to the skirt with unpressed pleats as well. It is also a rectangle. Pleats are used in place of gathers to reduce the circumference to the desired waist measurement.

*The Skirt with Sewn Down Pleats* The skirt that has either pressed or sewn down pleats is computed in a slightly different manner. Let us take the kilt for an example (Fig. 7–8C). In this case, first decide the desired distance of the flat panel in front (8″) and double that figure for overlap (16″). Then subtract the flat panel measurement from the total lower hip measurement (31½″). Now triple this resulting measurement (93″) and add the measurement for the flat panel and its overlap (93″ + 16″ = 109″). Two darts each are added to the flat panel and the underflap to bring in the waist sufficiently. A pattern for a kilt is illustrated in Figure 7–9.

*Skirts with False Fronts*

In Chapter 4 we saw a photograph of a Cavalier lady (Fig. 4–10). Her skirt was a fake of an underskirt and an overskirt. This technique is illustrated in Figure 7–10 (This would also work for the skirt in Figure 7–8B).

The skirt opening is hidden under the left overlap. This trick works very well for several periods and can also be used on a gored skirt. You will note the gradual train cut into the skirt rectangle. This is done for many periods including Renaissance, Cavalier, and Baroque. It gives a lovely line to the departing figure.

*The Circular Skirt*

A circular skirt does not really require a pattern. You can easily draft one from a simple procedure (remember C = Pi D). In order to determine the circumference of your skirt, you must determine the diameter, and to do that you must work with a few givens.

1. *Think of a circular skirt as a donut or as one circle inside the other, as illustrated in Figure 7–11. The inner circle is the waist; the outer, the hem.*
2. *We are given the circumference of the waist. In Jane's case, 26″. From this we must get its diameter (C = Pi D), or 26″ = 3.17 × ?. Therefore, 8½″ is the closest you could get by inches.*
3. *You also have a given in the waist-to-floor measurement of 43 inches plus one inch for hem (circular skirts don't require much of a hem) and ⅝″ for seam allowance, which totals to 44⅝ inches; but this is a radius, not a diameter.*
4. *Therefore you take half of your inner circle's diameter and you have a radius of 4¹⁄₁₆ inches, which is now added to the 44⅝ inches giving you a total radius of 48¹¹⁄₁₆ inches.*
5. *Using your blackboard compass or a tape measure on a pin, you can draw your two circles.*

THREE TYPES OF RECTANGULAR SKIRTS

B. A SKIRT WITH UNPRESSED
   PLEATS

C. THE KILT: A SKIRT WITH
   SEWN DOWN PLEATS

A. THE GATHERED SKIRT WITH A GATHERED FLOUNCE

**Figure 7–8.** *Three Types of Rectangular Skirts*

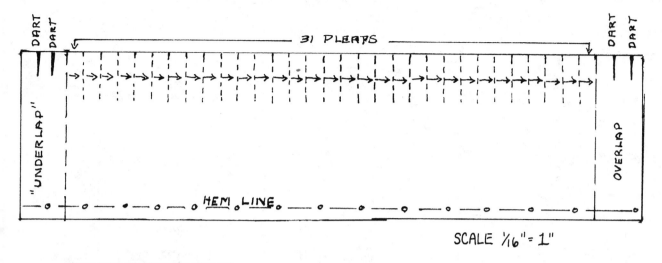

SCALE ⅟₁₆" = 1"

WAISTBAND

**Figure 7–9.** *A Kilt Pattern*

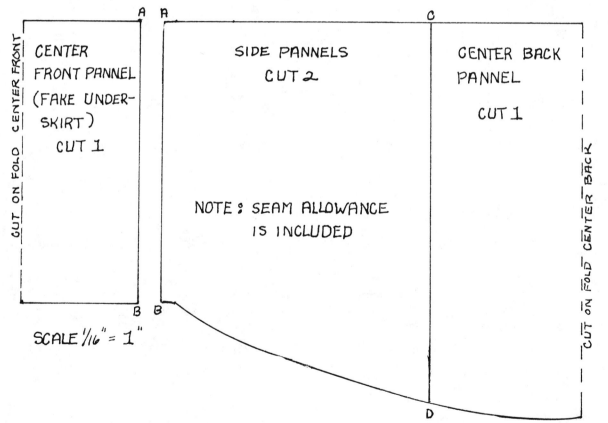

**Figure 7–10.** *A Pattern for a False Fronted Skirt with Unpressed Pleats*

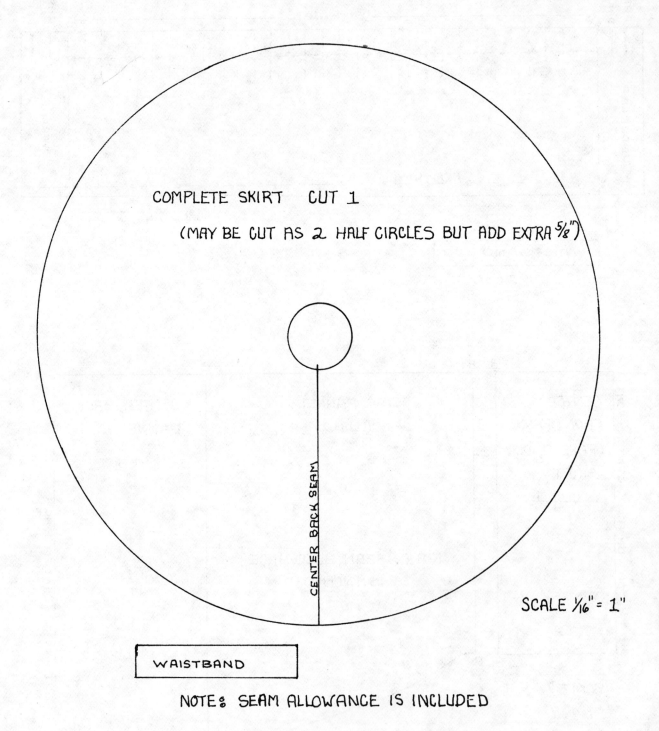

COMPLETE SKIRT    CUT 1

(MAY BE CUT AS 2 HALF CIRCLES BUT ADD EXTRA 5/8")

CENTER BACK SEAM

SCALE 1/16" = 1"

WAISTBAND

NOTE: SEAM ALLOWANCE IS INCLUDED

**Figure 7–11.**  *Drafting a Circular Skirt*

6. To construct, slit the circle up one radius. Sew the seam leaving a seven-inch opening for zipper or closure, add waistband, and hem.

*The Semi-Circular Skirt*

This too can be figured by mathematics without a specific pattern.

1. Make a semi-circle whose length equals the waist measurement plus 1¼ inches (27¼"). To do this, double the result (54½") for the "given," which in this case equals the circumference. Now you must find the radius (which is half of the diameter). The diameter for Jane would be approximately 14⅜ inches. Therefore, the radius would be 7³⁄₁₆ inches.
2. At point A on Figure 7–12, place the point of your compass, which is set for 7³⁄₁₆ inches; draw semi-circle B.
3. Now on your ABC radius from point B, measure down to C. This distance should correspond to the waist-to-floor (or calf or knee, as desired) plus one inch for hem and ⅝" for seam allowance at waist. This then makes the distance from B to C 44⅝ inches.
4. To draw semi-circle C, add the 44⅝ inches to the 7³⁄₁₆ inches (51¹³⁄₁₆"), making that your radius from point A.

*Gored Skirts*

Gored skirts are essentially skirts composed of wedges of a circle. We drafted a two-gored skirt (which is called an A-line skirt) in Chapter 6 (Figures 6–5 and 6–10).

A gore is a four-sided section of a garment that has two of its sides on opposite diagonals, as illustrated in Figure 7–13. Also illustrated there you will see a half-gore, a godet, and a gusset. A half-gore has

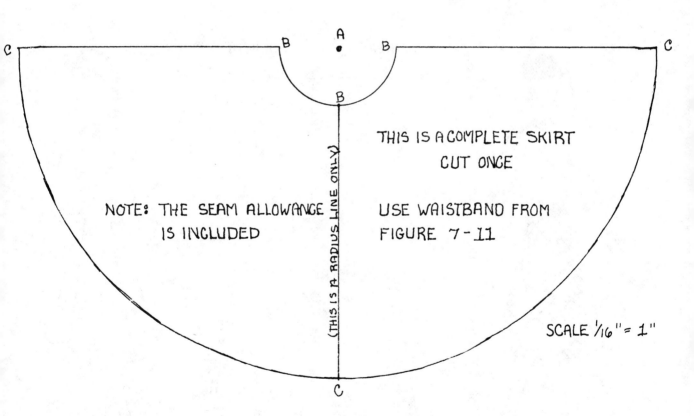

**Figure 7–12.** *Drafting a Semi-Circular Skirt*

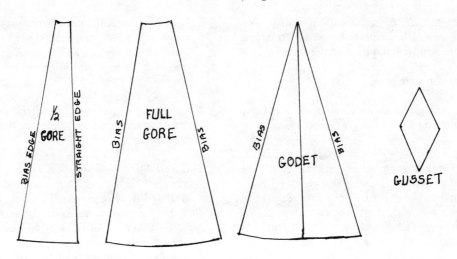

THIS IS NOT A SCALED DRAWING

**Figure 7–13.** *The Half-Gore, the Full Gore, the Godet, and the Gusset*

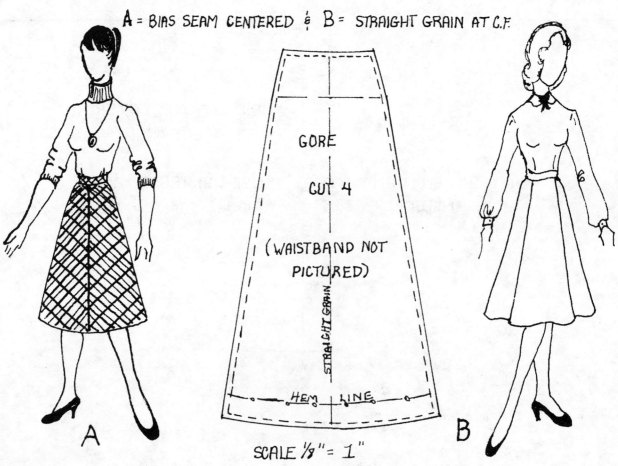

A = BIAS SEAM CENTERED & B = STRAIGHT GRAIN AT C.F.

GORE

CUT 4

(WAISTBAND NOT PICTURED)

STRAIGHT GRAIN

HEM LINE

SCALE ⅛" = 1"

**Figure 7–14.** *Four-Gored Skirt*

one side on the bias and one on the straight grain of the fabric. A godet is a triangular piece of fabric whose bottom side remains free and is used to give added fullness to the hem. A gusset is usually a diamond-shaped piece of fabric used to give extra ease in junction spots, such as the center crotch of a pair of pants or under the arm.

Perhaps because they all begin with G, many potential pattern drafters confuse these items.

*The Four-Gored Skirt*  Figure 7–14 illustrates and includes a pattern for a four-gored skirt. This skirt works well for bias cut plaids and chevron stripes.

*The Six-Gored Skirt*  Figure 7–15 is a six-gored skirt with godets added. If cut on the bias, this works particularly well for the 1930s look.

*The Eight-Gored Skirt*  The eight-gored skirt illustrated in Figure 7–16 works very well for adaptations to the belled skirt of the early 1900s.

When cut more fully it also works well for the Victorian fishtail hooped dress of 1865, as illustrated in Figure 7–17.

### Computing the Length of a Skirt to Go over a Hoop

Remember that when you have a skirt that goes over a hoop, *you must measure over this hoop* as your waist-to-floor measurement and then add seam allowance and hem. When worn over a hoop, the dress should just touch the floor. Nothing looks more tacky than seeing the hoop. The actress has several feet of moving room inside the hoop and really does not need to worry about her dress being too long.

### An Easily Adaptable Six-Gored Skirt

I have a simple system for cutting a six-gored skirt quickly. This skirt is very full at the bottom and only needs a little gathering or pleating at the waist to adapt to an 1895 bell, etc. It also moves well and I constantly use it for dancers. It is illustrated in Figure 7–18. The process is as follows.

1. *Compute the length needed, waist-to-floor. In Jane's case it is once again 45⅝ inches.*
2. *Cut across the folded fabric at that 45⅝" measurement, leaving the fabric folded, and repeat this step two more times until you have three pieces of fabric stacked up that measure 45⅝ inches on the fold and selvedge edges and 22½ inches (for 45" fabric) at the AB line and the DC line.*

3. *From point A, measure six inches toward point B and mark it letter E.*
4. *From point C, measure six inches toward D and mark it F.*
5. *Connect E to F.*
6. *Starting at E, measure down the EF line 45⅝ inches and put a mark so as to gently curve this, to "even-out" that which will become the hem line.*
7. *Starting at F, measure up the EF line and mark for the same curve as in step #6.*
8. *Cut all three layers at once; you then have three complete gores and six half-gores.*
9. *To construct, sew up your half-gores allowing seven inches on one straight edge for a closure. Now attach to the whole gores. Gather or pleat to a bodice or waistband.*

## Bodices

For some reason, bodices usually have an uneven number of pieces, starting with three and working all the way up to eleven. A two-piece bodice is as unusual as a seven-sided box. You can have a four-piece bodice but it is unusual, so we will be discussing the three-, five-, seven-, nine-, and eleven-piece varieties.

### The Three-Piece Bodice

We drafted the pattern for a three-piece bodice in Chapter 6. These same principles can be used for all the others. If you need a center front seam, you would then turn this into a four-piece bodice.

### The Five-Piece Bodice

The five-piece bodice has a center front, two side front, and two back pieces. This is scaled in Figure 7–19. If you cut a seam allowance down the center front instead of on the fold, you have a six-piece bodice.

### The Seven-Piece Bodice

The seven-piece bodice is illustrated and scaled in Figure 7–20. It has either the center front or the center back on the fold. If both are open, you have an eight-piece bodice. The basic pieces are center front on the fold, two side fronts, two side backs, and two center backs.

### The Nine-Piece Bodice

The nine-piece bodice is illustrated as it would adapt to a Rococo bodice and scaled in Figure 7–21.

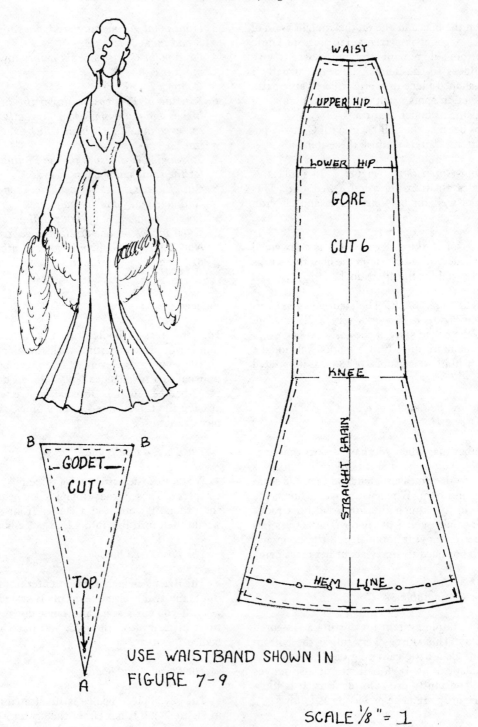

USE WAISTBAND SHOWN IN
FIGURE 7-9

SCALE ⅛" = 1

**Figure 7–15.** *Drafting a Six-Gored Skirt with Godets*

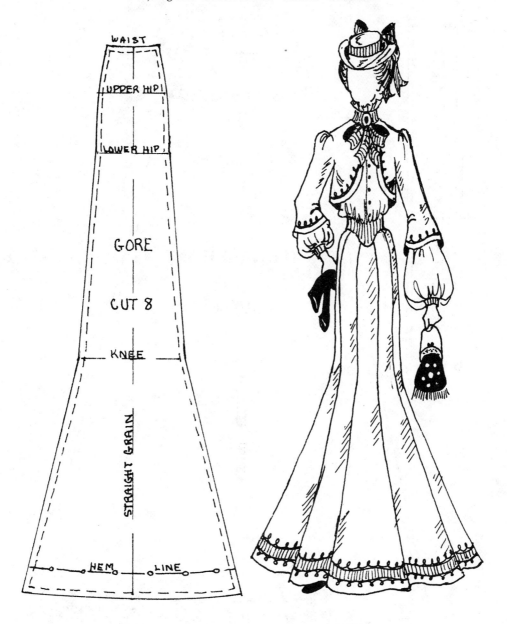

WAIST

UPPER HIP

LOWER HIP

GORE

CUT 8

KNEE

STRAIGHT GRAIN

HEM     LINE

NOTE: FOR A WAISTBAND, USE PATTERN OF FIGURE 7-9

SCALE ⅛" = 1"

**Figure 7–16.** *The Eight-Gored Skirt of the Early 1900s*

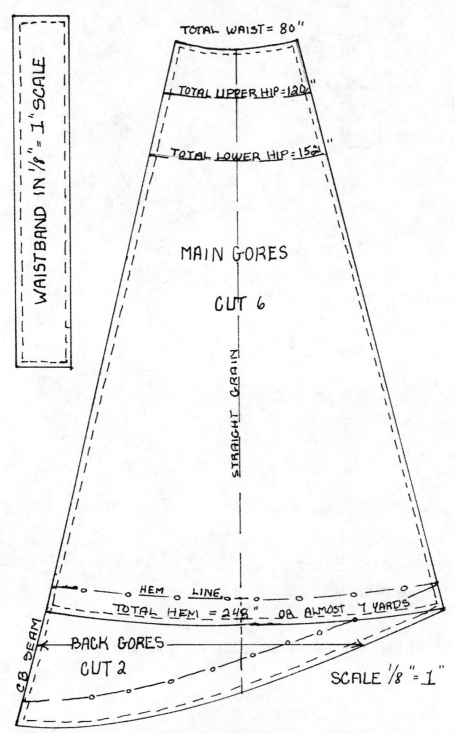

WAISTBAND IN ⅛" = 1" SCALE

TOTAL WAIST = 80"

TOTAL UPPER HIP = 120"

TOTAL LOWER HIP = 152"

MAIN GORES

CUT 6

STRAIGHT GRAIN

HEM LINE

TOTAL HEM = 248" OR ALMOST 7 YARDS

CB SEAM

BACK GORES
CUT 2

SCALE ⅛" = 1"

**Figure 7–17.** *Adaptation of an Eight-Gored Skirt for a Fishtail Hoop*

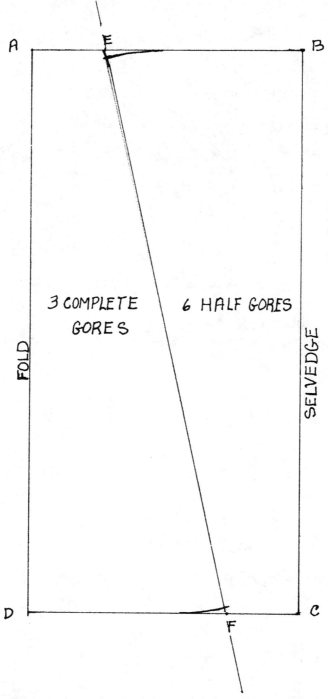

(CUT THIS IN A THREE PIECE "STACK-UP")

**Figure 7–18.** *Simple Six-Gored Skirt Construction*

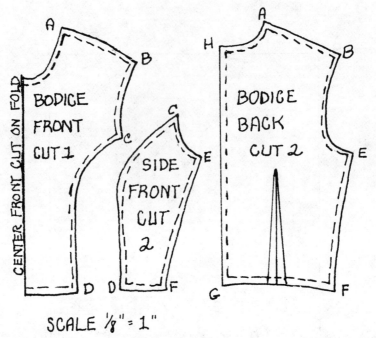

SCALE ⅛" = 1"

**Figure 7–19.** *A Five-Piece Bodice*

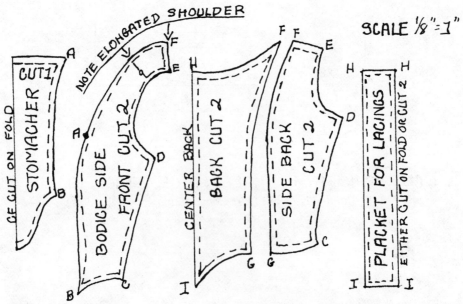

**Figure 7–20.** *A Seven-Piece Bodice Adapted to the Rococo Line*

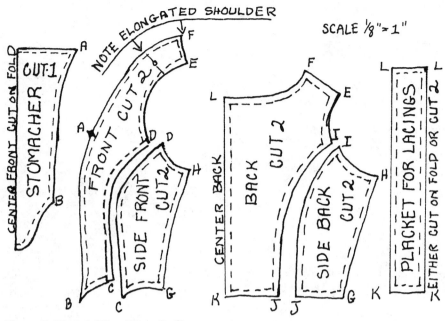

**Figure 7–21.** *A Nine-Piece Bodice*

This particular version has a center front piece cut on the fold, two side front pieces, two side pieces, two side back pieces, and two center back pieces.

### The Seven-Piece Bodice Adaptation

Figure 7–22 shows the seven-piece bodice adapted for a double-breasted Victorian riding habit and its scaled pattern. By putting a seam down the center back, we turn it into an eight-piece bodice.

### The Nine-Piece Bodice Adaptation

The Empire coat dress illustrated and scaled in Figure 7–23 shows the adaptation of a nine-piece bodice. In this case the waist was shortened as well.

### The "Off-the-Shoulder" Bodice

Both the Cavalier ladies and mid-Victorian ladies were very fond of bare shoulders, and cutting a bodice to fit well with no shoulder on which to hang it is a real art. Figure 7–24 is a basic adaptation of this.

### The Bolero

Jackets and boleros are really little more than variations on the theme of the bodice. A bolero is a short, fitted jacket that merely reaches the waist and is open in the front. It may or may not have sleeves. Figure 7–25 is an illustrated pattern of one.

### The Jacket

The jacket is a bodice that extends over the hips. This type of garment was called by the Victorians a "basque" when it was figure-hugging, as illustrated in Figure 7–26.

Sometimes the jacket was truly a bodice with a short skirt (called a "peplum") attached to it, as illustrated by the adaptation of the 1750 riding habit pictured in Figure 7–27. At other times the jacket was a loosely fitting over-garment like the ever popular blazer, made to be worn over a blouse and skirt.

There were even jackets that seemed to try to ride two styles at once. This is illustrated by the strange, almost semi-polonaise creation so popular in Republican France of the 1790s. As can be seen in Figure 7–28, this was not really a bolero, a bodice, or a peplum jacket, but a bit of all three.

### The Princess Line Garment

If the jacket is an extension of the bodice, then the princess line garment is its extension to the bottom

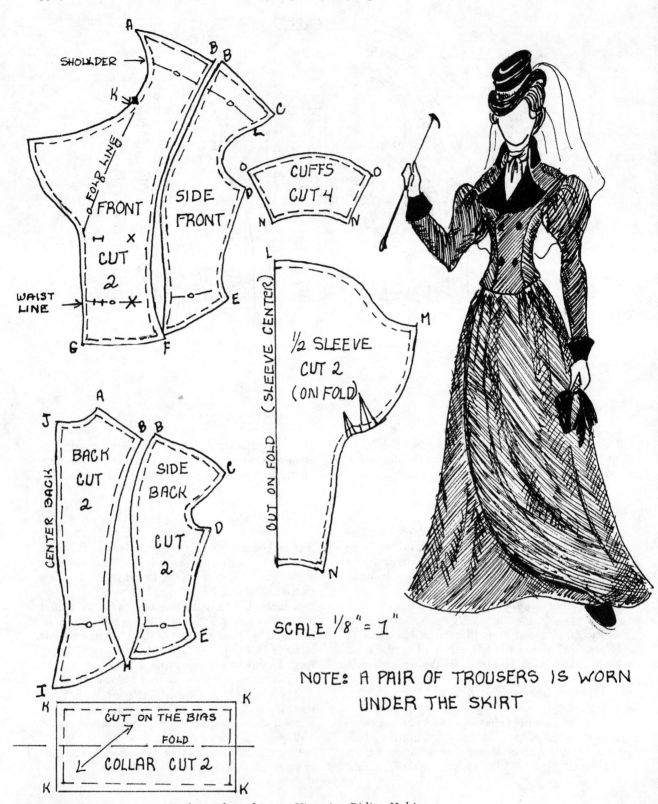

SHOULDER

K

FOLD LINE

FRONT
SIDE
FRONT

CUT
2

WAIST
LINE

G        F

CUFFS
CUT 4

½ SLEEVE
CUT 2
(ON FOLD)

CUT ON FOLD

(SLEEVE CENTER)

CENTER BACK

BACK
CUT
2

SIDE
BACK

CUT
2

SCALE ⅛" = 1"

NOTE: A PAIR OF TROUSERS IS WORN
UNDER THE SKIRT

CUT ON THE BIAS
FOLD
COLLAR CUT 2

**Figure 7–22.** *A Seven-Piece Bodice Adapted into a Victorian Riding Habit*

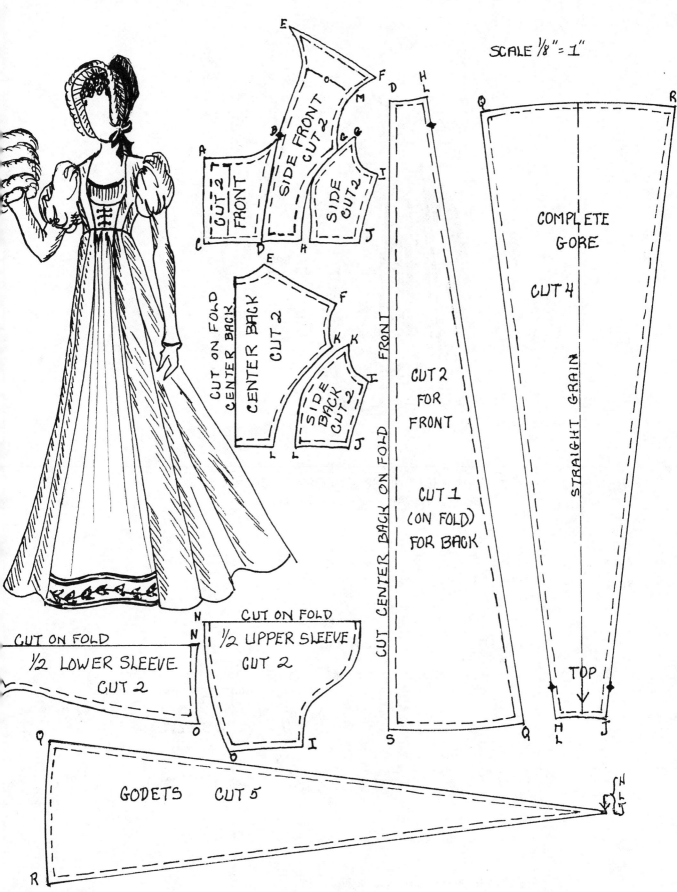

SCALE ⅛" = 1"

E

F

D  H  L

Q                    R

CUT 2
FRONT
CUT 2

SIDE FRONT
CUT 2

A  B

P  G

SIDE
CUT 2
I

J

COMPLETE
GORE

CUT 4

STRAIGHT GRAIN

C  D  H

E

CUT ON FOLD
CENTER BACK

CENTER BACK
CUT 2

F

K  K

SIDE BACK
CUT 2

H

CUT 2
FOR
FRONT

CUT 1
(ON FOLD)
FOR BACK

CUT CENTER BACK ON FOLD    FRONT

L  L

J

TOP

H  J
L

N

CUT ON FOLD
½ UPPER SLEEVE
CUT 2

CUT ON FOLD
½ LOWER SLEEVE
CUT 2

N

O

O

I

S                    Q

H

Q

GODETS    CUT 5

R

**Figure 7–23.** *A Nine-Piece Bodice Adapted into an Empire Coat*

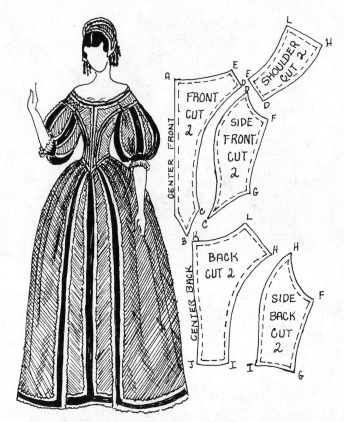

THIS PATTERN AND ILLUSTRATION IS BASED ON
VERMEER AND TER BORCH PAINTINGS; INCLUD-
ING PARENTAL ADMONITION, THE CONCERT, AND
A GIRL DRINKING WITH A GENTLEMAN

**Figure 7–24.** *An Off-the-Shoulder Bodice*

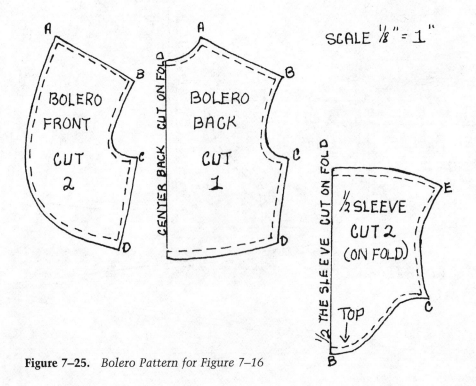

SCALE ⅛" = 1"

**Figure 7–25.** *Bolero Pattern for Figure 7–16*

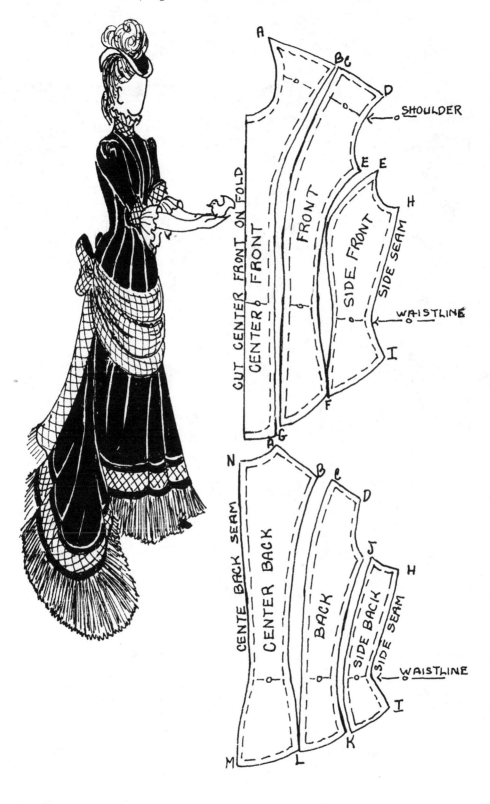

SCALE ⅛" = 1

**Figure 7–26.** *Drafting a Basque Jacket*

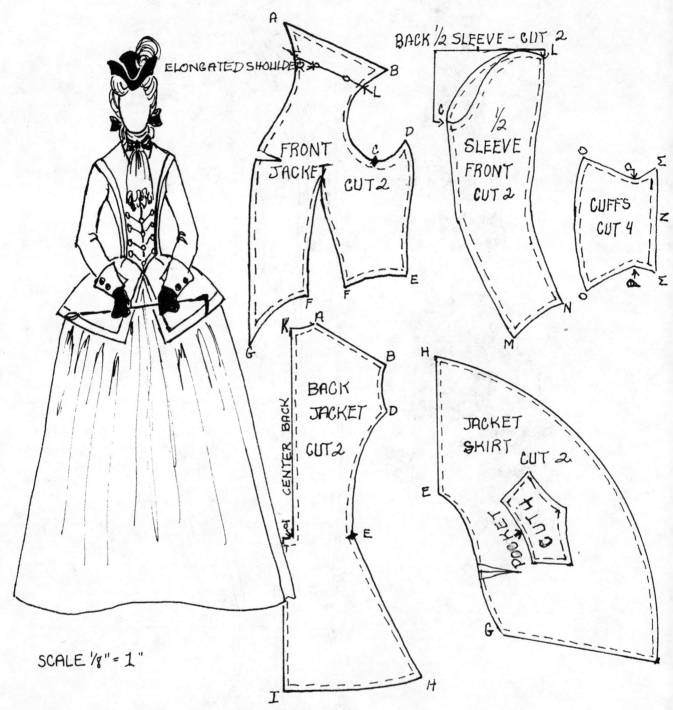

**Figure 7–27.** *Jacket Adapted from a 1750s Riding Coat*[1]

[1]Adapted from *The Cut of Women's Clothes* by Norah Waugh. Copyright 1968 by Norah Waugh. Used by permission of the publisher, Theatre Arts Books, 153 Waverly Place, New York, N.Y. 10014

1. JACKET SHOULDER – CUT 2
2. JACKET BOLERO LIKE FRONT –
   CUT 2
3. SIDE FRONT – CUT 2
4. SIDE BACK – CUT 2
5. CENTER BACK – CUT 2
NOTE: THIS IS AN ADAPTATION OF A STYLE
       CALLED "UNE ROBE A L'ANGLAISE"

SCALE 1/16" = 1"

6. CENTER BACK GODET – CUT 1
   ON FOLD AT LINE MP
7. BACK HALF SLEEVE – CUT 2
8. FRONT HALF SLEEVE – CUT 2
9. FALSE UNDER BODICE, CEN-
   TER FRONT – CUT 2
10. FALSE UNDER BODICE,
    SIDE FRONT – CUT 2

**Figure 7–28.** *Jacket of the Republican Era—1780s*

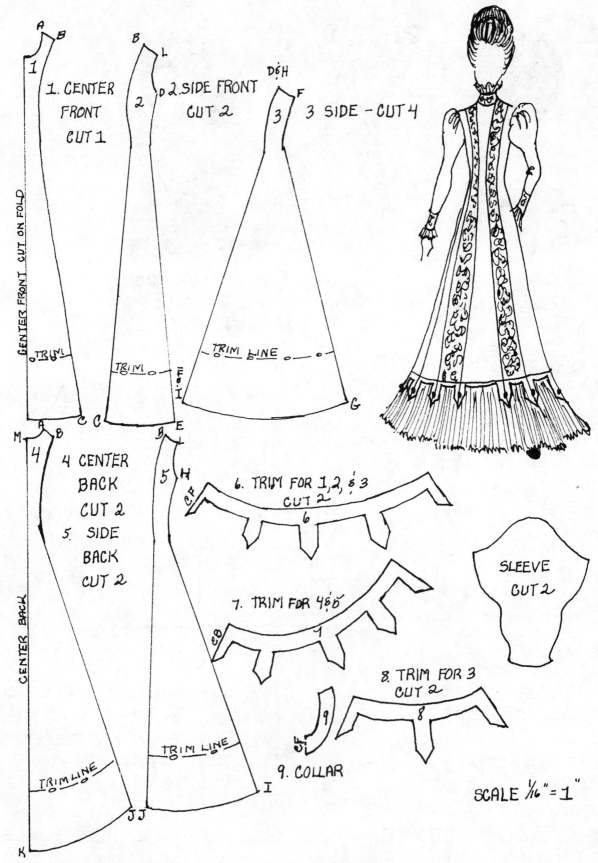

A
B
1
1. CENTER
FRONT
CUT 1
GENTER FRONT CUT ON FOLD
TRIM
C

B
L
D
2
2. SIDE FRONT
CUT 2
TRIM
F
I
E

D & H
F
3
3 SIDE – CUT 4
TRIM LINE
G

M
A
B
4
4 CENTER
BACK
CUT 2
5. SIDE
BACK
CUT 2
CENTER BACK
TRIMLINE
K

B
E
5
H
CF
TRIM LINE
I
J

6. TRIM FOR 1, 2, & 3
CUT 2
6

SLEEVE
CUT 2

7. TRIM FOR 4 & 5
CB
7

8. TRIM FOR 3
CUT 2
9
CF
8
9. COLLAR

SCALE 1/16" = 1"

**Figure 7–29.** *A Nine-Piece Bodice Adapted into a Princess Line Dress*

line, so to speak. You can literally take any bodice pattern and extend it to the floor and get a princess line dress.

This is exactly what was done with the nine-piece bodice of Fig. 7–20; it became the dress of Figure 7–29. If you are using the sloper method, use your bodice and skirt sloper together to achieve this.

**Blouses and or Shirtwaists**

At the turn of the century, as more and more women joined the work force, the adoption of "men-tailored" clothing into feminine styles became increasingly popular. This was by no means new. As you can see from the riding habit in Figure 7–27, this adaptation started many years earlier. The Victorian ladies wore blouses, and false blouse fronts called "dickeys," but when women began wearing a tailored shirt, they called them "shirtwaists" and buttoned them in the opposite direction from a man's shirt.

Whatever you wish to call them, they are nothing more than loosely fitting bodices extended just enough to have "tails"—the lower section that is tucked beneath the waistband of either skirts or trousers. They too are drafted from either the bodice sloper or drafted directly as you would a bodice or a shift. Now that we have taken care of the ladies, let's move on to the gentlemen.

# 8

# Drafting and Construction—
# Men's Garments

For the last several hundred years men have been wearing essentially the same basic pieces of clothing: a shirt, a pair of pants, a waistcoat, a coat, and a cravat, which today has become known simply as a tie. Even before this elemental breakdown men wore shirts, "hosen" (a type of pants), and doublet (a form of jacket). Before that both men and women wore robes, which were variations on the shift discussed in Chapter 7.

In this chapter we will discuss the men's garments by their component parts, the shirt, pants, vests, coats, and ties. A Renaissance doublet, a Gothic jupon, and a sac coat will all be treated under the general heading of coats.

## The Shirt

The easiest garment to make is the shirt. We will discuss four basic shirts commonly used in their periods and a few simple adaptations of them. They are the Renaissance, the Baroque, the Rococo, and the modern shirt. Modern shirts should always be bought because it saves much valuable construction time. Many modern shirts can be adapted to a period look.

*The Renaissance Shirt*  Figure 8–1 shows a basic Renassaince shirt that has been adapted to two different looks; Figure 8–1A depicts an Italian Renaissance shirt, and 8–1B shows an English one popular to the Elizabethans. Both are my adaptations gleaned from paintings. Shirt A is a composite of several Botticelli works, primarily the *Adoration of The Magi*. Shirt B is taken from an anonymous Elizabethan painting called *St. Bartholomew's Fair*. Figure 8–2 illustrates the pattern detail for both shirts.

*The Baroque Shirt*  Figure 8–3 illustrates and scales a Baroque shirt that is a composite made of several French fashion engravings from 1645 to 1663.

*The Rococo Shirt*  Figure 8–4 illustrates a Rococo shirt taken from *The Sign of Gersaint*, a painting by Watteau painted in 1721. By the 1780s it had changed very little except to lose most of its body fullness. The illustration and scaled pattern of the 1780 shirt in Figure 8–5 is a composite of several Hogarth paintings including those in the series called *The Rake's Progress* and *The Roast Beef of Old England*.

*The Adaptation of the Modern Shirt*

The modern shirt has not changed very much since the middle of the 19th century. Basically the collar, cuffs, and occasionally the shirt front have been modified.

*Modification of the Collar*  When it comes to collars, let us work backwards in time. The present pointed collar has been fairly standard since the 1930s. The depth of the point may vary but this is often not detectable in the proscenium stage. For arena staging, you can always cover a smaller collar with a larger one.

*The Button-Down Collar:* The button-down collar was popular from the mid 1950s through the early 1960s. You can always add the buttons and buttonholes to today's shirt collar if you are doing *Grease* or *Bye Bye Birdie*.

*The Rounded Collar:* During the early 1900s through the 1920s, young men wore a rounded collar. If you are in a proscenium house, you can but-

**A. AN ITALIAN RENAISSANCE SHIRT**

**B. AN ELIZABETHAN SHIRT**

**Figure 8–1.** *Two Renaissance Shirts*[2]

tonhole zig-zag a rounded end to a pointed collar and cut off. If your audience is too close for this, fold up the point, tack it, and slip it into another collar (collar cover) that has the rounded shape. You can always remove an old collar and add a new one.

*The Detachable Collar:* Many costume suppliers still make a wide variety of detachable collars, including rounded ones, wing tips, and the high starched collar of the 1790s to 1840s. All you need to do is remove the old collar from the shirt, but leave the collar band and add buttons or buttonholes for studs if you prefer. This enables you to use the detachable ones.

*The Wing Collar:* There is another alternative to the wing collar. Turn the existing collar straight up, fold down the collar points and top stitch across the fold to hold it. This sometimes looks quite effective. It depends on the depth of the point. Some collar points are too deep. Be sure to remove any collar stays.

*Modification of the Cuff* The shirt cuff can be modified by the addition of ruffles, or an over cuff can be added to make a regular cuff into a French cuff, if so desired.

[2]Adapted from *The Cut of Men's Clothes* by Norah Waugh. Copyright 1964 by Norah Waugh. Used by permission of the publisher, Theatre Arts Books, 153 Waverly Place, New York, N.Y. 10014

*Modification of the Shirt Front* To turn a plain shirt into a dress shirt, add ruffles or a fake tucked panel and sew fancy buttons on top of the buttonholes, with snaps beneath them. Stiffened fronts can be added and the front of the base shirt closed. Then slit it up the center back and add enough of an edge to be able to overlap and button it. Add a detachable collar.

You will note that I have not included a pattern for a modern shirt. You can buy printed patterns for this. You do not need to draft one.

**Vests and Waistcoats**

The waistcoat first came into being in the Baroque period, as a sleeveless undercoat that buttoned, when the exterior coat did not. It originally had a skirt but by the 1780s it had a skirt-like tab in the front and the back stopped just at the waist. Throughout the remainder of the 1700s it grew shorter and shorter until by 1806 it was just an inch or two below the waist in the front. It goes from a rounded front to a point or two points; from high-buttoned collarless to low-button double-breasted with a fake collar.

As the line and color of men's clothing became more somber, the waistcoat was the one garment that retained its former glory. It was often lavishly embroidered, striped and augmented with jeweled

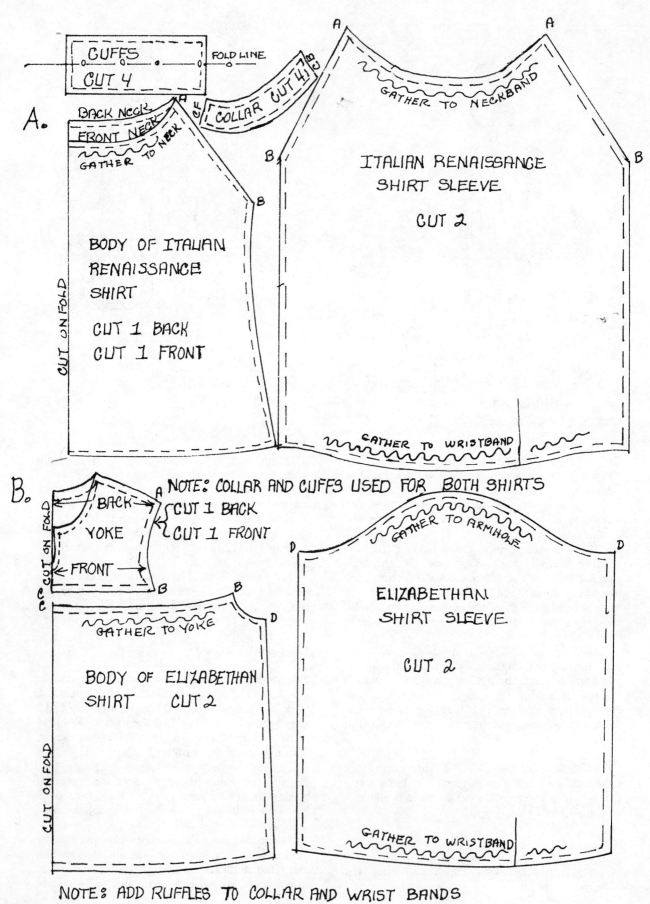

**Figure 8–2.** *Adapted Patterns for Renaissance Shirts*

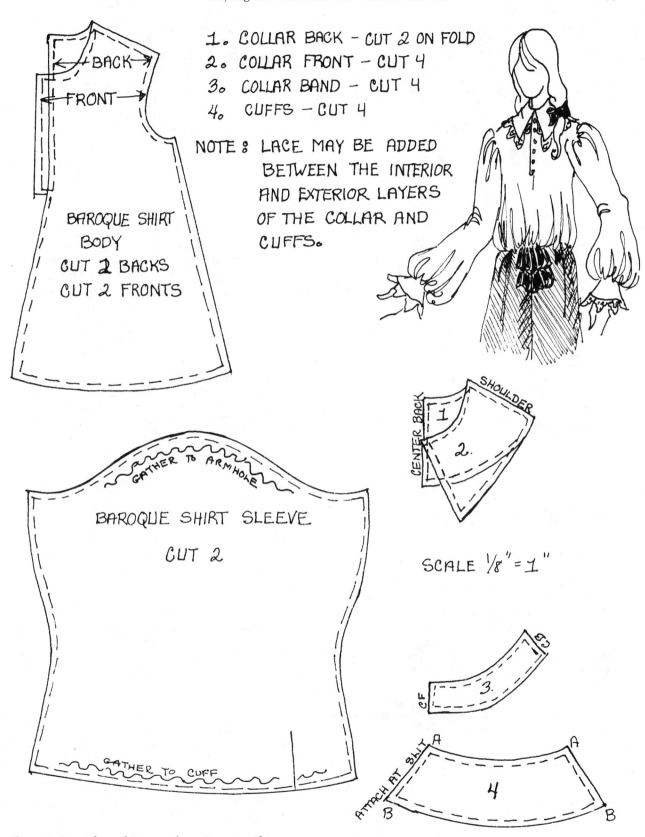

1. COLLAR BACK - CUT 2 ON FOLD
2. COLLAR FRONT - CUT 4
3. COLLAR BAND - CUT 4
4. CUFFS - CUT 4

NOTE: LACE MAY BE ADDED BETWEEN THE INTERIOR AND EXTERIOR LAYERS OF THE COLLAR AND CUFFS.

BAROQUE SHIRT BODY
CUT 2 BACKS
CUT 2 FRONTS

BACK
FRONT

BAROQUE SHIRT SLEEVE
CUT 2

GATHER TO ARMHOLE

GATHER TO CUFF

CENTER BACK
SHOULDER
1
2.

SCALE 1/8" = 1"

CF
3.

ATTACH AT SLIT
A
B
4
A
B

**Figure 8–3.** *Adapted Pattern for a Baroque Shirt*

**Figure 8–4.** *Early Rococo Shirt*

buttons. Then in the 20th century along came the three-piece suit all of the same fabric. This style is somewhat boring, but some of the vests were reversible so that the one side matched and the other side was of a complimentary color or pattern, a paisley, plaid, etc.

*The Skirted Waistcoat* The skirted waistcoat of Figure 8–6 is taken from a series of paintings by Pietro Longhi including *The Concert* and *The Dancing Lesson*. Also included is some detail from actual garments at the Museum of Costume in Bath, England. Note the elongated front shoulder line common to both coats and waistcoats of this period.

*The Tab-Fronted Waistcoat* The tab-fronted waistcoat of Figure 8–7 was also taken from garments of the costume museum in Bath.

*The Double-Breasted Waistcoat* Figure 8–8 shows two versions of a double-breasted waistcoat that can be made from one basic pattern. Letter A shows a low-cut rounded version with a fake collar. Letter B shows a high-cut V neck without a collar.

*The Single-Breasted Waistcoat* Figure 8–9 illustrates three versions of the single-breasted waist-

coat. Letter A is the high V necked version with notched collar and rounded at the waist. Letter B is the low rounded version with a single point often used for evening wear, and C is the modern V necked, two-pocket vest with two points at the waist. These can all be cut from one basic pattern using separate fronts. You can also use any combination of components you may desire. The pattern for this is seen in Figure 8–10.

**Pants**

Before men wore what we term pants, they wore a loose, similar garment called brais; these were worn to the ankle and gathered in by cross gartering. (In Volume I, Part Two a Barbarian silhouette shows this.) A simple pattern that will achieve this is shown in Figure 8–11. Then men wore simple "hosen" which in today's vernacular is synonymous with tights. The construction of tights is discussed in great detail in Chapter 10 as part of dance clothing.

*Pumpkin Hosen* We are going to start our progression of pants with "pumpkin hosen," the Renaissance garment illustrated in Figure 8–12. It is nothing but very full and very short pants with strips of a contrasting fabric on the outside, called panes. Not all hosen had panes. It is a matter of design choice.

There is a trick to sewing these hosen with the panes. Make the panes so that you have no vertical raw edges. Attach them upside down, sandwiched between the leg band and the leg, and stitch at 5/8" allowance. Then flip over and attach to the waist of the pants with a stay stitch. This is what gives the puff to the panes. If they are attached to the leg band like the waistband, their own weight tends to destroy the puff by its downward pull.

*Cannion* Cannion were hosen that came to the knee. They were sometimes worn under the pumpkin hosen and sometims worn alone. They were form fitting knee breeches that cupped the front of the knee cap. Figure 8–13 illustrates this. Both of these hosen made use of the codpiece.

*The Codpiece* The codpiece was first used by the Italian Renaissance gentlemen as a flap to cover a center front opening in the hosen. Originally it was merely a triangular flap. (This can be seen in Volume I, Part II, The Early Italian Renaissance Silhouette.) By the time of the English Renaissance (Volume I, Part II, English Renaissance, Tudor Silhouette), it had become a many splendored thing, padded, bejeweled, and obtrusive. You may or may not wish to use them. Two patterns for them are

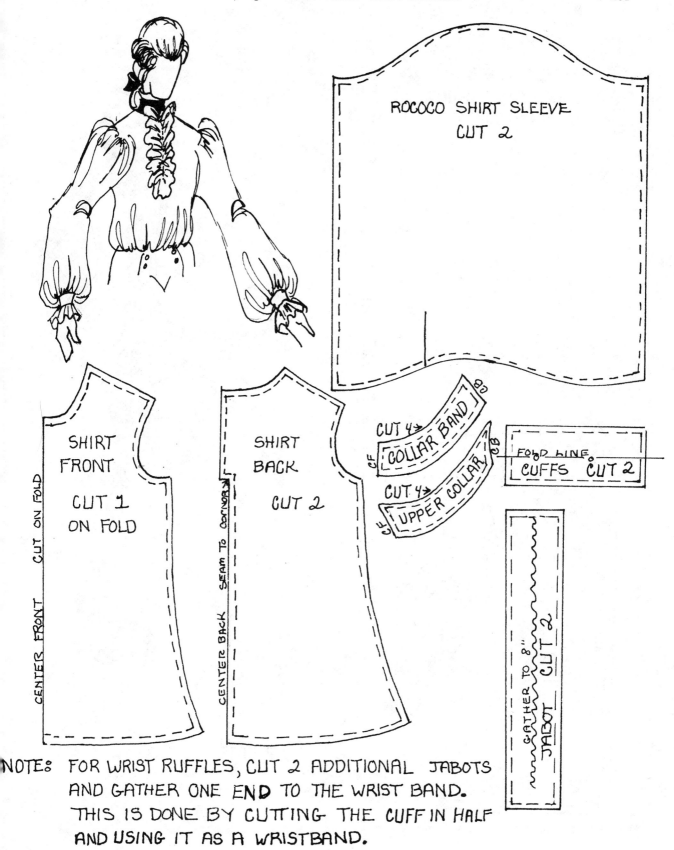

NOTE: FOR WRIST RUFFLES, CUT 2 ADDITIONAL JABOTS AND GATHER ONE END TO THE WRIST BAND. THIS IS DONE BY CUTTING THE CUFF IN HALF AND USING IT AS A WRISTBAND.

**Figure 8–5.** *Adapted Pattern for a Rococo Shirt*

NOTE: POCKETS MAY BE
STRICTLY DECORATION
OR PRACTICAL.

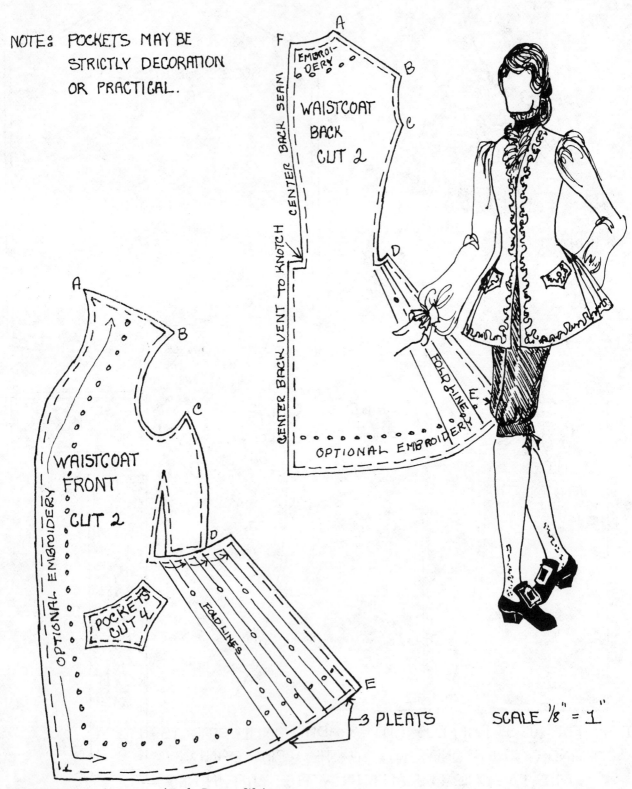

**Figure 8–6.** *Adaptation of Early Rococo Waistcoat*

**Figure 8–7.** *Adaptation of a Tab-Fronted Waistcoat*

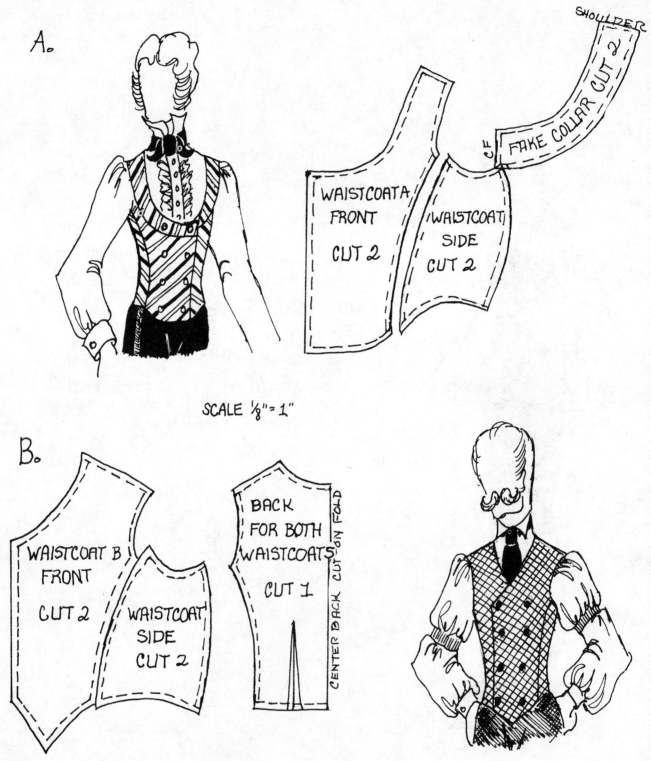

A.

WAISTCOAT A
FRONT
CUT 2

WAISTCOAT
SIDE
CUT 2

CF

FAKE COLLAR CUT 2

SHOULDER

SCALE ⅛"= 1"

B.

WAISTCOAT B
FRONT
CUT 2

WAISTCOAT
SIDE
CUT 2

BACK
FOR BOTH
WAISTCOATS
CUT 1

CENTER BACK CUT ON FOLD

**Figure 8–8.** *The Double-Breasted Waistcoat*

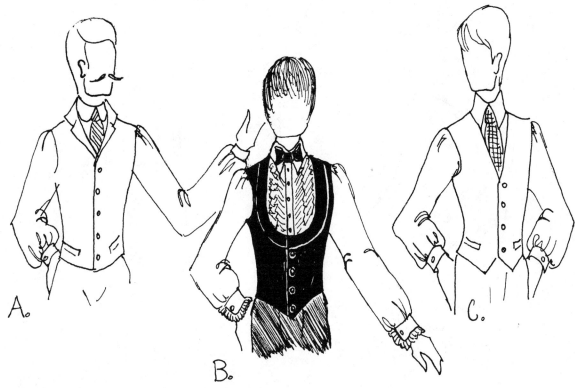

**Figure 8–9.** *Three Versions of a Single-Breasted Waistcoat*

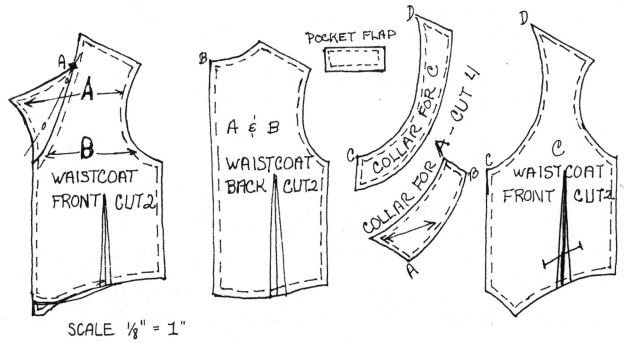

SCALE ⅛" = 1"

**Figure 8–10.** *Patterns for the Single-Breasted Waistcoats of Figure 8–9.*

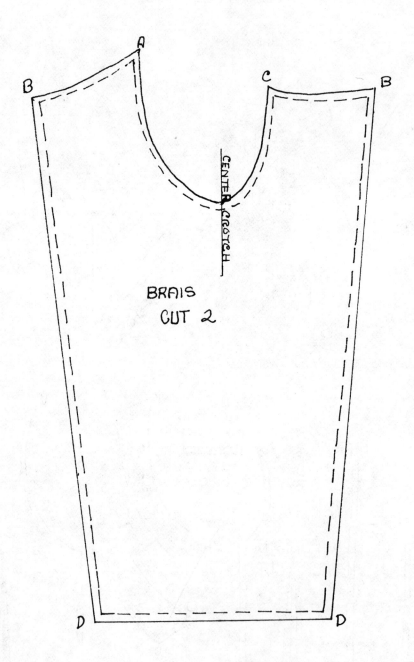

BRAIS
CUT 2

NOTE: MAKE A CHANNEL AT THE WAIST AND ANKLES
FOR ELASTIC OR A DRAW STRING

SCALE ⅛" = 1"

**Figure 8–11.** *Brais*

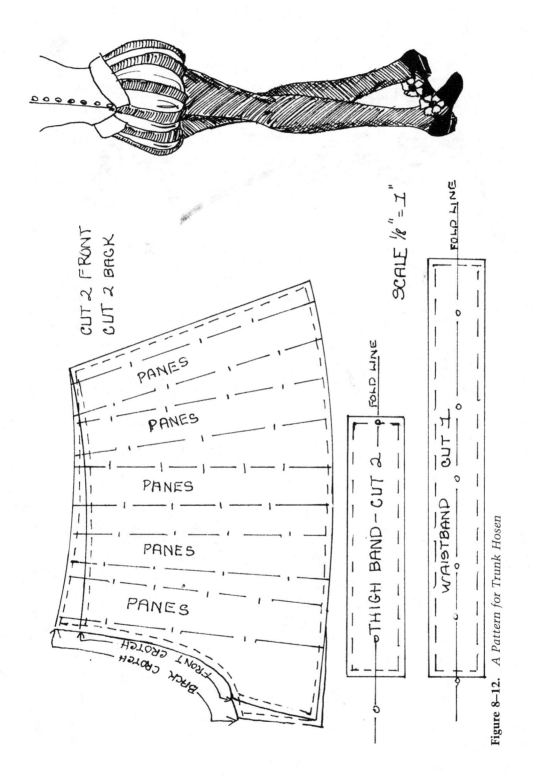

CUT 2 FRONT
CUT 2 BACK

PANES

PANES

PANES

PANES

PANES

BACK CROTCH

FRONT CROTCH

SCALE 1/8" = 1"

FOLD LINE

THIGH BAND - CUT 2

FOLD LINE

WAISTBAND CUT 1

**Figure 8–12.** *A Pattern for Trunk Hosen*

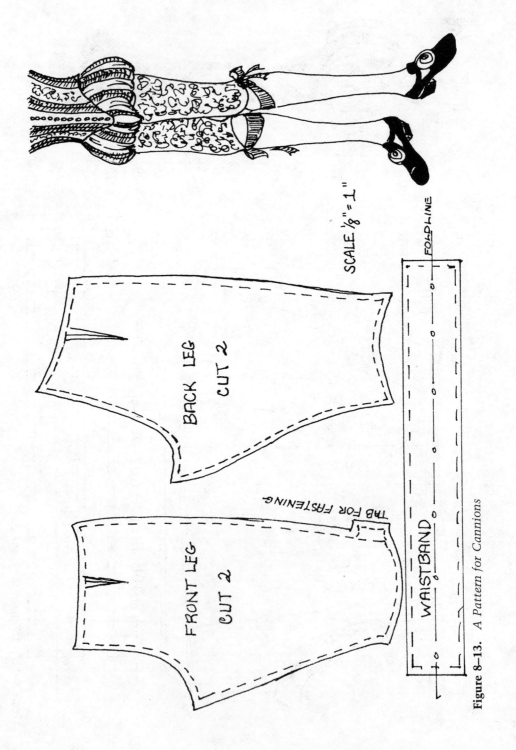

SCALE ⅛" = 1"

BACK LEG
CUT 2

FRONT LEG
CUT 2

TAB FOR FASTENING

WAISTBAND

FOLDLINE

**Figure 8–13.** *A Pattern for Cannions*

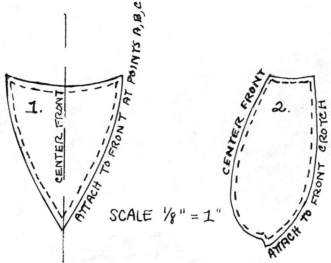

1. ITALIAN RENAISSANCE CODPIECE - CUT 1 EXTER-
IOR AND 1 INTERIOR PIECE, ONE USED TO FACE
THE OTHER

2. TUDOR CODPIECE - CUT 2 EXTERIOR & 2 INTERIOR

**Figure 8–14.**  *Patterns for Codpieces*

included in Figure 8–14 for those times when historical accuracy is needed. (These are adaptations from paintings of those periods.)

*Rhinegraves and Petticoat Breeches*  During the 1600s the style of breeches went from the extremely tight cannions to the very baggy Rhinegraves (also called Pantaloons) and stopped everywhere in between. That most ridiculous of Baroque male styles, Petticoat Breeches derived from those Rhinegraves, originally a Germanic style, became so full they looked like a skirt. They were trimmed in rows of horizontal ribbon loops and sometime skirts were worn over them. Figure 8–15 illustrates the three types just mentioned: A is the Cavalier banded breeches; B is the Cavalier straight-leg breeches; C is the Rhinegraves; D is the Petticoat variation with its accompanying over skirt and furbelows. Figure 8–16 scales patterns for Figure 8–15.

*The Rococo Breeches*  Figure 8–17 contains an illustration and scaled pattern for the Rococo breeches with a buckled kneeband. It also has the square fly that became popular in the mid-18th century. This same square flap can be adapted to bell-bottom pants for a sailor look.

This is a complicated, time consuming pattern. The same silhouette can be achieved by adapting the Cavalier straight-leg pattern to a kneeband and buckle; great time can be saved this way.

*The Directoire-Empire Breeches*  The pattern of Figure 8–17 can be adapted to the straight-legged, buttoned version of the Directoire and Empire periods. For an illustration of this see Volume I, Part II, The Empire Shilhouette.

*The Romantique Trousers*  There are two extremes to the trousers in the Romantique era: the baggy pantaloons with an instep strap (of the 1820s) and the extremely form fitting trousers of the 1830s, also with instep strap.

*Baggy Trousers:* Figure 8–18 is a basic pattern for the baggy trousers of the 1820s and their adaptation to "oxford bags" of the 1920s.

*Form Fitting Trousers:* The form fitting trousers can be cut from the leg sloper of Chapter 6 with ⅝" seam allowance added everywhere but the crotch curve; allow for one dart equidistant on the waist line and going perpendicular to it for four inches.

*The Modern Trouser*  Figure 8–19 is a pattern for the modern trouser with a straight leg. Also, on the dot and dash line is its adaptation to bell bottoms. It has a simple fly flap cut into the left side front and used as a facing. You can use any commercial pattern to cut a regular fly if you prefer.

*Riding Breeches and Jodhpurs*  Figure 8–20 illustrates both riding breeches and jodhpurs and their

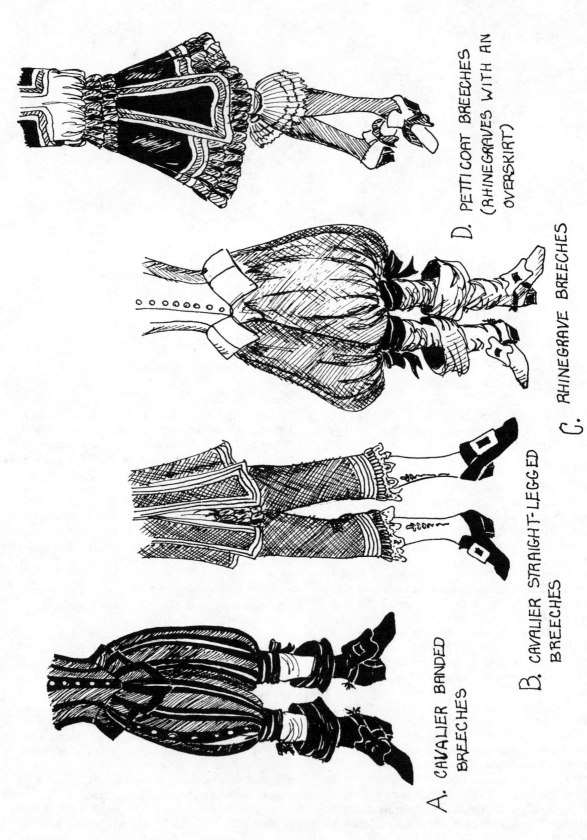

A. CAVALIER BANDED BREECHES

B. CAVALIER STRAIGHT-LEGGED BREECHES

C. RHINEGRAVE BREECHES

D. PETTICOAT BREECHES (RHINEGRAVES WITH AN OVERSKIRT)

**Figure 8–15.** *A Selection of Breeches*

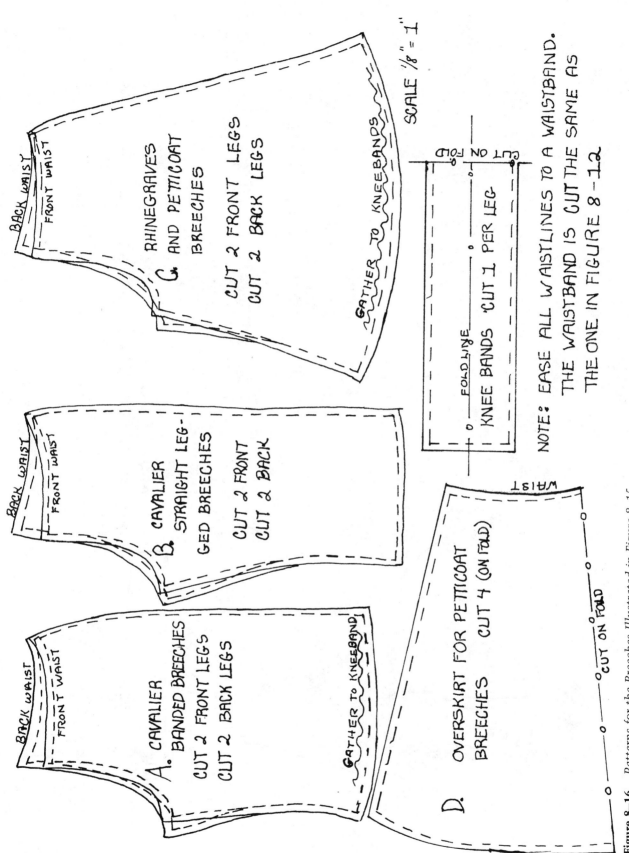

**Figure 8–16.** *Patterns for the Breeches Illustrated in Figure 8–15.*

BACK WAIST

FRONT WAIST

G. RHINEGRAVES AND PETTICOAT BREECHES

CUT 2 FRONT LEGS
CUT 2 BACK LEGS

GATHER TO KNEEBANDS

SCALE ⅛" = 1"

CUT ON FOLD

FOLD

FOLDLINE

KNEE BANDS CUT 1 PER LEG

NOTE: EASE ALL WAISTLINES TO A WAISTBAND. THE WAISTBAND IS CUT THE SAME AS THE ONE IN FIGURE 8–12

BACK WAIST

FRONT WAIST

B. CAVALIER STRAIGHT LEG-GED BREECHES

CUT 2 FRONT
CUT 2 BACK

BACK WAIST

FRONT WAIST

A. CAVALIER BANDED BREECHES

CUT 2 FRONT LEGS
CUT 2 BACK LEGS

GATHER TO KNEEBAND

WAIST

D. OVERSKIRT FOR PETTICOAT BREECHES    CUT 4 (ON FOLD)

CUT ON FOLD

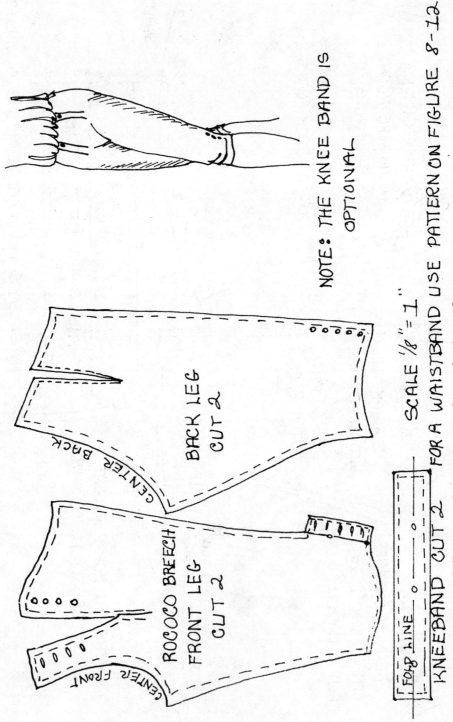

NOTE: THE KNEE BAND IS OPTIONAL

BACK LEG
CUT 2

CENTER BACK

ROCOCO BREECH
FRONT LEG
CUT 2

CENTER FRONT

FOLD LINE

KNEEBAND CUT 2

SCALE ⅛" = 1"

FOR A WAISTBAND USE PATTERN ON FIGURE 8-12

Figure 8-17. *Pattern and Illustration for Rococo Breeches with Square Flap*

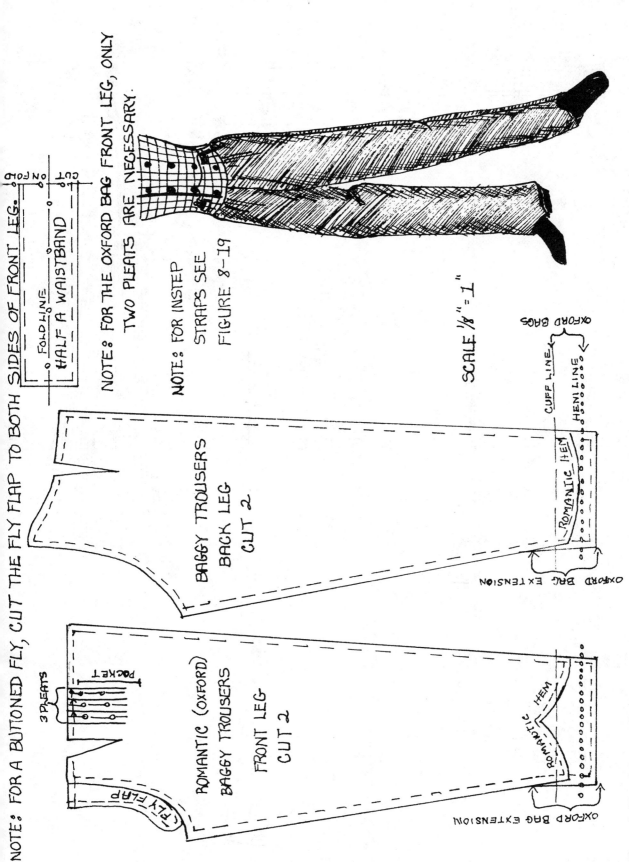

NOTE: FOR A BUTTONED FLY, CUT THE FLY FLAP TO BOTH SIDES OF FRONT LEG.

NOTE: FOR THE OXFORD BAG FRONT LEG, ONLY TWO PLEATS ARE NECESSARY.

NOTE: FOR INSTEP STRAPS SEE FIGURE 8–19

SCALE ⅛" = 1"

ON FOLD

FOLDLINE

CUT

HALF A WAISTBAND

BAGGY TROUSERS BACK LEG CUT 2

OXFORD BAGS

CUFF LINE

HEMLINE

ROMANTIC HEM

OXFORD BAG EXTENSION

3 PLEATS

POCKET

ROMANTIC (OXFORD) BAGGY TROUSERS

FRONT LEG CUT 2

FLY FLAP

ROMANTIC HEM

OXFORD BAG EXTENSION

**Figure 8–18.** *A Pattern for Romantic Baggy Trousers and Their Adaptation to Oxford Bags*

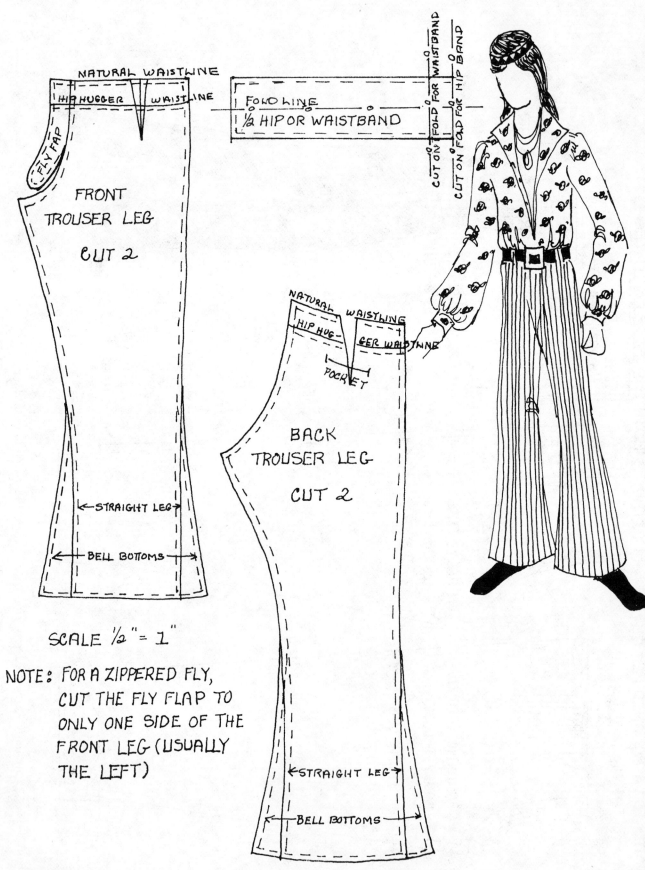

NATURAL WAISTLINE

HIP HUGGER   WAISTLINE

FLY FLAP

FRONT
TROUSER LEG
CUT 2

FOLD LINE
½ HIP OR WAISTBAND

CUT ON FOLD FOR WAISTBAND
CUT ON FOLD FOR HIP BAND

←STRAIGHT LEG→

←— BELL BOTTOMS —→

NATURAL   WAISTLINE

HIP HUG-   GER WAISTLINE

POCKET

BACK
TROUSER LEG
CUT 2

←STRAIGHT LEG→

←— BELL BOTTOMS —→

SCALE ½" = 1"

NOTE: FOR A ZIPPERED FLY,
CUT THE FLY FLAP TO
ONLY ONE SIDE OF THE
FRONT LEG (USUALLY
THE LEFT)

**Figure 8–19.**  *Straight-Leg Trousers and Adaptation to Hip-Hugger Bell Bottoms*

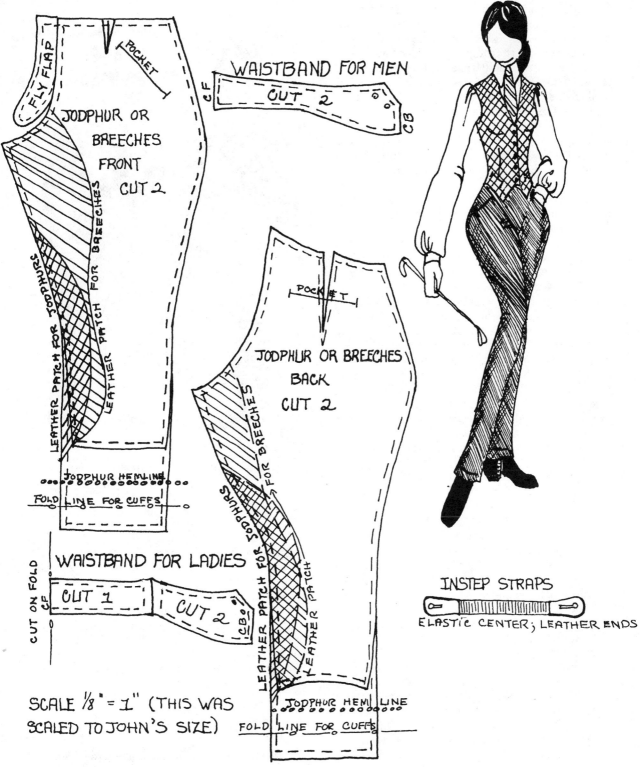

FLY FLAP

JODPHUR OR
BREECHES
FRONT
CUT 2

POCKET

CF

WAISTBAND FOR MEN
CUT 2

CB

LEATHER PATCH FOR JODPHURS

LEATHER PATCH FOR BREECHES

JODPHUR OR BREECHES
BACK
CUT 2

POCKET

LEATHER PATCH FOR JODPHURS

LEATHER PATCH FOR BREECHES

JODPHUR HEMLINE

FOLD LINE FOR CUFFS

WAISTBAND FOR LADIES

CUT ON FOLD

CF

CUT 1

CUT 2

CB

LEATHER PATCH FOR JODPHURS

LEATHER PATCH

JODPHUR HEM LINE

FOLD LINE FOR CUFFS

SCALE ⅛" = 1" (THIS WAS
SCALED TO JOHN'S SIZE)

INSTEP STRAPS
ELASTIC CENTER; LEATHER ENDS

NOTES: 1. FOR A ZIPPERED FLY, CUT THE FLY FLAP TO ONLY ONE SIDE OF THE
FRONT LEG
2. WHEN CUTTING LADIES' RIDING APPAREL, THE FLY IS UNNESSESARY.

**Figure 8–20.**  *A Riding Jodhpur or Breeches Pattern (Male or Female)*

patterns (letter A the breeches, letter B the jodhpurs). The difference is that the breeches are made to go inside knee-high boots and are worn when riding hunters and thoroughbreds. The boot gives added grip to the saddle needed for jumping and racing. Thoroughbred horses are a specific breed used in this country for hunters, jumpers, flat track racing, and steeplechasing.

Jodhpurs are trousers in that they come to the ankle, are worn over a low jodhpur boot, and are strapped under the instep. These are worn in this country in the show horse ring on American saddlebred horses, Arabians, Morgan horses, and Tennessee walking horses. The Tennessee walker is a member of the American saddlebred breed. The other two are distinct breeds on their own.

A jockey wears "silks" in the colors of the horse's owner. Figure 8–21 shows two jockeys in their silks. Figure 8–21A is a jockey who rides a thoroughbred on a flat track. He is wearing breeches, high boots, again for gripping purposes, as he will ride standing in his stirrups above the saddle in a crouching position. His shirt is tucked into his pants. His cap is steel-reinforced as are the velvet caps worn by all people who ride jumpers. The jockey in 8–21B drives a standardbred horse (also called "trotters") in trotting races. He rides in a two-wheeled vehicle called a sulky. His silk shirt is really a jacket, worn out over jodhpurs and his cap is quite different. These two riding trousers can be adapted to feminine use by the elimination of the fly front and the addition of a side zipper.

*Note:* The side saddle, which women still use occasionally, demands the wearing of a riding skirt—a wrap-around skirt with a draped front that *must* wrap right over left so that the slit is over the left leg. Trousers are worn under this which slip into a knee-high boot. It has not changed from the Victorian one shown in Chapter 7, except that the skirt is generally cut only double the circumference of the lower hip these days.

While on the subject of riding apparel, it would be wrong to exclude our western compatriots. Figure 8–22 shows the typical attire used when riding quarter horses; 8–22A pictures the male "get-up" and 8–22B the female. The cowboy sports the ever popular blue jeans, a notched yoke plaid shirt (which easterners call a "western" shirt), chaps, western style boots often refered to west of the Pecos as "chip-kickers," and a ten-gallon hat. These hats were used to carry water on the range and with typical tall-tale exaggeration, supposedly held ten gallons. Chaps are an overpant of leather covering the outside of the leg to protect it from cactus stickers and the prick of steerhorns on cattle drives. The woman's attire copies the man's except for her culottes, a divided pants-skirt adopted from the Argentinian gaucho's apparel as is the fringed bolero, and

A. THOROUGHBRED (BREECHES)   B. STANDARDBRED (JODHPURS)

**Figure 8–21.** *Jockey Silks*

her hat which is an adaptation of the caballero hat of Spanish origin. Culottes are often called 'gauchos' by westerners and are often made of leather. The woman and the man both wear neckerchiefs, usually a working man's red bandana. This had a practical reason in that it was pulled over the nose and mouth for protection against dust. Jeans can readily be purchased, and patterns for the other items can be found in the commercial pattern books.

### Coats and Jackets

Whether it was called a tunic, jupon, doublet, surcoat, coat, cote, jerken, or jacket, it is basically the same garment that covers the top portion of the body. A pattern will be given for the most generally used of these garments in each period. Though the sleeves will be included with these, discussion of them will be reserved for Chapter 9. Unless other-

**Figure 8–22.** *Western Riding Apparel*

wise specified, these patterns are composites that achieve the look of these periods.

*The Basic Tunic* As this is a garment much used by the danseur in ballet, I have included it in Chapter 10. It can be adapted for many things. For instance, add a skirt and puffed sleeves to the top of the waist and you have Henry VIII. It can be used as a sloper for several other styles as well.

*The Gothic Jupon* This gothic jupon has a darted front, sac sleeves, and the boat neck so popular in the early 1400s. The best way to achieve this is to use your basic tunic to the waist line as a construction lining. Sew your tucked front and back to their yokes and then to the construction lining. This trick will hold the darts (or pleats or folds) where you want them. This is illustrated in Figure 8–23.

*The Italian Doublet* Figure 8–24 illustrates the Italian doublet which comes just to the waist. The sleeves are tied to the armhole by means of laces called "points." The shirt sleeve is puffed through the openings.

*The Elizabethan Doublet* The Elizabethan doublet is illustrated in Figure 8–25. It has a tabbed

skirt and half-moon epaulettes that were used to cover the points. Today it is just as simple to attach the sleeve by machine.

*The Cavalier Jacket and Baroque Jacket* Figure 8–26A shows a pattern for the full Cavalier jacket that can be seen with the straight-legged pants in Figure 8–14B; 8–26B is a pattern for a Baroque jacket that would have been worn with the petticoat breeches seen in Figure 8–14D.

*The Baroque Skirted Coat* At the end of the reign of Louis XIV in France and during the reign of William and Mary in England, a style for an almost "princess line" coat came into fashion. This is illustrated in Figure 8–27. This developed into the extremely full-skirted coat with the elongated shoulder of the early Rococo.

*The Rococo Skirted Coat* This early Rococo coat is illustrated in Figure 8–28. From this came the modified skirted coat that can be cut from this same pattern by just eliminating some of the fullness. This eventually became the swallowtail coat of the Empire, the first of the tailcoats. This was taken from a garment at the Museum of Costume in Bath, England.

*The Tailcoat* The tailcoat should be subdivided into the swallowtail, and broadtail, and cut-away. These are all illustrated in Figure 8–30—A is swallowtail, B is broadtail, and C is the cut-away.
*The Swallowtail:* Figure 8–29 is a pattern for the swallowtail. This was adapted from a garment at the Philadelphia Museum of Art.[3]
*The Broadtail:* Figure 8–31 is a pattern for the broadtail. This was taken from a donated garment whose tailor's label read 1862.
*The Cut-Away:* Figure 8–32 is a pattern for the cut-away. This was taken from a donated garment.

*The Frock Coat* The frock coat was the 19th century's version of the coat with a skirt. There were double-breasted and single breasted varieties. For absolute authenticity the patterns for these in Frederick T. Croonborg's *The Blue Book of Men's Tailoring* is excellent.[4] Figure 8–33 is a simplified version that will achieve the same silhouette but without the elongated shoulder and complicated darts. Letter A indicates the double-breasted front; letter B shows the single-breasted front. You will find illustrations for the frock coat in Volume I, Part II, The Late Victorian (Sheath) Silhouette.

3. Philadelphia Museum of Art, *Fine Fashions*, 1979.
4. Frederick T. Croonborg, *The Blue Book of Men's Tailoring* (New York, Van Nostrand Reinhold Co., 1977), pp. 190–197.

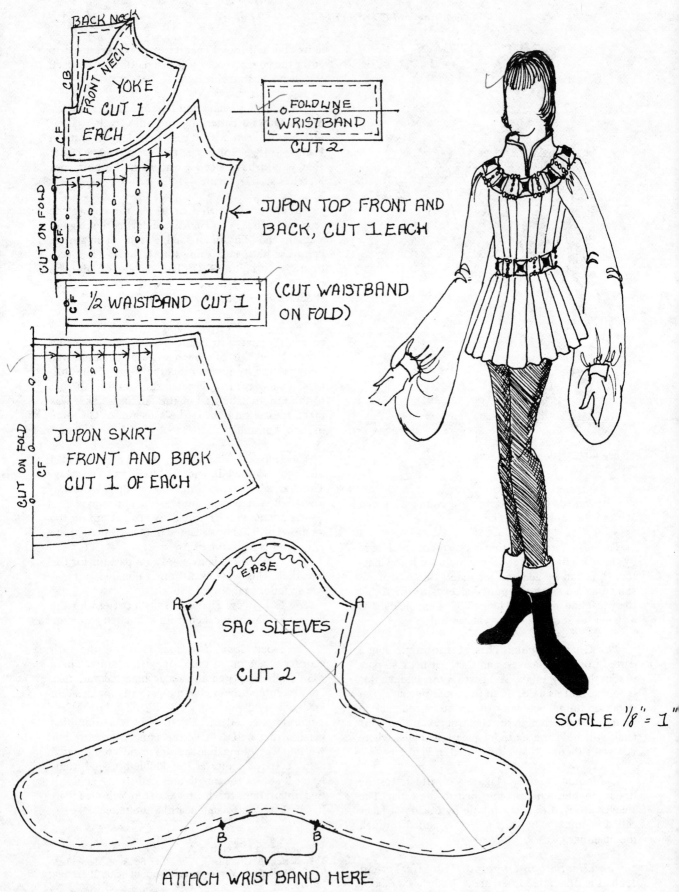

BACK NECK

FRONT NECK

CB

CF

YOKE
CUT 1
EACH

FOLD LINE
WRISTBAND
CUT 2

CUT ON FOLD

CF

JUPON TOP FRONT AND
BACK, CUT 1 EACH

CF    ½ WAISTBAND CUT 1    (CUT WAISTBAND
ON FOLD)

CUT ON FOLD

CF

JUPON SKIRT
FRONT AND BACK
CUT 1 OF EACH

EASE

A                    A

SAC SLEEVES

CUT 2

B        B

ATTACH WRIST BAND HERE

SCALE ⅛" = 1"

**Figure 8–23.** *The Gothic Jupon*

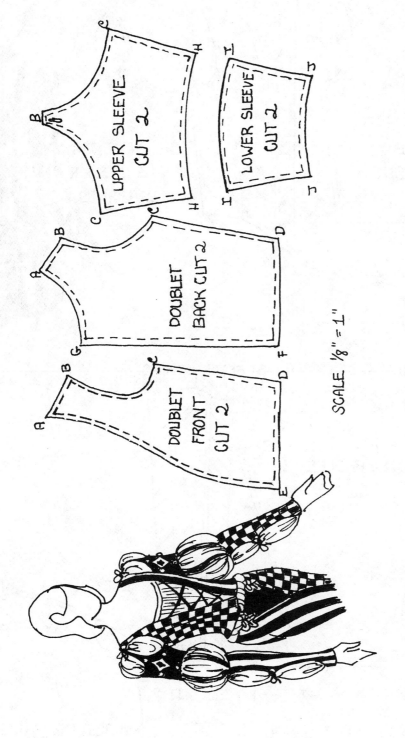

**UPPER SLEEVE CUT 2**

**LOWER SLEEVE CUT 2**

**DOUBLET BACK CUT 2**

**DOUBLET FRONT CUT 2**

SCALE ⅛" = 1"

NOTE: DOUBLET FRONT, BACK, AND LOWER SLEEVES CAN BE CUT FROM TWO DIFFERENT FABRICS FOR THAT PARTI STYLE

**Figure 8-24.** *Italian Renaissance Doublet*

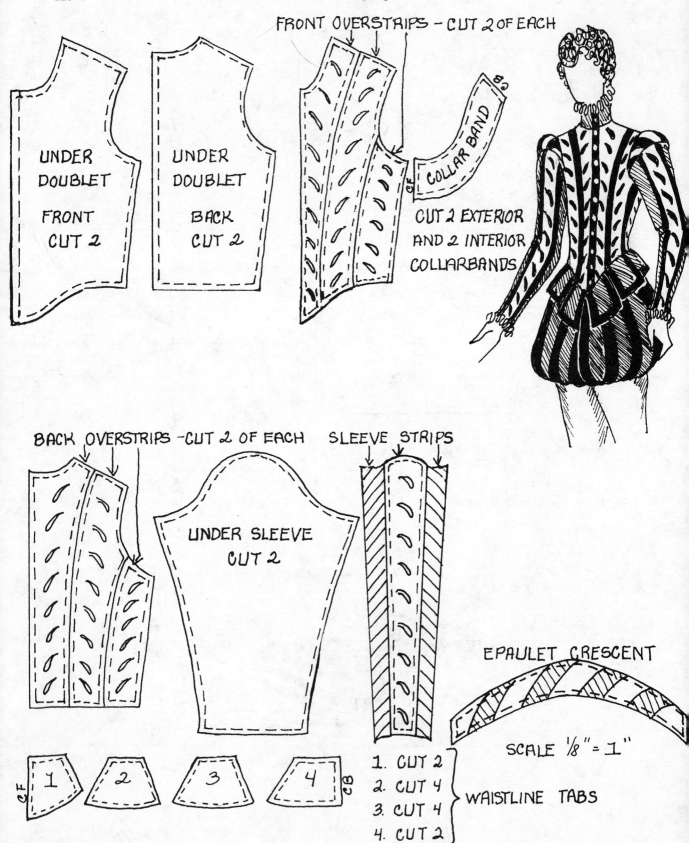

FRONT OVERSTRIPS – CUT 2 OF EACH

UNDER DOUBLET FRONT CUT 2

UNDER DOUBLET BACK CUT 2

COLLAR BAND

CUT 2 EXTERIOR AND 2 INTERIOR COLLARBANDS

BACK OVERSTRIPS – CUT 2 OF EACH

SLEEVE STRIPS

UNDER SLEEVE CUT 2

EPAULET CRESCENT

SCALE 1/8" = 1"

1. CUT 2
2. CUT 4
3. CUT 4
4. CUT 2

WAISTLINE TABS

**Figure 8–25.** *Elizabethan Doublet*

A.

BACK NECK
FRONT NECK
CENTER FRONT AND CENTER BACK

CAVALIER
JACKET
BACK & FRONT
CUT 2 OF EACH

NOTES: FOR SHIRT, SEE FIGURE 8-3
FOR SLEEVES, SEE FIGURE
9-26
FOR COLLAR, SEE FIGURE
9-3, #1

B.

Cavalier

CENTER FRONT AND BACK
BACK NECK
FRONT NECK

BAROQUE
BOLERO

CUT 2 OF
EACH (BACK
AND FRONT)

BOLERO SLEEVE
CUT 2

NOTES: FOR SHIRT, SEE
FIGURE 8-3

FOR PETTICOAT BREECHES
SEE FIGURES 8-15 AND
8-16

SCALE ⅛" = 1"

**Figure 8–26.** *Cavalier and Baroque Jacket*

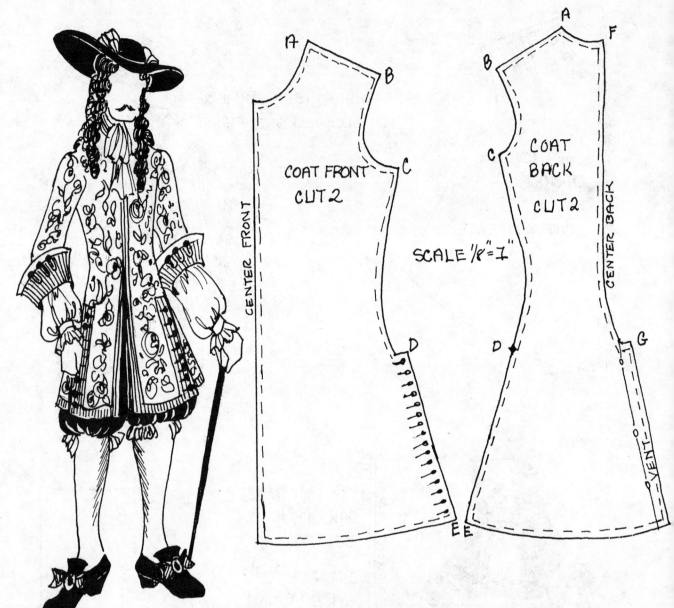

NOTE: THIS IS THE TYPE OF COAT ORIGINATED BY CHARLES II OF ENGLAND AND CARRIED THROUGH 100 YEARS MERELY WITH SLIGHT MODIFICATION.

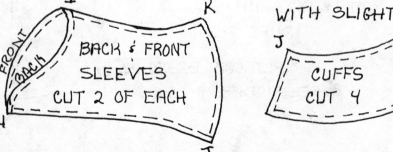

**Figure 8–27.** *Late Baroque Coat (William and Mary—1690)*

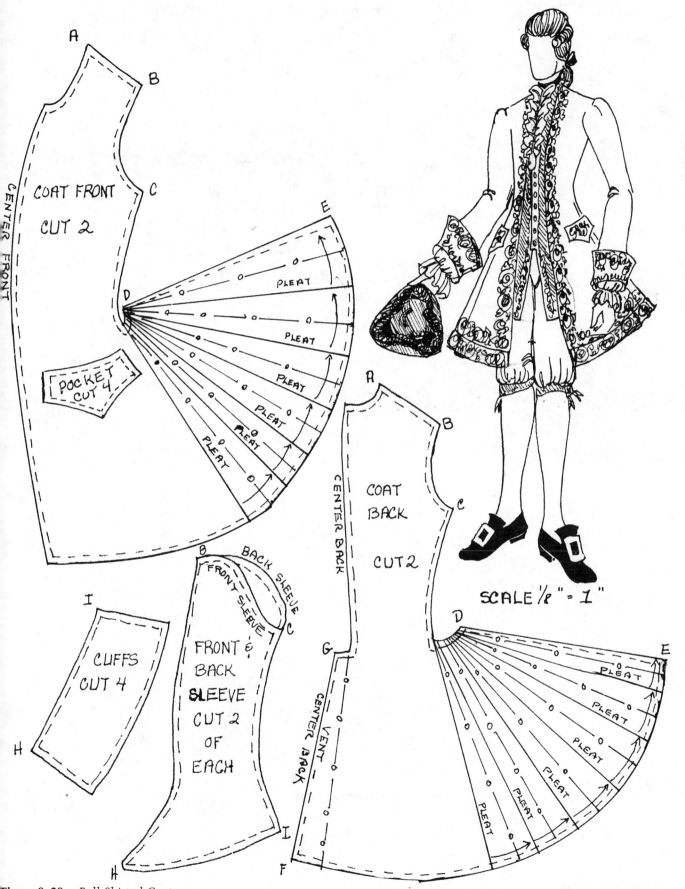

A

B

COAT FRONT
CUT 2

CENTER FRONT

C

D

E

PLEAT

PLEAT

PLEAT

PLEAT

PLEAT

PLEAT

POCKET
CUT 4

I

CUFFS
CUT 4

H

G

BACK SLEEVE

FRONT SLEEVE

C

FRONT &
BACK
SLEEVE
CUT 2
OF
EACH

I

H

A

B

COAT
BACK

CUT 2

CENTER BACK

C

D

E

G

VENT

CENTER BACK

PLEAT

PLEAT

PLEAT

PLEAT

PLEAT

PLEAT

F

SCALE ⅛" = 1"

**Figure 8–28.** *Full-Skirted Coat*

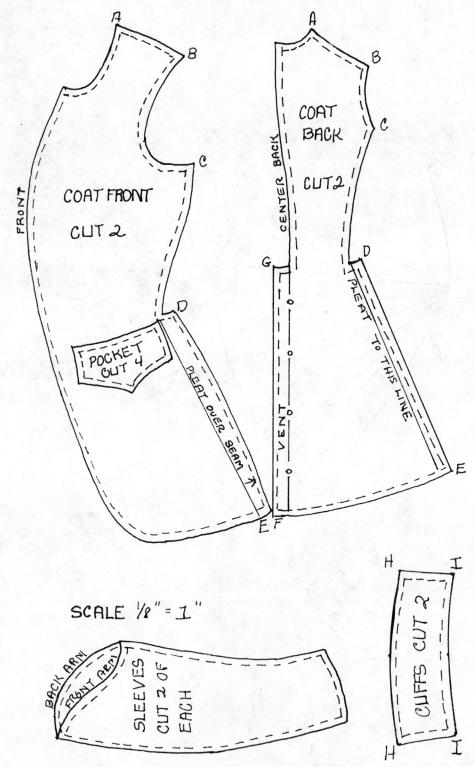

**Figure 8–29.** *A Pattern for a Swallowtail Coat*

A. THE SWALLOW TAILS

NOTE: OVER THE 19ᵗʰ CENTURY
THIS EVOLVED INTO THE
EVENING TAILS WHICH
ARE STILL WORN FOR
ULTRA FORMAL OCCASIONS

B. THE BROADTAIL

C. THE CUT-A-WAY

NOTE: THIS IS ALSO CALLED
"MORNING TAILS" AND
IS WORN FOR FORMAL
WEDDINGS IN THE DAY-
TIMES. IN GREY, THIS IS
PROPER ATTIRE FOR THE
RACES

**Figure 8–30.** *A Variety of Tailcoats*

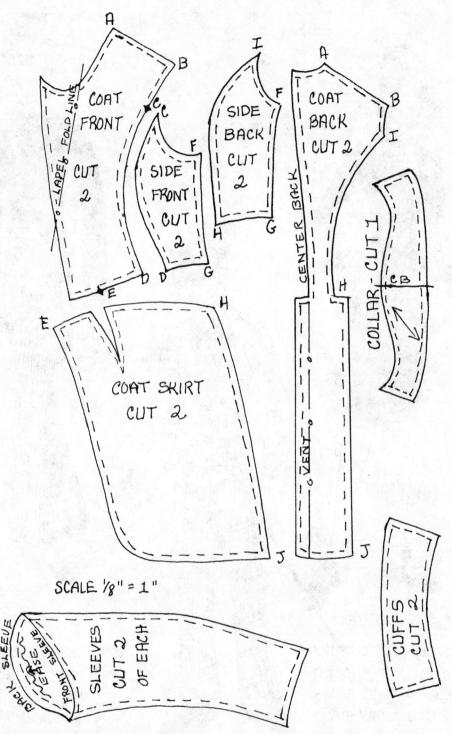

**Figure 8–31.** *A Pattern for a Broadtail Coat*

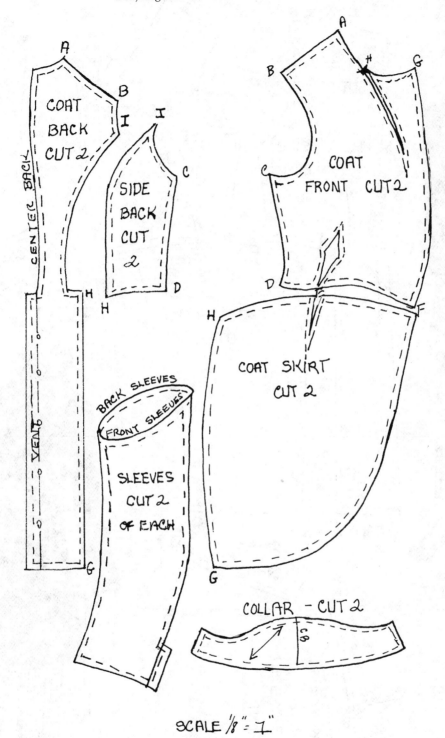

SCALE ⅛" = 1"

**Figure 8–32.** *Pattern for a Cut-Away*

COAT BACK CUT 2

CENTER BACK

SIDE BACK CUT 2

SINGLE BREAST ED COAT FRONT CUT 2

BACK SLEEVE

FRONT SLEEVE

SLEEVES CUT 2 OF EACH

CUFF CUT 4

POCKET CUT 4

SINGLE BREASTED COAT SKIRT CUT 1

VENT

SCALE 1/8" = 1"

COLLAR

CB

CUT ON FOLD

DOUBLE BREASTED COAT FRONT CUT 2

POCKET CUT 4

DOUBLE BREASTED COAT FRONT CUT 2

NOTE: THE COAT BACK AND SIDE BACK FITS WITH EITHER FRONT

**Figure 8–33.** *Two Versions of the Frock Coat*

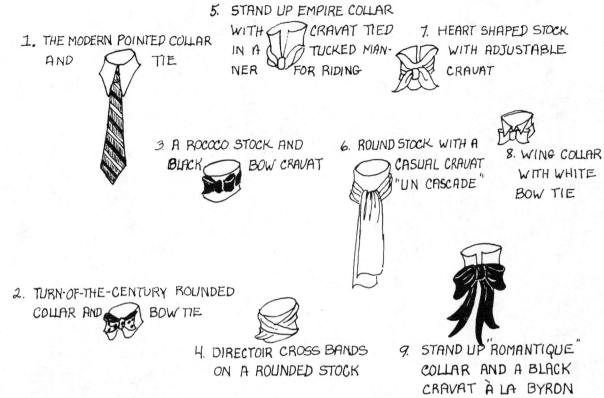

**1.** THE MODERN POINTED COLLAR AND TIE

**5.** STAND UP EMPIRE COLLAR WITH CRAVAT TIED IN A TUCKED MANNER FOR RIDING

**7.** HEART SHAPED STOCK WITH ADJUSTABLE CRAVAT

**3.** A ROCOCO STOCK AND BLACK BOW CRAVAT

**6.** ROUND STOCK WITH A CASUAL CRAVAT "UN CASCADE"

**8.** WING COLLAR WITH WHITE BOW TIE

**2.** TURN-OF-THE-CENTURY ROUNDED COLLAR AND BOW TIE

**4.** DIRECTOIR CROSS BANDS ON A ROUNDED STOCK

**9.** STAND UP "ROMANTIQUE" COLLAR AND A BLACK CRAVAT À LA BYRON

**Figure 8–34.** *A Selection of Cravats*

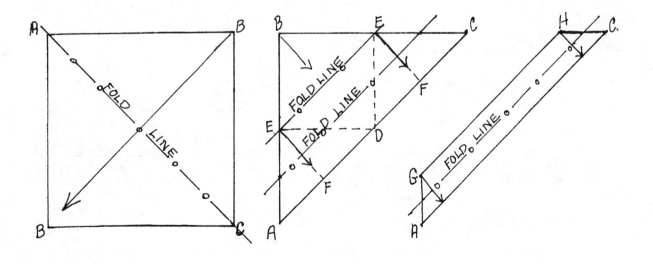

THIS IS AN UNSCALED DRAWING

**Figure 8–35.** *Folding a Cravat*

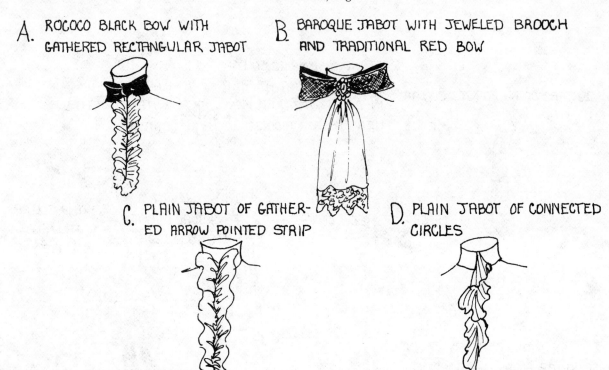

A. ROCOCO BLACK BOW WITH GATHERED RECTANGULAR JABOT

B. BAROQUE JABOT WITH JEWELED BROOCH AND TRADITIONAL RED BOW

C. PLAIN JABOT OF GATHER-ED ARROW POINTED STRIP

D. PLAIN JABOT OF CONNECTED CIRCLES

**Figure 8–36.** *A Selection of Jabots*

*The Sac Coat:* The sac coat was the Edwardian name for a sports coat and can be cut either double- or single-breasted from any contemporary suit coat pattern. The modifications are in the number of buttons, the curve or cut-away part of the center front, and the lapel. One can do this to existing garments as well.

### The Tie

The modern tie can usually be found in thrift shops for very little money. The tie itself has changed little in the last fifty years. It just gets wider or narrower by the decade. To make a wide tie more narrow, you simply have to refold it. To use a narrow tie for a wide one, open it up the whole way and face with another fabric. You will have to cut new interfacing as well.

Patterns are available for both the hanging tie and the bow tie in the commercial pattern books. A tie is also called a cravat; cravats go back quite a few years, right into the Rococo period. Figure 8–34 is a selection of a few cravats.

Most of these are merely ways of wrapping rectangles or bias strips around the neck and tying them. the rectangle is folded as shown in Figure 8–35. This method also gives a bias. This is important because it must curve around a circle (the neck) and lie flat. The bias cut facilitates this. Even today's ties are cut on the bias.[5]

### The Jabot

Figure 8–36 shows a selection of jabots. A jabot is a frill that hangs from the neck down the front of the shirt or blouse. In the early Rococo period, a jabot and a cravat might be worn together (Fig. 8–36A). There was a fashion for tying a jabot over a bow at the throat in the late Baroque (8–36B), and they were worn plain as well (8–36C).

Jabots were either a rectangle of fine cotton or linen lawn, or of lace. They sometimes were a series of circles sewn together onto a vertical strip (8–36D). Often the cravat was worn with a collar. Even before the jabot, there was the collar although it was often called the falling ruff. These were worn by both sexes. This leads us to our next chapter on unisex clothing.

5. Waugh, *The Art of Men's Clothes, 1600–1900*, pp. 119–120.

# 9

# Drafting and Construction: Unisex Garments

Perhaps the title of this chapter should use the word "bisex" garments because we discuss items that are cut the same, whether worn by men or women. These include collars, cuffs, sleeves, belts, aprons, capes, and the jumpsuit.

## The Collar

Collars have as much variety as the human imagination can conceive. Anything is possible if one follows a few basic construction and drafting principles.

1. *Always cut a collar either on the bias or with a convex curve that lines up exactly with the neck of the garment to which it is attached.*
2. *Except for a tailored suit collar that must roll (in which an undercollar is cut slightly smaller), all collars must be cut two times; once for the upper collar and once for the under collar.*

With this in mind we will now get down to specific cases.

### The Collar Band

The collar band can be used by itself or as a stand-up band to hold a ruffle or a falling collar. The neck ruffle of the Elizabethan shirt in Chapter 8 is one such case. The band is used by itself on the Italian Renaissance shirt (refer to Fig. 8–1). In the modern shirt, the collar band holds the pointed collar that turns down. A Mandarin collar is really a wider version of the collar band, as is the "stand-up" collar. Figure 9–1 illustrates two ways of cutting this.

*Inset Collars* Inset collars are those that fit into a collar band, but they may also be set into the neck of the dress or shirt by use of a neck facing. These include pointed collars, rounded collars, and splayed collars, as pictured in Figure 9–2.

*The Cowl Collar* A cowl collar is one purposely made too long for the neck so that it lies around the neck in several folds. It usually stands out, away from the neck. This is illustrated in Figure 9–3.

*The Boat Collar* A boat collar like the one on the Gothic jupon pattern in Chapter 8 (Fig. 8–22) also stands away from the neck, but it is stiffened and does not fall.

*The Shawl Collar* A shawl collar is usually one that goes from a point in the front to a drop shoulder and deep back, looking like a shawl. This is illustrated in Figure 9–4. This also refers to the collar used in a man's smoking jacket.

*The Bertha* The bertha is considered by some to be a collar. It is really a very deep ruffle that goes off the shoulder. The ruffle can be either a long rectangle or an enormous semicircle, as shown in Figure 9–5.

*Falling Bands* Falling bands and falling ruffs are essentially the same thing. These collars were worn separately over the garments. Some were attached to a band, some were not. Figure 9–6 shows a selection of these and their corresponding patterns. In this case the low neck curve indicates the front piece and the high neck curve, the back. These are generally cut with a shoulder seam and drafted the same way as any other shoulder.

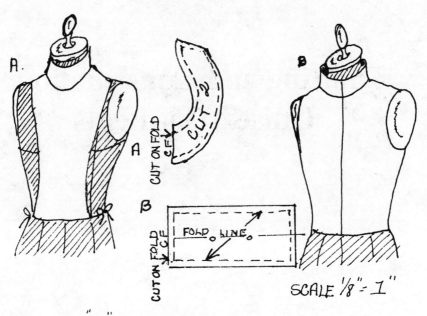

SCALE 1/8" = 1"

NOTE: COLLAR "B" MUST BE CUT ON THE BIAS

**Figure 9–1.** *Two Ways of Cutting a Stand-Up Collar*

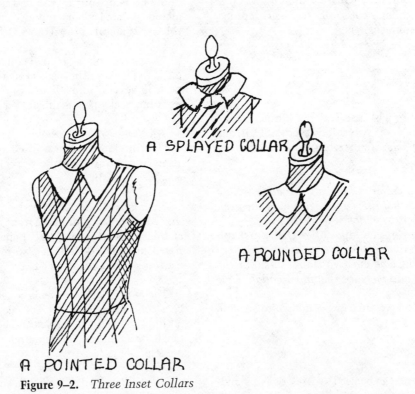

A SPLAYED COLLAR

A ROUNDED COLLAR

A POINTED COLLAR

**Figure 9–2.** *Three Inset Collars*

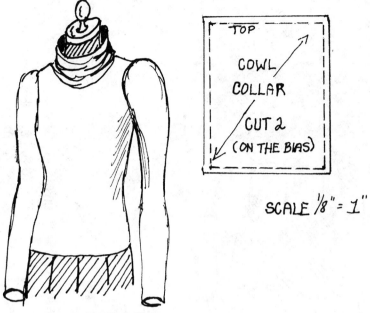

**Figure 9–3.** *A Cowl Collar*

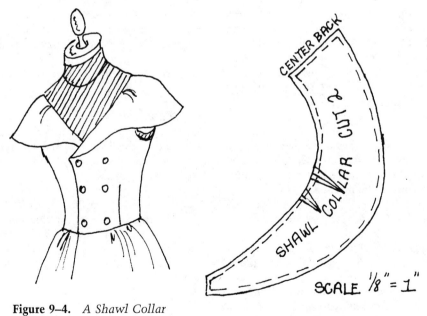

**Figure 9–4.** *A Shawl Collar*

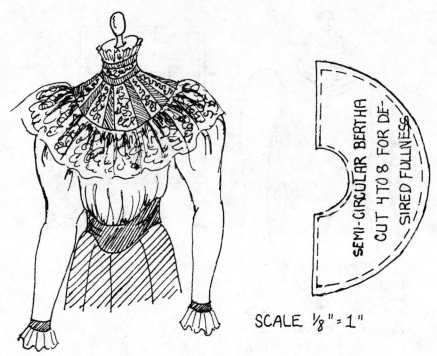

SCALE ⅛" = 1"

**Figure 9–5.** *A Bertha Collar*

*Preacher's Bands* Sometimes called preacher's tabs, these were marks of distinction for priests and preachers in the 17th and 18th centuries. Figure 9–7 illustrates them. Letter A shows the Protestant bands, and letter B the Catholic. This, of course, was general usage. Both Anglican and Lutheran churches wore style B at various times.

*Ruffs* Ruffs, like falling bands, were worn separately over the costume. They are time consuming to make but not impossible. You need a neck band that has been interfaced to make it sturdy. A pattern is not really essential. The method is as follows:

1. *Cut and make your neck band. Its depth determines the depth of your ruff.*
2. *Cut a rectangle four times the length of the neck circumference, plus 1¼ inches for seam allowance.*
3. *It is as wide as you wish. A cartwheel ruff has to go the distance from neck to shoulder. To this you add 1½ inches for hemming.*
4. *Hem all edges.*
5. *Run wires through each of the long side hems, and accordian fold the entire length of the material. Choose one wire edge to be attached to the band. Along this edge, tack each fold to the adjacent one at the middle so you have a series of figure eights. This tack is temporary.*

6. *Place the tacked edge against the neck band, as you release each temporary tack, retack the edge to the neck band adjusting the figure eights so they will reach around the entire band. This will cause the perimeter edge to spread in a fan shape. (See Fig. 9–8.)*

*The Picadil Collar* The Picadil collar is the stand-up collar so popular with the Elizabethans at the end of the 16th century. Figure 9–9 illustrates this and has a pattern, but this must be wired and sometimes boned.

*The Edwardian Stand-Up Collar* Figure 9–10 is an illustrated pattern for this boned choker of a collar. They were sometimes referred to as "dog collars."

## Cuffs

A collar is to a neckline what a cuff is to a sleeve. The attachment techniques are the same. The idea is to add detail to both areas. Collars and cuffs often correspond with each other in line. There is only one basic difference. A collar generally lies down and gravity keeps it in place. Some cuffs lie "up" and gravity is no help at all. Therefore, the cuff must be tacked to stay in place. As with collars some cuffs

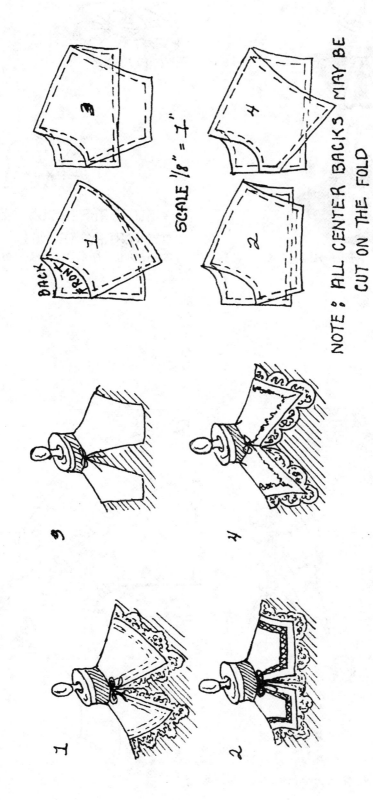

SCALE ⅛" = 1"

NOTE: ALL CENTER BACKS MAY BE CUT ON THE FOLD

Figure 9–6.  *A Selection of Falling Bands*

A.

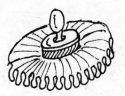

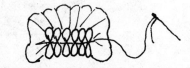

B.

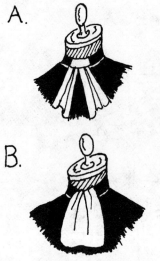

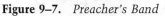

**Figure 9–7.** *Preacher's Band*

VIEW OF THE INSIDE NECK AND
TEMPORARY TACKING

**Figure 9–8.** *How To Tack a Ruff*

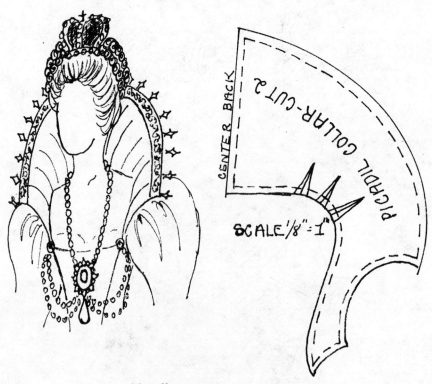

**Figure 9–9.** *The Picadil Collar*

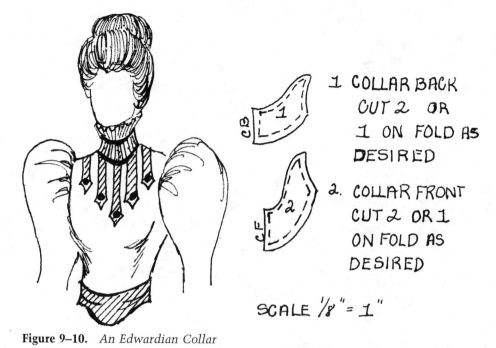

1 COLLAR BACK
CUT 2 OR
1 ON FOLD AS
DESIRED

2. COLLAR FRONT
CUT 2 OR 1
ON FOLD AS
DESIRED

SCALE 1/8" = 1"

**Figure 9–10.** *An Edwardian Collar*

are nothing but bands into which the sleeve is gathered. This does not have to be cut on the bias.

*The Cuff (Wrist) Band*  Figure 9–11 illustrates a cuff band and several variations. Like the collar band, the wristband may have a turn-up cuff added or a ruffle. The wristband is computed just like the waistband.

1. *Take the size of the wrist (Jane's is 6"), plus 5/8" for each seam, plus one inch for overlap fastening (6" + 1¼" + 1" = 8¼").*
2. *The depth is determined by the desired depth of the fold-over piece. If you want a finished band to be 1½ inches deep, doubled, add that to 1¼ inches for seam allowance and you have a depth of 4¼ inches.*
3. *If you are cutting a band that is not a fold-over, you must cut two pieces 1½ inches deep plus 1¼ inches for seam allowance (2¾").*
4. *If your finished cuff is to be deeper than two inches, you will want to splay the sides a bit. These three types of cuff band patterns are illustrated in Figure 9–12.*

*Wrist Ruffs*  Like neck ruffs, wrist ruffs are made to be attached to the wristband. The process is exactly the same as for the neck ruff.

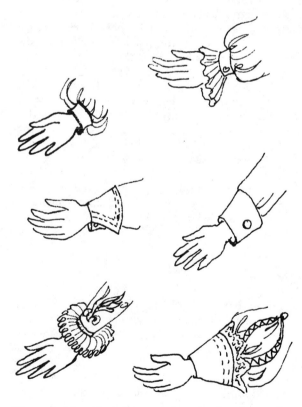

**Figure 9–11.** *Variations on the Wristband*

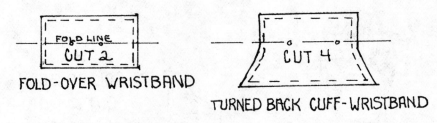

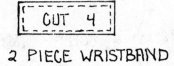

**Figure 9–12.** *Patterns for Wristbands and Cuffs*

*The Turn-Up Cuff* Turn-up cuffs include French cuffs, Pilgrim cuffs, and lace cuffs from the Cavalier period. They may be cut in one piece to be attached by a sleeve facing at the wrist or they may be attached to the wristband.

*The Falling Ruffle* During the Rococo period, and later in the Victorian period, sleeves were often finished in a circular ruffle pictured in Figure 9–13, with their corresponding patterns. Letter A is the single circle, B the double circle, and C is the egg-shaped one. These were generally used at the elbow. If they had been worn at the wrist, they would have fallen into the soup. They have great inherent movement and therefore should be used only in those places where they cannot impede voluntary movement.

**Sleeves**

Sleeves come in five basic types: the set-in sleeve, the dolman, the raglan, the tunic, and the kimono. These are illustrated in Figure 9–14.

*The Kimono Sleeve* This is one area in which I differ from *The Vogue Sewing Book*.[1] What is termed kimono sleeve in that book is really a tunic sleeve in that it is a variation of the basic Roman T shape of the early tunics. The kimono sleeve is

[1]*The Vogue Sewing Book* (New York: Vogue Pattern Co., 1975), p. 274.

nothing more than a hanging rectangle of fabric attached to a dropped shoulder or other sleeve piece.

*The Tunic Sleeve* The tunic sleeve is cut as part of the shirt or bodice body. A simple one is merely sewn up, generally with a gusset at the right angle of the underarm L-shaped seam.

*The Dolman Sleeve* The dolman sleeve is one that is also attached to the main upper body of the garment, generally from the waist in a slight upward curve. A dolman sleeve was being draped on the model in Figure 4–1 of Chapter 4. A sketch of this outfit, as it would look when finished, is shown in Figure 9–15.

Although I had to piece an addition onto the sleeve of the pattern because my muslin was only 40 inches wide, I could cut it out of the "Silesta" in one piece because it was 60 inches wide. This also gave me a very full skirt. Drafting from a draped form is by far the best way to achieve this sleeve.

*The Raglan Sleeve* The raglan sleeve is any sleeve extended from the neck, always on the bias. In Chapter 7 we talked about semi-raglan sleeves used when making a garment on a yoke. Figure 7–6 illustrates this. It is best to drape a raglan sleeve like the one illustrated in Figure 9–14.

*The Set-In Sleeve* The set-in sleeve is drafted and explained in Chapter 6. That was a simple straight sleeve. There are many variations that need consideration.

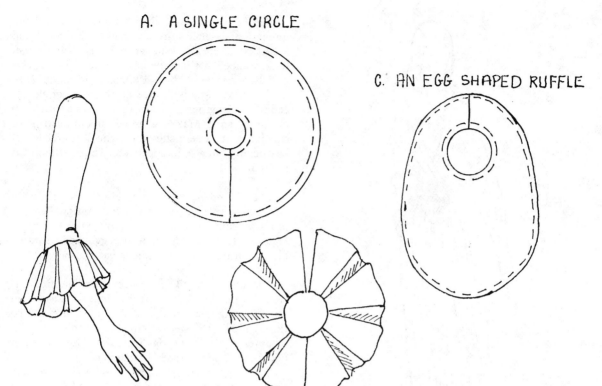

A. A SINGLE CIRCLE

C. AN EGG SHAPED RUFFLE

B. TWO CIRCLES (LETTER A) PUT TOGETHER

**Figure 9–13.** *A Variety of Falling Ruffles*

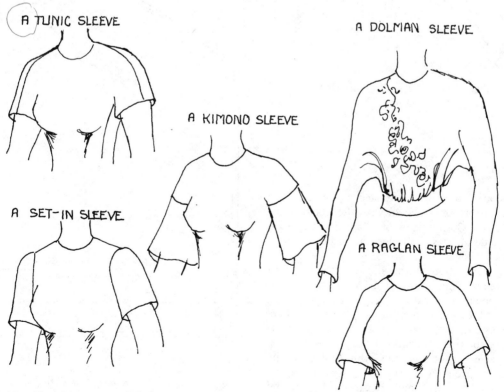

A TUNIC SLEEVE

A DOLMAN SLEEVE

A KIMONO SLEEVE

A SET-IN SLEEVE

A RAGLAN SLEEVE

**Figure 9–14.** *Five Basic Types of Sleeves*

**Figure 9–15.**   *The Dolman Sleeve*

*The Balloon Sleeve*   The balloon sleeve for the Italian Renaissance shirt of Chapter 8 (Fig. 8–1A and 8–2A) is essentially a raglan balloon. The English Renaissance shirt has the basic pattern for the set-in balloon sleeves (Chapter 8, Fig. 8–1B and 8–2B).

If a wrist ruffle is desired on this type of sleeve, add to the length extra inches that can be turned up inside the shirt. Make a channel for a drawstring or elastic about three inches above the bottom edge. A lace edging can also be added, etc. This is illustrated in Figure 9–16.

*The Houppelande Sleeve*   Figure 7–3 shows a houppelande sleeve pattern and illustration. Because of its enormity, the scale was reduced to $\frac{1}{16}'' = 1''$. Figure 9–17 shows the various dagging edges possible and in this case the scale is back to $\frac{1}{8}'' = 1''$.

*The Sac Sleeve*   The sac sleeve is a modified version of a houppelande with the bottom edge sewn up, allowing just enough room for the hand to go through. The sac sleeve with the Gothic jupon in Chapter 8 (Fig. 8–22) has fur cuffs. The fur is not necessary. The sac may be uncuffed.

The way you compute the "hand hole" is to take the hand measurement (John's is 8½") plus one inch

*Variations on a Set-In Sleeve*

There are full, balloon-like sleeves, and long sac sleeves, like the ones shown with the Renaissance shirts and the Gothic jupon of Chapter 8. There are houppelande sleeves, bell sleeves, pagoda sleeves, and puffed sleeves; there are baby doll sleeves and cuffed sleeves; there is the sleeve with the seam under the arm, and one with the seam at the back (like the one for the Watteau backed dress described in Volume I, Part II, in the Rococo silhouette); there are sleeves with two seams; there is the leg of mutton sleeve and there are parts of sleeves worn on top of other sleeves, such as the Gothic tippet and the Renaissance panes. All of the above are set into the armhole (or elbow in some rare cases of tippets and panes).

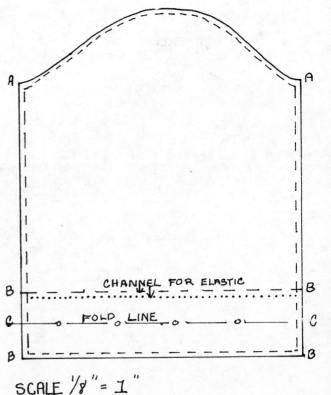

SCALE $\frac{1}{8}'' = 1''$

**Figure 9–16.**   *Construction of Full Sleeve with Self-Ruffle*

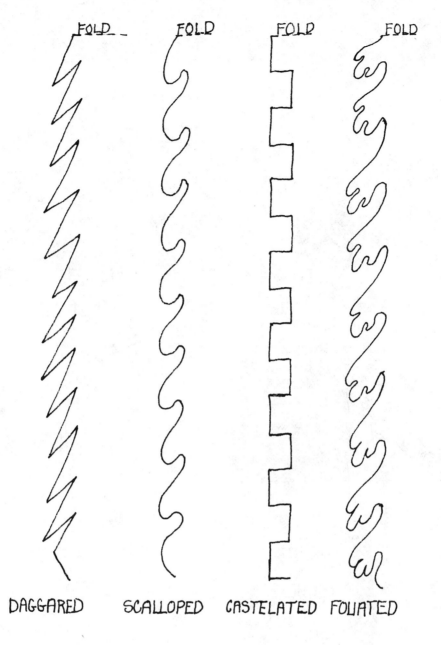

FOLD — FOLD FOLD FOLD

DAGGARED    SCALLOPED    CASTELATED    FOLIATED

SCALE ⅛ " = 1"

**Figure 9–17.** *Scaled Dagging Edges for Houppelande Sleeves*

for ease of getting in and out of it (9½"). If this were a straight sleeve, an extra 1¼ inches would need to be added for seam allowance (10¾").

*The Hanging Sleeve* Hanging sleeves are double sleeves. An interior sleeve comes to the wrist, which goes through a hole in an exterior sleeve. Some of these medieval and Renaissance creations still adorn the academic robes of certain universities. Most hanging sleeves can be cut from other patterns and slit in the center. This works for the houppelande, the sac, and the balloon sleeve. Figure 9–18 shows

the one Spanish variety that must be cut on a pattern all its own.

*Tippets* Tippets are also hanging sleeves. Figure 9–19 is a pattern for a Gothic and a Baroque tippet. The Gothic tippet was really little more than a decorative elbow band worn over another sleeve. The Gothic one is illustrated in the Middle Gothic silhouette in Volume I, Part II. The Baroque version is shown in Volume I, Part II, the Dutch Baroque silhouette.

**Figure 9–18.** *The Spanish Renaissance Hanging Sleeve*

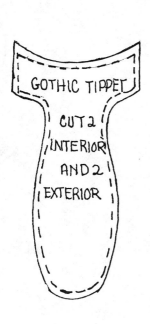

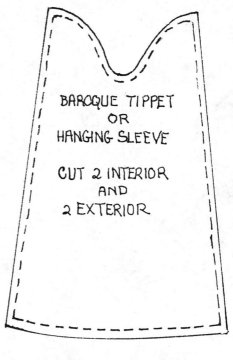

SCALE ⅛" = 1"

**Figure 9–19.** *A Pattern for a Gothic and a Baroque Tippet*

*The Pagoda and the Bell Sleeve* The bell sleeve is just what the name implies—bell-shaped. The pagoda is a variation on this theme. Both are illustrated and scaled in Figure 9–20.

*Puffed Sleeves* A puff sleeve is a balloon sleeve pattern cut extra long. Running through it are channels for either elastic or a drawstring that ties it to the arm creating a series of puffs. This is illustrated in Figure 9–21, along with a baby doll sleeve.

*The Baby Doll* The baby doll sleeve derived its name because of its relationship to the sleeves worn by very small girls and their dolls. It is really a one-puff sleeve.

*The Back-Seamed Sleeve* This is cut just like the straight sleeve variation discussed in Chapter 6. The seam is simply moved, as in the Rococo patterns in Figure 9–22. This is also done for a man's straight sleeve.

*The Two-Seamed Sleeve* You will find this sleeve with most of the more modern coat patterns in Chapter 8. They are drafted in the following manner (in this case you are drafting half a sleeve). We will be using John Doe's sloper, Figure 6–2.

1. Look at your straight sleeve sloper and divide it in half. (Fold it on the AE line.) Using point J on the GC line and E on the AE line as your 90° angle, measure 10° toward F and G.
2. Drop down on that same angular GC line one inch to a new point, letter M.
3. Using F and G as your 90° mark, move point G 10° further left to a new spot.
4. In a gentle concave curve, connect M to G.
5. Make a new ME line.
6. Add your seam allowance to the sloper and you have the inside arm piece.
7. Using the inside arm piece as a pattern, make a convex curve between H and A, extending A about one more inch to the right. Reconnect to L.
8. Extend point J one inch to the right and connect the new A to the new J and then connect the new J to E.

Do not add seam allowance again. This whole process is illustrated in Figure 9–23.

*The Leg-of-Mutton Sleeve* The leg-of-mutton sleeve can be cut two ways for the look of the 1890s. It can be cut in one piece, which usually takes a square yard of fabric per sleeve, or in two pieces, which may take less. Figure 9–24 illustrates these.

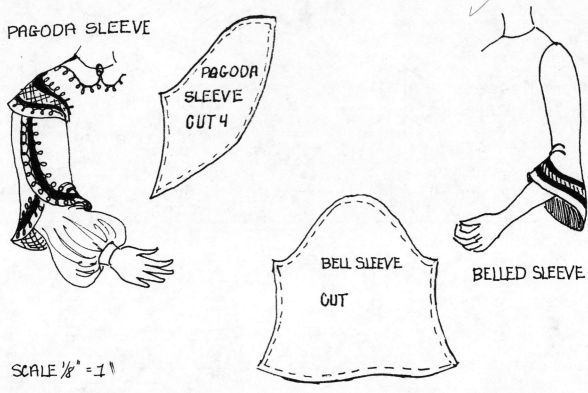

SCALE 1/8" = 1"

**Figure 9–20.** *Pagoda and Bell Sleeves*

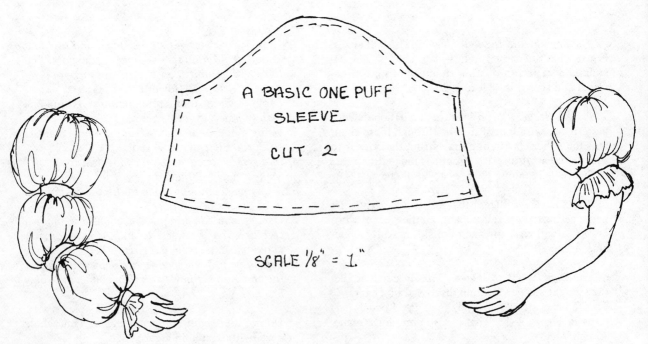

SCALE 1/8" = 1."

**Figure 9–21.** *Puff and Baby Doll Sleeves*

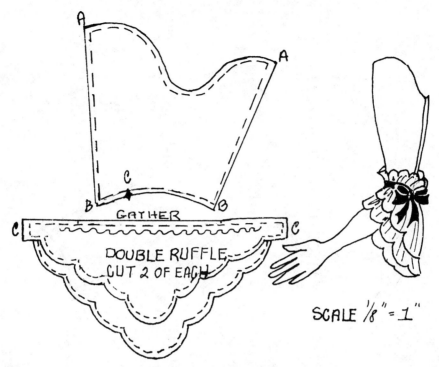

**Figure 9–22.** *A Rococo Sleeve*

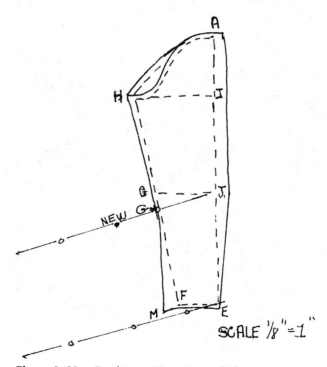

**Figure 9–23.** *Drafting a Two-Seamed Sleeve*

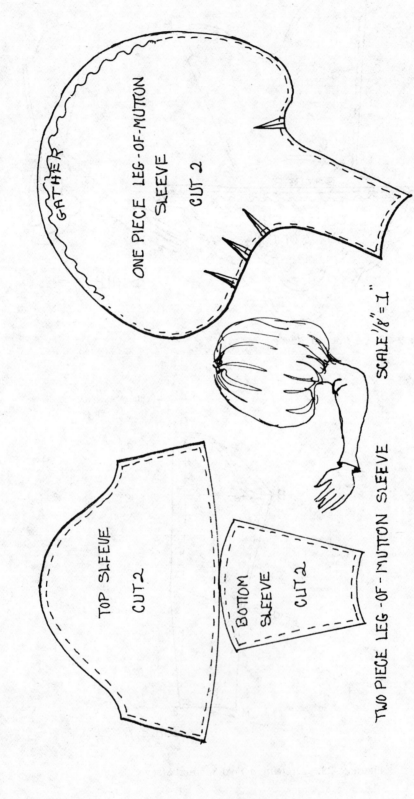

GATHER

ONE PIECE LEG-OF-MUTTON SLEEVE
CUT 2

TOP SLEEVE
CUT 2

BOTTOM SLEEVE
CUT 2

SCALE 1/8" = 1"

TWO PIECE LEG-OF-MUTTON SLEEVE

**Figure 9–24.** *Two Versions of the Leg-of-Mutton Sleeve*

*The One-Piece Leg-of-Mutton Sleeve* This can be gathered or pleated into the armhole. To keep the sleeves puffed out, pieces of twill tape the length of the shoulder-to-elbow measurement can be used inside the upper part attached at shoulder and elbow. This prevents the sleeve from falling down. (It works for the two-piece as well.)

My grandmother confessed that they used to stuff their sleeves with newspaper but, as her father owned a grocery store, she had access to paper sacks. She would blow up these paper sacks, tie them with string and use them. Then no printer's ink got on her dress or shoulders. It works like a charm, and rubber bands can be used to tie them off instead of string. (They do rustle when touched, which is distracting in a love scene. Plastic bags will do the same as will a small balloon.)

*The Two-Piece Leg-of-Mutton Sleeve* My favorite way of keeping the two-piece variety puffed is to put it on a straight sleeve construction lining. In other words, you are faking it but only the actress and her costumiere know. This follows the principle of all faked sleeves.

### The Faked Sleeve

This method is really the only way to assure yourself that a puff or slash is going to stay where you put it.

*The Renaissance Sleeve* Figure 9–25 is a pattern for a Renaissance fake sleeve with panes.

*The Cavalier Slashed Male Sleeve and the Cavalier Ladies Double Puff Sleeve* Figure 9–26 is a pattern for these two Cavalier sleeves. Regardless of type, the process of faking is always the same. Let us take the Renaissance sleeve for a working example. Please follow the diagrams in Fig. 9–25.

1. *First, let's count our pieces. We have an upper puff, an elbow puff, an upper fitted, and a lower fitted piece, plus five panes and two construction sleeves (11 in total).*
2. *Make and decorate the panes and put any decoration on the fitted pieces while flat.*
3. *Take the top puff and gather it to line IC and then to the top JAB line.*
4. *Stay stitch your bottom fitted piece onto its section, the "squarish" HDEFG part.*
5. *Place your panes upside-down along the HD line, evenly spaced.*
6. *Also upside-down, gather the bottom edge of the lower puff to the HD line.*
7. *Stitch across HD holding both the panes and the lower puff simultaneously.*

8. *Turn up the lower puff and gather to the IC line.*
9. *Put top edges of panes at the IC line. Stitch to hold.*
10. *Face the point edge of the upper fitted piece.*
11. *Now place the upper fitted piece upside-down (and so that the point goes towards the wrist) on the IC line and stitch across. This covers the bottom parts' raw edges.*
12. *Now fold it up and tack the point to the center.*
13. *You may wish to stuff your puffs with a little nylon netting. Do it now.*
14. *Take any little pleats on your puffs to make it conform to the JG and BE edges.*
15. *Face the bottom wrist.*
16. *Now sew up the underseam and ease into armhole.*

### Aprons

Aprons are worn to protect the clothing while one is doing dirty work today. This was not always the case. In the late Baroque era aprons were worn as decorative elements even by the nobility. The Victorian ladies wore them to show station and marital status. A Victorian widow wore a black apron long after the three year mourning period was up. Decorative aprons for both men and women were worn as part of nationalistic and folk dress. They can be divided into four main categories: the waist apron, the all-in-one apron, the bib apron, and the pinafore or over-the-shoulder apron.

*The Waist Apron* The waist apron can be a tiny bit of fluff for a French maid character, a long working apron, or a cobbler apron, all of which are illustrated in Figure 9–27. They are all a rectangle or semicircle attached to a waistband and you don't really need a pattern for that.

*The All-in-One Apron* The carpenter, the blacksmith, the butcher, and the chef all wear an all-in-one apron shaped basically the same way. The blacksmith's is leather, the chef's white, and the carpenter has one with extra pockets. Figure 9–28 illustrates this as well as the bib apron and pinafore.

*The Bib Apron* The bib apron differs from the all-in-one in that the upper part is a separate piece that is also sewn into the waistband and either pinned, buttoned, or strapped over the chest.

*The Pinafore* The pinafore is like a mini-dress that goes over another dress. This can be cut on any full skirt and bodice pattern. The one illustrated in Figure 9–28 is a princess line.

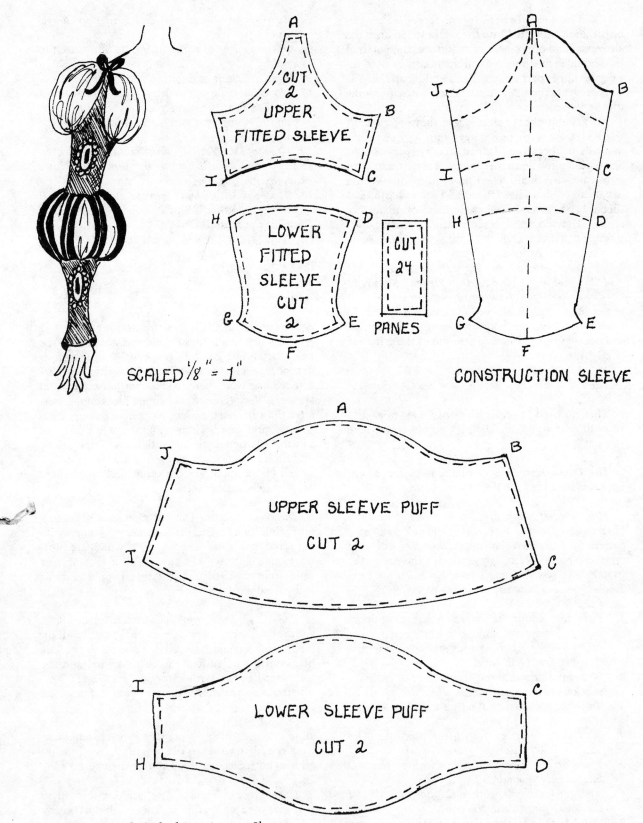

**Figure 9–25.** *The Faked Renaissance Sleeve*

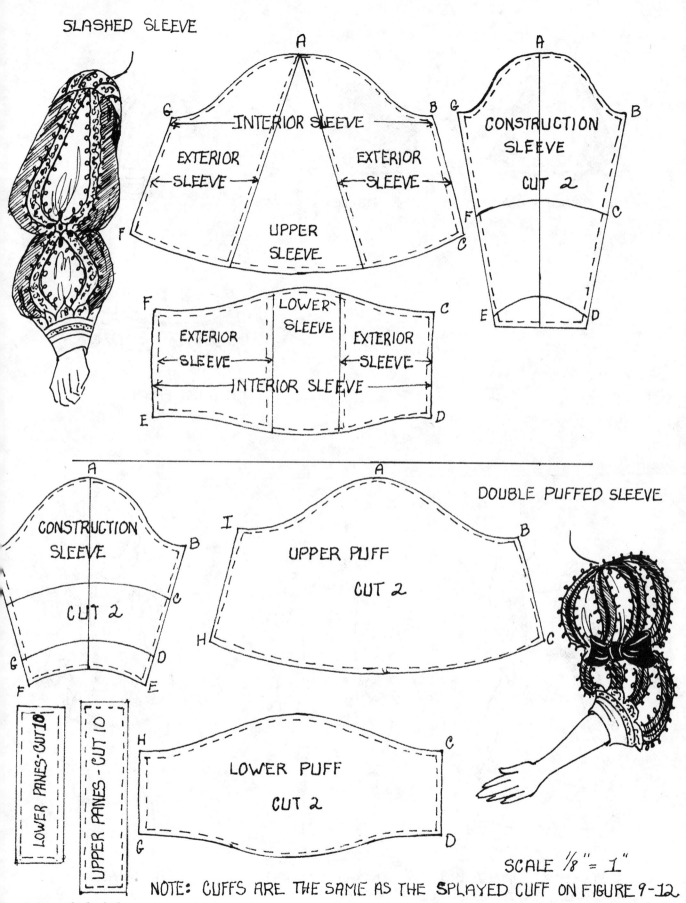

SLASHED SLEEVE

A

G · INTERIOR SLEEVE · B

EXTERIOR SLEEVE    EXTERIOR SLEEVE

UPPER SLEEVE

F    C

A

CONSTRUCTION SLEEVE

CUT 2

G · B

F    C

E    D

F    LOWER SLEEVE    C

EXTERIOR SLEEVE    EXTERIOR SLEEVE

· INTERIOR SLEEVE ·

E    D

A    A

DOUBLE PUFFED SLEEVE

CONSTRUCTION SLEEVE

CUT 2

B

C

G    D

F    E

I    UPPER PUFF    B

CUT 2

H    C

LOWER PANES · CUT 10

UPPER PANES · CUT 10

H    LOWER PUFF    C

CUT 2

G    D

SCALE ⅛" = 1"

NOTE: CUFFS ARE THE SAME AS THE SPLAYED CUFF ON FIGURE 9-12.

Figure 9–26.  *Slashed Sleeve*

THE FRENCH MAID'S APRON     THE COBBLER'S APRON

THE LONG APRON

**Figure 9–27.**   *Three Types of Waisted Aprons*

A PINAFORE WITH A BIB     AN ALL-IN-ONE     A PINAFORE

**Figure 9–28.**   *Three Types of Over-the-Shoulder Aprons*

## Belts

All belts are computed like you would a waistband, only they must be a little longer if buckled. They need a stiff interfacing. One must decide on their form of closure to accurately determine length.

## Capes

Most capes are actually a circle or components thereof. The same process used in determining circular and semicircular skirts works here, whether it is an exact semicircle used for a religious cope, or a short circle for a Spanish grandee. Even the Romanesque peliçon is just a big egg with a hole cut into it, as seen in the Romanesque description in Volume I, Part Two. There are two interesting historical deviations. One is the double caped "redingote." (The word redingote comes from riding coat or cloak.) The other is the inverness.

*The Redingote* Figure 9–29 shows the 18th century redingote associated forever with the highwaymen of their day, à la Ben Turpin and his horse, Black Bess (the Lone Ranger for English children).

DOUBLE CAPE "REDINGOTE" OF THE 1700's

A VICTORIAN COACHMAN'S COAT

**Figure 9–29.** *The Development of the Redingote*

This developed into the two-caped coachman's coat of Dickensian England a century later (also Fig. 9–29).

*The Inverness Cape*  The double-layered cape associated with Sherlock Holmes is really an inverness. There is a coat version as well. Both of these are illustrated in Figure 9–30.

**The Jumpsuit**

The last item of our unisex clothing is the jumpsuit, an all-in-one pants suit. This generally is of a knit fabric or has a front zipper. This is shown in the next chapter because it is so frequently worn by dancers.

THE INVERNESS CAPE: A SINGLE
BREASTED VERSION

NOTE: THE SLEEVES BELONG TO
      THE UNDERNEATH SUIT

**Figure 9–30.** *The Inverness Cape or Coat*

THE INVERNESS COAT HAS SELF
SLEEVES AND A DOUBLE BREASTED
FRONT.

# 10

# Drafting and Construction: Dancers' Costumes

Costume design is not limited to the world of the theater; it includes all aspects of show business, such as opera, ballet, night clubs, movies, and television; whatever comes under the general heading of "That's Entertainment!"

Dance is possibly the oldest form of theatrical expression, anthropologically speaking. It may have been for the dancer that the first costumes were designed, even if they were made of only bones and feathers. With the advent of the peculiarily American art, the musical comedy, all three muses performed at once in wedded harmony—dance, acting, singing. In show business parlance a person who performs with equal skill in all three areas is called a triple threat. The theatrical designer who creates for all these areas (opera, ballet, and theater) has become the triple threat of show business's technical side. With every one of these arts, certain knowledge must be gained if one's design or construction job is to be effective, and each art has its own terminology.

In this chapter we will discuss dance costumes as an entity unto itself but nothing stands truly alone. These costumes are adaptations of clothing to dancers' traditions and needs.

## What Are Dance Costumes?

Dance traditions define their costume terms. Dance can be defined in two parts, social dancing and dance as a theatrical art form.

*Social Dancing*  Social dancing is participatory. A person either alone or with a partner and/or group dances for the joy of self-expression. Ordinary clothing is worn, not a costume per se. This is just as true for the court pavan as for the Virginia reel. In the 1600s a social event of dance was called a "ball" and

people wore their best clothes to these occasions. Such clothing gradually evolved into what became known as "ball gowns" by the 1700s. In the 1800s certain social prerequisites became attached to habillements required for dancing functions. Women could bare their shoulders. Men wore white gloves, white tie, and tails. The ball gown of the 1800s evolved to the modern "evening dress" and the tails to the tuxedo. Today one still dresses up for an evening of disco, although the strenuous demands of disco dancing have brought the social dance clothes much closer to the dance costume.

*Dance as a Theatrical Art Form*  When dance is used to convey a thought, it becomes an art form. It is theatrical in that there are performers and the audience, two distinct groups who do not intermingle. This form evolved from entre act entertainments in opera to acts in themselves. This became known as "ballet." Ballet established certain traditions and terms, and even though theatrical dancing today includes tap, jazz, modern, mime, and very often folk dancing (which is really a form of social dancing adapted to the theatrical experience), the terms are generally the same. We shall use those terms to apply to a dancer's garments. These include the leotard, briefs, tights, tunics, bodices, and tutus.

## How Dance Costumes Differ

A dancer's costume must do everything any theatrical costumes must do—define character, place, time, and mood. It must also have one inherent quality other costumes may or may not need, movability. The movability is really a two-edged rule. The dancer must be able to move within the garment unhindered and the garment itself must move with the dance, to enhance the body movements.

This latter movement quality governs your design as well as the selection of fabric. The fabrics most frequently used in dance costumes are chiffons, silks, velvets, tulle, satin, and various fine cottons. The favorite fabric for most dance garments are any that stretch—knits of all sorts and the new synthetics such as spandex or lycra-based fabrics.

### The Knitted Garment

The knitted garments for dancers include leotards, tights, dance briefs, jazz pants, and the "all-in-one," which is the name for the dancer's jump suit. This garment is also called a body stocking. These garments are easily obtainable through retail dance supply stores, but you may not be able to achieve all that you would wish through ready-made items. With all the new stretch and sew fabrics and machine stitches, you can create your own.

Most knit fabrics today are four-way stretch. That means that they stretch in all directions. If you wish to use one that only stretches two ways, cut your pieces on the bias.

*Leotards* A leotard is the garment that fits the body from the shoulders to the crotch with two leg holes. Figure 10–1 shows a basic leotard pattern, scaled to Jane's measurements. Here is an instance when your sloper comes in very handy. A leotard may be cut to the body size with virtually no seam allowance. It should be sewn with only quarter-inch seams (with an overcast stitch), and the seam allowance used is taken into account by the nature of the stretch fabric used. This leotard has two basic pieces plus an optional sleeve. A tab placed center front can change the round neck to a deep V if so desired. This technique is also illustrated in Figure 10–1. Although this leotard is very popular and widely used, it has one disadvantage. It tends to flatten the breast completely.

The leotard illustrated in Figure 10–2 is made in the European manner with four basic pieces. Sleeves may be added if desired. You will also note the high cut to the leg line. This has become known as the "French leg." The rounded curve of the breast area allows for a more feminine look.

*The Shadow Panel* The one construction note that should be mentioned is the shadow panel. A shadow panel is an underlayer of a nude color or white stretch fabric that is put in the crotch area or, as in the case of the European leotard, up the center front. It is used under certain finely knit fabrics for reasons of modesty. Its necessity may depend on your choice of fabrics.

*Tights* "Tights" is a plural word signifying a pair of tights and shall be treated singularly. There-fore "tights" is a garment that fits the body from the toes to the waist. You can draft them using the leg sloper and adding the toe to it and a separate heel piece (Fig. 10–3). You can also draft it in the manner shown in Figure 10–4. In this case a simple way of getting the exact configuration of the leg is necessary (see Fig. 10–5). The process is as follows:

1.   *On brown paper draw a vertical line whose length corresponds to the waist-to-floor measurement, plus the length of the actors foot from the front of the ankle to the toe. This becomes your AB line.*
2.   *Measure two inches from A on a direct perpendicular to achieve F. Do the same from B to achieve C. Connect F to C so that the resulting line runs exactly parallel to the AB line.*
3.   *Measure from F on the direct perpendicular a length that corresponds to the thigh measurement, plus two inches. (For John Doe, this would be 22".) Do the same from B. These become points E and D.*
4.   *Connect E and D, achieving the ED line that runs exactly parallel to the FC and AB lines.*
5.   *Cut the paper into strips of one inch each from the ED line to the CF line.*
6.   *Have the dancer being measured lie down on your cutting table and place his or her heel on a stack of books so that the leg is raised but not bent.*
7.   *Pin the strip to the dancer's leotard from waist to thigh and then to the tights or down the leg. (Masking tape can be used as well.) This step must go down the center top of the leg and continue up to the waist on the same line.*
8.   *Now encircle the foot and leg with the strips, taping hem to the center strip.*
9.   *Gently lower the leg to the table and have the dancer sit up. Now pin the strip around the outside of the hip area to a similar spot on the back (not center back, but to the back leg seam for Fig. 10–4). Trim off excess paper.*
10.  *Cut paper strips around leg at center back.*
11.  *When this is laid flat, you have the configuration of the leg and outer hip area.*

*Stockings* The same process for determining leg configuration can be used for stockings as well.

*Dance Briefs* Dance briefs are the "panties" worn by the female dancer under a tutu, or by the male dancer when he is dancing bare-chested and bare-legged. Figure 10–6 shows illustrations and scaled patterns. Letter A shows a variety cut in four pieces, and letter B a one-piece version. Letter A may be used for either a woven or knit fabric. Letter B can be used for both types of fabric as well, but for a woven fabric it must be cut on the bias. The il-

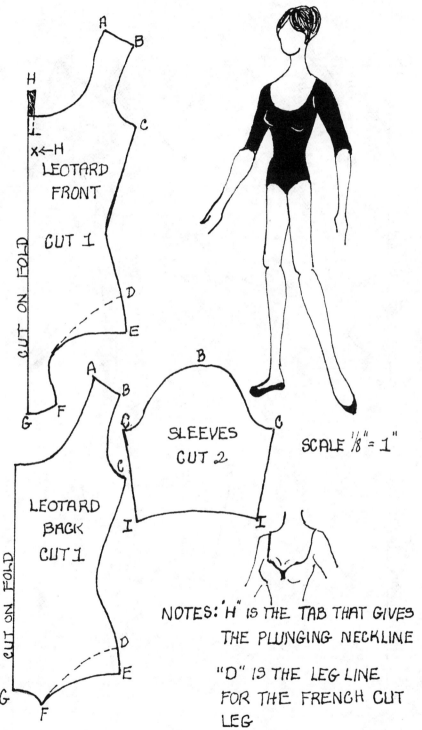

Figure 10–1. *The Basic Two-Piece Leotard*

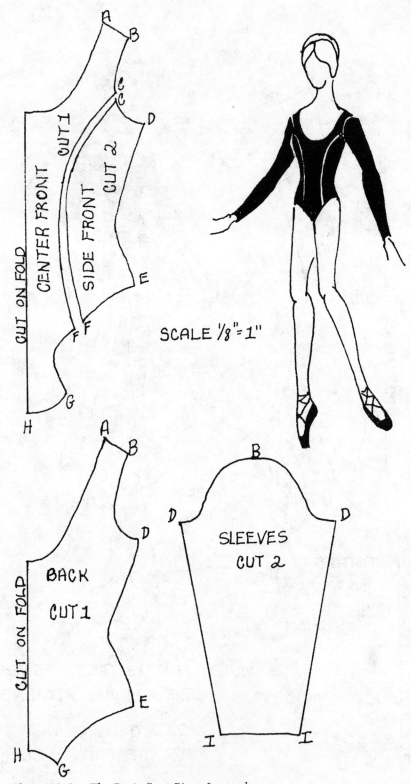

SCALE ⅛"=1"

**Figure 10–2.** *The Basic Four-Piece Leotard*

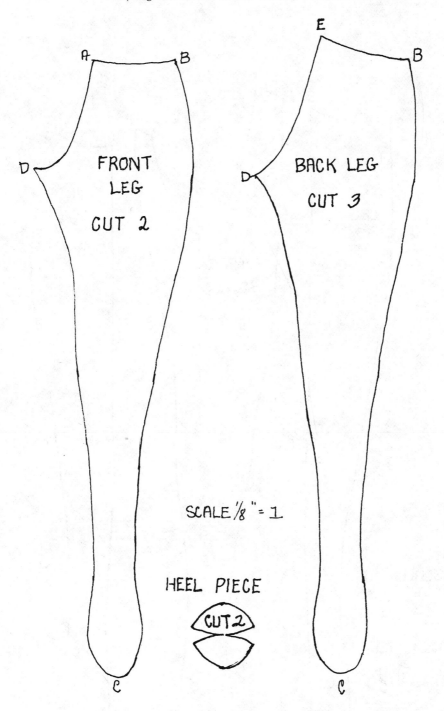

FRONT LEG
CUT 2

BACK LEG
CUT 3

SCALE ⅛" = 1

HEEL PIECE
CUT 2

NOTE: THIS PATTERN DOESN'T HAVE A BACK SEAM
BUT THERE IS AN INSEAM.

**Figure 10–3.** *Tights Pattern Made from a Sloper*

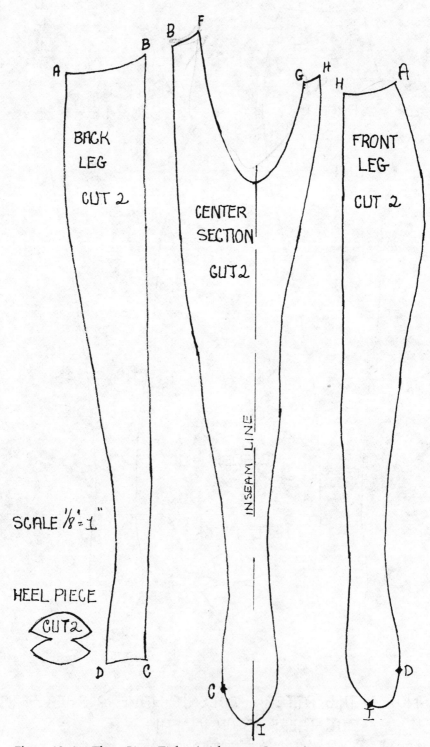

**Figure 10–4.** *Three-Piece Tights (without an Inseam)*

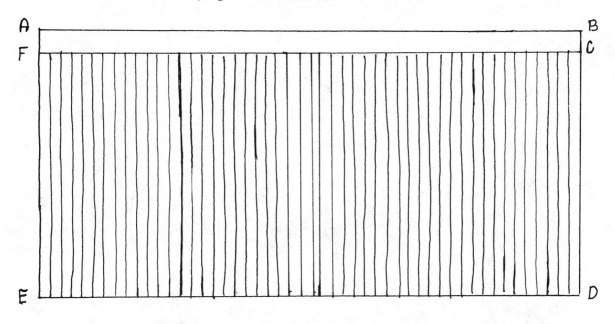

THIS IS NOT A SCALED DRAWING

**Figure 10–5.** *How to Measure for Making Tights*

lustration also shows the fanny ruffles worn under a Pavlova type tutu. These are worn to support the tutu in an upward rear lift. One construction note is to sew the ruffles on before you sew up the center back seam.

*The Dance Belt*    The dance belt is an extra firm athletic supporter worn by the male dancer under his tights. It can be bought in either white or black in any dance supply place. The white dyes easily.

*Jazz Pants*    Jazz pants are the flyless knitted bell-bottomed pants illustrated in Figure 10–7. They got the name because they are worn for jazz dancing, although they can be adapted to other dancing as well.

*The "All-in-One" Body Stocking*    The all-in-one body stocking was primarily a male dance garment in traditional ballet, but in jazz and modern dance it is worn by either sex. Figure 10–8 illustrates and scales this pattern for you.

*Decorating Knitted Garments*    Leotards and tights may be decorated by any of the methods described in Part Four but, whether painted or applied, decorating must be done on the dancer or a form—in other words, while the garment is stretched. That is the only way to control the design while corrolating it to the dancer's particular figure.

### Adaptation of Regular Pants to Dancing

Since we are on the general subject of garments for the legs, it is a good idea to discuss the adaptation of regular and easily available pants that certain situations require. The ballet *Fancy Free* involves three sailors. *Rodeo* requires cowboys. *Fall River Legend* requires a selection of everyday workmen's clothing. The musicals *Carousel, Anything Goes, On The Town,* and *Dames At Sea* also require sailors to dance, and dancing cowboys are legion in such shows as *Oklahoma, Paint Your Wagon, The Unsinkable Molly Brown, Wildcat, Annie Get Your Gun,* etc. Therefore being able to adapt jeans or sailor pants is a necessity.

In both cases the fabric used is sturdy, durable, and is stitched by the manufacturer with flat felled seams. Therefore, the older the fabric, the more pliable it is. If you buy new garments, wash them several times with a *little* bleach in the water.

If the dancing requirements are very strenuous, a gusset of a four-way stretch material can be used in the crotch intersection. This allows a little more stretchability for high kicking and athletic movements. If the dancing demands it, you can sometimes buy jeans of a new stretch fabric that looks like denim. Sailor pants can also be made of a stretch fabric.

There is one other trick that can be tried first. Give the garment to the dancer and have him wear

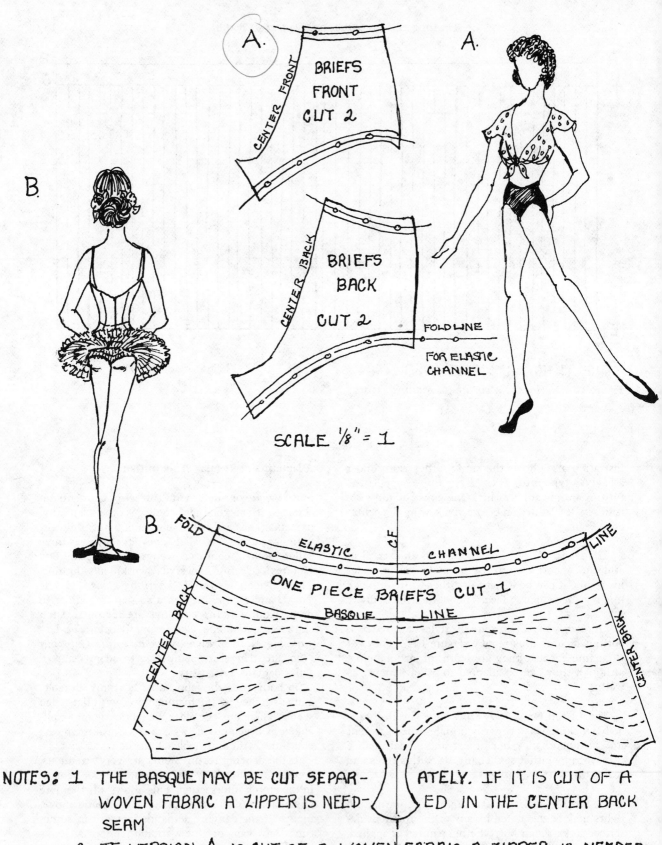

A.

BRIEFS
FRONT
CUT 2

CENTER FRONT

A.

B.

BRIEFS
BACK
CUT 2

CENTER BACK

FOLD LINE

FOR ELASTIC
CHANNEL

SCALE ⅛" = 1

B.

FOLD        ELASTIC    CF    CHANNEL    LINE

ONE PIECE BRIEFS CUT 1

BASQUE    LINE

CENTER BACK

CENTER BACK

NOTES: 1  THE BASQUE MAY BE CUT SEPAR-     ATELY. IF IT IS CUT OF A
WOVEN FABRIC A ZIPPER IS NEED-     ED  IN THE CENTER BACK
SEAM

2. IF VERSION A IS CUT OF A WOVEN FABRIC, A ZIPPER IS NEEDED
IN THE BACK SEAM

**Figure 10–6.**  *Two Versions of the Dance Briefs*

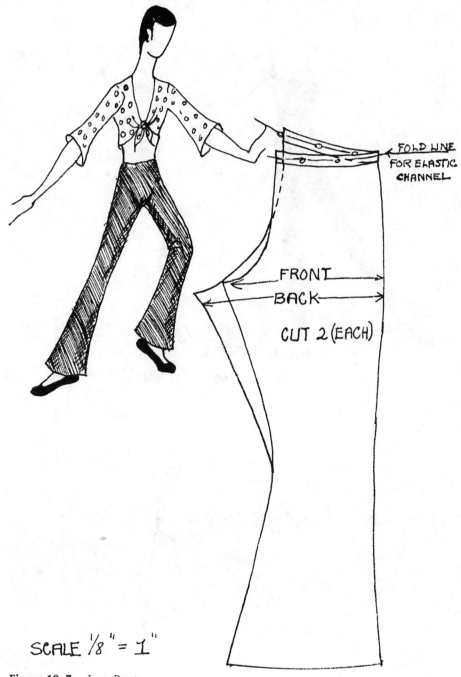

FOLD LINE
FOR ELASTIC
CHANNEL

FRONT

BACK

CUT 2 (EACH)

SCALE 1/8" = 1"

**Figure 10–7.** *Jazz Pants*

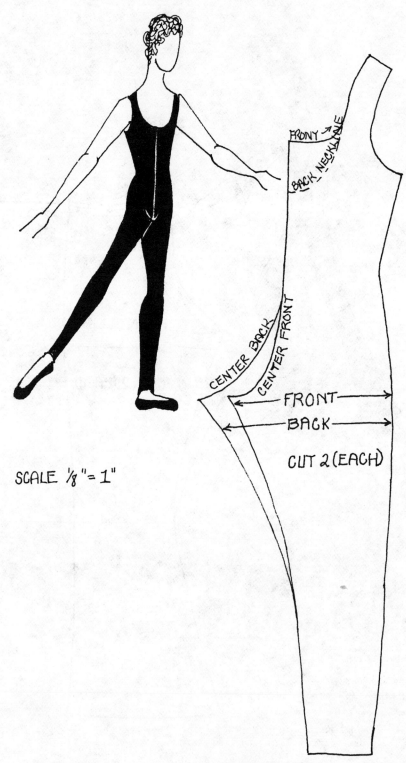

SCALE ⅛ "= 1"

**Figure 10–8.**   *The All-in-One Jumpsuit, or Body Stocking*

it in the shower and stretch it while damp. Then dry him with a blow dryer. A quick turn around in the shower is sufficient. He does not need to be soaking wet. The jeans will mold to the body. This takes about thirty minutes per dancer, so you must schedule accordingly.

## The Harem Pant

One other variety of pant is sometimes required by opera, ballet, and musicals of exotic settings; that is the harem pant. You would need them for the ballet *Scheherazade*, the opera *Abduction From The Seraglio*, and musicals such as *Kismet* and *The Desert Song*. Figure 10–9 is an illustrated pattern for this.

## The Male Dancer's Tunic

Figure 10–10 illustrates the classic male tunic from the ballet. You can adjust the neckline for the vested look pictured in Figure 10–11A, the military look in Figure 10–11B, or the romantic Gothic look in Figure 10–11C. The possibilities are endless and all are

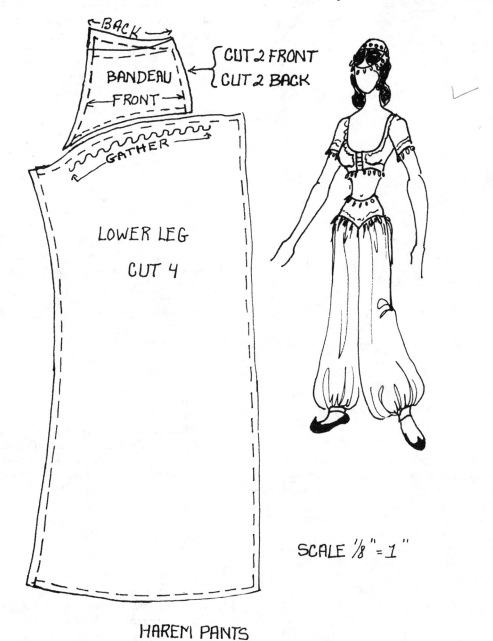

**Figure 10–9.** *Harem Pants*

**Figure 10–10.**   *The Classic Male Tunic*

cut and constructed in the same manner. The only thing that changes is the collar, the sleeves, and the extra seam in the front. This pattern also works well for a jacket to be worn over a shirt. A pattern for this tunic is in Figure 10–12, which shows both the two front-piece and the four front-piece versions. The two front-piece sleeveless version is also illustrated in Figure 10–10 by the classic male tunic.

### The Dancer's Shirt

The dancer's shirt illustrated in Figure 10-13A has sleeves remarkably like the one illustrated in Figure

9–21. It is cut very similarly to the yoked shirt of Chapter 6, but the bottom is a basque as opposed to a regular tail and the armhole opening is at least 22 inches. The yoke is open in this case. This pattern is illustrated in Figure 10–14. The shirt in Figure 10–13B is the Elizabethan shirt of Chapter 8, and Figure 10–13C is the classic bloused shirt you find in romantic ballets. Its pattern is illustrated in Figure 10–15.

As with the gusset in the crotch intersection of the pants, a diamond gusset at the underarm intersection is very helpful. Gussets are shown in Figure 10–16A. They are usually included in the sleeves of the male tunics or some male shirts. They are also put in form-fitting sleeves in female attire. For dancers, a gusset can be crescent-shaped (Figure 10–16B). Sometimes a little crescent-shaped opening is left on female attire. This is bound but merely left open, as shown in Figure 10–16C.

The third alternative is using sleevelettes. These are little puffs of fabric or tulle on pieces of elastic, placed on the upper arm so as to give an off-the-shoulder look when the arm is in a lowered position (Figure 10–16D). In fact, sleevelettes are not attached to the bodice at all.

*The Gusset*   The gusset, regardless of where it is needed, is drafted in the same manner. This is illustrated in Figure 10–17.

1. *A line is drawn, the measurement of which corresponds to the length of the desired opening. This becomes the AC line.*
2. *This line is bisected by a perpendicular line, DB, the length of which corresponds to the desired width of the opening.*
3. *The point of bisection becomes point E.*
4. *For the crescent gusset, only half a diamond is used and an arch connects A to C through either B or D as the dotted line on Figure 10–17 indicates.*

*The Sleevelette*   The sleevelette is merely a rectangle of fabric, seamed once with a channel at the top and bottom for elasticity. It should be cut three times as long as the upper arm measurement. The width may be as desired, but always figure in an extra two inches for puff.

### The Bodice

Figure 10–18 shows three basic bodices used in ballet. Letter A is the French bodice a la Degas; letter B is the classic one with the pointed front; and letter C is the romantique bodice with the rounded front. Letter D is the "pigeon" bodice, also French. All bodices are made of eight pieces except for children's

A. THE VEST AND SHIRT

B THE MILITARY TUNIC

C. THE ROMANTIC GOTHIC TUNIC

**Figure 10–11.** *Variations on the Basic Tunic*

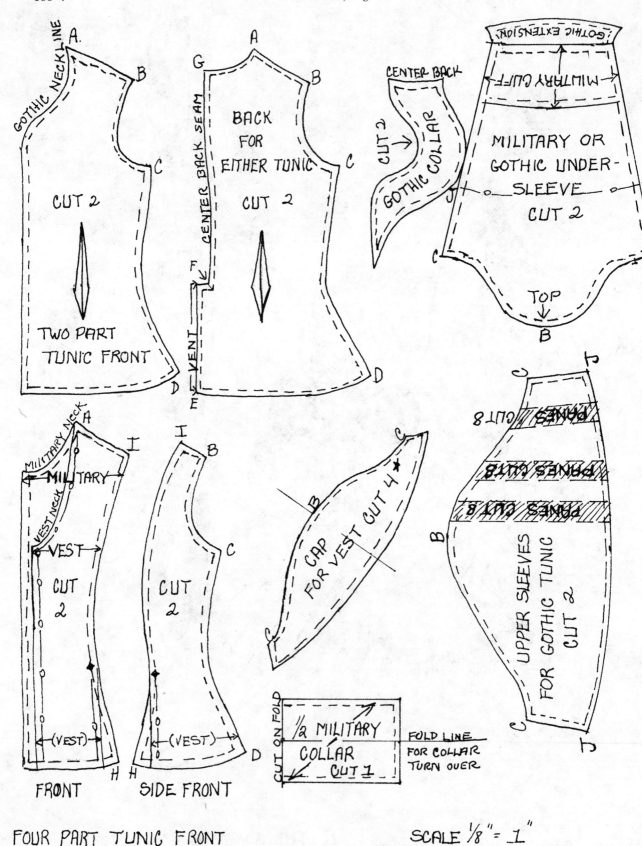

FOUR PART TUNIC FRONT

SCALE ⅛" = 1"

**Figure 10–12.**  *A Basic Tunic Pattern with a Choice of Fronts and Necklines*

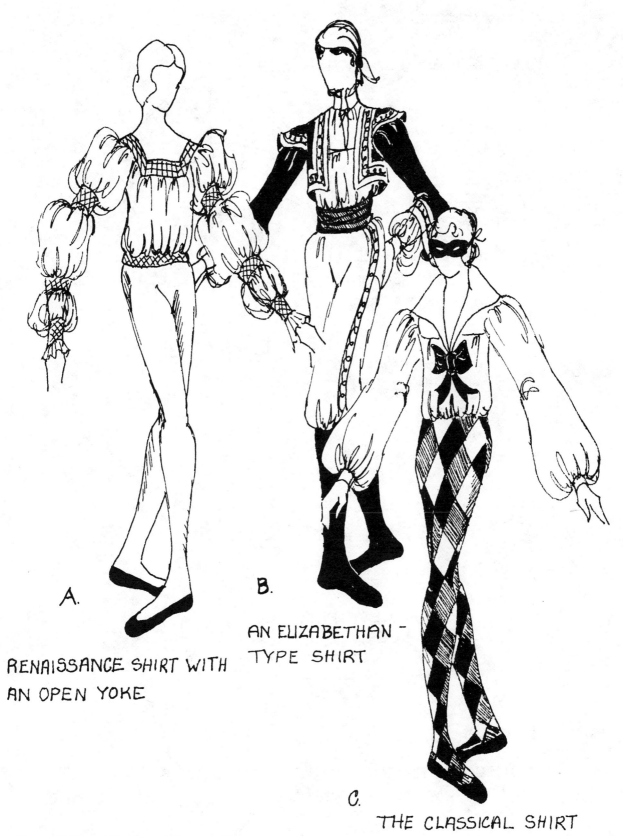

A.

RENAISSANCE SHIRT WITH
AN OPEN YOKE

B.

AN ELIZABETHAN -
TYPE SHIRT

C.

THE CLASSICAL SHIRT

**Figure 10–13.** *A Variety of Dancer's Shirts*

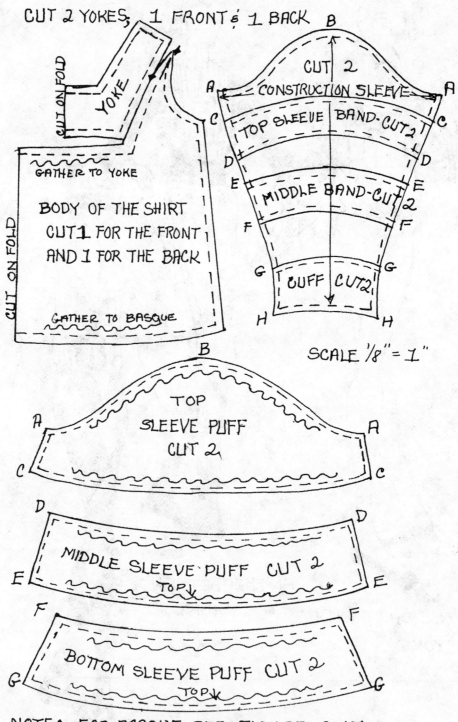

CUT 2 YOKES, 1 FRONT & 1 BACK

CUT ON FOLD
YOKE

GATHER TO YOKE

CUT ON FOLD

BODY OF THE SHIRT
CUT 1 FOR THE FRONT
AND 1 FOR THE BACK

GATHER TO BASQUE

B
CUT 2
CONSTRUCTION SLEEVE

TOP SLEEVE BAND-CUT 2

MIDDLE BAND-CUT 2

CUFF CUT 2

SCALE 1/8" = 1"

B
TOP
SLEEVE PUFF
CUT 2

MIDDLE SLEEVE PUFF CUT 2
TOP

BOTTOM SLEEVE PUFF CUT 2
TOP

NOTE: FOR BASQUE SEE FIGURE 10-15

**Figure 10–14.** *Shirt Pattern for Figure 10–13A*

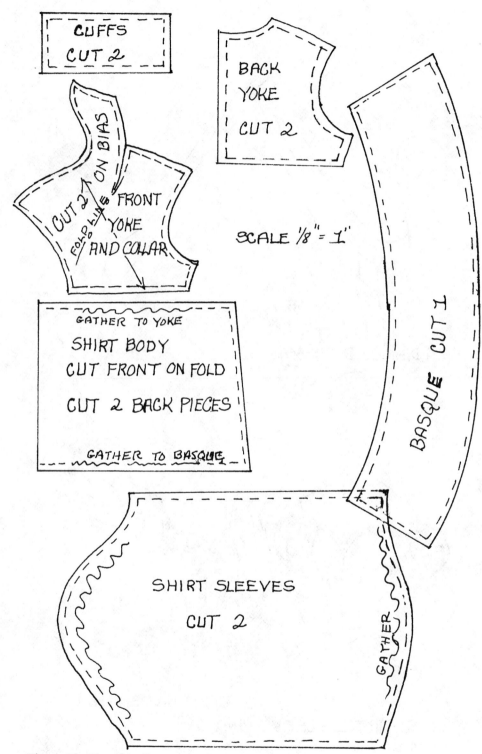

**Figure 10–15.** *Shirt Pattern for Figure 10–13C*

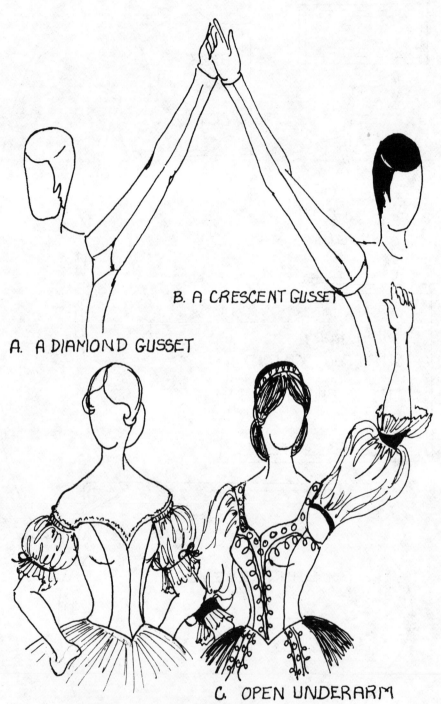

A. A DIAMOND GUSSET

B. A CRESCENT GUSSET

C. OPEN UNDERARM

D. SEPARATE SLEEVE PUFFS

**Figure 10–16.** *Solutions for Underarm Freedom*

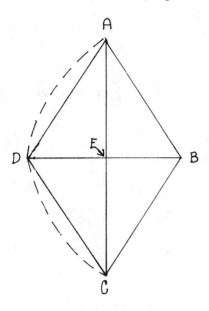

NOTE: THIS IS NOT A SCALED DRAWING

**Figure 10–17.** *The Drafting of a Gusset*

bodices which are made of four. Little girls have no need of a breast curve and their tummies are such that they need very little taken in at the waist by the division of the back pieces.

*The Classical Bodice* Figure 10–19 illustrates the pattern for both the classical bodice and the romantique one. A bodice is made and finished off as a separate garment. It is attached by hand to either the long or short tutu.

*The Romantique Bodice* Cut exactly like the classical, except the pointed front is omitted (Fig. 10–19).

*The Degas Bodice* Figure 10–20 illustrates the pattern for both the Degas and pigeon bodices. Unlike the two of Fig. 10–19, these bodices may be attached directly to their skirts. This is possible because neither is ever worn with the short tutu, only with knee or mid-calf length ones.

*The Pigeon Bodice* As with the classical and romantique bodices, the essential difference in the Degas and the pigeon is that the pigeon has a point. This must be compensated by the cut of a slight V at center front of the bodice neckline (Fig. 10–20).

*The Child's Bodice* A pattern idea for a child's bodice can be seen in Figure 10–21. This is unscaled. It is the previously mentioned four-piece variety.

Many bodices have self fabric "spaghetti" straps but if you wish a bare shoulder look, flesh-colored elastic works well. The elastic also takes grease and acryllic paints very well. If you wish some shoulder decoration, you can always build a yoke of nude illusion (or flesh-colored tulle). Figure 10–22 shows one such variation to the bodice theme. One note of construction detail: All bodices must be boned. The process is exactly the same as boning a corset, which was thoroughly described in Chapter 3.

**Skirts**

Naturally enough, dancers prefer skirts that move well and have a motion within them, such as circular, six- or eight-gored, or gathered skirts do. In dance parlance a gathered skirt becomes a tutu with a little adaptation.

*The Circular Skirt*

The circular skirt is often used over a multi-layered tutu whenever decoration is needed. This is because the multi-folds of the tutu would destroy the decorative element. This is illustrated in Figure 10–23, which shows a peasant costume done this way. The drafting and cutting of circular skirts for dancers are no different from the drafting and cutting of any like skirt explained in Chapter 6.

For a very full, marvelously floating effect, try putting two circles together and gathering them onto a waistband. A costume so constructed twirls and swirls seemingly forever. Remember, if you want the soft draping line of the circular skirt, you will most likely need a petticoat cut on the same pattern.

*The Cancan Skirt*

The cancan skirt is a circular skirt with ruffles in concentric circles on the inside that show when the skirt is lifted in the high kicking movements required. The cancan was a dance done in the village of Montmartre (now part of Paris) in the 1880s by a few laundresses. A bistro owner hired them. They scandalized all Paris because they only wore garters and stockings but no bloomers under those ruffled skirts. I do not advise this today. Make your dancers some ruffled short bloomers that can be cut on a pants pattern; Figure 10–24 is a scaled pattern for both skirt and bloomers.

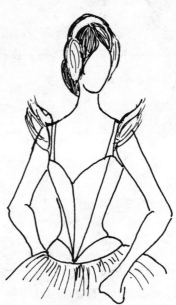

B. THE CLASSIC POINTED FRONT BODICE

A. THE FRENCH BODICE À LA DEGAS

C. THE ROMANTIC ROUNDED FRONT AND D. THE PIGEON BODICES

**Figure 10–18.** *Classic Bodices*

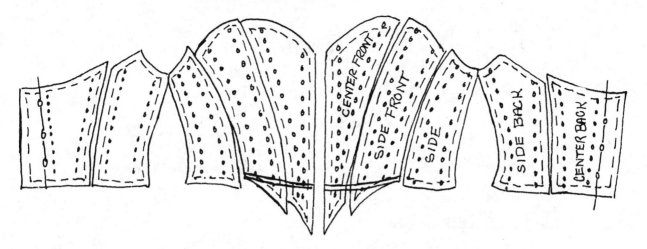

NOTES: 1. CIRCLE LINE INDICATES BONING CHANNELS

2. FOR THE ROMANTIC BODICE CUT AT DOUBLE SOLID LINE.

**Figure 10–19.** *A Pattern for the Classical and Romantic Bodices*

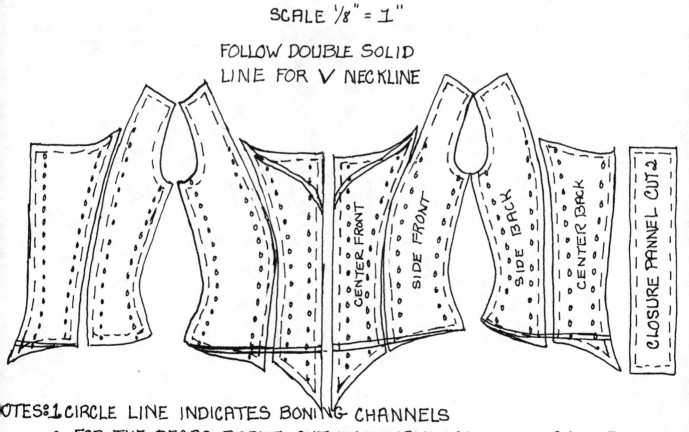

SCALE 1/8" = 1"

FOLLOW DOUBLE SOLID
LINE FOR V NECKLINE

NOTES: 1 CIRCLE LINE INDICATES BONING CHANNELS

2. FOR THE DEGAS BODICE CUT AT DOUBLE SOLID LINE AT HIP

**Figure 10–20.** *A Pattern for the Dropped Waist Pigeon or Degas Bodice*

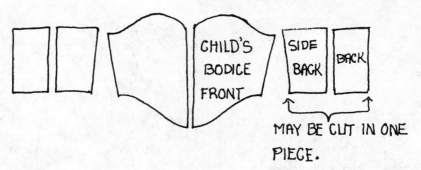

UNSCALED

**Figure 10–21.** *Child's Bodice*

**Figure 10–22.** *Bead Work on Nude Illusion*

**Figure 10–23.** *Circular Skirt*

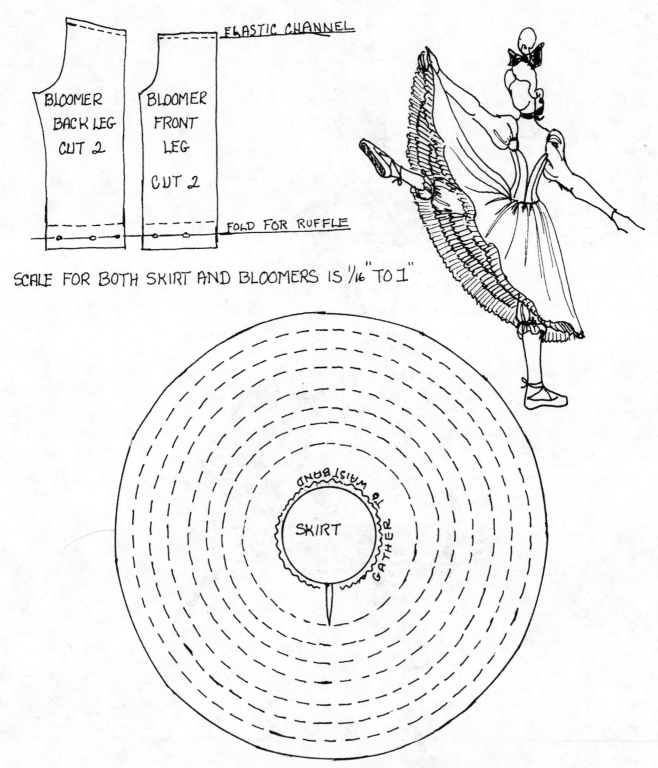

ELASTIC CHANNEL

BLOOMER BACK LEG CUT 2

BLOOMER FRONT LEG CUT 2

FOLD FOR RUFFLE

SCALE FOR BOTH SKIRT AND BLOOMERS IS 1/16" TO 1"

SKIRT

TO WAISTBAND

GATHER

NOTE: THE DOTTED LINES INDICATE PLACEMENT OF ROWS OF RUFFLES.

ALWAYS WORK FROM THE BOTTOM TO THE WAIST.

**Figure 10–24.** *Pattern for a Cancan Skirt and Bloomers*

*The Short Tutu*

The short tutu can be made in three ways—the dancing school variety, the cartwheel, and the Pavlova type.

*The Dancing School Variety* Because of the expense and difficulty of making a classical tutu, many dancing schools resort to a variety that achieves the silhouette but avoids the classic proportions. This is nothing more than four layers of net and/or tulle gathered and sewn to a basque very close to a waistband. In fact, the top layer should be caught into the waistband.

What is a basque? This has not the same meaning here as we encountered when discussing jackets in Chapter 7. The dancer's basque is an upper hipband to which layers of skirt are attached. (In Europe this is also referred to as a petersham band.) Figure 10–25 shows the drafting of one of these. The drafting of the skirt layers follows the following procedure.

1. *The bottom layer should be a rectangle at least four times the width of the upper hip measurement, plus 1¼ inches per seam, and for the average female about eight inches deep. Tulle and net are usually 72 inches wide. For Jane you would need 128" + 2½" (two seams at 1¼" each) = 131" for this layer.*
2. *The next ruffle would be approximately the same width (131") but two inches deeper because it has moved up two inches.*
3. *We again move up two inches for the next ruffle. The circumference of the hip at this point is 28 inches. This is multiplied by four for 112" + 2½" give you a rectangle of 114½" by 12" deep.*
4. *The last layer is computed by taking four times the waist measurement (126") plus 2½" = 128½" wide by 13½" deep. We have only moved up 1½ inches this time.*
5. *Now add the waistband.*

*A word of construction caution* When sewing rows of ruffles or any sort of concentric layering, always work from the bottom up. Note: This can be worn over a pair of commercially bought dance briefs, or like the classical tutu, attached to dance briefs of your own construction.

*The Cartwheel Tutu* The cartwheel tutu is often called the plate. Make your own basque and to its bottom edge sew a double ruffle of net. Each ruffle should be four times the upper hip circumference plus 1¼ inches for each seam (131"). The waistband is added to the basque. Then a circle of fine buckram is cut so that the inner opening is equal to the upper hip measurement in circumference (32")

NOTE: THIS IS AN UN-SCALED DRAWING

**Figure 10–25.** *Short Tutu of the Dancing School Type*

and the outer circle is 12 inches on a radius from the inner circle. The inner circle is cut away leaving a doughnut-like plate. This is then covered with an exterior fabric and decorations, and is then sewn onto the basque at a *slightly* down center angle. This is illustrated in Figure 10–26. This may then be

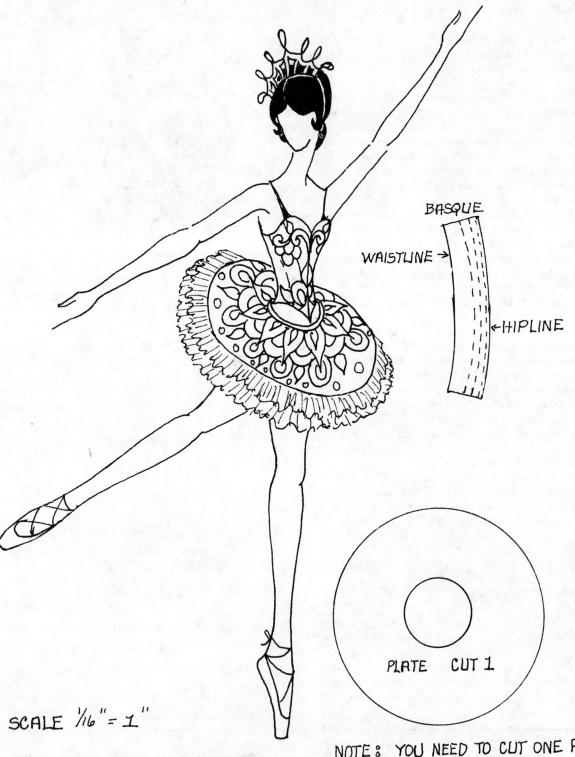

BASQUE

WAISTLINE →

← HIPLINE

PLATE    CUT 1

SCALE ¹⁄₁₆ ″ = 1 ″

NOTE: YOU NEED TO CUT ONE PLATE
OF A STIFFEND FABRIC AND
ONE OF YOUR DECORATIVE
FABRIC.

**Figure 10–26.**   *The Short Cartwheel Tutu*

sewn to the ruffled briefs pictured in Figure 10–6. (The briefs may also be worn separately.)

*The Pavlova Tutu* This is made almost exactly like the cartwheel variety but the plate is not used. Instead one more ruffle of double net is used two inches above the first and 14 inches deep. This is illustrated in Figure 10–27. Figure 10–28 shows a short tutu with a tail. This is often used for bird and animal characterizations and merely uses an ellipsoid shape to the bottom edge of the rectangle (also in Fig. 10–28).

*The Long Tutu*

The long tutu can be made to the knees or to the mid-calf. It seems to be a matter of tradition as to

CONSTRUCTION OF "TAILED" TUTU BY ELLIPSOIDAL RUFFLES. THIS IS NOT A SCALED DRAWING

**Figure 10–28.** *Tutu with Tail*

**Figure 10–27.** *The Pavlova Tutu*

which ballets take which length. The longer tutu is the older in "balletic" historical tradition, so perhaps it goes by the age of the ballet, but it is also a matter of directorial choice (see Fig. 10–29). These too are made on the basque and can be made like the dancing school variety short tutu or dropped on the basque like the Pavlova. If it is to be worn with either of the French bodices, it must be the dropped variety.

Regardless of tutu variety, they must all be hand sewn to the bodice. Use a small locked whip stitch to attach the briefs to the basque and the same on the inside of the waistband to the inside of the basque. For added security take a slip stitch to the outside edge of the bodice.

All tutus must be hook-and-eyed up the center back. Why? The center back or center front are the spots that get even tension during all movements. The center front is usually decorated. Hooks and eyes are the most secure fastenings, and dance costumes require maximum security. If a peasant costume requires an apron, it should be attached to the waistband of the tutu.

Costuming dancers is very demanding because of all the requirements of fit and movement. A short tutu alone takes almost forty hours to construct. They are very expensive. The going professional rate starts at $500, but if the tutu is well made, it will be worth every cent.

**Figure 10–29.** *The Long Tutu*

# 11

# Fittings, Alterations, and Layouts

Now that you've drafted your sloper or pattern, you will want to cut the garment. Before doing this, however, you should have a fitting session, maybe two. If you have used the sloper method, you will want to fit the sloper before you cut your pattern. If you've draped the form instead of an actor, you should make adjustments for his particular body. You will also want to do this if you've done your pattern by the flat drafting method.

## Fittings

### Fitting the Sloper

Since the sloper is without seam allowance, how does one fit it to the actor's body? There are two ways. Have the actor wear leotards and tights and pin it to those, or use three-inch wide masking tape.

For the masking tape method, lay the sloper shoulder-to-shoulder for the front and back pieces and tape. This acts as your hanger. Now hang it on the actor's shoulder and tape the sides. For excess room you can slash the sloper as needed. Such room is often needed for a bust dart placement for the full-figured woman. If you are doing a "waist down" sloper, such as pants or a skirt, tape the straight edge seams first and then wrap the body.

The importance of each fitting cannot be stressed too much. The more problems you can solve at these early stages, the fewer you have to alter later. That simple statement is all too often overlooked in a rush toward completing the garment. It is truly a penny wise–pound foolish situation.

### Fitting the Pattern or the Mock-Up

The mock-up will already have been sewn with a loose machine basting stitch. One should also sew the pattern together this way including all darts, gathers, etc., but in sections: the top or bodice pieces, the bottom, and the sleeves. These sections make adjustments easier. Remember when doing your machine basting, *do not lock your seams by backstitching.* You will want to take the basting apart. An unlocked basting needs only to be pulled out; it need not be ripped. This fitting can be done seam-side out, but remember that the sides are reversed.

### The Final Fittings

The final fittings are done to the costume itself. All alterations must be completed at this time. With luck, the costume will not need anything major. You will need to mark your closures (buttons, hooks and eyes, snaps, etc.) and the exact hem.

## Alterations and Adjustments

For the most part costumers consider alterations and adjustments the same thing. The old home economics theory was that an adjustment referred to something small, like taking in a dart or a seam, and an alteration meant a big item, such as the addition of a seam or a gusset.

The basic rule of thumb in alterations is that whatever you do to make something smaller, you can do the opposite to make it bigger. This is eminently sensible as long as you remember that every rule has its exceptions. The first and most important exception is that you can always take out excess fabric, but you cannot add to what is not there.

In other words, the only solution to cutting a pattern or garment too small is to stock plenty of fabric because you will have to cut it over.

*To Decrease a Pattern* The following list contains things you can do to make your pattern smaller.

1. *Add a center back or center front seam to that which had previously been cut on a fold.*
2. *Add, extend, or take a dart. This is usually done to pairs of darts, but may not necessarily be done this way.*
3. *Lift up the shoulder seam to shorten.*
4. *Cut off excess at the waist.*
5. *Take in the gathering or double pleat.*
6. *Remove a panel from a gored skirt.*

*To Increase a Pattern* This list shows ways of making your pattern bigger.

1. *Let out darts.*
2. *Let out seams (a little).*
3. *Let out the gathers or pleats.*
4. *To make a garment longer, add a shoulder piece or lower the hem.*
5. *Add a gusset, godet, or panels.*
6. *Add a crescent to increase the sleeve or armhole curve.*

I will not attempt to explain individual cases because the cases are as numerous as there are individuals. A good sewing book will be your best guide in this, as it should be for your layout instructions.

### Layouts

Layout is a manufacturer's term for the placement of the pattern on the fabric so as to use the least amount of cloth to achieve the design. This is governed by four things: the size and shape of the pattern pieces, the type of fabric, the width of the fabric, and its pattern or design.

*The Layout for the Type of Fabric* Certain fabrics have a definite direction. This includes all plush or piled fabrics, and certain luster synthetics. These are called one direction fabrics. Certain uneven plaids have to be cut this way as well. It simply means that all pattern pieces have to be placed so that the top of each piece is always in the same direction as the ones before and after it. This is illustrated in Figure 11–1. (Plaids also require a certain amount of excess yardage in order to match the vertical and/or horizontal lines.)

*The Layout for Size and Shape of Pattern Pieces* Some pattern pieces are simply too big to cut double on the vertical fold. You may wish to open your fabric and fold it horizontally. For example, let's say we are cutting a Gothic shift that is 116 inches in circumference around the skirt hem. You have a 36-inch wide fabric that comes off the bolt folded to 18 inches wide. It may be 36″ × 180″ (5 yards) long. You open this and fold it to a shape 36″ × 90″. You will discover that this is called "cutting on the horizontal fold". The fold line looks vertical, but keep in mind that you are folding across the width of the fabric and that makes it horizontal. You may still cut double (see Fig. 11–2).

Occasionally a piece must be cut absolutely flat, one piece at a time. This problem is illustrated in Fig. 11–3.

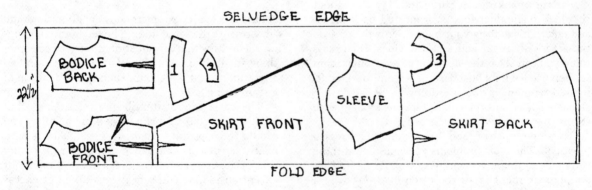

**Figure 11–1.** *Layout for Cutting Directional Fabric*

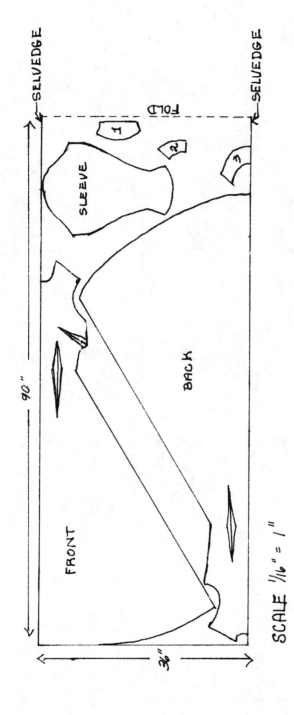

SCALE $^1/_{16}'' = 1''$

1. SLEEVE FACING
2. BACK NECK FACING
3. FRONT NECK FACING

**Figure 11-2.** *Layout for Cutting on the Horizontal Fold*

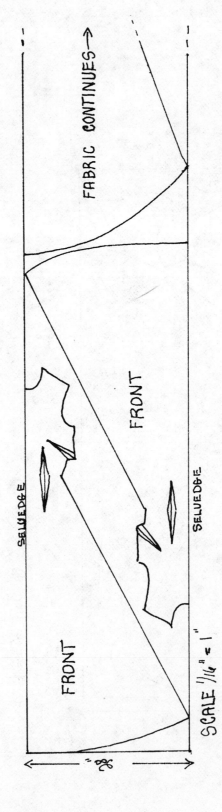

**Figure 11-3.** *Layout for Cutting One Piece at a Time*

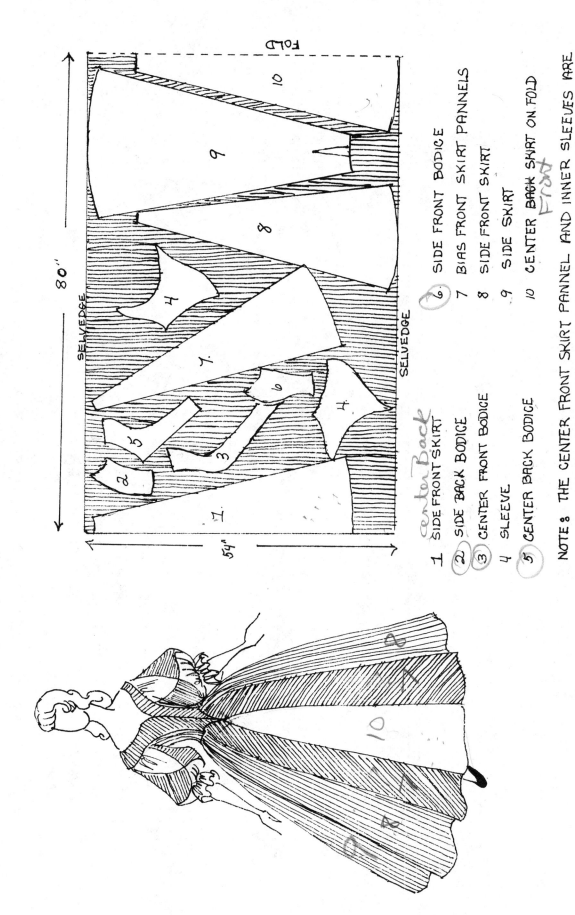

**Figure 11–4.** *Layout to Achieve Bias Stripes*

SCALE ⅟₁₆″ = 1″

80″

54″

FOLD

SELVEDGE

SELVEDGE

center Back

Front

1 SIDE FRONT SKIRT
2 SIDE BACK BODICE
3 CENTER FRONT BODICE
4 SLEEVE
5 CENTER BACK BODICE

6 SIDE FRONT BODICE
7 BIAS FRONT SKIRT PANNELS
8 SIDE FRONT SKIRT
9 SIDE SKIRT
10 CENTER BACK SKIRT ON FOLD

NOTE: THE CENTER FRONT SKIRT PANNEL AND INNER SLEEVES ARE CUT FROM ANOTHER FABRIC

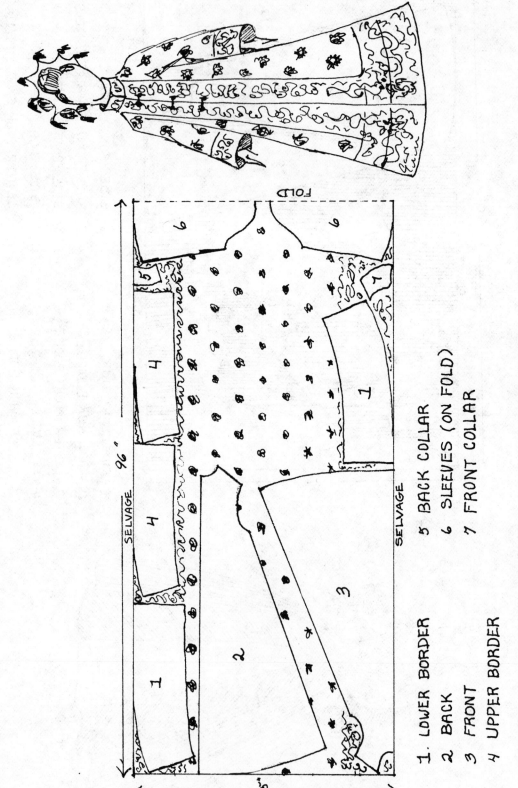

SCALE ¹/₁₆" = 1"

SELVAGE

96"

SELVAGE

FOLD

45"

1. LOWER BORDER     5. BACK COLLAR
2. BACK     6. SLEEVES (ON FOLD)
3. FRONT     7. FRONT COLLAR
4. UPPER BORDER

NOTE: FACINGS CAN BE CUT FROM OPEN SECTION BETWEEN BORDERS

**Figure 11–5.** *Layout for Cutting a Border Printed Fabric*

*The Layout for the Width of the Fabric*　You may need to do this for normal-sized pattern pieces if the width of your fabric is particularly narrow. Some oriental silks are only woven 28 inches wide. Even 36-inch wide fabric may be too narrow for certain shaped pieces.

*The Layout for a Specific Pattern or Design*　You may want to achieve a specific effect by playing with the textile decoration. You might wish to create chevron stripes out of vertical ones, bias plaids, or work a border print in a specific manner. Figure 11–4 shows the layout for achieving chevron stripes to create the illustrated design. Figure 11–5 shows a layout for the border print used to create the garment therein illustrated. These layouts are very helpful in determining exact yardage needed. Keep them on file for budgeting future shows.

# THREE

# The Construction of Accessories

*How simple life would be if we only had to worry about a dress or a suit that just covers the middle of the body. Such clothing saves us from the cold and heat of the elements, but as long as there is a human ego we will all be like the lady at Banbury Cross, "With rings on her fingers and bells on her toes." That particular lady made music wherever she went. The "music makers" of the costume trade are the accessories.*

*Included in this section is "how to" information on hats, shoes, armor, jewelry, masks, animal heads, and some costume props. Perhaps because the items are smaller, they seem to attract more creative thinking. The reward of a job well done is quickly gratifying. I am just as guilty as my employees. I'd far rather work on one My Fair Lady hat than cut out five maids' uniforms for the same show.*

*Without the proper proportion of rain and sunshine the garden doesn't grow. Accessories may be the sunshine of the costume trade, but they are only one part of an overall design concept.*

# 12

# The Construction
# of Hats and Headdresses

The latest fashion magazines show a resurgence of hats. Nothing so readily completes an outfit as the proper hat or headdress. For thousands of years headdresses achieved what no other item of apparel was able to do quite so readily—instant recognition of face and status. A crown symbolizes the king; the tri-tiered tiara, the pope; the helmet, the soldier; and a bit of frilly white nonsense, the maid. Certain hats symbolize certain periods of time; the pointed conical hat and veil brings to mind knights in armour and fair maidens in Gothic distress. The mop (or mob) cap reminds us of the French Revolution. Certain hats have become synonymous with certain places. Can one think of Mexico without picturing the sombrero or a Frenchman without his beret?

Even in our own century, wearing hats was prevalent until the 1960s and '70s. A lady always wore a hat to church, to town, to tea, to a garden party. It was only with the advent of bouffant hair styles that hats went out of fashion. Much of the same thing happened during the bouffant styles of the 1770s and 1780s. Now that hairstyles have become more natural, hats are returning. Therefore we needs must know and be accomplished in the millinery arts.

## Restoration of Period Hats

The easiest solution to the problem is finding the correct period hats, either through donations, thrift shops, or backlogged stock. Often these hats have been badly stored and creased and crushed almost out of recognition. But restoration is usually quite simple. Flat brims can be ironed out, and a little spray starch can often help. The easiest way to iron a rolled brim is on a tailor's roll or ham. I have upon

occasion taken a bum roll and tied it into a circle, inverting a brim onto that, and have ironed or steamed it out. Steaming can do wonders to restore hats. The crown can be stuffed to hold its shape with scraps and then steamed, but then it must sit until completely dry. A new coat of felt stiffener can be applied.

Using felt stiffener requires a word of caution, however. It should be used in a well ventilated area. If ventilation is poor, use clear varnish as a felt stiffener. The varnish is applied with a brush, usually to the exterior of the felt. One or two coats can generally be absorbed without changing the hat's appearance. If more is applied, a shiny look appears. To avoid this, one may coat the inside of the hat. One should always use this inside technique when stiffening velvet. Some straw hats can be steamed out and restiffened, but other straws are very perishable.

## Adaptation of Old Hats and Hat Forms

If restoration does not solve your problem, you will have to build your hat. Don't throw away that old straw hat that won't steam out. The brim may still be useful. New hats can indeed be made out of old ones. Also there are many ready-made hat shapes and frames that can be adapted for period use. Figure 12–1 shows several such shapes. The black velvet hat in the upper right-hand corner was turned into the 1914 hat pictured in Figure 12–2. It was merely steamed, pressed, and redecorated, and the brim was tacked up.

The basic straw shape in the lower right of Figure 12–1 cost three dollars in 1978 at the local variety store. It is adapted into the Victorian bonnet seen in

**Figure 12–1.** *Hats that Can Be Adapted*

**Figure 12–2.** *Adptation of Black Velvet Hat into 1914 Hat*

**Figure 12–3.** *Victorian Bonnet*

Figure 12–3. The straw was painted red with acryllic paint. A wedge was cut out of the center back brim just under the crown. The inside of the brim was faced with white eyelet gathered around the inside crown. All raw edges of brim and crown were cov-

ered with a blue bias tape. Yellow, white, red, and blue flowers, and blue ribbon decorated the inside and outside of the brim.

The typical Florida straw sun hat in the upper left of Fig. 12–1 is available for very little in almost

**Figure 12–4.** *Turn-of-the-Century Lady's Boater*

**Figure 12–5.** *Adapted Straw Hat (1)*

any Florida drugstore. It became the basis for my turn-of-the-century lady's boater pictured in Figure 12–4. I removed the extraneous fabric and hat band. Then I cut the crown off two inches below the top, and lowered it to the brim level. To secure the brim in its new shape, I trimmed it down in the center front and slit the center back to the crown base. This allowed me to overlap the back brim, achieving the turned-up shape. It was then covered in a navy blue gabardine to match its accompanying outfit, after which it was trimmed with pale blue moire ribbon onto which was stitched some old navy grosgrain looped edged ribbon. Blue silk cornflowers were nestled around the brim, and a big ribbon bow was put on the outside of the back brim anchoring it up to the crown.

The hat in Figures 12–5 and 12–6 is made from the shape in the lower left corner of Figure 12–1, plus the brim from an old straw hat whose crown had been completely crushed in storage. This shape, as pictured in Figure 12–1, is one of those softly floppy bridesmaid's hat shapes available in most fabric stores or bridal shops. It is made of a sheer straw-like fabric (probably synthetic). Although the basic shape was fine and the color perfect (a peach that exactly matched a dress I designed for a production of *Carousel*), it could not be stiffened. The extra brim sewn to it gave it the proper stiffness. The straw hat was inserted inside the peach hat, and both were machine stitched together in a zigzag stitch around the outer edge of the brim. I tacked the lower crown edges together by hand, and hand-tacked the crown together in several places. Therefore the peach crown reshaped the bashed-in crown of the straw. The exterior was then trimmed in cinnamon velvet ribbons and peach to pink flowers.

**Figure 12–6.** *Adapted Straw Hat (2)*

All four of the previously mentioned hats were adapted by modification of a basic shape—lowering a crown and narrowing a brim, or cutting the brim to achieve a new direction.

**Other Modifications**

The two hats in Figure 12–7 and 12–8 were basic shapes that were modified by adding on new brims. Both of these hats were made for a production of *A Flea in Her Ear*, which the director wanted set in

**Figure 12–7.**　*Basic Shape Modified by Adding New Brim (1)*

**Figure 12–8.**　*Basic Shape Modified by Adding New Brim (2)*

the style of 1912–1914 when hats were indeed grandiose. You may recall that this is the time period of *My Fair Lady* as well.

For the hat in Figure 12–7 we started with the same basic straw shape seen in the lower right of Figure 12–1. To this was added a new egg-shaped brim whose crown opening was slightly off center. The two brims were stitched together and the new brim was then reinforced with hat wire. The whole hat was then covered in gold satin which had been interfaced with muslin. Black ostrich plumes and a pleated pink frou-frou were added. The brim was

then bent and shaped for the desired effect. Finally, it was tacked upward to the crown for added security.

This particular hat is an example of creating something for a definite hair style; a bouffant Gibson girl effect which would hold it in place with the aid of an Edwardian 14-inch long hatpin. This hair style was not available to the present model.

This same process was used to modify the hat in Figure 12–8, in which an even bigger oval brim was added to the straw base, wired, covered, and trimmed. This creation points to the success of hat wire in achieving a series of curves without the added help of upward tacking.

## Hat Construction

If you cannot find, refurbish, or adapt to achieve your goal, you must construct from scratch. Hats are constructed according to one of three basic principles. Either they are molded, built from a series of cut pieces, or draped.

Besides supplies of buckram, hat wire and ready-made hat forms and frames, clear varnish, and felt, you should also keep on hand head blocks (wig blocks), hat molds, wire cutters, needle-nose pliers, curved hand sewing needles, and a sailor's leather palm (the last because it takes a lot of force to pierce several layers of felt and buckram with a needle). White glue, large T pins, and a wide variety of ribbon, veiling, and artificial flowers, jewels for decoration, etc., are also required. A hand steamer and a hand-held hair dryer can be useful.

## Molded Hats

Many hats that are molded on a form are referred to in the millinery trade as "blocked." A hat mold is termed a hat block. One such hat block is pictured on the left side of Figure 12–9. Many shapes of hat blocks can be bought through millinery supply houses.

The basic method of hat construction is that the felt, buckram, or straw is wetted and stretched over the block and held in place by pins, string, or both. These blocks are made of balsa wood and readily hold pins. When the felt has thoroughly dried, it is removed from the mold and should retain its shape. It is then stiffened, trimmed, and decorated.

Most men's hats, like the three straw hats pictured in Figure 12–1, are molded in this fashion. But these blocks take up a great deal of room, and as previously stated, the work area needs to be well ventilated. If you have a relatively small operation, you are far better off buying blocked hats. Several

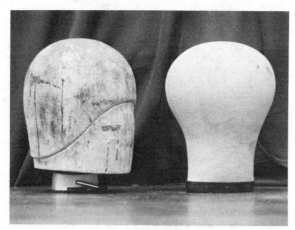

**Figure 12–9.** *Hat Block (left) and Wig Block (right)*

costume houses in the United States sell excellent ready-made period hats which with proper care and storage methods will last through many shows.

There is another solution to molding certain exotic shapes. One can cover wig blocks with plastic cleaner bags and then mold plasticine clay to the desired form. Then shape the felt or buckram over this form. (The wig block is on the right of Fig. 12–9.)

I have had great success with upside down clay flower pots as a mold for a truncated conical hennin. The head size can be increased by a folded roll of newspaper placed around the bottom rim. The trouble with plastic flower pots occurs when either varnish or felt stiffener is applied. These ingredients cause the plastic to bubble. I have even used an upside down wastebasket as a mold for barrel helmets.

**Hats Constructed of Several Pieces**

The hats that are built of several pieces have their basic method of construction as well. A basic shape or series of shapes must be cut from a supportive surface. This can be cardboard, Acta, buckram, horsehair, woven straw, or felt, depending on one's desire for quality and degree of stiffness. These shapes are then connected, wired if necessary, and covered in the desired fabric.

Constructed hats generally fall into one of several categories. The first, and perhaps the easiest to make, includes close fitting caps and coifs. The second includes the brimless crown shape. Crownless brim shapes comprise the third category, and the fourth combines any two of the above. Therefore, a coif with a brim attached becomes a bonnet; a coif with a veil in back becomes a French hood; a crown with an attached brim becomes a Pilgrim's hat or the beplumed hat of a dashing Cavalier.

*Coifs*

Let us discuss the coif. Present day baby bonnets are miniature coifs, and patterns for them can be enlarged to fit the adult head. This is what was done for the felt and gold lamé coif pictured in Figures 12–10 and 12–11. Multiple yarn braids were added which turned this hat into a partial wig thereby making it a headdress. This particular creation was worn by a dancing girl in a rather futuristic version of Lorca's *Blood Wedding*. A scaled pattern for this coif can be found in Figure 12–12.

The French hood modeled in Figure 12–13 is an adaptation of this same coif pattern. It uses the front piece of the coif, but this time it was cut of buckram, and wire was added to shape it to hug the ears. A simple liripipe hood was added to the back. A pleated trim covered the front piece. Gold braid, beads, and pearls were used as decoration to cover the seam. This liripipe hood is very little more than a basic stocking cap pattern slightly modified (You will find this pattern illustrated in Fig. 12–14.)

**Figure 12–10.** *Baby Bonnet Pattern Enlarged to Fit the Adult Head*

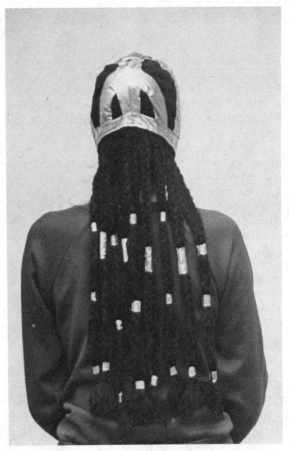

**Figure 12–11.** *Hat in Figure 12–10 As a Headdress*

BASIC COIF PATTERN -
SCALE ¼" = 1"

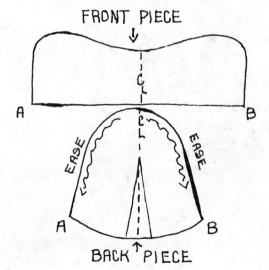

**Figure 12–12.** *Basic Coif Pattern*

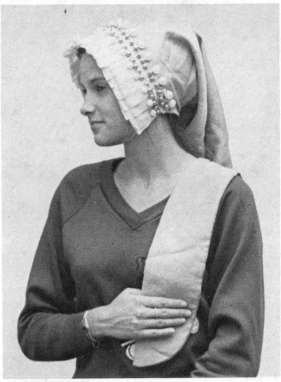

**Figure 12–13.** *French Hood*

Another close fitting cap that is basic in construction is the tonsure cap or yarmalke. It is generally made of six small, round-sided triangles. These same six triangles can be elongated to obtain various pointed headdresses such as Gothic helmets, pope's tiaras, and Eastern mystic headdresses. Several of the helmets pictured in Chapter 15 used this pattern. It is not always necessary to use six sides. Sometimes four sides will suffice.

The sleep helmet pictured in Figure 12–15 shows this cap combined with a headband and ear flaps. It was constructed for the wife in a production of *I Do, I Do*. A scaled pattern for this tonsure cap and its helmet adaptation appears in Figure 12–16.

*Brimless Crown Shapes*

Excellent examples of brimless crown-shaped headdresses are the two miters pictured in Figure 12–17. For the miter on the right, a basic shape, shown in Figure 12–18, was cut out of buckram. This was then covered in green velvet (interfaced with muslin) both inside and out. Gold brocade was appliqued to the outside, and the short ends were then sewn together. Afterwards, gold braid was glued on, and a double thickness of a separate green velvet piece shaped like a rounded diamond, was cut (see Fig. 12–19). The two layers were sewn together

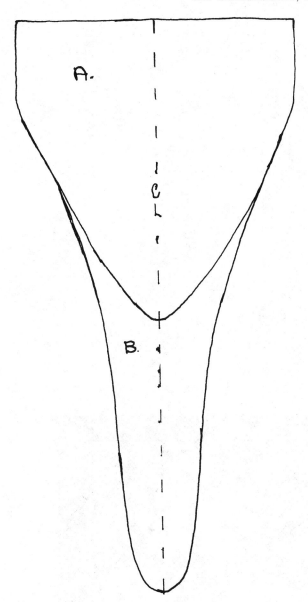

**Figure 12–15.**   *Sleep Helmet*

A. STOCKING CAP

B. LIRIPIPE ADAPTATION

SCALE ¼" = 1"

**Figure 12–14.**   *Stocking Cap Pattern and Adaptation*

leaving a small opening for turning rightside out. This then was sewn inside the miter's open crown. The miter was then decorated with jewels and pearls. This particular miter is a bishop's of the early Roman Church. An archbishop's miter is higher and often lacks the inside piece.

The miter on the left of Figure 12–17 was also an early Christian one but generally associated with the Eastern Church. Although the shapes vary, the construction process is the same. Poster board was used to stiffen this miter, however. The shape was essentially that of two horns brought together with the aid of a tacking thread at the top. (Scaled patterns for these miters appear in Fig. 12–20).

Making a king's crown is, of course, the simplest of all brimless crowned headdresses. It is a cut shape, connected and decorated. It has no top, no interior, it is really nothing more than a decorative headband.

*The Crownless Brim*

Nothing better exemplifies the crownless brim than the Gothic roundel. This is nothing but a large stuffed fabric doughnut worn on the head. The Valois bonnet so popular in Elizabethan England and Renaissance France is actually a variation on this basic structure, because it is a brim attached to a headband onto which is gathered a circle of fabric.

By comparison, this same gathered fabric circle is the basis for the mob (mop) cap, but in this case the gathering stitch or channel is placed an inch or two inside the perimeter of the circle and then gathered to the desired circumference of the head.

SCALE ⅛" = 1"

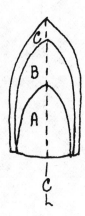

A. TONSURE (SKULL) CAP : CUT 6
B. BASIC HELMET SHAPE : CUT 6
C. FOOTBALL SHAPED HELMET : CUT 4

**Figure 12–16.** *Basic Skull Cap and Adaptations*

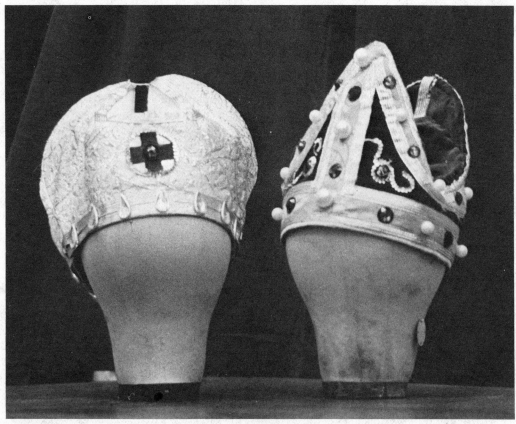

**Figure 12–17.** *Miters (Brimless Crown Shapes)*

**Figure 12–18.** *Basic Shape for the Western Church's Miter*

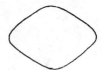

**Figure 12–19.** *Round-Ended Diamond Piece for Interior of the Miter*

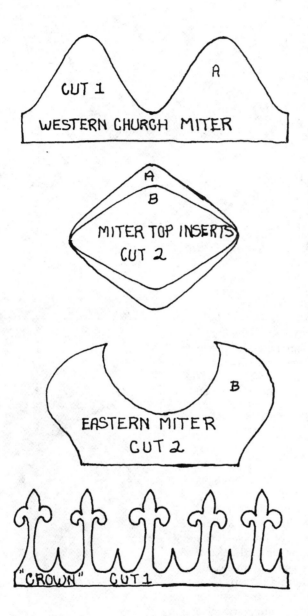

A. TOP INSERT FOR WESTERN CHURCH MITER

B. TOP INSERT FOR EASTERN CHURCH MITER

SCALE ⅛" = 1"

**Figure 12–20.** *Scaled Patterns for Two Miters and Crown*

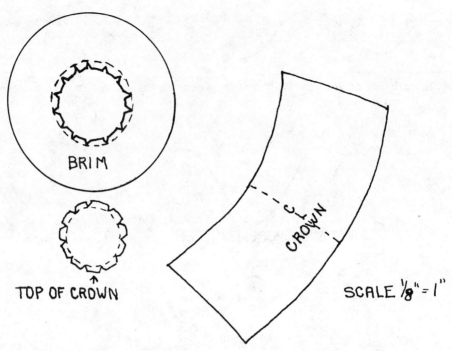

**Figure 12–21.** *Basic Pattern for Pilgrim Hat*

### The Combined Shape

The combined shape that comes most readily to mind is the pilgrim hat, a truncated conical crown attached to a flat circular brim. As previously stated, all or the crown part can be molded or blocked. A pattern for the cut and construct version can be found in Figure 12–21.

### The Draped Headdress

The last form of headdress construction is essentially drapery. A babushka is a draped headdress, as are whimples, veils, barbettes, and gorgets. A turban, another example of a draped headdress, is usually a rectangular piece of cloth that can be wound around the head in an infinite variety of ways. It can be wound each time it is worn, or the milliner can wind it around a head block and tack it permanently into place. He or she can even cut a pattern from this. This was what was done to create the basis for the turban in Figure 12–22. This creation was also used in the aforementioned production of *Blood Wedding*. An extra gold lamé underbrim was added to the green velvet turban as were the quilted and stuffed wings. These wings were held in place by a tacking thread, much as the horns of the Eastern miter were held in place.

It is important to note that millinery supplies sell ready-made wire frames upon which all sorts of creations may be draped.

**Figure 12–22.** *Turban used in* Blood Wedding

### The Crocheted or Knitted Hat

There is one other method of hat construction, that is the knitted or crocheted one. You can see a crocheted cloche in Figure 12–23. The crochet technique can also be used for snoods, cauls, nets, and a wide variety of trim techniques.

**Figure 12–23.** *Crocheted Cloche*

**Figure 12–24.** *Crocheted Net Holding a Hairpiece*

Both knitting and crocheting use yarn in a series of connected loops to achieve a garment. These loops are connected by two needles in the knitting process and by one hook in the crocheting process. Patterns and instructions can be found in numerous lady's magazines, or in your local knit and needle-work shop or department.

In Figure 12–24 you will see how a crocheted net can hold a hairpiece that was attached to a coif-like front brim. The actress's own hair came through the back and over the bottom of the hairpiece, which looked like part of her hair but stayed in place much more comfortably than if it had been hairpinned.

I regret to admit that this chapter touches only the tip of the iceberg in the art of millinery. Covering the subject completely would necessitate another book. I hope this chapter has given you a starting point, a way of thinking to stimulate your creative imagination.

# 13

# The Construction of Footwear

## New Shoes for Old

Is the easiest way around the problem of period shoes simply to find them? At a conference several years ago, one costume designer was delighted to receive 250 pairs of old shoes dating from 1880 to 1930. She spoke on and on about her wonderful antique shoes until another costumiere asked if all her actresses had antique-sized feet. Aye, there's the rub, in both a figurative and literal sense.

We have bigger feet than our grandparents had. In the mid-1920s the average woman's shoe size was a 6. It is now 7½ or 8. Therefore, those wonderful old-fashioned high-buttoned shoes that one occasionally finds in Aunt Minny's attic just take up shelf space in costume storage. You are far better off to take them apart, cut a pattern from them, put the pattern in a manila envelope, and store it. Use poster board for shoe pattern pieces because it gives a firmer edge when cutting new leather.

Now find a good cobbler who will work with you and make a couple of pairs. I have an arrangement with a local cobbler: I cut the leather and he makes the shoes. I also cut patterns for him; we trade our labor costs and only charge for materials. He is also very helpful at adapting shoes into period styles. He can change heels, put on platforms, put on high tops, cut toes out or put them in, and add or subtract any number of straps.

If you do not have to watch every penny of the budget, or if your organization is given an unexpected donation, period shoes can be bought new. Capezio's in New York will supply you with Wellington boots, high-buttoned shoes, or Scottish gillies, but these are special order items and you must give them six to ten weeks notice. Certain period footwear styles have remained constant, and it is only a matter of knowing where to shop. The cowboy boot of the 1880s looks just like the cowboy boot of the 1980s (minus a few rhinestones, perhaps). The riding boot has not really changed since the 1700s, nor has the low jodhpur boot changed since the 1840s. These two items are readily available at riding apparel stores throughout the Eastern seaboard.

The most basic shoe shape for women is either the ballet slipper or the low-vamped, small-heeled (1½" to 2") shoe called in the theater trade "character" shoes. Usually available in black and white, these are available from any number of dance supply houses. For the Broadway production of *A Chorus Line*, Capezio brought out a flesh-color shoe that has become very popular. Capezio also makes a ballet-like shoe top put on a regular leather sole and flat heel; it is called the "folk dance" slipper and comes in black, white, and red. Included in Capezio's catalogue is a soft suede shoe that works very well for most Gothic shows (see Fig. 13–1).

For Gothic pattens or clogs, go to Dr. Scholl or earth shoes. Sandals' availability depends on the season. If you know you are going to do a Greek or Roman play in January, plan ahead and buy a supply of sandals in July. Sandals are also the easiest form of footwear to construct. Once again, have a talk with your favorite shoemaker.

## Build If You Must

If the above suggestions still do not satisfy your needs, you will have to build your own footwear. Some basic supplies that you should have on hand are an awl, a leather punch, a straight and a curved hand sewing leather pointed needle, leather needles in sizes 14 through 20 for your sewing machine, the sailor's leather palm (already mentioned in Chapter 12), and buttonhole twist thread in black, white, and beige for hand sewing. The sewing machine will also need heavy duty thread.

**Figure 13–1.** *Rhythmics—Gothic-Looking Shoes Sold by Dance Suppliers*

It is not always necessary to use real leather. Shoes can be made of almost every conceivable fabric. However, sturdier materials like vinyl, suede cloth, felt, upholstery weight velvets, corduroy, or velveteen are preferable. If a lightweight fabric is necessary, interline it with a sturdy one. Above all, remember that the fabric should be sturdy but *pliable.*

All footwear follows a basically simple method of construction. There is always the sole or bottom of the shoe and then the upper section. The vamp is that part of the upper section that covers only the top of the foot, instep to toe. The entire upper section is generally made and then (right side to right side) sewn to the sole inside out. Then the shoe or boot is turned rightside out. This is the process used in making the lady's Gothic pointed-toed slipper and the man's Gothic pointed-toed boots shown in Figures 13–2 and 13–3; the square-toed Renaissance shoes of Figure 13–4; and the high boots of Figure 13–5. The Renaissance toes keep their shape best if they are stuffed a little or padded and quilted.

The Indian moccasins of Figure 13–6 are almost the inverse of this process in that the sole wraps up to become the heel and toe cover and only a tongue-like vamp suffices for the top.

The webbed feet of Figure 13–7 are merely modifications of a basic slipper pattern. You may never need to costume an actor in webbed feet, but the pattern is included as an example of what can be possible.

It is naturally assumed that you are using pliable fabrics that lend themselves to being turned inside-out. If heavy leathers are used, the sole must be stitched on by a cobbler or cobbler's sewing machine.

## Modification of Footwear

Sometimes a whole shoe or boot need not be built. An added piece may be the trick to turn a contemporary shoe into a period one. We are all familiar with the trick of adding a false tongue and buckle on a black elastic band over an ordinary black men's tie shoe, and voila! You have the buckled shoes of our founding fathers.

In the early 1970s men began once again to wear heeled shoes, or at least what was called in the 1940s Cuban heels. I bought one pair in every size from

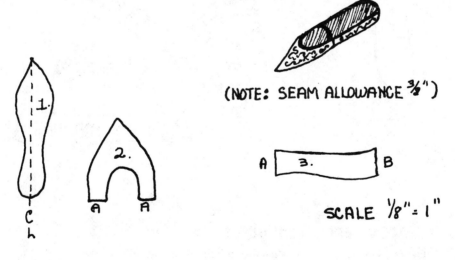

(NOTE: SEAM ALLOWANCE ⅜")

SCALE ⅛" = 1"

1. SOLE - CUT 2
2. FRONT VAMP - CUT 2
3. SIDE AND HEEL - CUT 4

**Figure 13–2.** *Pattern for Lady's Gothic Pointed-Toe Slipper*

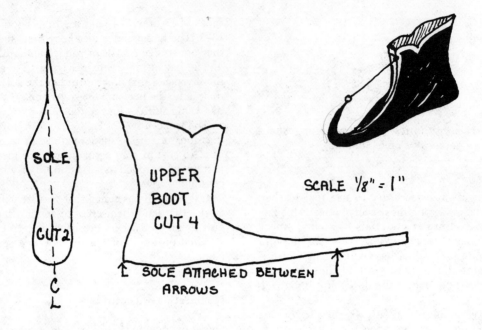

SCALE ⅛" = 1"

SOLE ATTACHED BETWEEN ARROWS

(NOTE: SEAM ALLOWANCE ⅜")

**Figure 13–3.** *Pattern for Man's Gothic Pointed-Toe Boot*

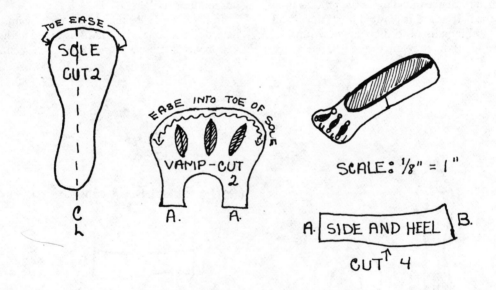

SCALE: ⅛" = 1"

(NOTE: SEAM ALLOWANCE ⅜")

**Figure 13–4.** *Pattern for Man's Renaissance Squared-Toe Shoe*

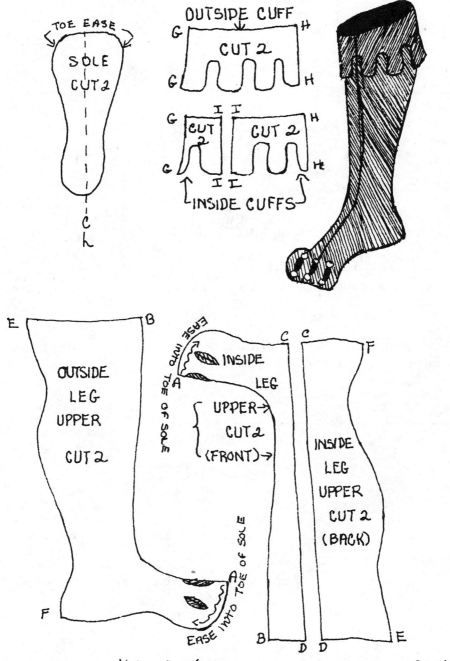

SCALE ⅛" = 1"   (NOTE: SEAM ALLOWANCE ⅜")

THIS BOOT GOES ABOVE THE KNEE 4½" BUT
IT MAY BE SHORTENED AS DESIRED.

**Figure 13–5.**   *Pattern for Man's Renaissance Boot*

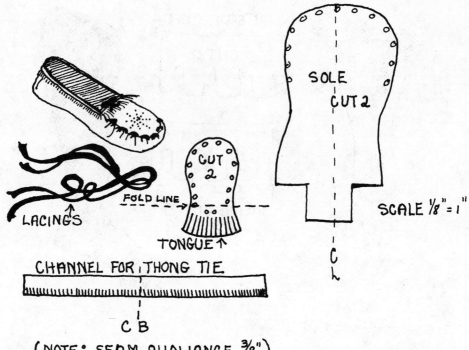

**Figure 13–6.** *Pattern for Indian Moccasins*

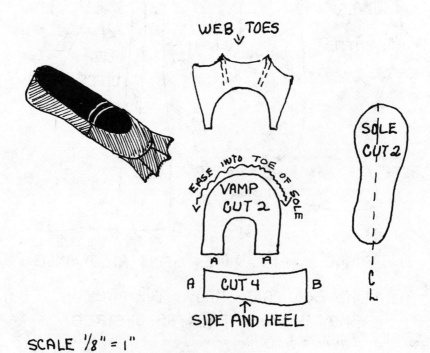

**Figure 13–7.** *Pattern for Webbed Feet*

7½ to 12 and have been adding bows, buckles, and red tape to the heels for every Baroque show we've done since.

Another form of modification is the spat and gaiter illustrated in Figure 13–8. You will find patterns for both of these in Figure 13–9.

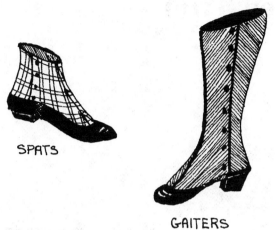

SPATS

GAITERS

**Figure 13–8.**  *Spats and Gaiters*

When making tight fitting boots, the technique for drafting a tights pattern described in Chapter 10 can be adapted for this purpose as well. High-heeled cowboy boots with an added cuff at the top make excellent Cavalier boots. Even high-heeled shoes can be given a new top to turn them into the fold-down boots called "slops" in the mid-Baroque era. In this case your base shoe or boot dictates your pattern.

### Best Foot Forward

Like hats, their counterpart at the other end of the body, the proper footwear can do much to complete the outfit. It should be part of the overall design. If it is a case in which the foot is only glimpsed from time to time, the shoe should be as unobtrusive as possible. If the footwear is purposely outlandish (slops, or a pointed toe with bells, or webbed feet), a reasonable facsimile or the item itself should be given the actor at the earliest possible moment in the rehearsal period. It all boils down to a matter of putting your best foot forward.

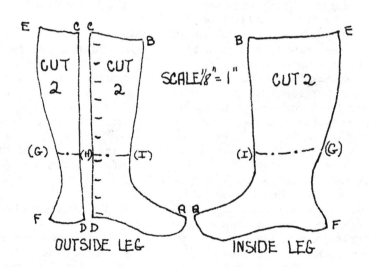

FOR SPATS CUT OFF AT (—•—•) DOTTED LINE

(NOTE: SEAM ALLOWANCE ⅜")

**Figure 13–9.**  *Pattern for Lady's Spats and Gaiters*

# 14

# Construction of Jewelry and Jeweled Trim

Remember the moment in Moliere's *The Miser* when Harpagon finally gives in on all points to secure the return of his jewels and gold? Gold and jewels have held an endless fascination since the time of Croesus. It is the one area of costume construction that generally fascinates the most because the glittery, sparkling rewards are almost instantaneous. You don't have to wait until an enormous costume is finished. Jewelry, although only part of the overall outfit, is a creation in itself. Further fascination comes to the costumer in being able to fake gorgeous things out of almost nothing.

Every costume shop should attempt to keep as much costume jewelry on hand as can be reasonably used, stored, etc. Items of costume jewelry that look "period" should be kept as they are. The rest is fair game for adaptation, reuse, modification, and so forth.

We have all heard the grand stories of various performers who wore the real thing on stage. Indeed, one Russian ballerina, who in her heyday was mistress to the czar, was famous for wearing real diamonds! Excluding budgetary prohibitives, this is totally unnecessary. Sometimes rhinestones sparkle more and dramatic action should in itself be a precaution.

Except for an occasional pair of pierced earrings or a wedding band, I generally caution our performers either not to bring valuable jewelry to the theater, or to check what they have with our stage manager who has the only access to a *locked* area.

Another problem with actual jewelry is one of scale. Can it be read in your theatrical house by your audiences? This "maxim" controls all your actions whether collecting, using, or creating. Depending on readability, almost anything from soda straws and

elbow macaroni to junk from the scene shop floor can be turned into jewelry. It all depends on what you do to it. What can be done with practically nothing seems to have an endless variety.

### Use of Actual Metals

The cross down center in Figure 14–1 was cut from actual metal, in this case 1/16" thick brass. Brass is a good substitute for gold, and aluminum works as a substitute silver. In the case of this cross, a bit of crude detailing was added with black enamel paint, and a hole punched in the top. The chain was crocheted from a relatively thick gold elastic cord obtained in a craft shop. Granted that on close inspection this looks crude, but it read very well from our auditorium which seats approximately 600 people.

### Balsa Wood and Hot Glue

Please note the cross down right in Figure 14–1. This was made of balsa wood that had hot glue dribbled over it in thin strings so that it read like filigree. It was then sprayed with a gold metallic paint. A small screw eye was screwed into the top so that it could hang on a ribbon.

Hot glue can be applied this way to any number of surfaces, including leather, buckram, and stiffened felt. Hot glue is also useful for the application of such other items as cord and string, jewels and beads, or variously shaped pasta, etc.

It is important to remember that dry hot glue returns to its milky beige color and is not clear. For this reason, you might wish to use it only when you

**Figure 14–1.** *Stage Accessories "Faked" for Production.*

are going to paint over it. I prefer glues that are clear when dry if there is any chance that the glue might be seen.

### New Jewels from Old

In the case of the somewhat ambassadorial decoration on the baldrick up center in Figure 14–1, an old pin was redone in plastic beads and a piece of gold braid was gathered, rosette fashion, around it and attached prong by prong with gold cotton thread. The same was done for the pin at the center top of the Romanesque girdle pictured in Figure 14–2.

### The Buckram and Braid Method

The squared cross and two diamonds in the left of Figure 14–1 are jeweled trim in preparation to be attached to a costume. They are made from buckram and braid. In the case of the squared cross, a three-inch square of buckram was cut and sprayed with metallic gold paint. It then was allowed to dry completely. A cross of red felt was glued on, as was the red stone in the center. Then plain gold braid was glued around the edge. This was later applied to an archbishop's miter.

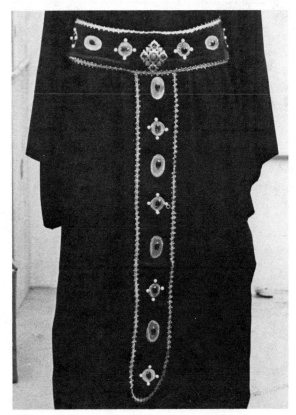

**Figure 14–2.** *Bejewelled Romanesque Girdle*

The two diamonds were two of thirty-six that were later appliqued to a king's robe. Again the basic diamond shape was cut from buckram. A repeat of this shape was also cut from magenta velvet ribbon and zigzagged onto the buckram. The gold braid and center jewels were then stitched on.

In many cases either aluminum or nylon screening can be substituted for the buckram. The aluminum screening must be cut with tin snips and its edges bound in a little masking tape to prevent abrasiveness to the fabric or the performer's skin. The nylon screening can be cut with scissors and is non-abrasive, but not as stiff as the aluminum.

Why use glue for the squared cross and not for the diamonds? The diamonds would be applied to a costume that would need to be dry cleaned. Dry cleaning fluid destroys many glues and it certainly removes a great deal of metallic paint. This simple thought must be kept uppermost in mind when planning your jeweled trim.

The same method was used for the jeweled trim in Figure 14–2 with one difference. Instead of buckram as a base, I used some lovely metallic gold vinyl I found by the yard (54 inches wide, too) in a craft shop. This same gold vinyl was used to create the collar and belt in Figure 14–3.

**Figure 14–3.** *Collar and Belt Made of Gold Vinyl*

## Where To Secure Supplies

Your local crafts store should be your greatest help in securing cord, beads, pearls, stones, pin fasteners, earring backs, balsa wood, a variety of glues, buckram, paints, and the hundreds of other items included in this end of costume production.

Another, though perhaps strange, source for supplies is a friendly medical doctor or, if you are in a metropolitan area, a good surgical supply house. Tongue depressors are a great help in jewelry making, used either as supports or by themselves. In the next chapter on armor construction, you will see uses for such medical items as plaster bandages and surgiflex. Alginate, essentially a dental product, is used in making castings.

The tongue depressor cross in Figure 14–4 was one of several made for a production of *Becket*. Two tongue depressors were painted brown, cross-tied with string, and attached to a crude rosary-like set of beads worn around the waists of the monks. The cross was slipped through the loop at the other end and held by a bead to the desired circumference of the waist.

Your scrap and trim box is another excellent source of supplies. That is where the piece of black lace and connected black eyelet trim in Figure 14–5 were found. The upholstery braid and curtain rings were found in our prop room. The washers and nails came from the scene shop floor.

## The Stiffened Lace Method

A Victorian dog collar was created from the upholstry braid shown in Figure 14–5. Bias tape in a matching color was used to cover the ragged ends to which hooks and eyes were added. Several coats of gold metallic spray paint and a coat of clear varnish were then applied. A plastic cameo from old thrift shop jewelry was glued to the center front.

The same method was used on the black lace shown in Figure 14–5. After the varnish dried, I glued alternating red stones and pearls onto the center of each scallop to make the necklace seen down center in Figure 14–6.

This is basically the same method used to create the parure of jewelry in Figure 14–7. The black connected eyelet of Fig. 14–5 was cut apart in various ways to create the bracelet, necklace, and earrings. The chain of the necklace was crocheted with a very fine crochet hook and fine gold elastic thread. The nice part of this is that it avoids worrying over a catch as it will stretch to fit over the head. A loop of this same thread will be attached to the end of the bracelet so that it will "button" over the large pearl. Earring backs will be glued to the earrings.

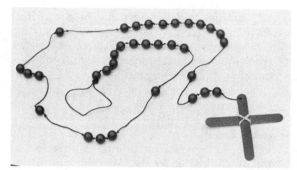

**Figure 14–4.** *Cross Made of Tongue Depressors*

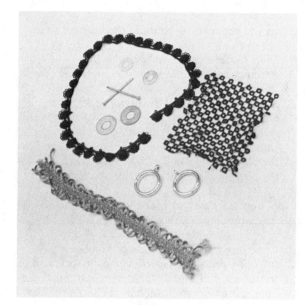

**Figure 14–5.** *Supplies from Scrap*

**Figure 14–6.** *Jewelry Made from Stiffened Lace Method*

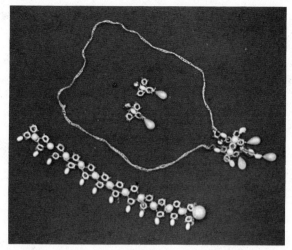

**Figure 14–7.** *More Examples of Stiffened Lace Method*

### Junk from the Scene Shop Floor

The necklace up right in Figure 14–6 is made from washers and curtain rings from the scene shop and prop room. The washers were sprayed with gold paint and then glued to the one side of the curtain rings. The gold coins were then glued on top of the washers. A chain was crocheted of metallic yarn to which the rings were attached.

That hat ornament in the center of Figure 14–6 was made from one of the nails pictured in Figure 14–5 plus two hooks normally used to attach drapes to a traverse rod, two large pearls, and a jeweled button. The hooks were hot glued onto the nail and then wrapped in a little masking tape. This was then sprayed gold. The pearls and button were then glued on with clear jeweler's glue. If pin backs are not big enough for your purpose, a common safety pin can be attached to the back of a brooch as seen on the one in Figure 14–6 to the left of the hat ornament.

### Methods Not Pictured

There are many other methods to achieve similar results and one cannot picture them all. Also some techniques used in jewelry are used elsewhere as well. Papier maché, Acta, castings, and macrame are four such techniques.

#### Papier Maché

Papier maché is the use of paper strips or pieces in combination with white glue to build up a hard surface of many layers. The strip method of papier maché is discussed in detail in Chapter 17. For jewelry purposes one needs to use small pieces of paper instead of strips. Out of them can be formed a dough that can be rolled, cut, twisted, and so forth. Also available is a pre-mixed product called "Celluclay" to which you merely need add water. When dried this can be drilled, lightly sanded, painted, and varnished.

### Acta

Acta, a commercial product, is a lightweight glue-impregnated paper. Dry, it can act as buckram. Wet, it can be stretched, molded, cut, curled, and shaped. It can be painted with various paints, inks, and dyes. Fabric can be placed on it and when wet, Acta bonds to that fabric.

### Macrame

Macrame is the art of tying string into a series of knots and braids to achieve a pattern. The texture is achieved by the type and thickness of the cord or string used. Beads can be worked into this as well. One of the best examples that comes to mind was Guinevere's wedding dress in the film version of *Camelot.* It appeared to have been macramed with hundreds of tiny seeds and shells added.

Macrame can be used to create Egyptian collars, all sorts of belts, chains, and heavy trim. It is even one way of making hats and chain mail.

### Castings

Let us look at a hypothetical situation for a brief moment. You are doing a production involving some actual historical figure and you wish to reproduce, as accurately as possible, a painting of that individual. Anne Boleyn comes to mind, perhaps in a production of *Anne of a Thousand Days.* You want to recreate her famous initial necklace "B" with three drop pearls. The easiest way to do that is by casting. Jewelers have many processes for this, all involving molten metals. Budgetwise, you cannot afford that so you must cast something like papier maché, plaster of paris, or plastic wood. The process of casting for a plaster positive is pictorially described in Chapter 16 on the making of masks.

Plaster is rather heavy and perishable for jewelry. Plastic wood would be a more viable choice. Now for the molding process:

1. *First of all, a positive should be made or modelled in clay on a piece of flat wood or masonite. For this purpose plasticine clay can be used, but ordinary children's modelling clay will do. Your "B" would be formed of this.*
2. *Now line a box with tin foil. The box, of course, must be a little bigger than your clay positive on all four sides, and deep enough to hold it without crushing the clay.*
3. *Generously grease the clay positive with petroleum jelly or "Green Soap," a liquid soap obtainable at any pharmacy.*
4. *Now prepare some plaster of paris, following label directions for pouring consistency, and pour in just enough to fill two-thirds to three-fourths of the box.*
5. *Invert the clay positive into the plaster so that the wood piece under the clay is now resting on top of the box.*
6. *Let stand to dry. Twenty-four hours are usually recommended.*

Then you are ready to unmold the clay negative.

1. *First, invert the box so that it is up.*
2. *Remove the box. It should come right off the tinfoil.*
3. *Now peel the tin foil away from the plaster.*
4. *Gently remove the plaster negative from the clay positive. If enough petroleum jelly was used, this should be easy. If not, take a blunt knife and cut the clay off the wood block. Then gently dig out the clay, making sure to remove all of it.*

Now you are ready to make your plastic wood (or other material) positive.

1. *Generously grease the plaster negative.*
2. *Into this press the plastic wood. It is advisable to use a small nail or large needle to make any holes necessary for attachments while the wood is still soft.*
3. *Let it dry. Depending on the thickness used, plastic wood takes between two days and a week to dry completely.*

Next you will have to unmold the positive.

1. *Your blunt edged knife should gently loosen the sides of the plastic wood.*
2. *It can be drilled, gently sanded, painted, and varnished to a bright shine.*

(Some people find themselves allergic to the chemical components of plastic wood.)

### Hatomold

There is a new medium on the market from West Germany called Hatomold, a marvelous flexible plastic molding material that comes in three types of flexibility, depending on its use.

K50 is the hardest and is used for making jewelry and scenic moldings (I also use it for making puppets.) When you order it, you also receive the material with which to make the negative cast, as well as the K50 for the positive. This negative does not require greasing before the positive is poured. When set, the positive may be drilled, nailed, and painted with various types of paint. While still in its soft form, it can be colored by adding Tondosol Universal Color Paste to it.

M60 Hatomold is used to construct flexible masks by the process illustrated in Figure 16–7. It is medium soft in comparison to K50 and P100. P100 is soft and is used in makeup techniques for bald heads and wig hair lines, artificial noses, scars, and blisters.

Both Hatomold and Tondosol Universal Color Paste are products of A. Haussmann GmbH u. Company, 2000 Hamburg 70, P.O.B. 700804, West Germany. As we are now able to dial direct overseas, the phone number is 011-4940-660896. However, it may also be purchased through Rosco Laboratories, Inc., 36 Bush Ave., Portchester, NY 10573; phone 914-937-1300.

### Sculptured Pieces of Bread Dough and Salt Plaster

Perhaps your production of *Anne of a Thousand Days* is being done in an auditorium that seats 1200 instead of 300 and your replica need not be extremely detailed. In that case you may wish to merely mold a "B" and be done with it. Two substances work very well and can be easily done in any basically stocked kitchen or kitchenette area of the shop. These are bread dough and salt plaster.

. The bread dough is simply flour mixed with enough water to make it workable. You can model the dough into the "B" on the wood block and let it sit to dry (remember to put the necessary holes in it while it's still wet). If an oven is available, model the "B" on a small flat cookie sheet and bake it dry in a slow oven (150° to 200°F).

This bread dough will take inks, vegetable dyes, paint, and then varnish for shine and hardness. Try varnishing the plain dough and when that is dry, spraying it with a metallic paint. A second coat of varnish can then be applied. This gives a very good metal shine.

The same process can be done with salt plaster. Salt is mixed with just enough white glue to make a dough. It must stand to dry in the open air, however, as applied heat melts the salt. Salt plaster can be dyed with vegetable dyes and then varnished, and the salt crystals give a wonderful glistening effect. The added advantage of the white glue, vegetable dye, and salt combination is that it becomes opaque or slightly translucent. If rolled in small balls, jewels can be made of this, or beads if they are strung while still slightly tacky. For the best effect of clear color,

the vegetable dye can be added directly as the dough is mixed.

### Sawdust and Glue Dough

Another way to sculpt pieces of jewelry is by making a dough out of sawdust and Weldwood glue. Sawdust is always easy to get from the scene shop. Weldwood glue is a powdered glue manufactured by Allied Chemical Corporation. Sift sawdust to remove large particles. Mix the sawdust and powdered glue and moisten with water until you get a dough. Other dry industrial glues may be substituted.

This can be dried in a 150°F oven for four to eight hours. It can then be sanded, drilled, chiseled, and painted. It is lightweight and very durable.

### Making Your Own Jewels and Beads

Sometimes you are faced with the problem of having to make your own jewels. This is particularly true when large stones and beads are needed. As we have seen, the salt plaster is one construction method, but there are several others including ceramic clay, pasta, sea shells, hardened glue, and varnished candy.

You are probably thinking, "Oh come on! Varnished candy indeed!" But it works. I once saw a gorgeous costume displayed at a theater conference; it had the loveliest green and red gemstone rings in which a pearl nestled. Upon close inspection they were Life Savers. Candy *must* be varnished or shellacked. If not, theatrical lights melt them. Dipping them in Elmer's glue also seems to prevent melting. An interesting effect can be obtained by dipping the candy in glue and sprinkling it with rock salt.

Fired ceramic clay beads are easy to make, if you have access to a kiln (ceramic clay can also be molded and fired as well). The beads can be glazed and refired or stained, or painted with acrylic or enamel paints and then shellacked.

Sea shells can be painted with pearl luster nail polish and thus transformed into Baroque pearls. This technique also works for ceramic beads. I have used all kinds of shells for texture and sprayed them with metallic paint as well.

Pasta stars, shells, and elbow macaroni can be inked, painted, or dyed with vegetable dye and then dipped in white glue (remember it dries clear) or varnished. The varnish makes them a little stronger and less likely to crack. I have even painted plastic straws with acrylic paint, cut them into pieces, and strung them as beads.

My latest discovery was purely accidental. I had left some pearlized white acrylic paint out in a nice round globule at home one day when I got called to the phone. I forgot about the paint and rushed off to work. When I returned that evening, it had dried out completely leaving me a lovely large Baroque pearl. Acrylic paint is now made in metallic gold, silver, bronze, and copper. I've been using pearlized acrylic paint for studs and jewels ever since the accidental discovery. If applied wet to a porous surface such as fabric it holds without the aid of glue. If it is put on a sealed surface such as a plate or cookie sheet, when dry it can be peeled off and glued on to whatever you wish.

Elmer's or Sobo glue can be used in much the same manner. It can be poured into a mold (tin or glass only), mixed with vegetable dye, and left to dry. It can then be peeled off and reglued as a jewel. For sparkle, add a little piece of tin foil to the bottom of the jewel.

### Equipment Required

Each process requires its own equipment, but you should have on hand fasteners, wire cutters, a rhinestone setter, studs, grommets, and jeweler's wire. The wire need not be actual gold, but you will need wire in several gauges in both a gold and silver color. It is also a good idea to have a very fine electric drill with a sander attachment. A small toaster oven is also a nice addition.

We have mentioned crocheted chains. We discussed crocheting in the chapter on hat construction (Chapter 12) and we will be using this technique again in the next chapter. For this reason you should keep on hand several crochet hooks of various sizes.

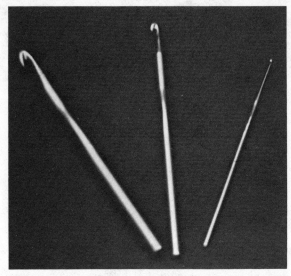

**Figure 14–8.** *Crochet Hooks Used to Construct Chains*

In Figure 14–8 you will see three such hooks. The one on the right was used to make the fine chain for the necklace in Figure 14–7. The one in the middle is used for jewelry chains and hat patterns. The one on the left is a Hero size 12, used to crochet chain mail and very heavy chains.

# 15

# The Construction of Armor

I am amazed at all the recent controversy over the amount of violence on television. Violence is being treated as a phenomenon peculiar to 20th century idiot box entertainment. Violence and dramaturgy have been inexorably linked since the early Greek tragedies.

When there has been violence, people have striven to protect themselves from it; the type of protection is dictated by the type of violence. For thousands of years violence was enacted on a one-on-one basis, employing some form of spiked and/or pointed instrument including arrows, spears, swords, daggers, etc. This necessitated the protection of the individual body in an encasement that would withstand being pierced. This protection comes under the general heading of armor.

As warfare changed, the protection changed. The use of guns brought an end to the use of armor. The greatest protection against the gun is camouflage. With the emergence of the Atom bomb, shelters are built underground.

Dramaturgy, however, is more often concerned with what *was* than what *is*, and therefore armor plays a significant part and must be constructed for any number of plays.

## Dual Classification of Armor

There is a dual classification of armor within the theatrical structure. Sometimes it is classified as a prop and sometimes as a costume. Who makes what often becomes confusing. Some resident theater companies employ one person as an armorer who does it all, taking his designs from both the costume and set designer. In most university situations, the rule seems to be "He who designs it, makes it." I prefer to regard armor as a costume if it is worn by the actor, and as a prop if it is merely picked up and carried.

Armor itself falls neatly into two basic types—hard pieces and soft pieces. Hard pieces include such items as hard helmets, breastplates, riveted plate armor, swords and shields, or anything that resembles plate metal. Soft pieces include padded and studded leather and chain mail, basically anything pliable in nature.

### Hard Armor

There are many ways of making hard pieces and the choice of which to use often depends on the requirements of its specific use. As an example, the sparkling armor used by Miles Gloriosus in *A Funny Thing Happened On The Way To The Forum* is strictly for show. No actual fighting goes on. When I did the show in 1977, I used a gold and silver eyelash lamé interfaced with felt. It was cool, pliable, and never failed to get its laugh.

A production of *Macbeth* will require some definite broadsword dueling when Macbeth and Macduff finally go at it. Their armor has to withstand the stresses, strains, and blows of actual fighting.

The preferable techniques for active use of armor are fiberglass, stiffened felt, or celastic. Papier maché and the plaster bandage techniques are fine for passive uses.

*Papier Maché* The papier maché method and its derivative products, such as Celluclay and Acta, are discussed in great detail in Chapters 14 and 17. These may be also adapted to armor construction. One separate problem with armor construction, however, is the making of breast or back plates. Have the actor come in for a two- to three-hour session with you. Have him wear a close fitting leotard or T shirt. Take a cleaner's plastic bag and cut neck and armhole openings. Slip him into it and scotch tape it to conform to his body.

Now have him lie down in a comfortable position, and taking glue-impregnated strips, build up the breast plate on him, drying each layer with a hand-held hair dryer until you get the desired thickness.

After this is completely dry, the actor can stand up and the plastic bag can be cut down the center back. He can then slip out of it. The plastic bag is then removed from the inside of the breast plate.

If a back plate is desired, the actor must lie comfortably on his stomach and the process is repeated. After the back plate is dry, the plastic is cut up the center front and the actor slips out of it.

The decoration can then be added. For an extra smooth hard look, a coat of Gesso can be applied and dried before painting. The Greek breastplate in Figure 15–1 was done this way. The decoration was rope and grommets. It was purposely distressed to look as though it had been through the Trojan War.

*Plaster Bandages*  The same process can be used for plaster bandages. The advantage of the plaster bandage is that it dries harder and more quickly, and you need less of it for the same degree of hardness. Also the plaster can be used as either a negative or positive cast of the actor's form for other processes, such as fiberglass, celastic, or stiffened felt.

This plaster cast becomes a negative cast if the outside is used. Celastic and stiffened felt both tend to shrink so I suggest using the positive side. Fiberglass fabric stays fairly well to size and this can be used on the negative side.

*Celastic*  Celastic is a commercial product, a fibrous paper that becomes malleable when soaked in acetone. It should be torn in pieces about two inches

wide, and several strips should be torn on the bias to facilitate going around curves. The torn edges melt into a smoothness that cut edges will not achieve. Some cut strips can eventually be used to cover raw edges around neck and armhole openings.

A few words of caution about the use of celastic are these:

1. *For easy removal, cover the plastic form with tinfoil first.*
2. *The chemicals impregnated into the celastic and the acetone can cause skin irritation. Use rubber gloves (hospital latex gloves are wonderful).*
3. *Acetone eats plastic. Pour it into a porcelain, glass, or stainless steel receptacle (bowl).*
4. *Use the acetone in small amounts as it evaporates quickly. It is also a good idea to use it in a well ventilated area.*
5. *Once dry, celastic must be cut with a knife or tin snips.*

After the plate has dried any roughness can be smoothed by sanding, and any holes can be filled with plastic wood.

*Stiffened Felt*  The felt best suited to armor construction is industrial felt three-eighths to a half-inch thick, but regular (decorator) felt can be used in several layers although this is a slower process. To save time later in the painting process, dark colors (grey, brown, black, dark green, or blue) are the most serviceable. The higher the proportion of wool fiber the better the finished product will be.

Cover the form in a plastic cleaner bag and then stretch the dampened felt over it, nailing it down until dry. A sizing of white glue and water is used to dampen the felt which gives a stiffened surface when dry. If a more pliable surface is desired, plain water can be used for dampening. After the felt form has completely dried, it can be painted with shellac.

This method is particularly effective in faking certain embossed designs. A design can be built up with clay on top of the plaster cast, which is then covered with stretchy rolled plastic that will conform to the design. The felt may then be placed over it as illustrated in Figure 15–2.

If industrial felt is unavailable, you can use the sizing method of dampening each layer of decorator felt and the sizing will dry and hold it together. Always shellac any layered felt pieces for added strength. It might also be necessary to shellac it inside and out. Then paint can be applied in any number of techniques.

*Fiberglass*  Fiberglass is virtually indestructible. Basically it consists of a loosely woven fillament made of glass that is coated with a clear plastic resin.

**Figure 15–1.**  *Breastplate Made with Papier Maché*

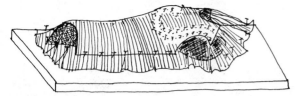

**Figure 15–2.**　*Stretched Felt over an Armor Cast*

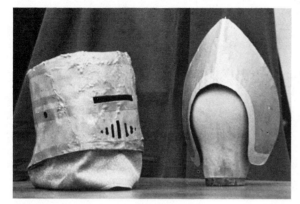

**Figure 15–3.**　*Fiberglass Helmets*

Consider the two helmets in Figure 15–3. The barrel helmet on the left was made by molding the glass fabric over a waste basket and bending the back out in a sort of duck tail effect. It was then painted in the fiberglass resin. Once this was dry, a felt lining was glued inside and sponge rubber pieces were fitted to make it rest comfortably on the actor's head. The eye and mouth slits were carved out and holes were drilled into the side so that the actor could hear. (This was one of four such helmets worn by Becket's murderers in Anouilh's play *Becket*.) The silver knit lamé gorget was added to the bottom. The rough battered texturing was achieved by mixing sawdust into the paint.

The football type helmet on the right side of Figure 15–3 was made of buckram and felt according to the pattern in Chapter 12, Figure 12–22. Then a piece of the glass fabric was stitched over it, and the resin was applied. It was very smooth and needed practically no sanding. (It too was lined in felt for the actor's comfort.)

Let us compare the helmets with the kingly helmet in Figure 15–4. This was used by King Arthur in *Camelot*. The crown is detachable and was worn in the knighting scene by itself. The helmet was made of papier mache, and fiberglass resin was merely painted onto it, thereby making it durable but also lightweight and comfortable. The mouth slits on this were merely painted because Arthur had no lines when wearing it.

I discovered that regular fabric will take fiberglass resin, so I fiberglassed all my fairy wings for a pro-

**Figure 15–4.**　*Papier Maché Helmet with Detachable Crown, used in* Camelot

duction of *A Midsummer Night's Dream*. This led me to try fiberglass resin applied directly to felt.

In Figure 15–5 you will see the helmets, sword, and shield used for the 1979 production of *Macbeth* at Florida Atlantic University. The helmet on the right is pliable suede cloth trimmed in silver leather and gold buttons. It hugged the head, and only the cross, which was supported by a piece of a tongue depressor, needed stiffening. The helmet on the left was constructed by the same technique, but when finished it was stuffed with newspaper and dipped into the resin and allowed to dry. It is hard as a rock on the outside. The felt interior is soft and comfortable to wear. Also the fiberglassing prevented the buttons from coming off.

The shield was made of posterboard covered in the glass fabric and painted with the resin. Then it was studded and painted. The inside was lined in felt, and straps were attached.

The sword was made from sheet aluminum cut in two pieces. The hilt of the blade was fitted

**Figure 15–5.** *Fiberglass Helmets used in* Macbeth

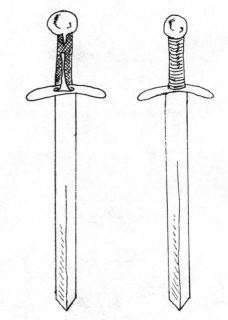

**Figure 15–6.** *The Making of a Broadsword*

through the T bar and then encased in two pieces of wood. A wooden finial was also encased at the top between these same two pieces. This was bound in brass wire and the whole handle was dipped in the fiberglass resin. This process is illustrated in Figure 15–6. The aluminum used was a quarter-inch thick. Because there is something exciting in hearing the clang of metal in stage fighting, we used aluminum. We painted the shield in Figure 15–5 to look like studded leather, but we put metal squares around the outer rim for sound purposes. However, even dull edged aluminum can be dangerous, and all such equipment should be used with caution.

All the processes so far described can be used equally as well for smaller pieces like gauntlets, epaulettes, greaves, and gorgets.

### Vacu-Form Armor

Before leaving the subject of hard armor, we must discuss vacu-form pieces, a relatively new process of forming plastic shapes in pre-existing molds. Pre-molded pieces can be purchased either unfinished or completely finished from two sources: Costume Armor, Inc. P.O. Box 325 Shore Road, Cornwall on Hudson, New York 12520, or Tobins Lake Studio, 1650 Seven Mile Road, South Luan, Michigan 48178. The finished pieces are ready for the stage but if you prefer to incorporate your own decorated motifs, you would prefer to purchase the unfinished pieces and finish them yourself. The only objection to buying armor would be an educational one. In a university situation your students need to know how to construct it for themselves.

### Soft Armor

When thinking of soft pliable armor pieces, chainmail always comes to mind immediately. One should also remember that man protected himself with leather and animal skins long before chainmail was invented.

*Leather Armor*   Leather can be quilted, padded, studded, woven, laced, plaited, fringed, and beaded in a variety of techniques and combinations. You may use real leather or any of a number of substitutions including vinyl, naugahyde, ultra-suede, suede cloth, oilcloth, and even brushed denim or un-waled (uncut) corduroy.

Leather, vinyl, and suede cloth also take well to acryllic paints used undiluted from the tube. This gives a superb leathery surface. The glue or acryllic process when applied to the abovementioned woven fabrics prevents ravelling at the cut edges.

The Romanesque armor in Figure 15–7 was made from a soft plastic leather that was appliqued, quilted, and studded with plastic disks. Several special techniques are required when sewing leather or leather substitutes. You should use leather pointed needles, both in your machine and for handwork. A leather point is illustrated in Figure 15–8.

Most of the suede or leather fabrics have a "wrong" side that will go easily through your sewing machine's feed. Problems often arise when the minute, rubberized particles build up on the machine needle. A tiny dab of petroleum jelly on the needle tip will help this.

**Figure 15–7.** *Romanesque Armor Made of Soft Plastic Leather*

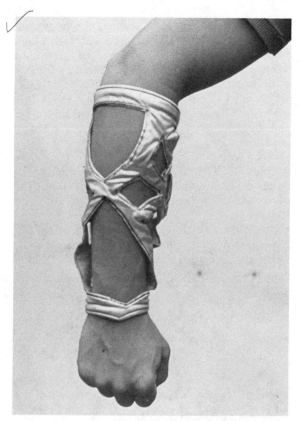

**Figure 15–9.** *Padded Openwork Armguard*

**Figure 15–8.** *Leather Pointed Needle*

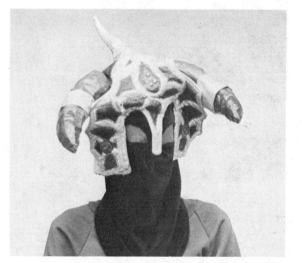

**Figure 15–10.** *Death's Mask and Headdress used in* Blood Wedding

Often, when top stitching on the leather side is required, the leather does not want to feed properly and gets stuck in one place, bunches up, or skips stitches. This can be solved by pinning strips of waxed paper to the underside. After stitching, rip off the paper.

Leather or leatherette fabrics can be used in conjunction with felt for the quilted and padded look seen in Figures 15–9 and 15–10. Figure 15–9 shows a padded and openwork armguard (decorative and used for strictly passive purposes). Figure 15–10 was Death's mask and headdress used in a production of *Blood Wedding*. This was made by the same process as the armguard but was not cut out into openwork. After this headdress was made, the entire piece was dipped in fiberglass resin for durability.

*Chain Mail* The most realistic looking chain mail is knitted with a stockinette stitch and used purl-side out. A simple chain crochet stitch also works very well. The texture is achieved by the size of the cord, string, or yarn and the size of the knitting needles or crochet hook. Although the results look most like the real thing, it is indeed a time consuming process. An example is shown in Figure 15–11.

Many knit fabrics available today can save hours of time. Once again, your choice is dictated by the degree of "readability" you desire. A new yarn called cloisonné is also available in metallic gold and silver.

Once again, with the cooperation of a friendly physician or medical supply house, there is an alternate method for constructing chain mail. That is a product called surgiflex (Fig. 15–12), a tubular stretch knit that is put on top of pliable bandages to hold them in place. I discovered this when I developed a severe allergy to adhesive tape while healing from a leg injury. Surgiflex comes for specific stretchable widths—finger, arm, leg, and torso. Torso is the best for our purposes as it will conform to all parts. It can be cut and will not ravel. It does have one disadvantage, however, and that is its white color. It must be sprayed first with a dark tone and then with a metallic. It also must be sprayed stretched, either on the actor or on a form.

Figures 15–13 and 15–14 show a third alternative. This is a metallic net casement cloth available by the yard from window and advertising supply houses. It can be used in conjunction with or under fabric, as demonstrated in Figure 15–13, or by itself as in Figure 15–14. Figure 15–14 is a section of a pair of "chain mail" brais to be worn over tights.

**Figure 15–11.** *Crocheted "Chain Mail"*

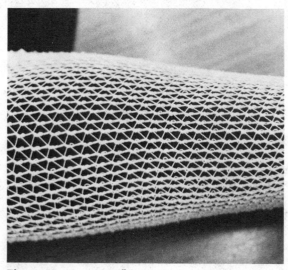

**Figure 15–12.** *Surgiflex*

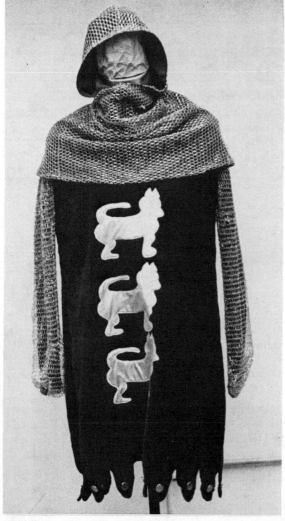

**Figure 15–13.** *Metallic Net Casement Cloth used in Conjunction with Other Fabric*

**Figure 15–14.** *Metallic Net Casement Cloth used by Itself*

### Painting Techniques for Armor

Often, whether constructing hard pieces of armor or soft pieces, a painted finish is required. The techniques employed depend upon the material used. If the material is light naturally, then a dark matte coat should be used before the metallic paint or powder is used. The metallic paint should be used sparingly, allowing the darker texture to come through. Greens work very well as an undercoat to bronzes. Browns work well under copper and gold. Black works best under silver, and just a dash of silver over black gives a good iron look. For knitted or crocheted chain mail, a dark yarn or string is preferred. A ship's chandler store can always supply you with either dark green or black net cording.

If you are using cloisonné yarn or metal pieces, you may wish to age them. A light dusting of the hues mentioned above works very well. A clear matte finish acrylic spray will give to metal a nice dull luster that may be the right color but too reflective. Fiberglass resin also dulls the metal somewhat. FEV, a material to be discussed in Chapter 19, can be used as a metallic paint.

### Plated Armor

Plated armor is composed of many small hard metal pieces linked together. It began as "fishscale" armor and goes back to early Babylonian times. It can be made from any number of materials. The pop tops from beer and soft drink cans are easily linked together, as illustrated in Figure 15–15. Interlinked grommets that have been snipped open, linked, and then glued shut with a clear jeweler's glue as illustrated in Figure 15–16, can also be used.

Please look once again at Figures 15–6 and 15–7. The square disks on the edge of the shield in Figure 15–6 and the round disk's studding in Figure 15–7 were bought already linked as plate. Disks like this could be cut of any number of materials and linked together. All that is needed is the material and a little imagination. Hard pieces that need plates added to them should be molded and then riveted together as actual armor was riveted.

In emergencies we often wish for a knight in shining armor. You may never need one, but you will at least be adequately prepared to produce one on demand.

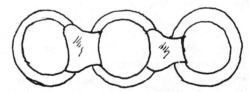

**Figure 15–15.** *Chain Mail from Linked Pop-Tops*

**Figure 15–16.** *Chain Mail from Linked Grommets*

# 16

# Construction of Masks

The mask is such an integral part of theater that its very symbols are the masks of comedy and tragedy. In our culture, masks date from the ancient Greeks. In Oriental cultures masks are just as important a tradition. Since the invention of theatrical makeup, the mask plays less of a part in both cultures. Yet in makeup terms the face is often called "the masque."

### The Philosophy of the Mask

The philosophy of the mask changes a bit from period to period. The Greeks used it to symbolize a specific emotion, which was heightened to carry to the last row of the amphitheater. The Greeks' masks were of various materials—wood, ceramic, clay— and some religious and death masks were gold. In this latter category the mask of Agamemnon comes to mind.

Shakespeare made use of masks over and over; *Romeo and Juliet's* masked ball, *Love's Labours Lost's* romp in the forest, etc. Some historians believe that *The Tempest* was written and first performed as a court masque for James I. Here the word seems to change not only its spelling, but its intention, as well. These were stories or allegories of magical and/or mystical themes performed by the court itself wearing masks to represent those themes. As theater became more commonly popular, this type of masque gradually declined into the masquerade, which was merely a ball at which masks were worn.

The commedia dell'arte used the mask as character identification, so that regardless of the name given a particular character, the audience knew that underneath, it was really a Harlequin or Pantalone or Columbina. Then along came Moliere in France and Goldoni in Italy, who incorporated these stereotypical characters into their plays, but freed them from their masks.

It is interesting to note that as the actor on stage became free of this device, the public began to adopt the mask as part of its everyday apparel. Both women and men of 17th century France and 18th century Italy (particularly Venice) adopted the wearing of black masks when abroad after dark. Was it at this time that the wearing of masks began to take on its sinister qualities, the philosophy being that its wearer had something to hide?

In the musical *The Fantasticks* during the song "Round and Round," there is a recitative between El Gallo and Louisa. Louisa says, "That man! Look out, he's burning! My God, he's on fire!" El Gallo says, "Just put up the mask and its pretty." Louisa, looking through her mask says, "Oh, isn't he beautiful! He's all sorts of orange, red-orange. That's one of my favorite colors."[1]

This may be a reverse perspective but the idea certainly seems to express our modern philosophy that the mask has become a sort of blinder to the world's great problems. The mask no longer keeps the viewer hidden from the world. It keeps the world out. Whatever its philosophy, the mask is formally entrenched into the theatrical tradition.

### Types of Masks

There are essentially five types of masks. Figure 16–1 shows three masks of the commedia delle'arte. Both El Capitano to the left and Pantalone (with beard) at right are full-face masks. The Harlequin mask in the center is known as a three-quarter mask because it covers the eye area and nose. A mask that covers only the eye area is called a half-mask. Figure 16–2 shows a commercially made rubber molded mask that covers the entire head. This could also be

[1]Tom Jones and Harvey Schmidt, *The Fantasticks* (U.S.A.: Metro-Goldwyn-Mayer n.d.).

**Figure 16–1.** *Three Masks of the Commedia dell'arte—Full-Face (left and right) and Three-Quarter (center)*

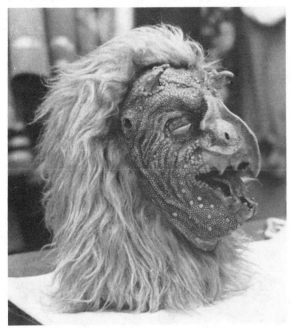

**Figure 16–2.** *Full Head Mask*

were said to have been frequently sculpted out of ceramic clay, then fired and glazed or painted. This takes one special piece of equipment, a kiln. At universities the art department might have a kiln. In other situations, finding a kiln may prove impossible. A good substitute might be Celluclay.

Celluclay is processed paper pulp and glue to which you merely add water and knead to the desired clay-like consistency; you can then sculpt with it. After it is completely dried, it can be sanded for smoothness, then painted and shellacked or spray sealed (inside and out). It is a form of papier maché.

Our Commedia masks in Figure 16–1 were made of leather as a class project by a student named Dikran Hazirjan. Florida Atlantic University and I are indebted to him for his excellent research and craftmanship. Procedural steps were as follows:

1. *He first carved balsa wood positives.*
2. *He sealed these wood positives with several coats of varnish.*
3. *He soaked his leather until it became pliable and stretched it over the positives, nailing the edges down. El Capitano's was done in two pieces vertically divided from forehead, through nose to chin.*
4. *After the leather had completely dried, he trimmed away the excesses, and with a hand sewing leather needle and buttonhole twist (or carpet) thread, he sewed the two halves of El Capitano's face together. He sliced the inside chin and tuck-stitched it together again, which raised it to its present pugnacious tilt. He also sewed on Pantalone's nose and beard.*

classified as an animal head. In Fig. 16–3 we see the "lollipop" mask. These are masks on a stick and are merely held to the face and not tied to it. The full face mask to the left has the stick in the center position. The half mask to the right has the stick on the side.

Masks can be made of almost anything. We have already spoken of the ancient Greeks' masks. Two such masks are illustrated in Figure 16–4. These

**Figure 16–3**  *Lollipop Masks*

GREEK (FROM A 6TH CENTURY VASE)

ETRUSCAN - 5TH CENTURY GOLD WORK

**Figure 16–4.**  *Some Ancient Masks—Greek and Etruscan*

5. *Next he stained the leather the colors needed— a black for Harlequin, a reddish color for Pantalone. El Capitano is natural leather.*
6. *He added leather thongs for ties to the sides. He also added Pantalone's beard, which is lambswool cut to fit the chin. The fur side is out. The leather is next to the actor's skin.*

### Masks Adapted from Available Forms

Many times masks can be adapted from readily available forms; the Halloween half masks of cheap

satin make a good base. Costume rental agencies carry these masks all year round and sell them for a very nominal price. The half mask in Figure 16–3 was just such an adaptation. It was merely painted with glue, white felt was stretched over it, and the edges were clipped and glued to the inside and decorated with ribbons and flowers. That particular half mask is called a cat's eye, as opposed to the standard half mask. These two variations are illustrated in Figure 16–5.

The full-face mask in Figure 16–3 was made of buckram and Acta covered with a copper colored "eyelash" fabric on the outside, and lined in muslin

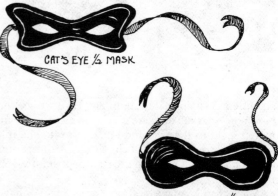

CAT'S EYE ½ MASK

REGULAR HALLOWEEN ½ MASK

**Figure 16–5.**  *Variations of the Half-Mask*

on the inside because "eyelash" fabric scratches and could be dangerous near the eyes. This was then trimmed in gold braid, black feathers, lace, rhinestones, and pearls. Most of the techniques used in jewelry making can also be used here. This lollipop mask, as well as the mask shown in Figure 16–6, were used in the Florida Atlantic University production of *Romeo and Juliet*.

The mask in Figure 16–6 was also done on a buckram and Acta base, but the pieces added to it were wired, stuffed, and quilted, so that they could be shaped and bent as desired. This was made out of black and green velvet, silver lamé, red felt, rhinestones, and gold braids. The wires were inserted into the interior of various leaf-like appendages and quilted into place.

## Molded Masks

The commercial mask in Figure 16–2 is a latex creation, made by pouring latex into a plaster negative mold. Since we have talked about two types of molds, a positive and a negative, perhaps we should define them and describe their uses.

### The Positive Mold

A positive mold looks like the finished product. It can be made of balsa wood, as described in the leather mask making process, in which case it would have to be carved. It can be made of clay, either ceramic (and fired), or plasticine. It can also be cast in plaster of paris. From this positive either

**Figure 16–6.** *Mask used in* Romeo and Juliet

IT IS NECESSARY TO USE 2 POSITIVES, ONE INSIDE THE OTHER TO MAKE A PLASTER NEGATIVE WHICH IS MOST LIKELY IN SECTIONS AND BANDED TOGETHER FOR POURING

THE SAME PROCESS IS USED TO MAKE PLASTER MOLDS FOR POURING CERAMIC AND PORCELAIN SLIP

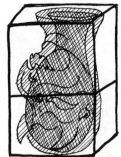

**Figure 16–7.** *The Casting of a Poured Latex Mold*

another positive can be made by stretching something over it (leather, Acta, or felt), or it can be used to make a negative mold.

### The Negative Mold

The negative mold is the positive turned inside out, so to speak. For the commercial head mask a clay positive was cast into plaster, making a negative. Then the latex was poured into the negative mold. This allows for mass production of the same thing. This process is illustrated in Figure 16–7.

### Casting the Actor's Face

Regardless of the type of mask, it must fit the actor's face. If possible, a positive cast of that face can be a great help. Once you have that, it can be built upon, the contours can be changed by the addition of plasticine clay, and then a moulage (a latex liquefied by heat) mask can be painted on top to get another positive from it. This technique is illustrated in Figure 16–8 and is used by the actor frequently as part of his makeup craft. Various methods of doing this are described by Richard Corson in his book, *Stage Makeup* and by Michael Westmore in *Theatrical Makeup Techniques for Stage and Screen*.

Another method of making masks is the Alginate method. (Figures 16–9 through 16–12 show this process.) Alginate, sometimes called Gelltrate, is the product dentists use to make dental impressions. It is cold to the touch and is usually mint-flavored.

Michael Westmore describes an Alginate process in which the Alginate is applied to the face and then held by plaster bandages. This process takes a much longer time than the one below and is far more uncomfortable. The process below has the actor's face covered for only forty-five seconds and so might be

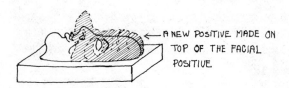

← A NEW POSITIVE MADE ON TOP OF THE FACIAL POSITIVE.

NOTE: IF THE SECOND BUILD UP IS PROPERLY GREASED WITH PETROLEUM JELLY A NEW ALGINATE NEGATIVE CAN BE MADE OR A NEW PLASTER NEGATIVE TO BE USED AS PART OF THE LATEX PROCESS

**Figure 16–8.** *Use of the Positive Facial Cast in Mask Making*

**Figure 16–9.** *Preparing Box for Alginate Method*

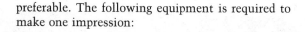

preferable. The following equipment is required to make one impression:

1. A full can (24 oz.) of Alginate
2. At least 6 ice cubes
3. A large plastic bucket
4. A wooden stirer (a kitchen spoon or painter's stick)
5. A racer's bathing cap
6. Petroleum jelly
7. A roll of tin foil
8. A box big enough for the head to fit into, with a semicircle cut out of one edge for the neck
9. Water
10. 5 lbs. plaster of paris
11. A can or two of high gloss, clear acrylic sealer

Note: This is a messy process, so be sure to have the actor wear old clothing; something low necked is advisable.

1. *Preparation of Box (Fig. 16–9):* Cut out semi-circle for neck. Place face in it. If box is more than two inches longer than head, cut a piece of cardboard to shorten end. Cover the inside with tinfoil.
2. *Preparation of Face (Fig. 16–10):* Cover hair, ears and all hairline with bathing cap. Grease edge of cap, face, and under chin with plenty of petroleum jelly. Put a little plug of facial tissue in each nostril, but not enough to distort the shape.
3. *Preparation of Alginate:* Mix one can of Alginate to 1⅓ cans of water, plus six or more ice cubes. The ice water retards the set-up time of the Alginate. Mix with a wooden spoon and get as smooth as possible. If two people can do it, one to pour slowly and the other to mix, it works better. This is mixed in the plastic bucket. Pour into foil lined box.
4. *Casting (Fig. 16–11):* Test the Alginate before the actor puts his face in; it should be just on the

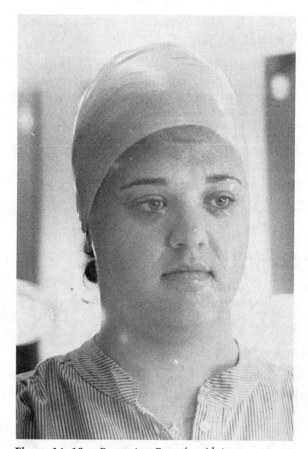

**Figure 16–10.** *Preparing Face for Alginate*

verge of setting, a little springy, but still squashable. Have actor sit and place his head in box for the minimum of forty-five seconds. (Any person should be able to hold their breath that long.) Caution him to keep his face in an expression of repose. He should remove his head in a slow, fluid motion, first wiggling his facial muscles to be released from the Alginate (Fig. 16–12).

**Figure 16–11.** *Casting for Alginate Method*

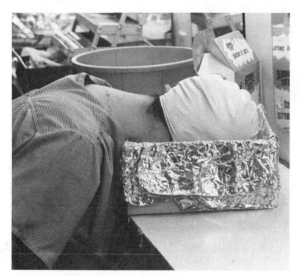

**Figure 16–12.** *Making Facial Impression in Alginate*

**Figure 16–13.** *Plaster "Positive"*

5. *Preparation of Plaster of Paris: Clean out all the Alginate from the plastic bucket. Dry. Put in powdered plaster of paris and add water until it is of a thick pourable consistency, like that of a thick milkshake. Pour into alginate negative. Let set for approximately three to seven days. If it is left in a hot, dry room it will take three days. In air conditioning it usually takes five.*

6. *Unmolding: Invert and unmold (Fig. 16–13). Dry completely. Any little air holes may be either sanded away or filled in with a little plaster paste.*

7. *Sealing: For convenience, use an acrylic high gloss sealer that may be sprayed on. It would take two or three coats. Let each coat completely dry before doing the next.*

The advantage of this method is its speed; the actor does not have his head in the dark very long and the molds are extremely accurate. This same process can also be used for jewelry making.

Now that you have the Alginate cast, a mask can be made by papier maché right on top. This is essentially the same process described in Chapter 17. Celluclay can be used; so can stretched felt, Acta, celastic, or moulage.

### Moulage

Moulage is a *heated* rubber substance that can be painted onto a positive form as thin or as thickly as needed. Moulage takes greasepaint and acrylic paints very well. It does not react well to oil-base paints. The papier maché will take any paint, as will celastic, Celluclay, or Acta.

Masks are often worn in conjunction with elaborate headdresses. Many mask construction techniques are used for headdresses as well, but for construction they must be treated like hats. For this, consult Chapter 12.

# 17

# The Construction of Animal Heads

Every costume shop has been asked at one time or another if it could loan or rent out an Easter Bunny, Turkey, Great Pumpkin, Big Bird, and so forth. People portrayed animals in connection with religious rights from ancient times, including the jackal-headed priests of Egypt and the minotaur dancers of Crete.

### The Portrayal of Animals

Aristophanes wrote plays about frogs and birds. Shakespeare turned Bottom into an ass. Faust called up all manner of creatures from the underworld, and both Dorothy and Androcles had lions for friends. Thornton Wilder made use of a dinosaur and mammoth. James Thurber saw unicorns in his garden. The animal characterization is no stranger to dramaturgy.

Sooner or later every costume designer will have to know how to build an animal costume, and the hardest part will undoubtedly be the head. The rest of the animal will have to conform somewhat to human characteristics (two arms, two legs, and a torso), or at least half a body. In the musical *Gypsy* the character Louise (Gypsy as a child) portrays the back half of a cow in a vaudeville routine. In the musical *Camelot* the opening scene was resplendent with actors, who wore their own horses. Two of the most fascinating examples in recent dramaturgy are the six actors playing horses in *Equus*, and the lizards in Albee's *Seascape*.

The foregoing does not even take into consideration mascots for various high schools and colleges, promotional animals, parades, ice shows, etc.

### The Animal Head—Cousin to the Mask

Animal heads, like their cousin the mask, can be made from stiffened felt, leather, cloth, or papier

maché. They can be poured of latex or rubber. The pouring process is exactly the same as that described for the latex mask in Chapter 16.

*The Papier Maché Method of Construction*

The papier maché method, in conjunction with fabric or felt, seems to have the greatest flexibility during the construction process, and, made correctly, is the most durable for its weight. It is not as light as the latex or rubber head, but it does not tear or rot apart as easily. It is certainly not as heavy as leather and if properly ventilated is not as hot as either of the others. It can be painted and sealed, have fabric glued to it, and can be adjusted to workable parts. Figures 17–1 through 17–8 show the construction of the head of a mascot for Atlantic High School of Delray Beach, Florida. It is a green "Seahawk".

*Materials Needed*   Figure 17–1 shows the materials needed:

1. *Newspaper cut in 1½" to 2" wide strips.*
2. *Florist wire*
3. *Electrician's wire*
4. *Hot glue gun*
5. *Chicken wire*
6. *Wire cutters (tin snips may be substituted)*
7. *Masking tape ½" wide*
8. *White glue (Elmer's or Sobo)*
9. *Bucket*
10. *Nylon screening*
11. *Large-eyed sharp sewing needle. Embroidery needles are useful as is heavy duty thread if something needs to be attached by stitching.*
12. *A blow hair dryer*

*Constructing the Frame*   Figure 17–2 shows a series of wire circles that have been made from the florist wire. The large ovals in the front center are

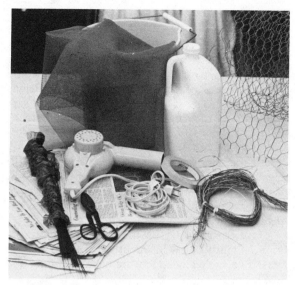

**Figure 17–1.** *Materials Needed for Constructing Animal Head*

**Figure 17–2.** *Florist Wire to be Used in Animal Head Construction*

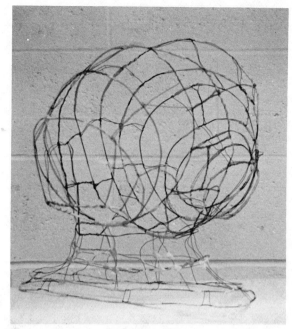

**Figure 17–3.** *Wire Assembled to Give the Head Its Shape*

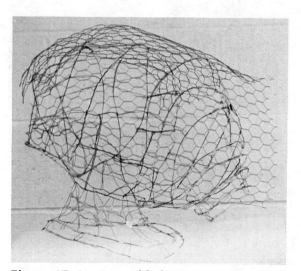

**Figure 17–4.** *Assembled Wire Covered with Chicken Wire*

for the shoulders. The larger circles are for the front and top of the head. The small circles (left) are for the back of the head, and the strangely shaped item in the center is the beak.

These circles must be wrapped in masking tape for added strength. Then they are wired together with more florist wire. The electrician's wire can effectively cross tie each junction. A dab of hot glue can also be used for this purpose. Since both the electrician's wire and hot glue leave bumps, a little more overlay with masking tape can smooth this a bit. In Figure 17–3 we see the assembled wire that gives the shape of the head.

This is then covered with chicken wire, which is snipped and bent to the desired shape and attached with either hot glue or electrician's wire. We can see this in Figure 17–4.

*External Shaping Additions* Now is the time to add external appendages, such as a beak. The performer needs to see out through the beak, so a piece

of nylon screening is inserted into the inside of the beak and is sewn around the edge with a large-eyed needle and heavy duty thread; this is then trimmed. The beak is then attached to the head (see Figures 17–5, 17–6).

*Viewing Holes* The nylon screening is now placed strategically for eyeholes through which the performer can see straight ahead. I once portrayed Nana the dog in a children's theater production of

**Figure 17–5.** *Beak Construction*

**Figure 17–6.** *Beak Attached to Head*

*Peter Pan* and can attest from firsthand experience that an actor must be able to see his feet and straight ahead in order to navigate properly. Side peepholes may also be necessary, depending upon the given situation.

*Hearing Holes* As with the helmet described in Chapter 15, talking inside one of these heads is like talking down a rain barrel. Hearing may also be impeded, in which case tiny holes for hearing may have to be considered. These can be allowed for at this stage, or may be drilled after the head is completed.

*Addition of Mouthpiece or Movable Parts* A megaphone-like instrument may also be built into the head. Figure 17–7 illustrates this process. If this device is used, it must be inserted at the point in which the wire frame is assembled. Once the chicken wire is attached, you cannot get your hands in to do the necessary work. The same principle applies to any moving parts like hinges or attachments. Their pulleys are of course attached after construction.

An ordinary kitchen funnel is generally sufficient. Larger varieties are available for larger heads. Correct placement of funnel depends on the size of the funnel needed and the actor's mouth area when inside the head.

Have the actor try on the frame and place the funnel slightly below his mouth. There should be at least two inches between the edge of funnel and lower lip.

*The Maché Layer* Figure 17–6 also shows the laying on of newspaper strips that have been immersed in a solution made of equal parts of white glue and water. These strips are laid a layer at a time. The first layer goes horizontally; the second layer is placed vertically; and the third layer is a series of diagonal crisscrosses, cutting out the screened places. One or two layers should then be placed on the inside. A hand-held blow hair dryer is a wonderful help. Dry each layer outside and inside, as pictured in Figure 17–8, until the whole head is covered (Figure 17–9).

*The Final Painting and Decoration* The head is then painted and any additional pieces may be added, such as the Seahawk's feathered cockscomb, which was soft cotton and very "flyable" when the Seahawk is leading a cheer. We see the finished head in Figure 17–10.

Figure 17–11 shows the Mammoth head from Florida Atlantic University's production of *The Skin of Our Teeth*. It had a topknot of hair made of silvery grey yarn, long false eyelashes (plastic, from a local magic shop), and a movable trunk that at the moment is looped over a tusk. The tusks were wrapped in the honey-colored plastic tape that movers use on packing crates. The trunk was made from a pink plastic "Slinky" (a spring toy that goes up and down stairs). The pink Slinky was encased in a muslin tube and attached to the head after the papier maché was applied. It was first glued in place and then reinforced by stitches of string just below the screen-viewing window between the eyes.

*Disguising the Viewing Hole* When painting with medium to dark colors, the nylon screen really disappears, as you can see in Figures 17–10 and 17–11. If the paint dries over a hole in the screening,

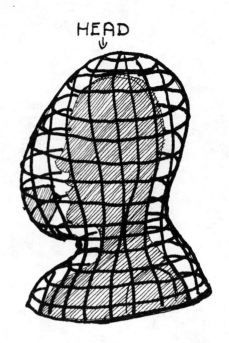

HEAD

CORRECT PLACEMENT OF FUNNEL
DEPENDS ON THE SIZE OF THE FUNNEL
NEEDED AND THE ACTOR'S MOUTH AREA
WHEN INSIDE THE HEAD.

PUNCH OUT 2 HOLES EQUIDISTANT AROUND FUNNEL FOR THE
HOLES # A PICTURED BELOW. DO THE SAME FOR # B.

THE FUNNEL IS ATTACHED TO THE HEAD
BY WIRING IT TO THE OUTER STRUCTURE
THROUGH HOLES A AND B.

FUNNEL

CUT HANDLE (IF THERE IS
ONE) AND NECK OFF
FUNNEL. MASKING
TAPE ANY RAW
METAL EDGES

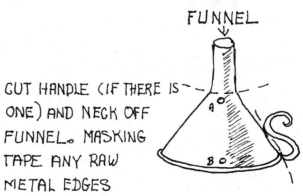

**Figure 17–7.** *Insertion of Megaphone-Like Device into Animal Head*

**Figure 17–8.** *Drying the Maché Layer*

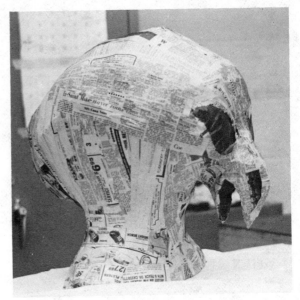

**Figure 17–9.** *Entire Head Covered with Maché*

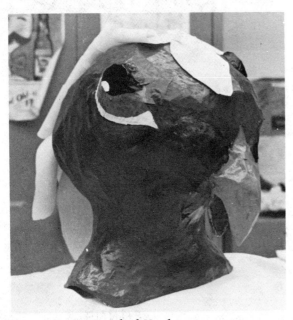

**Figure 17–10.** *Finished Head*

**Figure 17–11.** *Mammoth Head*

a pin prick will take care of it. If you dry your paint with the hair dryer, the air pressure automatically clears the holes. If white or pastel colors are used, the screen area tends to look dark. Simply cover it with a piece of white or pastel organza and hold the edges down with glue. The actor can see through the organza (but not through chiffon). Match the organza to the color of your head. It may be spray textured, but do not paint it a solid color.

The papier maché will take almost any paint. The nylon screening is not overly durable under too many coats of enamel. Various acrylic paints work well and if a glossy look is desired, spray with a gloss acrylic sealer.

*Sealing the Head* Always seal the inside of your head as well as the outside. The spray sealer is much quicker than varnish and dries faster. There is a reason for this. It prevents mildewing and it also prevents insects from feasting. Cockroaches are very fond of the milk and flour in the glue, and termites like the wood pulp in the paper.

*Sculptured Efffects* Three dimensional sculptured effects can be made from the papier maché pulp method (the Celluclay already described in Chapter 16) and applied to the strip covered head. Newspaper torn in small pieces and mulched with the glue and water solution will also work. Bread dough sculpture is another solution (see Chapter 14). Some manufacturers use a layer of muslin strips as the top crisscross layer. Papier maché strips can be curled on a pencil, dipped in glue, and placed on the head. When the pencil is slowly removed, you have a hanging curl. Hairdresser's plastic rollers can be used to create big banana curls. Yarn can be glued in sections and worked like a wig, or dipped and used stiff when dried. Pasta can be used as it is in jewelry making. The possibilities are endless.

### Alternative Construction Techniques

*Fabric*   One does not have to use papier maché. I have made the wire frame and instead of covering with chicken wire, I lashed it together with electrician's wire. Then I draped muslin over it, and using the same techniques described in Chapter 4, I draped a pattern for the ass's head (Fig. 17–12). The entire underjaw is screen, as well as a peephole center front. Muslin was used as a pattern to cut the fur fabric. I then constructed the muslin as the lining, which was sewn to the inside first, when I could still see what I was doing. The fur fabric exterior was then made by hand. It was lightweight and had a very realistic flexability to it.

The eyes were stuffed circles of painted sheet muslin; the eyelids, felt semicircles with stiffened and curled felt eyelashes; and the nostrils were semicircles of fur fabric lined in pink felt.

Muslin takes all kinds of paints and dyes and can be lit from the inside for some very eerie effects. Still, it is not as durable as papier maché and will not take the added weight of moving parts.

## Construction of Moving Parts

*Gravitational Pull*   The most commonly requested moving parts are closable eyes and openable

**Figure 17–12.**  *Ass's Head*

mouths. To achieve these, we put to use a very elementary principle of physics, gravitational pull.

When a puppeteer wishes to walk the puppet, he or she raises the leg with a string. It falls by itself while the puppeteer raises the other leg. Therefore, to use this principle you must decide the look you wish your animal to have 85 percent of the time, because it will be counterbalanced for the exception. In other words, if you wish an eye to wink, it will be open for 85 percent and closed for 15 percent. If you want your crocodile to snap at Captain Hook, his mouth will be closed the 85 percent and open only 15 percent. The next consideration is that the performer must be in complete control of these movements. If not, both of you may indeed have the tiger by the tail.

*Winking Eyes*   When working with the eyes, the simplest solution is to have both eyes close simultaneously. This is done by using two rolling balls attached by a cord which is worked by an elastic string that goes to a pad under the performer's chin. When his mouth is closed, the eyes are open. When he drops his jaw, the eyes are closed. The winking effect is achieved by merely turning the head a three-quarter profile to the audience, who will see only one eye shut. This method is illustrated in Figure 17–13.

The eyeball must rotate on a strong wire axis (coat hanger wire) which is attached to the structure while still in its chicken wire stage. The pulley strings are nylon fishing filament for the part that goes to the center bottom of the pupil and elastic thread for the half that is inside the head. These are attached by hook and eye to the chinstrap. This allows the actor to put the headstrap on before putting on the animal head. When using this method, be sure that the animal head neck is large enough for the actor to get his hand up to hook lines to the chinstrap. This method works very well for extravaganzas (mascots, ice shows, circuses). However, if the performer must talk, it obviously is not the best choice, because his eyes would be blinking with every word.

Figure 17–14 shows a hand-controlled method. The easiest way is to have both eyes in synchronization and controlled by one hand. It is possible to have each hand control one eye at a time. It is also possible to have one hand control the eyes and the other control the mouth. The controlling strings go inside the neck of the lower costume, down the arms to plastic rings, which slip around a finger. When the hand is in a fist position, the eyes are closed (or the mouth open).

*Talking Mouths*   Figure 17–15 shows the hinged mouth and its string. This string is often taken under the chin, through a tiny hole in the neck, and

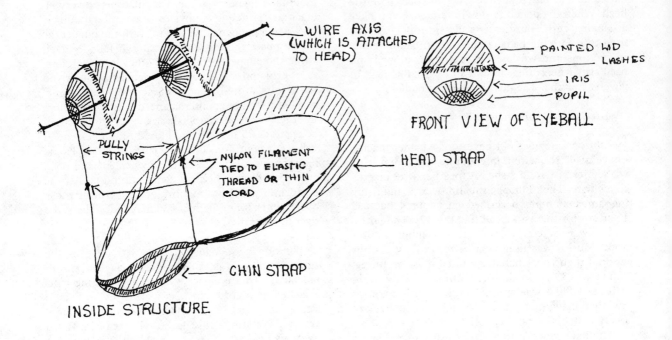

WIRE AXIS (WHICH IS ATTACHED TO HEAD)

PAINTED LID
LASHES
IRIS
PUPIL

FRONT VIEW OF EYEBALL

PULLY STRINGS

NYLON FILAMENT TIED TO ELASTIC THREAD OR THIN CORD

HEAD STRAP

CHIN STRAP

INSIDE STRUCTURE

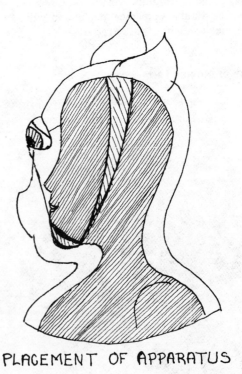

PLACEMENT OF APPARATUS

**Figure 17–13.**   *The Chinstrap Method of Movable Eyes*

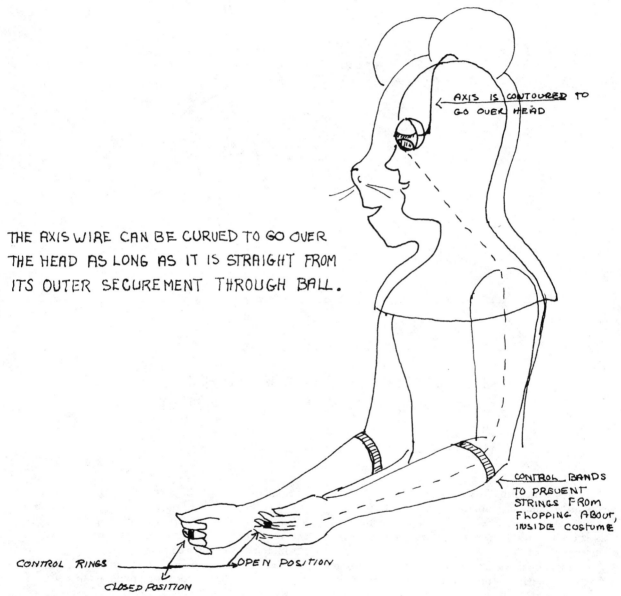

AXIS IS CONTOURED TO
GO OVER HEAD

THE AXIS WIRE CAN BE CURVED TO GO OVER
THE HEAD AS LONG AS IT IS STRAIGHT FROM
ITS OUTER SECUREMENT THROUGH BALL.

CONTROL BANDS
TO PREVENT
STRINGS FROM
FLOPPING ABOUT,
INSIDE COSTUME

CONTROL RINGS

OPEN POSITION

CLOSED POSITION

**Figure 17–14.** *Hand-Controlled Eyes*

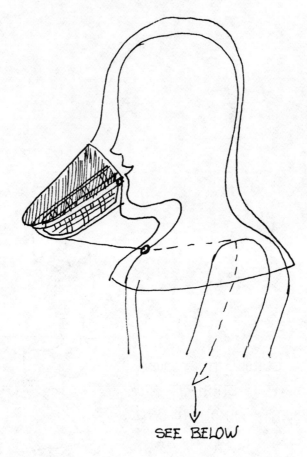

SEE BELOW

THIS IS CONTROLLED BY ONE HAND BUT IN THE
SAME MANNER AS ILLUSTRATED IN FIGURE
17-14

**Figure 17–15.** *A Movable Mouth (Lower Jaw Hinge)*

then down the arm. Any visible portion of string should be made of nylon (clear) fishing line. Once this is inside, it can be attached to an elastic cord as the cut end of the fishing line is often very scratchy.

Often animal costumes have gloves or mittens that serve as paws or hooves, etc. If this is the case, the ring on the elastic cord must go on the finger before the paw. If the actor's hand is used, elastic cord will take either liquid or grease makeup. Paint the plastic ring with acrylics. Acrylic paint may also be used on the elastic cord if it is necessary to have it match a particular costume.

This same clear fishing line can be used to control any number of costume problems, to say nothing of tails and wings, etc.

# 18

# Construction of Costume Props

A costume prop is any item that is not actually worn but carried by the actor or actress. Props include such diverse items as fans, purses, muffs, canes, watches, parasols and umbrellas, eyeglasses, gloves, and variously assorted boxes for patches, snuff, etc. Artificial flowers and fruit are also frequently used in dresses and millinery, as well as being carried in nosegays or corsages.

Whenever possible, buy these items. In the long run it is considerably less aggravating. But sometimes you cannot find enough, or just the right thing, and then you are forced into construction or reconstruction.

### Fans

Fans can be divided into two basic types, folding and non-folding. Folding fans need some form of hinged frame. The most common is the type that spreads out like the fingers of the human hand. The other radiates out from a central point like those Japanese paper wheels one gets in fancy rum drinks at Polynesian restaurants. Both of these are illustrated in Figure 18–1.

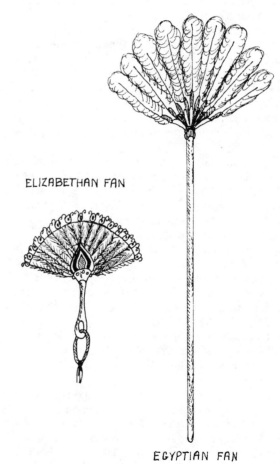

ELIZABETHAN FAN

EGYPTIAN FAN

**Figure 18–2.** *Lollipop Fans*

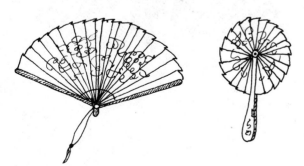

**Figure 18–1.** *Two Types of Folding Fans*

The second type of fan is the lollipop fan. This is stationary in size and shape and is held by some means of a handle centrally placed. Palm frond fans are an example of a lollipop fan. So are the Elizabethan and Egyptian fans illustrated in Figure 18–2.

*Repairing Folding Fans* Folding fans are extremely difficult to make from scratch because the folding handle is usually delicate and hard to carve. They are not hard to enlarge or repair, however.

The materials needed depend upon the repair needed. If all parts of the fan are in working order but the hinge pin is missing, a small pearl-headed straight pin will do. Pearl- or glass-headed pins are usually available in craft shops or fabric stores. You will also need a loose pearl or glass bead of equal size to the one on the pin.

Stack up the handle and intermediate spokes and temporarily tie them together. Insert the pin through the holes and snip off the pointed end about one-eight-inch beyond the depth of the folded handle. Put a drop of jewelers glue on the snipped end and insert onto the other the pearl or glass bead. You can knot a delicate cord at each side between the pearl and handle for a wrist hanger. Now untie the ties. Your fan should work.

If your handle is perfectly good but the face is shot, you must replace it. To obtain a pattern, pin the old face flat down onto paper or muslin and trace it. To make absolutely sure your spokes will be spaced evenly, trace their positions on a piece of brown paper before the old face is removed. This is used to align the spokes on the back side of the new face. Now carefully remove the old face. Cut a new face and glue it on.

The material for the new face may be paper or silk or lace. If you wish to decorate the face, do so. Then lightly size the fabric with a little spray starch and, using a press cloth, iron the fabric. If paper is used this is not necessary. (Have you ever tried rice paper? It's lovely and delicate.)

Now carefully fold and tie shut. Steam lightly and let dry for at least 24 hours. If you have at your disposal one of those tiny shoed, long handled travel irons, you can press each fold edge and skip the steam and drying process and you will achieve a greatly more flexible fold.

To enlarge the fan, you must replace the spokes and cut a proportionately bigger face. Never throw away a fan handle or spokes!

*Constructing Lollipop Fans* To construct the lollipop fan, you need a dowel rod and a fan-shaped wedge. The top of the dowel rod is slit and the wedge is inserted and glued into it. The wedge is then decorated in any number of ways. This is briefly illustrated in Figure 18–3.

*Repairing Feather Fans* Feather fans are somehow very theatrical, even when not used in burlesque. The feathers are usually glued to short spokes, leaving the feather shaft as an extension. These are then tied together with some form of cording. If this cording is broken, attach a thread to the

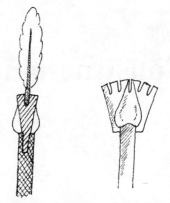

CROSS SECTION AND FRONT VIEW

**Figure 18–3.** *Constructing Lollipop Fans*

broken spot and with a fine crochet hook chain the thread to the next spoke or spikes. At each spoke encircle and connect the chain.

*Repairing Carved Fans* The Orientals make several varieties of carved folding fans as illustrated in Figure 18–4. These spokes are connected by two series of flat cording. Soutache braid makes an excellent substitute. Knot one end. Weave it through the opening and knot the other end. To ensure doing it correctly, take out the old ribbon, one spoke at a time, and run in the new the same way.

These are often made of ivory or cinnabar and might be considered too valuable for stage use. There are many attractive plastic and camphor wood copies, however.

## Purses

Purses have also been called pouches, reticules, and in today's vernacular handbags or simply bags. They

**Figure 18–4.** *Carved Fan Connected by Ribbons*

can be made of all sorts of material—wood, leather, canvas, needlecraft, and macrame. Almost any type of fabric is used. They come in any shape (square, sack, round, etc.) and size from the ridiculous to the sublime. In the following I shall attempt to explain some of the basic shapes most often required by the costume designer. They are the simple sack, the reticule, the clutch purse, and the box purse.

*The Simple Sack*   The simple sack is illustrated in Figure 18–5. The accompanying diagram is not a scaled pattern. Fold your fabric along line D so that the "right" sides meet and you are looking at the "wrong" side. You must stitch side seams going from D to C and then from B to A, leaving the space from C to B open.

Now fold the fabric along line B and stitch it to line C. Make another row of stitching five-eighths of an inch above line C for a channel. Feed two drawstrings going in opposite directions, one starting at each of the side openings.

*The Reticule*   There are two types of reticules, the round, "pouch" bottomed one and the sack variety that is attached to a petal, tortoise shell, or wooden frame. Figure 18–6 illustrates the round bottom one. Cut the circle to your desired circumference. The length of the upper piece must equal this circumference, plus 1½" for seam allowance. Sew up the seam of the upper section going from D to C

and from B to A, leaving the sp                B free.

At this time you must make                distantly centered from the sear                lines C and B. Now you must fo                B and sew line A to line C. Make a channel as you did for the sack purse. The next step is to sew the upper section to the bottom circle. Lastly, feed in your two draw strings. (By leaving a small opening on your seam between B and C, you will have your second opening for your second string.)

*Framed Sack Reticule*   The frame of a reticule is only its top structure, which provides a sturdy base for a chain hanger and a hinged snap opening. This usually has either links or small holes in it, so that a sack can be attached. Figure 18–7 illustrates one such example with a scaled pattern. This was taken from a chatelaine purse dated 1847 on its sterling silver frame.

These frames can be bought at most needlecraft stores. They are often found in antique shops, and at flea markets, garage sales, and Aunt Minnie's attic. You must have your frame in order to properly gauge the size of your sack.

*The Clutch Bag*   The clutch bag is the easiest of all types of purses to make (see Fig. 18–8). Cut the rectangle out of an exterior and a lining fabric. Bag them flat and press for a smooth edge. If you are

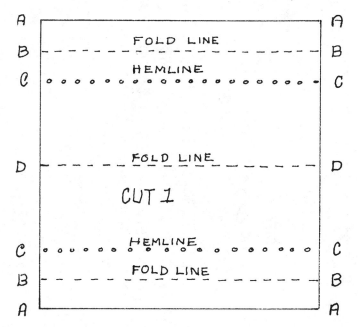

SCALE ⅛" = 1"

**Figure 18–5.**   *Illustration and Scaled Pattern for a Simple Sack Purse*

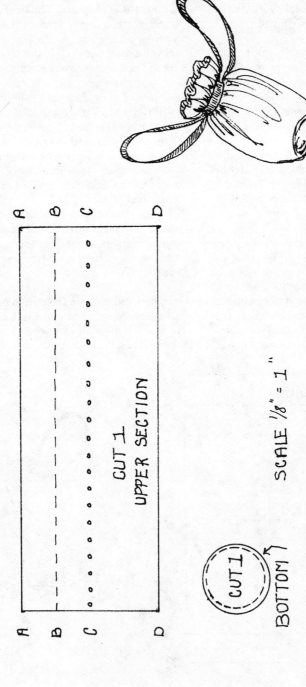

A
B
C
D

CUT 1
UPPER SECTION

A
B
C
D

CUT 1
BOTTOM

SCALE ⅛" = 1"

NOTE: AN ALTERNATIVE METHOD FOR CREATING A CHANNEL
IS TO SEW A PIECE OF RIBBON, 1" WIDE, TO THE
EXTERIOR THROUGH WHICH DRAWSTRINGS MAY BE RUN.

**Figure 18–6.** *Illustration and Scaled Pattern for Drawstring Reticule*

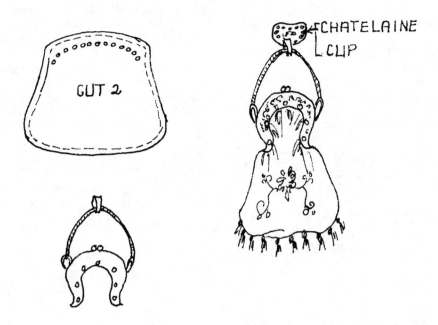

SCALE ⅛" = 1"

NOTE: THE CLIP AT THE TOP OF THE CHAIN WAS FOR ATTACHMENT TO A BELT

**Figure 18–7.** *Illustration and Scaled Pattern for a Victorian Reticule*

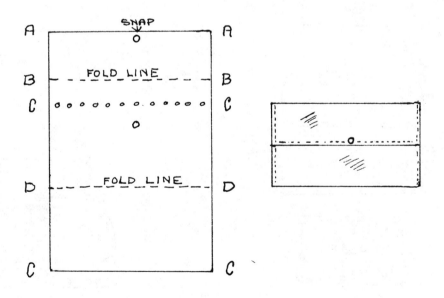

SCALE ⅛" = 1"

**Figure 18–8.** *Illustration and Scaled Pattern for a Clutch Purse*

using leather you can pound the edges. Now fold on line C so that D is about one inch below line B. Seam the sides. Fold at line C and fasten with a center closure, a snap, a gripper, or a loop and toggle.

*The Box Purse* There are two types of box purses—one with two separate side pieces, but the main body of the purse is all in one piece as in Figure 18–9, and those with a boxed bottom as illustrated in Figure 18–10. The sewing techniques are the same as those previously discussed.

## Muffs

Muffs occasionally have inner zipper compartments that act as a purse, but their intended purpose was as a hand warmer. More often than not, these were made of fur. (You will find techniques in sewing fur in Chapter 23.) The muff is nothing more than two rectangles of fabric, each sewn into a cylinder, and placed one inside the other. An interliner of stuffing is added for extra warmth. This is illustrated in Figure 18–11. If you wish a zipper compartment in

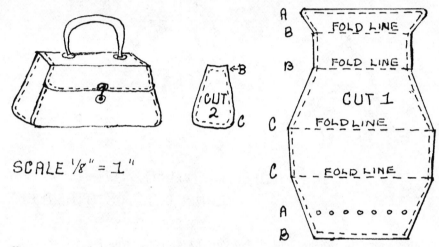

**Figure 18–9.** *Illustration and Pattern for a Box Purse in One Basic Piece*

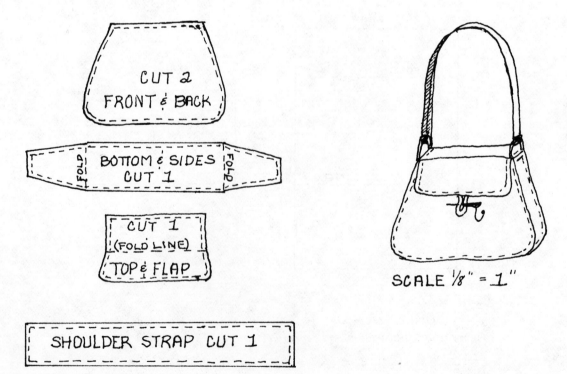

**Figure 18–10.** *Illustration and Pattern for a Five-Piece Purse*

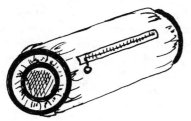

**Figure 18–11.** *A Muff with a Zipper Pocket*

either the interior or exterior, it must be made before the rectangle becomes a cylinder. It is usually constructed like a pocket in any dress.

### Canes and Walking Sticks

The difference between a cane and a walking stick is in the length. Along with these come an assortment of oddities such as shepherdess crooks, archbishops crosiers, and Tiny Tim's crutch.

In Volume I, Chapter 11, I talked about finding a French porcelain faucet knob and using it as a cane handle. Doorknobs make good tops; so do handles from broken umbrella frames and other broken canes. The important thing to remember is to find or make the top first and then select the proper sized dowel rod to fit it. Any number of styrofoam balls

can be attached to a dowel, covered in papier maché strips or plaster bandages, and then sanded smooth and painted.

### Crooks and Crosiers

Shepherdess crooks are a little more difficult to make. The easiest way is to use a simple wooden cane and add onto the bottom with a piece of dowelling. The crosier is an ornamental crook. Start with the crook and using jewelry techniques add the ornamentation.

### Watches

The best thing to do about watches is to keep a supply of non-working watches of all types on hand. They should include pocket watches, wrist watches, and the ladies' Victorian watches that were worn either on a chain around the neck or on a pin. Fake pocket watches can be built from a round piece of balsa wood, a paper front appropriately painted, a washer the same circumference as the wooden round, and a small screw eye. This is illustrated in Figure 18–12.

If you have a fairly large proscenium house in which there is some distance between the audience

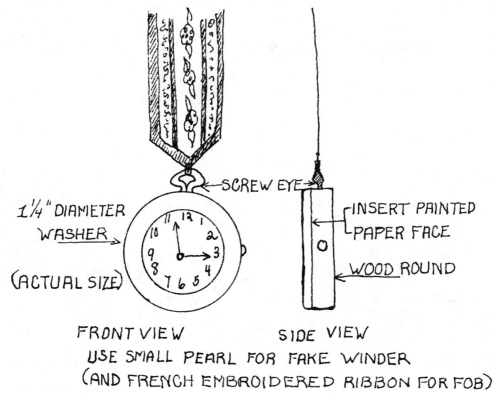

**Figure 18–12.** *How to Fake a Watch and Fob*

and the performers, other fakery is possible. I have found that from a distance lockets often look like watches and can be attached to pins or fobs. They have the advantage of opening. If the performer does not have to open the watch but merely glance at it, any number of disks can be used.

The watch fob can be made of ribbon or fabric. If a metal mesh is desired, use fine aluminum screening and cover the raw edges in masking tape. A little gold (or silver) paint will take care of it. (For a little more "how to" information consult "The Buckram and Braid Method" of jewelry construction, Chapter 14.)

### Parasols and Umbrellas

How like the English language to mix up its root syntax for essentially the same item. "Parasol" is a direct stealing of a French noun which literally means "for the sun." The French, in their infinite wisdom, call the same item used for the rain a parapluie. Practitioners of the English language go to an obscure German root for umbrellas. Even the Pennsylvania Dutch, whose literal anglicization from German is delightfully quaint, call an umbrella a "bumbershoot." However you call it, and whatever its purpose, its construction is the same.

Oriental paintings prove that parasols were used in ancient China. They were also known to the classic Romans, but they were built in a stationary outstretched manner. We will never know exactly who invented the collapsible variety, but whoever it was should be blessed. I once tried to build a workable umbrella frame. It was a total failure, and a great waste of precious time. Therefore, my advice is never throw away any frame in workable condition.

Handles can be changed, and the shaft and frame spray painted a new color. Tops can be remade.

The best pattern for a new top is one section of the old top. If it is in shreds, iron it onto some fusible interfacing to hold it together long enough to cut your muslin pattern piece. This is best sewn on the "baby lock" machine.

Here is a reminder about spraying the frame another color. Of course you would spray it when opened. Just make sure *it is thoroughly dry* before closing it.

### Eyeglasses

Eyeglasses can be easily and cheaply bought so you need not bother with construction. Period glasses, granny, "Ben Franklins," lorgnettes, or monocles illustrated in Figure 18–13 can be purchased from any number of costume supply houses or magic shops. Antique shops sell them cheaply because prescription lenses are useless to anyone else.

I have an optometrist friend whose hobby is collecting antique frames, and he is very generous about lending them. Many places that sell frames will lend them to you for program credit. They are also willing to repair and insert plain glass lenses for a nominal fee and sometimes free of charge.

*Quick Repairs* The one thing about eyeglasses is that they seem to break half way through the run of a production. Quick repairs are needed. A small silver or brass safety pin will act as a temporary hinge pin. If the ear piece becomes rough and snags the hair or scalp, a drop of hot glue will solve the matter.

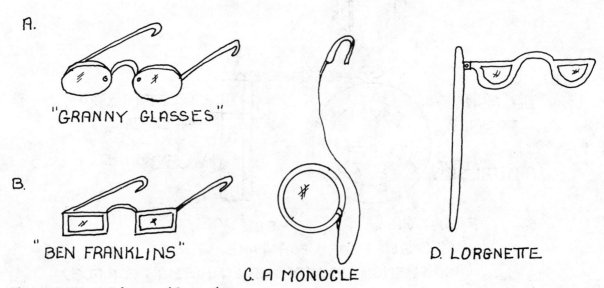

A. "GRANNY GLASSES"

B. "BEN FRANKLINS"

C. A MONOCLE

D. LORGNETTE

**Figure 18–13.** *A Selection of Spectacles*

## Gloves

Gloves were a derivation of medieval gauntlets, which were used in battle and in the sport of falconry. Gloves were certainly used when riding as well. Some historians credit Queen Elizabeth I for the popularization of glove wearing for all occasions. We can categorize gloves into three groups—gauntlets, regular gloves, and partial gloves. All gloves are difficult to make and should be bought whenever possible. Keep a supply of all types on hand.

*Gauntlets*     Gauntlets can be made by attaching a cuff to an already existing pair, such as gardening gloves. These can be metalized or leatherized using one of the methods already discussed in Chapter 15 on the construction of armor.

*Partial Gloves*     Partial gloves include mitts and mittens. A mitt is a Victorian invention of lacey gloves with no fingers or thumb past the first knuckle. One usually finds these in bridal shops. If necessary you can use a crochet pattern for gloves and just end the fingers at the first knuckle.

Mittens have the thumb and a palm that covers the four fingers simultaneously. These can be bought in any store that has skiing equipment.

## Assorted Boxes

Assorted boxes that become costume props include snuff boxes, patch boxes, cigarette cases, pillboxes, and powder compacts.

*Pill Boxes*     Snuff, pill, and patch boxes are all essentially about the same small size and can be used interchangeably. Today we buy them as pill boxes which are easily and inexpensively obtainable.

*Snuff Boxes*     Snuff is still obtainable at a tobacconist, but a few unrolled cigarettes will suffice. Remember that snuff was used to clear the nasal passages, so a snuff box must be accompanied with a handkerchief.

*Patch Boxes*     Little metallic shapes are being sold once again as patches for punk rock attire. Patches can be made by using tiny shapes of felt, velvet, or sequins and securing them to the skin by eyelash adhesive. The patch box was always accompanied by a little bottle of glue. Just decorate an eyelash adhesive bottle.

*Powder Compacts*     Since the invention of pressed powder (powder in a cake), cosmetic manufacturers have been making plastic throwaway compacts cheaply, and these will do in many instances. Some metal compacts for loose powder can still be bought at department stores. The use of these is recent enough that they are easily obtainable in thrift and second hand shops. So are cigarette cases. New cigarette cases and cigarette holders can be purchased from the tobacconist.

## Artificial Flowers

These days beautiful silk flowers are manufactured so well that you have to touch them before you can tell if they are artificial. They can be cut and used for hat decoration, garment ornamentation and costume props. They are also extremely expensive!

Plastic flowers are cheaper but they literally weigh more and thereby tend to droop and pull the fabric of a costume. Frankly, for costume purposes, they look tacky. For these reasons you may wish to build your own flowers. Included in this chapter are illustrations with accompanying patterns for eight basic types of flowers—the round-petaled flower, the irregular petaled round flower, the sawtooth-edged flower, the cluster flower, the point-petaled flower, the spike-petaled, the star flower, and the trumpet flower. Some flowers have two or more shapes of petals in combination, as well as patterns for leaves and calyx.

*Basic Structure Of All Flowers*

All flowers have six basic parts in common—the calyx, the petal, the stamen, the pistil, the stem, and the leaf. The stamen has two parts, the anther and the filament. The pistil has four parts, the stigma, the style, the ovary, and the ovule. This is illustrated in Figure 18–14, as well as the leaf-like spathe.

*Supplies*     To make any flowers you will need some specific supplies.:

1. Fabric—This may be paper, silk, felt, or cotton. A woven fabric will fray at the edges. To prevent fraying, you may do one of the following.
   a. Before cutting, outline your petal edges in glue as described in Chapter 20 under Applique Techniques.
   b. Paint your petals with acrylic paint.
   c. Stretch your fabric on a frame and size with a solution of equal parts of white glue and water. Let it thoroughly dry. Then cut your petals, leaves, calyx, etc.
2. Florist wire
3. Needlenose pliers that are also wire cutters
4. Florist's green paper tape

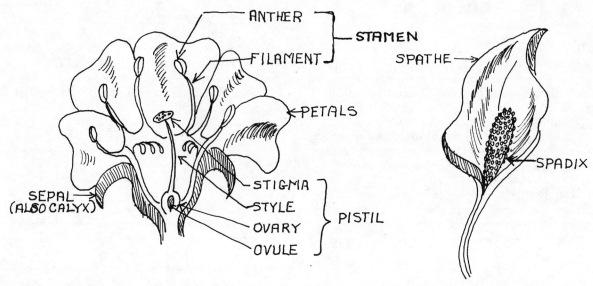

**Figure 18–14.** *Diagram of a Flower and Spathe*

5. *Pistils and stamen—These can often be bought in craft shops. They can also be made in one of the following manners.*
   a. *Jewelers fine wire topped with a small glass bead or seed pearl*
   b. *Wire topped in a little drop of hot glue or bread dough and then painted*
6. *Small sharp scissors*
7. *Fuzzy pipe stem cleaners in yellows, brown, and black*
8. *"Cover yourself" buttons in various sizes*
9. *A book showing color photographs of a variety of flowers—Florist shops give out books showing sample arrangements and sometimes lovely flower calenders. Seed catalogues are also good sources. Your library will have books on the subject, botanically classified, as well as under the art of flower arrangement.*

*Flower Construction*

For whatever flower is made, there is one general rule of thumb: start building from the inside out. It's not nice to fool Mother Nature, but we just won't tell her we've borrowed her system.

You must make your center and attach it to a florist wire. Then attach other petals until you have built up the desired amount; then add the calyx. A few drops of white glue should serve as an anchor. For those flowers that need wired petals, make sure all the wire ends go through the calyx. You only need one fine wire to wrap all of them together. Now add your leaves at various intervals along the stem and wrap the whole stem in green florist's tape. For hat and garment decoration you will need very little stem. A wire loop is often more advantageous.

*Round-Petaled Flowers* Round-petaled flowers include roses, pansies, peonies, gardenias, camellias, violets, and various flowering trees such as apple and cherry. The differences among them are in the size of the petal, the color, and how many are required (see Fig. 18–15).

*Irregular Petaled Flowers* Irregular petaled flowers include poppies, cosmos, and hibiscus (see Fig. 18–16).

*Sawtooth-Edged Flowers* Sawtooth-edged flowers include carnations, bachelor's buttons, and cornflowers (see Fig. 18–17).

*Cluster Flowers* Cluster flowers include wisteria, lilacs, geraniums, and hydrangea. These flowers are so time consuming to make that it is cheaper to buy them.

*Pointed-Petaled Flowers* Pointed-petaled flowers include daisies, asters, and mums. Both daisies and asters have a button center that can be constructed by making a piece of a pipe stem cleaner into a button-sized pinwheel and gluing it onto a "cover yourself" button. Glass beads can be glued on for further texture if desired.

Asters are shorter petaled than daisies and are double- or triple-layered.

Mums are multi-layered and their petals turn up. This shape can be achieved by spray starch and gentle directioning with the hand (see Fig. 18–18).

*Spike-Petaled Flowers* Spike-petaled flowers include lilies of all types and tulips. These long petals sometimes need additional wiring to bend the leaves

PETALS

BUD
→ →ROLL→

LEAVES

SEPAL

NOTCHED
PETAL

ROSE, LEAVES & BUD

WILD ROSE
(ALSO BLOSSOMS OF FLOWERING TREES)

DOGWOOD

THESE PETALS, SEPAL, AND LEAVES
ARE ACTUAL SIZE

**Figure 18–15.** *Illustration and Patterns for Round-Petaled Flowers*

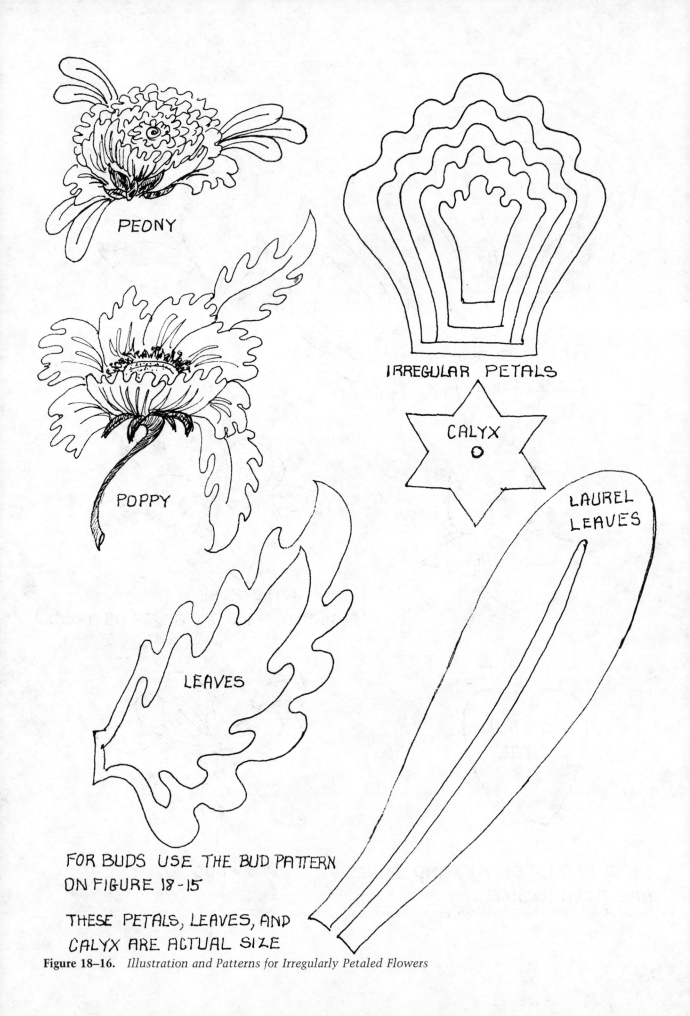

PEONY

POPPY

LEAVES

IRREGULAR PETALS

CALYX

LAUREL LEAVES

FOR BUDS USE THE BUD PATTERN
ON FIGURE 18-15

THESE PETALS, LEAVES, AND
CALYX ARE ACTUAL SIZE

**Figure 18-16.** *Illustration and Patterns for Irregularly Petaled Flowers*

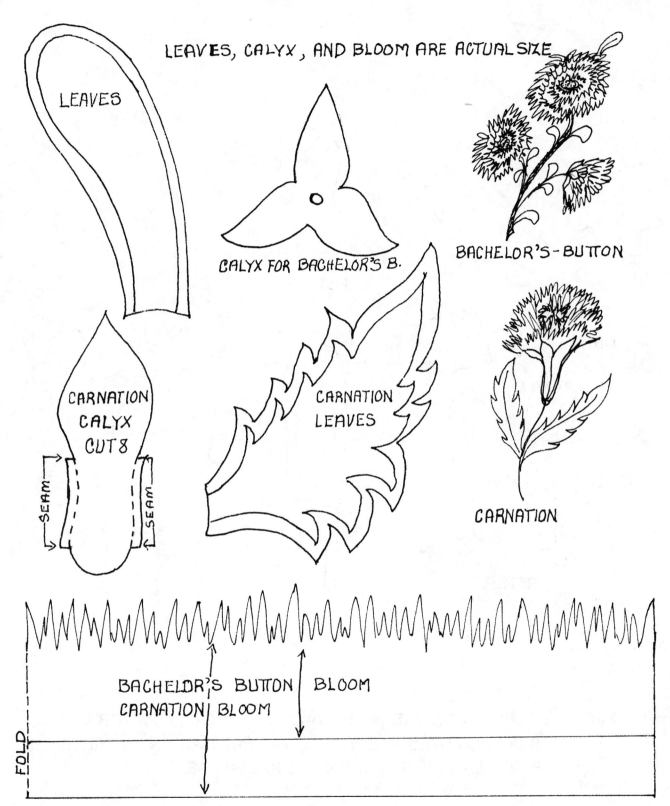

LEAVES, CALYX, AND BLOOM ARE ACTUAL SIZE

LEAVES

CALYX FOR BACHELOR'S B.

BACHELOR'S-BUTTON

CARNATION CALYX CUT 8

SEAM     SEAM

CARNATION LEAVES

CARNATION

BACHELOR'S BUTTON BLOOM
CARNATION BLOOM

FOLD

NOTE: THE LONGER THE BLOOM IS CUT—THE FULLER THE FLOWER

**Figure 18–17.** *Illustration and Patterns for Sawtoothed Flowers*

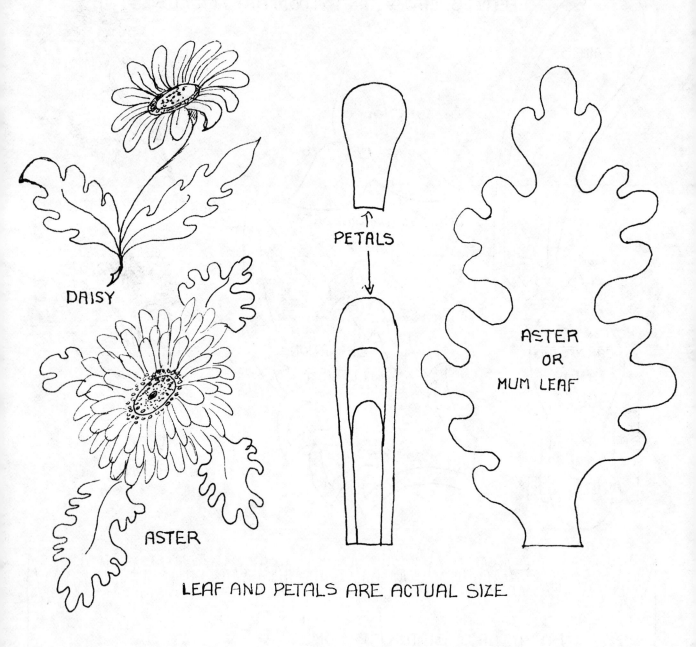

DAISY

ASTER

PETALS

ASTER
OR
MUM LEAF

LEAF AND PETALS ARE ACTUAL SIZE

NOTE: FOR CALYX USE THE BACHELOR'S BUTTON CALYX PATTERN
FOR DAISY LEAVES USE THE "LEAF" PATTERN ON FIGURE 18-16
FOR CENTER USE A BALL FROM BALL FRINGE

**Figure 18–18.** *Illustration and Patterns for Daisy-Like Flowers*

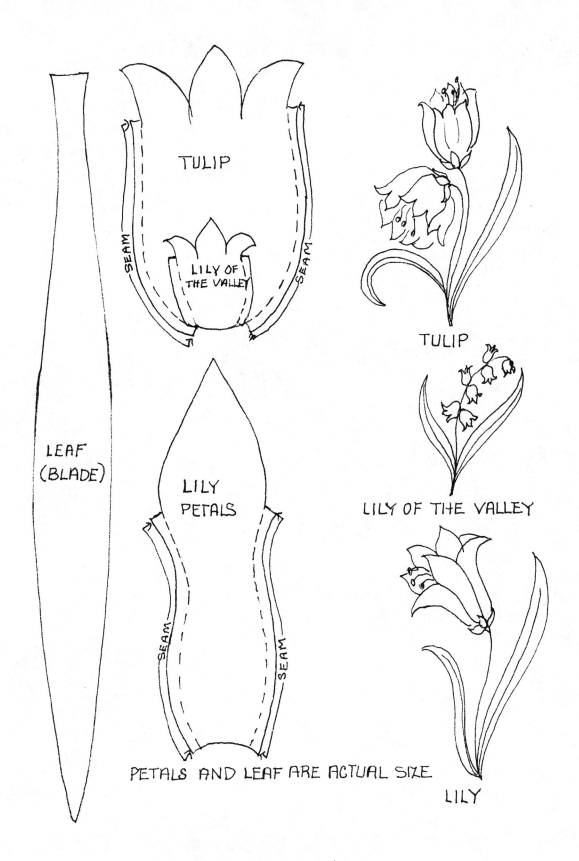

TULIP

LILY OF
THE VALLEY

LEAF
(BLADE)

LILY
PETALS

SEAM

SEAM

SEAM

SEAM

TULIP

LILY OF THE VALLEY

LILY

PETALS AND LEAF ARE ACTUAL SIZE

THE BLADE MAY BE ELONGATED TO ANY LENGTH

NOTE: FOR CALYX USE THE PATTERN ON FIGURE 18-16

**Figure 18–19.** *Illustration and Patterns for Tulip-Like Flowers*

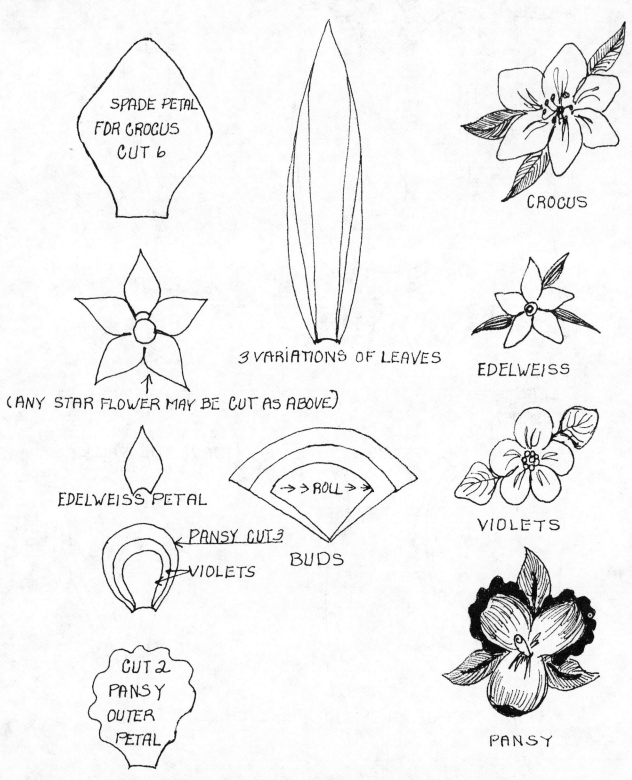

SPADE PETAL FOR CROCUS CUT 6

3 VARIATIONS OF LEAVES

CROCUS

(ANY STAR FLOWER MAY BE CUT AS ABOVE)

EDELWEISS

EDELWEISS PETAL

→ → ROLL → →

BUDS

PANSY CUT 3

VIOLETS

VIOLETS

CUT 2 PANSY OUTER PETAL

PANSY

NOTE: SPADE PETALS CAN BE USED AS LEAVES FOR VIOLETS. THE STAR FLOWER CUT AS ONE UNIT MAY BE USED FOR SEPALS. ALL PETALS, LEAVES AND BUDS ARE ACTUAL SIZE

**Figure 18–20.** *Illustration and Patterns for Star-Like Flowers*

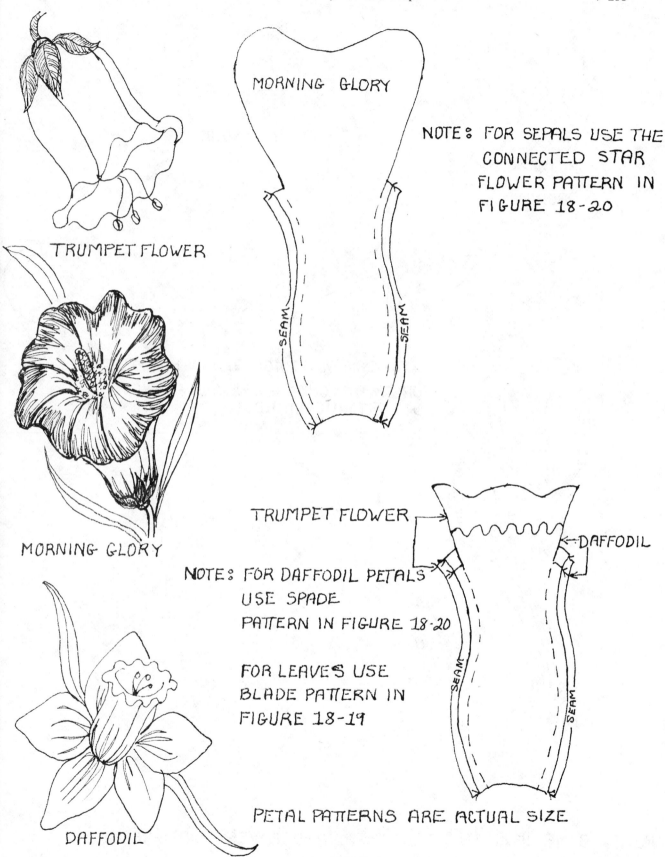

TRUMPET FLOWER

MORNING GLORY

MORNING GLORY

NOTE: FOR SEPALS USE THE CONNECTED STAR FLOWER PATTERN IN FIGURE 18-20

TRUMPET FLOWER

DAFFODIL

NOTE: FOR DAFFODIL PETALS USE SPADE PATTERN IN FIGURE 18-20

FOR LEAVES USE BLADE PATTERN IN FIGURE 18-19

PETAL PATTERNS ARE ACTUAL SIZE

DAFFODIL

SEAM

**Figure 18–21.** *Illustration and Patterns for Trumpet-Like Flowers*

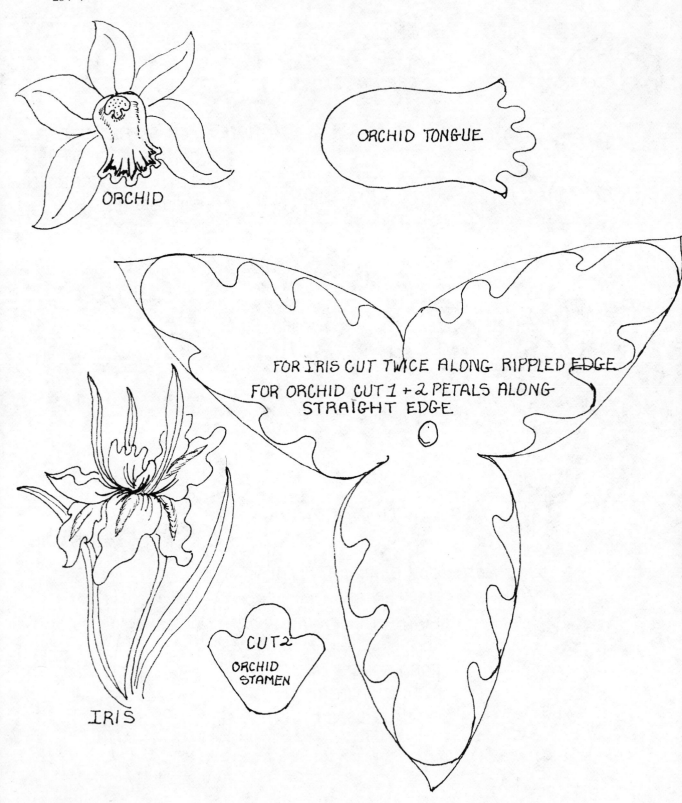

ORCHID

ORCHID TONGUE

FOR IRIS CUT TWICE ALONG RIPPLED EDGE
FOR ORCHID CUT 1 + 2 PETALS ALONG
STRAIGHT EDGE

IRIS

CUT 2
ORCHID
STAMEN

NOTE: COMBINE WITH OTHER SEPAL AND LEAVES AS DESIRED

**Figure 18–22.** *Illustration and Patterns for Combination Flowers*

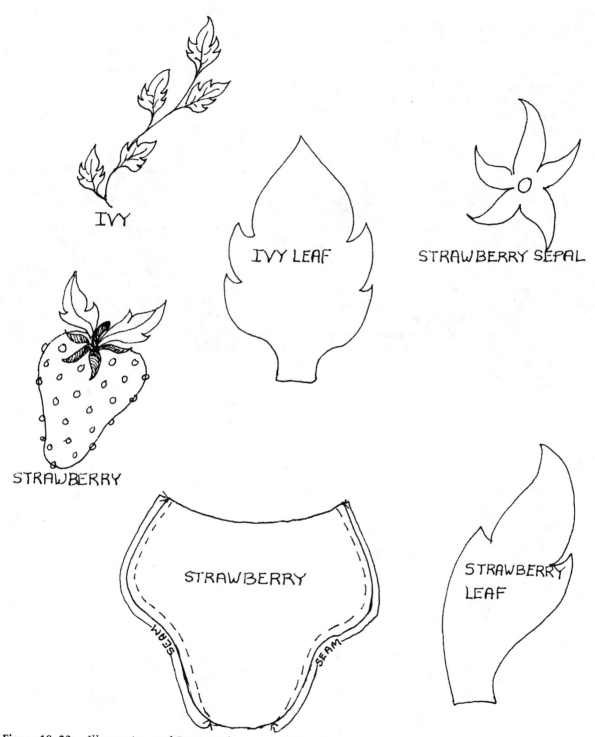

**Figure 18–23.** *Illustration and Patterns for Ivy and Strawberry*

to the desired shape (Fig. 18–19). If wire is needed, it should be glued to the individual petal leaving a tail. All these tails are then placed around the center wire and, along with pistil, stamen, etc., are wrapped in green tape and taken through the calyx.

*Star Flowers*   Star flowers include dogwood, crocus, azaleas, and gladiolus. The star for the dogwood is really more of a cross. The crocus is a single six-pointed star. Azaleas are double six-pointed stars. Impatiens and jasmine would be five-pointed stars. Gladiolus is a double three-pointed star, and iris is a three-pointed tongue-shaped flower combined with two spike petals (Fig. 18–20).

*Trumpet Flowers*   Trumpet flowers require a little stitchery, as marked in Figure 18–21. These would include trumpet vines, gloxinia, and morning glories. Gloxinia is a velvet-like blossom in shades of pink, red, and purple. Velvet should be used as the fabric.

*Combination Flowers*   As previously mentioned, the iris has a combination of petal types. Daffodils combine a small trumpet center with six spade-shaped petals. Orchids have a tongue-like center petal with five outer petals of various shapes and lengths depending on the variety. These are illustrated in Figures 18–21 and 18–22.

The iris also requires a fuzzy shaft partway down its tongue-shaped petals. This is done by a piece of yellow pipe stem cleaner.

*Leaves*   Each flower illustration has its accompanying leaf pattern, but Figure 18–23 shows the ivy and lemon leaf patterns and a pattern for the calyx.

## Artificial Fruit

Artificial fruit can be bought relatively cheaply in plastic and glamorized. Dip it first in glue and then tiny glass beads. Small fruits can be made of bread dough with wire attached while the dough is still soft. The making of bread dough is described in Chapter 14.

There is one velvet fruit that always looks charming and is easy to make—strawberries. Figure 18–23 is an illustrated pattern for this. The body of the berry should be red velvet gathered to a green velvet ribbon a quarter-inch wide. The calyx is green felt and the seeds are tiny seed pearls. It takes a little fiber fill for stuffing.

# FOUR

# Methods of Fabric Design

With the thousands of fabrics available these days, you may still want or need to create your own pattern, specific color, texture, or motif. Plays involving gothic armies demand this. You cannot be haphazard with heraldic identification. Greco-Roman plays demand specific motifs which are difficult to find. The cost of those luscious oriental fabrics may be prohibitive, and it is cheaper to hand paint inexpensive taffeta for the same effect.

Fabric design includes texture as well as color, and divides itself neatly into three basic categories: woven, cut and applied.

Woven designs include tweeds, plaids, checks, and brocades. It is possible to weave your own, but unless you're Penelope and have a twenty-year wait until Ulysses' return for opening night, you'd best confine yourself to buying these fabrics.

Cut designs include all types of velvets, velours, corduroy, and eyelet. These fabrics are also more easily bought than created, but the technique can be applied to costume construction.

We are concerned primarily with applied design, that which is added to a fabric to create a motif. There are two ways to add design: textile design and needlecraft.

For further clarification of stitching techniques I have included a chapter of illustrated stitches most commonly used in needlecraft and costume sewing techniques.

# 19

# Textile Design

Textile design has two basic categories: dyeing techniques and painting techniques. Dyeing techniques include "all over" dyeing, dye painting, batik, and dye printing. Painting techniques include freehand painting, block printing, stencil work, flocking, and silk screening.

## Dyeing Techniques

At best dyeing is an inexact science. Have you ever run out of fabric and tried to match it from a new bolt of the same type? All knitters know how frustrating it is to match skeins of yarn. Yarn manufacturers put dye lot numbers of their skein labels for just that reason. If commercial manufacturers have this problem in a highly controlled situation, you are certain to encounter it as well.

This is not necessarily a problem. One may not always achieve the original intent, but one might prefer the color one gets by accident. Either way, dyeing techniques are invariably a challenge to one's creative ingenuity.

Regardless of the techniques involved, a few basic requirements regarding knowledge and equipment must be obtained.

### The Nature of Dyes

At the risk of sounding a bit like that childhood game of twenty questions, all dyes are either animal, vegetable, or mineral in origin. To these we must add one other category achieved through modern progress, chemical. An example of an animal dye is Tyrian purple, a dye extracted from a snail-like shellfish known generally as the *murex brandaris*. The ancient American Indians found a similar dye in the shellfish *purpura lapillus*. It was estimated that it took a little more than 25,000 of these creatures to make one ounce of dye. Is it any wonder

that it was so expensive that it was relegated strictly to imperial use?

The example of a vegetable dye that comes most readily to mind is indigo, a plant originally from India. The ancient Roman name for this plant was *indicium*, reflecting its place of origin. Its generic name is *indigoferae* and it is a member of the pea family. The anil plant of the West Indies also produces a similar dye.

A mineral dye would be one like sulphur, which yields yellows and blacks, or minerals extracted of metals such as chromium, copper, and iron.[1]

*Oxidation*   One often hears the term "oxide" in conjunction with a dye or pigment color, such as the color chromium oxide green. Many dyes and pigments change color when allowed to aerate.

*Mordants*   Dyes also change color when mordants are used. A mordant is any agent used in conjunction with a dye to both set and/or change the color. The word derives from the French verb *mordre*, which literally means "to bite." In the context of dyeing, it means more generally "to take hold."

A list of commonly used mordants would include:

1. *Sulphuric acid (oil of vitriol)*
2. *Acetic acid (vinegar)*
3. *Uric acid (urine)*
4. *Sodium sulfate (Glauber's salt)*
5. *Sodium chloride (common table salt)*
6. *Sodium carbonate (soda)*
7. *Potassium chloride (sea salt)*
8. *Potassium hydroxide (found in common soaps; also called caustic potash)*
9. *Potassium nitrate (saltpeter)*

[1]Veila Birrell, *The Textile Arts* (New York: Harper Brothers, 1959), pp. 383-386.

*Chemical Dyes*  Chemical dyes originally started in an effort to produce a wider spectrum of colors, such as prussian blue developed by a German named Diesbach in the early eighteenth century. In the early nineteenth century aniline dye was discovered by Unverdorben in Holland. The chemical formula for aniline is $C_6H_5NH_2$. Although originally derived from the anil plant, it is now a compound derived from benzene, $C_6H_5$.[2]

These chemical dyes definitely produce a more stable coloring process and for the costumer's purpose we shall concentrate mainly on them.

*Required Equipment for Dyeing*

As you are probably not dyeing huge bolts of fabric but just enough for one or two outfits at a time, you could make do with some very basic equipment including the following:

1. A large soup kettle or vat
2. Hot plate or stove
3. Automatic washing machine
4. Automatic dryer
5. Plastic bowls, dishpan, and laundry baskets
6. A quart size measure
7. A cup measure that includes ounces
8. An ounce scale and a gram scale
9. An electric timer (your dryer may have one)
10. Ironing board
11. Iron
12. Brown wrapping paper
13. Cheese cloth or old cut up nylon stockings
14. Terrycloth toweling
15. Sponges
16. Stainless steel pots or kettles
17. Rubber gloves
18. Wooden spoons
19. Dip sticks
20. A dowel rod at least 30 inches long for stirring and lifting
21. Household bleach
22. Scouring powder
23. Color remover
24. A selection of dyes
25. Salt
26. White vinegar

*Selection of Dyes*  A selection of various household dyes should be kept on hand. Household dyes are sometimes referred to as "union" dyes. It is possible to buy these in your local grocery or drug store by the packet. One packet is approximately one ounce and will dye approximately five yards of fabric. Some of the common brands are Rit, Tintex, and Putnam. These can often be bought directly from

the manufacturer in bulk quantities of one pound, five pounds, or more. The savings when buying in quantity is considerable, provided you have the storage space. All union dyes should be stored in a sealed tin or opaque plastic container, as light and air can fade or change the color. Both Rit and Tintex contain salt. Rit also comes in liquid form.

All three may be purchased in bulk. Tintex is acquired from Knomark, Inc., Jamaica, New York, 11434; Rit from Best Foods: CPC International Inc., Indianapolis, Indiana, 46221; and Putnam from Putnam Color and Dye Corporation, P. O. Box 1267, Galesburg, Illinois, 61401.

Putnam sells hot water dyes to which you add the salt. They also sell a selection of cold water dyes (excellent for dye painting). One convenient thing about dyes in packet form is that the packet is gelatin and it dissolves right in the vat or washing machine, which is very neat for the room and the fingers.

When using any dye, the directions on the label should of course be read completely for the most advantageous usage. It is also a good idea to wear rubber gloves. A few general rules apply to most household dyeing.

*Intensity of Color*  Intensity of color is controlled by three things: amount of dye in ratio to the amount of water and fabric, the temperature of the water, and the amount of time in the dye solution.

The hue's intensity depends on the amount of dye to the volume of water and poundage of fabric. For example, if you were to dye five yards of fabric in a washing machine full of water with one ounce of dye, you would get a given tint of the hue. To darken this hue, you could use two ounces. But if you were to dye eight yards of fabric in the same amount of water to one ounce of dye, your fabric would probably be a lighter tint of the original hue. It might take two ounces of dye to the same volume of water to get the eight yards of fabric to be the same tint that the five yards were with one ounce of dye. Your dye instructions may require you to measure the amount of dye and weigh your fabric.

With hot water dyes, the hue deepens in ratio to the heat of the water. One gets a pastel tint with hot tap water, which seldom goes over 100°F. One gets a middle tint in a washing machine whose hot cycle temperature generally does not exceed 140°F. For the deepest shades, boiling of 212°F is sometimes necessary, particularly when certain navy blues, bottle greens, and blacks are desired. Fabric must be boiled in a vat.

Intensity also deepens in proportion to the amount of time the fabric is left in the dye solution; the longer the time, the darker it gets, but this can be deceiving because fabrics will only absorb so much dye.

[2]Ibid., p. 388.

*Desirable Fabrics for Dyeing* We have all tried to dye fabrics that simply will not dye or absorb the dye evenly. To ensure an even shade, fabrics of natural fibers are preferred—i.e., cotton, silk, linen, wool, and hemp. Cotton, silk, and linen will take boiling far better than wool. Nylon is one synthetic that dyes very well at medium temperatures. Polyester and acetate fabrics dye poorly, if at all. The trouble comes with fabrics of fiber combinations, particularly those with so much natural fiber and so much synthetic.

I once attempted to dye a 35 percent cotton/65 percent polyester fabric. The 35 percent took the dye and the 65 percent stayed its original color. In this particular instance it was a happy accident because the 35 percent was a cotton backing and the pale overlay of the 65 percent gave the effect of a marvelous antique silk.

To insure yourself against disaster, always dye a sample or swatch. This swatch must be treated exactly as you intend to treat the total yardage.

*Preparation of Fabric* To insure your fabric for maximum effect, you should remove all sizing and preshrink the fabric as much as possible, always remembering that boiling fabric will most likely increase the amount of shrinkage, and in the case of wool it may loosen the fiber. Your fabric should be rinsed in clear water first and then immersed in the dye solution.

After you achieve the desired intensity, you should rinse the fabric in cold, clear water to remove any excess dye; just rinse it until the water squeezed out runs clear. It is important to remember that the dried fabric will be at least one shade lighter than the wet fabric.

*Preparation of Dyes* Sometimes you can buy the exact pigment you need, or you can achieve your color by its varying intensities. In other cases it is necessary to blend pigments to get the desired color. You can premix small quantities of the pigments with a little water to test the color, but be sure to use accurate measurements and to correlate them to proportions that can conveniently be increased.

Let us take a hypothetical example of a teal blue. You may discover that three grams of prussian blue to one gram of yellow ochre, plus a half-gram of burnt sienna to a half-gallon of water brought to boiling will dye a half-yard of fabric just the right color if boiled for three minutes. You wish to dye five yards that exact color. Therefore it will take 30 grams of prussian blue to 10 grams of yellow ochre, plus five grams of burnt sienna to five gallons of water, and the fabric must be boiled an equal time of three minutes.

It is also handy to keep a "recipe" book which has the dried sample of fabric and your private formula so that you can do it again without experimentation.

If you are dye painting, you may wish to mix a dye paste. This is done by using a little water at a time until you achieve the desired color and consistency. This paste should be strained through a nylon stocking to avoid any undissolved crystals that might "explode" at a later time, leaving a little extra "bloop" of color.

*Over Dyeing* Over dyeing is the process by which you take a fabric of one color and tint it with a second color to achieve a new color. You might need to match an already existing piece of yardgoods and can find a similar fabric but not quite the same shade. Over dyeing can solve this if you are careful and use your common sense.

*Setting Dyes* If you have carefully followed the direction of your hot water dye labels, you should have no problem in setting your dyes. Occasionally a dark color will continue to bleed or run. This is particularly true of navy blues, blacks, and various shades of reds. Even the commercially dyed fabrics in these shades tend to bleed and should always be washed separately. Sometimes a little white vinegar in the rinse water will help set these colors.

*Alternative Dyes*

There are several alternative types of dyes that work very well either as an all-over dye or for specific dyeing techniques.

*Cold Water Dyes* As previously stated, Putnam has developed an excellent permanent cold water dye, but its color range is somewhat limited.

*Vegetable Dyes* There are four vegetable dyes that I love for certain tinted effects—coffee, tea, red wine, and Welch's concord grape juice. Coffee and tea will give cream and vanilla tints to white fabric. Boiling the fabric in these will set your color. Red wine, particularly sparkling Burgundy or fizzy Cella Lambrusco, give a beautiful pink tint. A little salt helps set it, even cold. I believe the carbonation also helps set the color. White fabric boiled in concord grape juice or even concord grape wine gives a beautiful bluish lavender. Regular food coloring is also a vegetable dye that can be set with specific mordants (usually white vinegar).

*Silk Dyes* There are beautifully vibrant silk dyes that work very well for silk screening, silk painting, tie dyeing and batik. These may be purchased in bulk from Screen Process Supplies Manufacturing Co., whose current address is 1199 East 12th St., Oakland, California 94606.

*Sun Developing Dyes* The same company makes a product called Inkodye which develops in the sunshine (a great product for those of us in Florida or California!). This is just plain fun to use as a paint. Use a flour and water paste as a resistant for those areas you wish to leave white. Now paint with various dye colors the design areas. Put the wet fabric out in the sunshine to dry. The colors become brilliant. When the fabric has completely dried, wash it in warm soapy water to remove the resistant and any excess dye. This product is available at many art stores, as is premixed resistant. You can make your own, however, by gradually adding one cup plus two or three tablespoons of flour to one cup of water. Blend until smooth and use a nozzle plastic bottle as an applicator. It is literally so simple that children take great delight in it and the effects can be quite beautiful.

*Permanent Inks* Permanent inks, often called indelible, make good dyes for dye painting small areas.

### Tie Dyeing

Tie dyeing is the process of either pleating, twisting, tying with wax coated threads, knotting, or folding a piece of wet fabric and dipping it into a dye solution so that the thickness and shape of the thusly caused irregularities absorb the dye at greater or lesser degrees of intensity. The underlying principle is that the thicker the fabric, the slower its absorbtion rate becomes. As with most dyeing, one must always work from the lightest shades to the darkest shades. An example of a tie dyed silk can be seen in Figure 19–1.

### Dye Painting

Dye painting is simply painting techniques achieved with dyes. These techniques are usually freehand but some resistant substance must be used if you desire to keep your color areas from running into each other. One such resistant was discussed in connection with the Inkodye product.

Plain old Elmer's glue or Sobo glue works well and dries clear but shiny. For a leaded glass effect, black acrylic paint works well. White acrylic paint works well for a more startling contrast. Clear acrylic gel also is effective, but be sure the dye you are using is compatible with acrylics. Inkodye is not.

### Batik

The word "batik" is an ancient Malayan one meaning "to design." The process is basically the same as that used in the intricate Easter egg painting of Russian and middle European countries. When used in the decoration of pottery, it is called negative painting.

The underlying principle is that a beeswax-paraffin solution is used as a resistant medium. The temperature of the dyes must not be too hot or they will melt the wax. (The Putnam cold water dyes are excellent for this.) Starting with the lightest color the design is built up. Wherever the wax is, the color does not penetrate. Therefore each different colored part of the design requires a separate waxing.

The fabric pictured in Figure 19–2 is batiked. The lightest shade is yellow. That means that all the yellow portion was waxed out, leaving only the figured areas free. The next color is a bright pink. More

**Figure 19–1.** *Tie Dyed Silk*

**Figure 19–2.** *Batiked Fabric*

wax would be added to preserve that color, and the final brown color would remain.

Your fabric needs to be stretched wet over a frame until taut. This frame may be any embroidery hoop or quilting frame but should be stainless steel. You also need a hot plate or stove to keep your small pan of wax melted. The wax may be applied with brushes of various sizes, or it can be dripped from a toothpick or pin.

When all the dyeing steps are completed, the wax is removed by placing the fabric between two layers of brown paper (wrapping paper or even grocery bags) sandwich fashion. This "sandwich" should be placed on a stack of newspaper and then pressed with a moderately hot iron. The wax will melt into the papers. it may be necessary to repeat this process several times until all the wax is gone. The fabric should be washed in a little clean water and cold water soap and rinsed. The soap will help set your dyes.

*Crackle Batik*  Crackle batik looks like fine spidery lines and is made by painting the entire surface with wax, letting it dry, and crushing it so it literally cracks. This is then dipped into the dye solution. Wherever the cracks are, the dye leaves its pattern. The paraffin content in the wax accounts for its brittleness. A brittle wax is more desirable for this crackle process than for regular batik.

*Crayon Batik*  This is another fun process and simple enough for children to enjoy. (In fact, I first did this in Girl Scouts.) Draw with crayons, or better still drip melted crayons onto your fabric. Remove the wax as previously described. To set the color, a mordant of equal parts water to white vinegar can be used. Just dampen a pressing cloth in this solution, place it over your crayon batiked cloth, and press with a warm iron.

**Dye Printing**

Almost all commercially printed fabric is printed with dye. Hand printed fabric can either use dye or paint, depending on use and personal preference. The three most common methods of commercial printing are photo printing, roller printing, and commercial silk screening.

*Photo Printing*  The fabric in Figure 19–3 has been photo printed. The easiest way to tell photo printing when buying your fabric is to look at the back. In the photo printing process the back of the fabric looks almost pure white, as if the dye had not penetrated all the way through. The fabric does not have a photograph on it. Photo printing is merely a new way of transferring the design to the roller process.

**Figure 19–3.** *Photo Printed Fabric*

There is a way to transfer a photo from a newspaper or printed book to fabric. You must dip the photo in a solution of a quarter-ounce pure soap flakes (Ivory Flakes works the best) in two ounces of boiling water. Cool this and slowly stir in two ounces of pure turpentine. Carefully blot excess solution off photo with paper towels. Now place the photo face down on clean flat fabric. Put a paper towel on top and rub over the entire back with a wooden spoon. Carefully remove all paper. The photo will have transferred itself to the cloth. Let it hang to dry for 24 hours. It is washable. Iron on the "wrong" side. One word of caution: This only works with *printed* photographs, not others. It is the printer's ink that transfers.[3]

*Roller Printing*    Enormous cylinders are engraved and then inked with dye and pulled across the fabric. The engraving is time consuming and

[3]Francis J. Kathan, *The Hand Decoration of Fabric* (New York: Dover Publications, 1959), p. 159.

costly. Lithography is often employed. A separate roller is required for each color. The fabric in Figure 19–4 has been roller printed. There are eight shades, excluding the white, which was probably its original color, as its back or "wrong" side is also white, but there is more of a dye penetration. That would mean eight separate rollers were used.

Modern commercial printing methods are so clever that it is sometimes very hard to be absolutely sure about the method used. As already demonstrated, different fabrics absorb dye differently. Looking at the "wrong" side is not always a foolproof test.

*Commercially Dyed Silk Screen*    The fabric pictured in Figure 19–5 is one that I saw being printed in Japan. It is silk screened silk which was dye impregnated. Each color demands its own screen and there are ten separate colors. It was printed in ten-yard lengths. For costume purposes, however, the silk screen process seems to work better as a painting technique and I will treat it as one.

## Painting Techniques

Whatever the technique you use, you should be familiar with certain general principles involved in all textile painting. For maximum results fabrics composed of natural fibers work the best. These fibers are porous and will absorb and hold onto the paints better. This does not mean you cannot paint on synthetics, but it is always a good idea to test your paints on a swatch of the desired fabric.

*Textile Paints*

Many varieties of premixed textile paints are available in art and craft stores.

*Tube Oil*    You can paint with tube oils that have been mixed with clear lacquer. Turpentine is used in this case as a thinner. It should be used sparingly as it will "ring" (bleed in an outward circle) if too thin. For blended fabrics that may contain some synthetic fibers, be sure you use gum turpentine, not any thinner made from a petroleum base as this tends to melt certain acetate and polyesters. Acetone tends to bubble acrylic fibers.

*Acrylic Paints*    I personally am very fond of tube acrylic paints because you can use them as they are on leather or vinyl. You can dilute them with water for fabrics that are washable or can be dry cleaned and do not need any particular setting process such as steaming, heat, or chemical solutions. Diluted with enough water, they also make excellent paints for air brush techniques.

**Figure 19–4.** *Roller Printed Fabric*

**Figure 19–5.** *Silk Screened Fabric*

There are two disadvantages. On nonporous surfaces they may peel. They must be ironed on the "wrong" side if painted item needs pressing.

*FEV* FEV is an abbreviated term that stands for French Enamel Varnish, a mixture of aniline dye pigments and clear shellac diluted with denatured alcohol. Dye pigments do not have to be used, though liquid shoe polish (except white) can be used. Bronzing powders can be added for metallic effects. This is a tricky substance, however. Too much alcohol and it will flake off the fabric; too much shellac and it becomes stiff as a board. If white shellac is used, the color is opaque in nature. For a pearlized effect, you can mix powdered mica into white shellac with a drop or two of dye for a tint. Always test this on a fabric swatch. This may be either washed or dry cleaned.

*Enamels* Pure fibers work very well with regular enamel paints, either brushed on or sprayed straight from the can. This also works on rayon, nylon, and some polyesters. One should be very careful with certain acetates and acrylic fibers. Again, test first.

*Free Hand Painting*

Free hand painting is self explanatory. If you are painting leather or vinyl or something equally as stiff, you do not necessarily have to stretch your fabric. If you are painting a softer material, you must stretch it so that it cannot ripple and thus cause distortions. For medium weight fabrics an embroidery or quilting hoop will do. For organzas or chiffons I prefer a tight stretching over a solid, somewhat absorbent surface such as matte board or illustration board. This will absorb the excess paint that falls through the finely woven threads and prevents any "ringing" that otherwise might occur.

The two heraldic tabards pictured in Figure 19–6 were painted primarily with acrylic paints straight from the tube. The long tabard on the left was white vinyl, chevron striped in sky blue. The fleur-de-lis emblem was originally painted with gold enamel, as were the narrow chevron stripes between the white and blue, but the enamel bubbled the vinyl surface so gold braid was used to cover the "blooper" and an appliqued fleur-de-lis was used.

The short tabard on the right was made of white chamois and also painted with acrylic straight from the tube. The studding circles were painted with gold enamel and caused no ill effect, but the leather did not absorb the paint evenly; some spots seemed more absorbent than others. This tabard was painted after the fiasco of the left-hand tabard and we pretested all the paints, but there was no way of predicting those sponge-like spots. Both tabards were

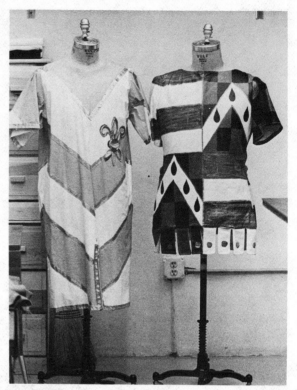

**Figure 19–6.** *Painted Fabrics*

painted freehand, but the various straight edges were marked with masking tape.

When doing specific area painting, it is wise to cut your flat pattern pieces out and then paint them while flat. The bird and flowers pictured in Figure 19–7 are painted on silk organza. In this case a double layer was used and worn over gold lame in imitation of the effects achieved by Japanese silk paintings. This was originally on the skirt of my evening gown that was damaged beyond repair. (Rather than completely destroy my hand painting efforts, I cut out this spot and framed it.) In this case, a specific area of the finished garment was decorated.

I often paint flowers with loose brush strokes, omiting any outlining or drawing step, but I cannot seem to do animals that way. I need to draw a proportioned outline. For many years I used oil pastel pencils for this purpose, white on dark colors and pale blue, yellow or pink on lighter ones. Now tailor's chalk pencils are available in the notions section of all fabric stores; these are even better and they have a little brush attached to the eraser end. They also come in blue, pink, and white.

## Block Printing

Block printing is the process in which paint is rolled onto a block that holds a design. The block is then inverted onto the fabric and "stamped" or pounded

**Figure 19–7.** *Painting on Silk Organza*

to make a firm imprint. These designs are carved on the block either as a negative or positive impression. Figure 19–8 illustrates a negative impression, and Figure 19–9, a positive one.

The underlying principle is that the raised area of the block leaves the impression. The block can

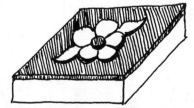

**Figure 19–8.** *A "Negative" Block for Printing*

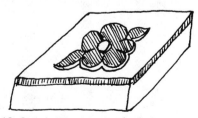

**Figure 19–9.** *A "Positive" Block for Printing*

be made of any carvable material, but wood and linoleum are generally the most widely used. Rough the surface with sandpaper and coat with white paint. Your design can be drawn on freehand or transferred with carbon paper. Any *sharp* tools can be used to carve the design. Linoleum carves more easily when warmed slightly. Put your paint on any flat, glazed surface large enough to accommodate your roller. If your design is to be repeated at regular intervals, these areas should be marked on your fabric. Make sure that your block has an exact right angle by which you may correctly aline your repeat. If two or more colors are desired, it is necessary to carve separate blocks, one for each color.

Once again, the fabric should be stretched over cardboard or illustration board that acts as a pad to absorb excess paint. The fabric in Figure 19–10 is a positive block print from Africa.

### Variation to Block Printing

I adapted a variation to block printing. I must confess that I got the idea from a television commercial advertising a way of printing a design on walls by using a carved hand roller. I covered my rolling pin with sheet floor corking which I had

**Figure 19–10.**   *Block Printed Fabric*

carved. I rolled it in the paint and then directly on my fabric. A strip of ⅟₃₂″ thick brass put where the ends met acted as a stopper. Without the brass strip the design repeated as long as the paint held out.

## Stencil Painting

Stencil painting can be a very useful tool for the costume designer. It allows exact repetition of bold patterns to be done quickly. It also enables you to use negative and postive techniques over a much larger area than block printing and to use many things as stencils.

*Negative Stencils*   An example of negative stenciling is used in making striped fabric. Lay the fabric out on the table, mark straight lines with a 48-inch-long T square, and lay masking tape along these markings. Then spray the fabric with paint (or dye if a light shade is desired). One can sometimes paint over it with a roller dipped in heavier paints if necessary. After the fabric is dry, just remove the tape. *Voila!* Stripes!

In other words a negative stencil is using something to prevent absorbtion that by its very absence creates a design. If more than two colors are desired in your striping, more masking tape can be added on top of the previously painted area and the process repeated. Variation is determined by the width of the intervals. This principle is illustrated in Figure 19–11.

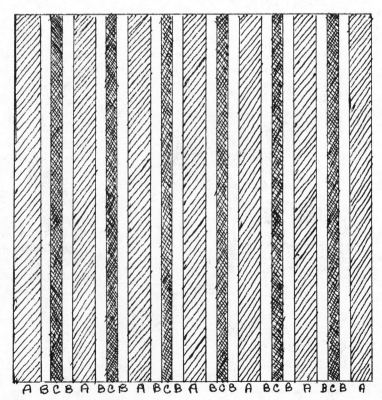

A. THIS STRIPE WAS MADE WITH 2″ MASKING TAPE. THIS STRIPE WAS A YELLOW-GREEN

B. THIS STRIPE WAS THE BASE (YELLOW) FABRIC

C. THIS STRIPE WAS MADE WITH 1″ MASKING TAPE. THIS STRIPE WAS A PEACOCK BLUE

A  BCB A  BCB A  BCB A  BCB A  BCB A  BCB A

**Figure 19–11.**   *The Masking Tape Method of Stenciling Stripes*

The same principle of negative stencil painting can be used to create a polka dot pattern by evenly spacing notebook hole reinforcements. The fabric can be spray dyed, dried, and then the little rings removed. The center of the ring is then painted another color. This gives three colors to the pattern—the newly dyed background color, the ring in the fabric's original color, and the third color of the painted center. This painted center would be an example of a positive stencil. This is illustrated in Figure 19–12.

*Positive Stencils*   The usual way of creating a positive stencil is by cutting a design out of substantial paper or thin plastic that can be cut either with very sharp scissors or an exacto knife. The open cut area can be air brushed with either dyes or paints, or roller painted. If a very sharp line is desired, it is best to draw your stencil outline and brush in by hand. This takes a little longer but the results are usually worth it. The fabric shown in Figure 19–13 was done this way. This was how the pattern for the replica of the dress from the Duc du Berry's *Book Of The Hours* was done. This can be viewed in toto in the frontispiece; its source is shown alongside. An illustration of the stencil for this is shown in Figure 19–14.

There was a second reason for drawing the stencil outline first in this particular instance. Two colors were used. The diamond-like design was a darker shade of the background while the connecting circles were painted metallic gold. Normally two stencils would be needed for direct painting of a second color. This circumvents that step altogether.

**Flocking**

Flocking is the name industrially used for the addition of extraneous particles to a design. Often the design is done in clear glue and fiber particles are dusted on top of the entire surface. The glue dries and the excess particles are blown away, leaving only those that made contact with the glue.

This basic principle can be used for any number of odd effects. It's a great way to "glitz" a costume. Dust on metallic glitter or mica, tiny opalescent glass beads, tiny pearls, or even sequins. The basic design can be brushed on either freehand or by stenciling.

**Silk Screen Technique**

Silk screening is a form of stencil work. A piece of silk organza is stretched over a frame. Onto this a

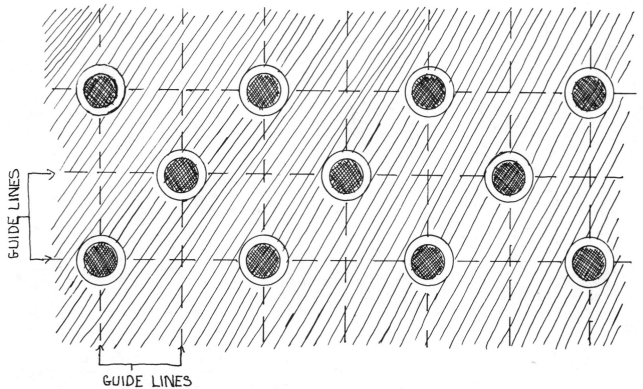

**Figure 19–12.**   *Polka Dots Made by Stencil and Hand Painting Techniques*

**Figure 19–13.** *Positive Stencils on Fabric*

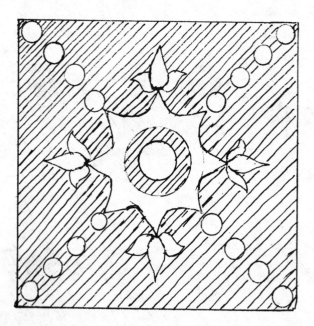

SCALE ½" = 1"

**Figure 19–14.** *Stencil Pattern from the Duc du Berry's* Book of the Hours

design is painted with a resistant medium. Paint is then pushed through onto a receiving fabric which is thus printed. The fabric pictured in Figure 19–15 is an example of commercially painted silk screen work. Compare this with the dyed silk screened work previously pictured in Figure 19–5. The painted silk screened fabric has been extensively developed in two particular areas of the United States, Key West and the Hawaiian Islands. Lily Pulitzer fashions use this type of fabric almost exclusively.

*Materials Needed*

There are several different methods of silk screen preparation, so the following list of materials should be treated merely as a general guide:

1. *Silk organza for mesh*
2. *A frame*
3. *Resistant material*
4. *Newspapers*
5. *Brown paper*
6. *Paints*
7. *Squeegee*
8. *Fabric*
9. *Masking tape*
10. *Tacks*
11. *Cleaning Solutions*
12. *Brushes and pencils*

*The Mesh* For the best results pure fiber silk organza should be used as the mesh. It will take either water soluble or solvent soluble resistants and cleaners. If you don't know the fiber content or cannot afford the pure silk, test a little piece of your organza first. This fabric is then stretched over a frame and securely tacked down. For a clean edge, cover this tacking with masking tape.

*The Frame* In costume work it is most beneficial when the frame covers the entire width of the fabric. This width becomes the length of the frame. It is convenient to keep a supply of frames in lengths of 36, 45, 54, and 60 inches since these are the most commonly used widths of dressmaker fabrics.

The width of your frame is determined by the desired width of your repeat motif. I personally prefer frame widths to be 24" to 28". Those widths create a convenient repeat most readily adaptable to flat pattern pieces. Judicious placement of most pattern pieces will fit that width. The exception would be full or widely gored skirts. I discovered this convenience when I invested in some gorgeous Japanese "obi cloth." (The obi is the wide waistband and little back pillow that Japanese women wear over their kimonos.) Obi cloth is an extra heavy brocade, often

**Figure 19–15.**  *Painted Silk Screened Fabric*

over embroidered, that is woven in widths of only 24 to 28 inches. It is also extremely expensive, not only because of its workmanship but because it takes twice the length of ordinary fabric to make a dress.

*Resistant Materials*  Your resistant materials are used to block out your design. First draw your design (or trace it if you are copying something). Then use either a solution of white glue and water, lacquer, or shellac as block-out resistants. Paint around the design, so that the paint only goes through that area. White glue dries clear and is difficult to see. A drop of washable food coloring in it will tint it and enable you to see exactly what you are doing. When this is dry, hold it up to the light and check for little pin holes left by tiny air bubbles. Fill these in with more resistant.

*Preparation of the Table*  You should cover your table with newspapers first and then a layer of brown wrapping paper taped down to form an absorbent padding under your fabric. If you are only doing small areas, blotter paper is excellent. The reason the brown paper is needed is to prevent the newspaper ink from getting on your fabric.

*Selection of Paints*  Any one of the previously mentioned paints can be used as long as it is compatible with the resistant material. When in doubt, test first; it saves the gnashing of teeth. The paint must be of milkshake consistency. When using acrylics, empty a tube of color in a coffee can, adding just enough water to have it pour. Enamel paints are the right consistency from the can.

There is a hobby store paint that works very well for silk screening; it is called Flo-Paque and is manufactured by Floquil, Inc. It is premixed to the right consistency, is opaque, and even comes in metallic colors. When ironed it becomes washable although the metallic gold and silver seems to lose its shine if washed in strong detergents. The paint is then poured out into the well created by inverting your frame onto the fabric. Use a squeegee to push it through the mesh. (Squeegees can be bought in hardware stores.) Your squeegee should be big enough to fit exactly inside your frame. It can also be made by a piece of flexible rubber nailed between two pieces of wood.

*Cleaning Solutions*  Your frames can be cleaned off and used for the additions of other colors or stored for use another time. Detergent and water will clean off the white glue. Mineral spirits or solvents will clean off the lacquer or shellac. Be sure to read labels and test, if necessary.

### Advantages and Disadvantages of Silk Screening

For costume work silk screening has both advantages and disadvantages. The advantage is mainly that you can do large areas quickly. For small areas this process is too time consuming and stencil work or block printing should be used. Also, the frames take up storage space and the work area required may be too extensive for the size of your shop.

### Other Methods of Silk Screening

Other methods of silk screening include lithograph crayon, water soluble and solvent soluble tusche, and stencil film. These products are available at arts and crafts store and come with directions. There are numerous books on the subject in your library.

Figure 19–16 shows the bodice of a Renaissance outfit with a combination of applied techniques. The stomacher and lower sleeves have been hand painted, appliqued, edged in braid, and beaded with pearls. The bead work and appliques are part of the needlecraft techniques described in the next chapter.

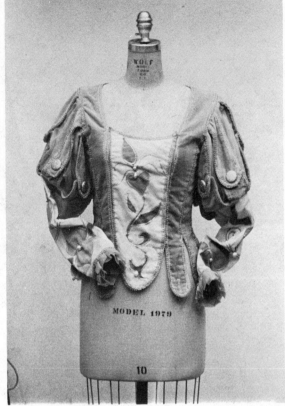

**Figure 19–16.** *Renaissance Bodice with a Combination of Applied Techniques*

# 20

# Needlecraft Techniques

Needlecraft techniques are those methods of applied design that are done with an eyed needle and some sort of yarn or thread. These include needlepoint, petit point, gros point, bargello, cross stitch, crewel embroidery, drawn work, cut-out work, and trapunto.

In China some of these techniques go back 3000 years. Ancient oriental Emperors left certain elaborately worked pieces in their wills to their heirs. Murals on the walls of Egyptian tombs show women doing needlework. This art is mentioned in the Old Testament—"fine linen with embroidered work from Egypt" (Ezekiel 27:7).

Mathilda, the wife of William the Conqueror, celebrated her husband's victories by embroidering the Bayeux Tapestry. Technically speaking it is not tapestry at all, but crewel embroidery on linen measuring 20 inches by 230 feet.

Geoffrey Chaucer, as secretary to John of Gaunt, Duke of Lancaster, mentions in an inventory list of items destroyed by the Savoy castle fire the sad loss of the "Arthurian Tapestry" that had been embroidered by Eleanor of Acquitaine. It had supposedly been passed down through six generations, and was said to have covered an entire wall in its depiction of King Arthur and the Knights of the Round Table.

The invention of steel needles in the mid-fifteenth century gave great impetus to the needle arts. The list of queens who were noted practitioners include Elizabeth I, her arch rival Mary, Queen of Scots, and her mother Anne Boleyn. Ann Boleyn's petit point was even admired by her detractors.

There was such a popular demand for embroidered dress goods during the English Renaissance that Elizabeth I granted special privilege to the "Boiders Guild," men who earned a living by doing this for commercial profit.

In Victorian England all types of "stitchery" were prized. The inventions of machines during this time seemed to give all types of handwork greater importance. The later Victorians were prone to guild the lily somewhat. Embroidery was done with the locks of a loved one entwined with the thread. Needlepoint was combined with a glass bead on every stitch to give texture to the design. All sorts of drawn work, cut-out work, and embroidery were combined on the same creation augmented by tassels or fringe.

In the early twentieth century, the mania for machinery almost totally replaced handwork, but with the increase in leisure time, a renewed interest in and appreciation of these skills became evident.

Bobbin techniques are also included in this chapter. While strictly speaking this is not a needlecraft, it does include thread and yarn techniques that are "kissing cousins" to some of the needlecraft techniques.

Bobbin techniques include tatting and certain forms of lace making. These techniques have lost out to machines. It is included here because as costumieres, you should be able to recognize it when you find it. Then, too, if you understand the basic techniques involved, you might be able to repair it or adapt these for your own creative uses.

## Overlayed Canvas Needlecraft

Overlayed canvas needlecraft includes petit point, needlepoint, gros point, bargello, and latch hooking; those crafts that involve the working of yarn over a loosely woven but highly sized fabric called a "canvas." This is not the canvas used for sails or in the scene and costume shop. This canvas is bought by how many spaces it has to the inch. Latch hooking and gros point are done on canvas that has four to six holes per inch. Needlepoint uses canvas that generally has eight to twelve holes per inch. Petit point uses fourteen to as many as twenty-four to the inch.

*Latch Hooking*   Latch hooking is used generally in rug making or for thick tufted areas. It employs a latch hook instrument and heavy yarn cut in short pieces which are looped over the right-angled junction of warp and woof threads. This method can be used for making yarn wigs in costume work. You must soak the canvas in vinegar water to remove the sizing and then shape it to the head by darting and tucking. The raw edge can be bound in soft elastic. Just remember always to latch your wigs starting at the bottom and working up row by row.

*Petit Point, Needlepoint, and Gros Point*
Needlepoint, petit point, and gros point are all essentially the same stitch. The difference is in the type of thread or yarn and the number of stitches done per inch.

Figure 20–1 shows a piece of Victorian needlepoint depicting a gentleman in Rococo attire talking to a maiden over a garden wall. This was worked in a combination of stitches and threads. The majority of the picture is done in wool needlepoint, but the faces were worked in silk petit point.

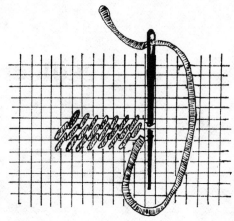

**Figure 20–2.**   *The Basic Needlepoint Stitch*

Figure 20–2 illustrates the basic needlepoint stitch, which is diagonally over one. Many other stitches are used in combination with needlepoint these days, but they are technically not needlepoint. They are adaptations of other stitchery techniques.

*Tapestry Stitch*

One variation to the needlepoint stitch does need mention; that is the tapestry stitch. Figure 20–3 pictures a pillow done in this stitch. As you see, it creates a ridge.

Please do not confuse this stitch with tapestry work. Tapestry is a weaving art. The tapestry stitch was made to imitate that look. It is really an over-one, up-two stitch, as illustrated in Figure 20–4.

Needlepoint is quite time consuming (petit point even more so). I do not recommended that you do much of it, but you should know enough to be able to repair a needlepoint purse, vest, or pillow prop. Gros point can be done fairly quickly and is sometimes useful in costume work.

*Bargello*   Figure 20–5 shows a needlework in process. It, too, is a combination of stitcheries and threads. The onion-like center design is done in bargello. The threads are a combination of wool, cloisonne silver yarn, and DMC embroidery floss. Cloisonne yarns are discussed in Chapter 17 on jewelry making. DMC is a brand name that has become generic for a cotton floss that has the look of silk.

The background is done in needlepoint but with this variance. The diagonal direction of the stitch was purposely changed in each quarter to focus toward the center. Generally the diagonal direction always goes one way. The essence of bargello is that it is an arrangement of stitches in a straight vertical

**Figure 20–1.**   *Victorian Needlepoint*

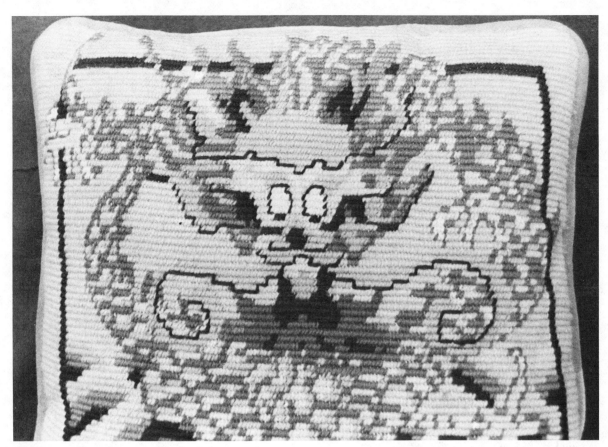

**Figure 20–3** *Tapestry Stitch*

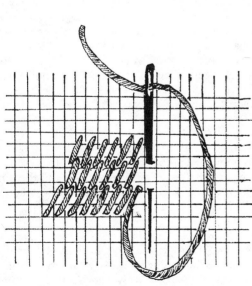

**Figure 20–4.** *The Tapestry Stitch (Over-One, Up-Two)*

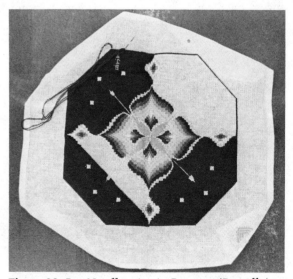

**Figure 20–5.** *Needlepoint in Progress (Bargello)*

or horizontal line. Patterns and variations are endless and any needlecraft store will have books on the subject. Bargello goes quickly and is useful for suspenders, vests, purses, etc.

## Embroidery

Embroidery is any of a thousand stitches used on woven fabrics and with any number of yarns and threads; silk, DMC®, and wool are the most readily available in this country. The embroidery techniques easily adaptable to costume work are cross stitch, crewel, satin stitch, and smocking.

*Cross Stitch* Figure 20–6 shows a cross stitch pillow done in wool of a heavy weight square woven linen fabric. Because of its direct application to the fabric, this is a useful costume tool. This particular type of cross stitch is done from a graph in which you count squares of symbolized colors. Figure 20–7 is the finished product of the graph in Figure 20–8.

You *must* have a square woven fabric. In this case the linen warp and woof threads were heavy enough to be seen with the naked eye. Ginghams and evenly squared plaids also work.

The rose pictured in Figure 20–8 was done in this technique on a green linen background, but the square weave was much finer so DMC was used; then only three threads to the floss were used, as compared to the six threads used in the bargello design of Figure 20–4.

At the end of most pattern books, you will find an "accessories" section in which they sell transfer patterns for all types of embroidery including cross stitch. This can be done on any fabric.

Purists of embroidery technique will tell you that you should be sure all your top cross-over stitches are worked from the same diagonal. At the risk of suggesting a bad habit, I feel it pertinent to point out that for stage purposes no one will ever see it that closely to tell the difference.

**Figure 20–6.** *Cross Stitch Pillow*

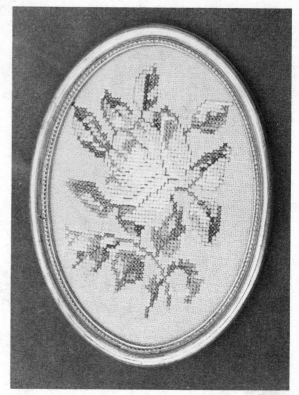

**Figure 20–7.** *Rose Cross Stitched from Graph in Figure 20–8.*

*Crewel* On the subject of crewel the purists again pontificate that the design must be worked out in a wool yarn of a specific crewel twist, like the piece of Indian crewel pictured in Figure 20–9. In today's parlance crewel has become the popular term for all kinds of stitchery techniques involving a certain group of stitches worked either singly or in combination with one another. Figure 20–9 was done entirely in one stitch—the chain stitch.

Chapter 21 is an illustrated glossary of stitches most commonly used in crewel work and general costume sewing. You will be surprised at how many so called "embroidery stitches" you've been using in everyday sewing for years but for different purposes.

*Feather and Fern Stitches* Figure 20–10 shows an example of a pillow I made as a child, using only two basic stitches, the feather stitch and the fern stitch which is really a variation of the straight stitch. This makes good peasant detail.

*French Knots* Figure 20–11 shows an example of Chinese embroidery almost exclusively done in what are called French knots. How the Chinese stitch became French is truly a ponderable question. However, it certainly points out the bicultural nature of the art.

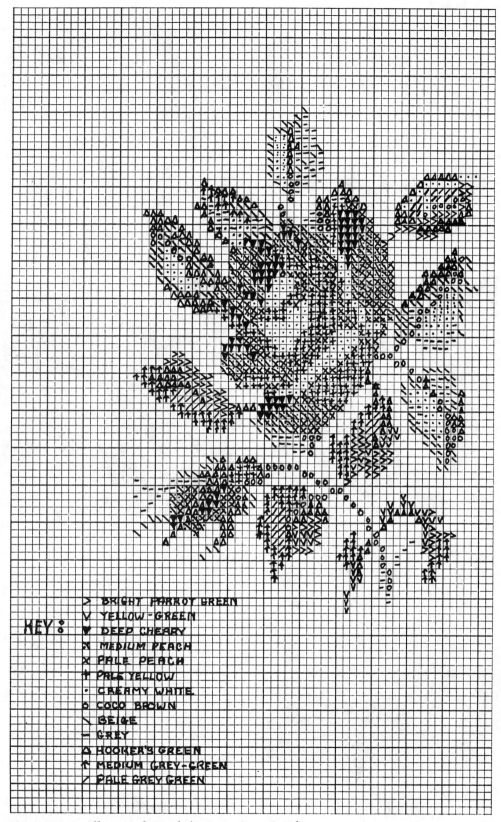

**Figure 20–8.** *Illustrated Graph for Rose Cross Stitch*

**Figure 20–9.** *Indian Crewel*

*Satin Stitch* Figure 20–12 shows an example of modern Japanese satin stitch embroidery. Both this and the Chinese piece are silk threads on silk fabric. Whether these two are done by hand or machine is impossible to tell by looking.

The Chinese embroidery was done on a pair of pants donated to Florida Atlantic University. The satin stitch was on an inexpensive kimono I bought in Japan. Its cost indicates it might have been machine-made.

The long and short stitch used primarily on the machine-made Mexican embroidery of Figure 20–13 can be duplicated either by hand or on some of the new sewing machines. If you wish to do this, your machine must be able to use two needles at once and be used without the presser foot. It should also

**Figure 20–10.** *Pillow of Feather and Fern Stitches (made by the Author)*

**Figure 20–11.** *Chinese Embroidery Done in French Knots*

**Figure 20–12.** *Japanese Satin Stitch Embroidery*

**Figure 20–13.** *Machine-Made Mexican Embroidery*

be able to free feed so that you can move the design. Your instruction book will give you all the details.

Some fabric stores carry certain spools of embroiderer's thread for this purpose, even to monochromatic shading on a single filament.

*Smocking* Smocking is taking a pattern of stitches and extending it at regular intervals so that the stitch gathers the fabric into a design. Smocking transfer patterns are also available in most pattern books.

*Running Stitch Embroidery* Figure 20–14 shows running stitch embroidery. As this demonstrates, a thread is run through a woven fabric in what seamstresses would term a basting stitch. One side of the fabric is the exact reverse of the design on the other side. There is not necessarily a right or a wrong side. In the example pictured, the background striped fabric is wool while the running stitch is a shiny cotton cord-like thread. According to its label, this was made in Mexico. It is impossible to be absolutely sure if it was made by hand.

## Other Needlework Techniques

There are other needlework techniques that, strictly speaking, are not those of embroidery. These include applique, patchwork, beadwork, fagotting, cut-out work, quilting, and trapunto.

**Figure 20–14.** *Running Stitch Embroidery*

*Applique*

The art of applique is the cutting of small pieces of colored fabrics into various shapes, arranging them upon or around one another on a separate background fabric in such a manner as to form a design, and then sewing them down with a variety of stitch techniques. Figure 20–15 illustrates this basic idea.

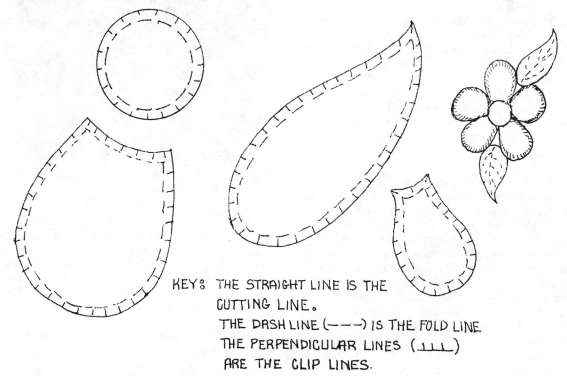

KEY: THE STRAIGHT LINE IS THE CUTTING LINE.
THE DASH LINE (– – –) IS THE FOLD LINE.
THE PERPENDICULAR LINES (⊥⊥⊥) ARE THE CLIP LINES.

**Figure 20–15.** *Applique Techniques and Illustration*

To do this properly, your shaped pieces must be cut a quarter-inch bigger all the way around than the desired finished look. This quarter-inch is then turned and pressed so as to make a tiny hem. Remember to clip all curves before turning and pressing. A slipstitch (sometimes called blind, or hidden stitch) is used to sew it down with a regular thread. Decorative stitches may also be used.

*Applique Short Cuts for the Costume Designer*   This process is terribly time consuming for the costume designer. There are several ways of cutting down on this: felt applique, glue outlined applique, "stitch-witchery" applique, and machine buttonhole stitch appliques. At this time, we costumieres should bow down and pay proper tribute to the unsung hero of the sewing machine zigzag stitch for its countless uses, particularly in applique work.

*Felt Applique*   Figure 20–16 shows Madame Ernestine's first act dress from *Little Mary Sunshine*, which was entirely felt applique work both on its dirndl bodice and apron. The advantage of felt is that it does not ravel, so no extra quarter-inch is necessary. Also, it can be glued on if you so desire, instead of sewn. In this case one color of felt was glued on top of another to build up textures as well as colors.

*Glue Outlined Applique*   To save on the quarter-inch hem turning for applique that is cut from fabric that ravels at the edges, an edge of glue can be applied. The process for this is simple: First, lay the fabric out flat on the table, then draw the shapes you desire. Now trace around the shapes with white glue. Let it dry completely. Then cut immediately along the glued edges. Place on your background fabric and machine zigzag. Set your zigzag stitch width so that your needle goes over the glued edge. Elmer's smallest nozzle-nosed bottle makes the finest edge. You just have to refill your bottle more often.

*"Stitch-Witchery" Applique*   Stitch-Witchery® is a fiber glue that can be bought by the yard, either in strips (used mainly for hems) or in 24-inch widths, which is what we desire for this process. Stitch-Witchery is actually a bonding technique.

Cut out your applique shapes, minus the quarter-inch hem. Lay them on the stitch-witchery and with a pencil trace the shapes. Cut out these pieces. Now arrange your design, sandwiching the stitch-witchery between the applique fabric and the background. Cover with a press cloth and bond with your steam iron. *Do not move your iron back and forth!* Just place the iron over the design, hold, and lift. Replace the iron and repeat, if necessary.

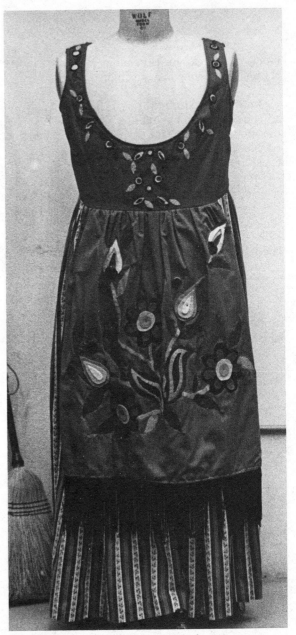

**Figure 20–16.**   *Felt Applique Work*

The manufacturers of this product claim that it is both washable and dry cleanable. It is, one or two times. After that the edges begin to lift. You may wish to zigzag the edges if your costume is going to get a lot of wear or have a long run. If it is only to be worn for two or three performances, you will not need this added step.

*Machine Buttonhole Stitch Applique*   Figures 20–17 and 20–18 show good examples of buttonhole stitch applique. The buttonhole stitch on most mod-

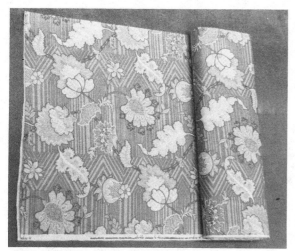

**Figure 20–17.** *Upholstery Weight Cotton*

**Figure 20–18.** *Machine Buttonhole Stitch Applique Using Flower Design Shown in Figure 20–17*

ern machines is nothing more than a very tight zigzag stitch. The fabric in Figure 20–17 was an upholstery weight cotton from which I cut the imitation crewel styled flowers and leaves. With a drop or two of white glue on the back of each flower in strategic places, I placed them to create the design in Figure 20–18. The glue was allowed to dry overnight. The next morning the edges were sewn down with a buttonhole zigzag stitch. The finished costume can be seen in Chapter 4, Figure 4–10.

### Patchwork

Patchwork is really a form of applique. The sewing and cutting techniques are the same. The difference

is that it does not necessarily have a background fabric. When an under fabric is used (but not always seen), the patches are connected by the slip stitch or any of several decorative stitches such as the feather stitch, the couching stitch, the chain stitch, or the blanket hem stitch. When no background fabric is used, the patches are merely seamed together. For the costumiere this can be done quickly by machine.

Figure 20–19 shows a machine patchwork pillow. The fabrics used were all non-raveling—a plastic lame, nylon velours, and suede cloth. While going through the scrap box at the end of a show, the colors appealed to me so I cut a circle of muslin, overlayed the various pieces, and zigzag stitched them onto the muslin.

You can use the same technique in costume work quite effectively. Take your muslin construction lining, place your patches, and zigzag accordingly. Some of the new machines with the fancy stitches also take embroidery threads. They are fine for this kind of patchwork, particularly the feather and old-fashioned buttonhole stitch (not zigzag, the couching stitch).

Figure 20–20 is an example of several applied techniques used in a patchwork quilt. This was designed and worked by Alice Provonsha. She calls it "Flower Beds." You will see appliqued areas surrounding the flower bed. The flowers have been quilted by an outline embroidery stitch and embossed in the trapunto manner.

### Quilting

As shown in Figure 20–20, quilting can be achieved by several of the aforementioned techniques. It is

**Figure 20–19.** *Machine Patchwork Pillow*

**Figure 20–20.**  *Patchwork Quilt Utilizing Several Applied Techniques*

basically a textured technique made by the sandwiching of a bulky filler between two flat pieces of fabric, tacking it in such a way that the stitch forms a design. This can be seen in Figure 20–21.

### Trapunto

Trapunto is also a quilting technique usually done to a printed fabric for a bas-relief effect (see Fig. 20–20). The area to be extended is outlined stitched through a backing fabric. Small cuts in each area are made in the backing and small pieces of filler are pushed through, usually with a fine crochet hook. Polyester fiber fill and cotton batting can be used for this, as well as the padded layer of regular quilting. I personally prefer to use pieces of old nylon stockings for my own trapunto work because they seem to slide into tiny spaces with greater ease.

### Beadwork

Beadwork is a design achieved by the application of tiny pieces of glass, sequins, pearls, and stones. Fig-

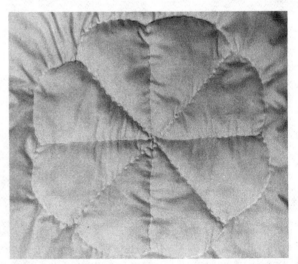

**Figure 20–21.**  *Quilting Design Formed by Stitching*

ure 20–22 is an example of hand done beadwork designed by Mrs. Provonsha as part of a class project. The iridescent dark beads are round, the pearls are called oats, and the long ones are silver bugle beads. When sewing by hand, a special beading needle and

**Figure 20–22.** *Beadwork—Direct Application*

NOTE: EACH BRAND OF SEWING MACHINE HAS ITS OWN VERSION OF THIS

**Figure 20–23.** *A Sequin Foot*

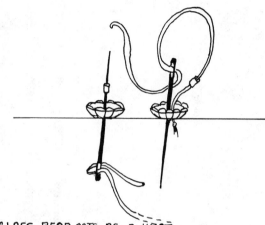

A GLASS BEAD ACTS AS A KNOT

**Figure 20–24.** *The Technique of Sewing Sequins*

monofilament beading thread are required. If the bead hole is large enough, mercerized thread can sometimes be used with a regular needle.

Figure 20–22 is an example of direct application. Sometimes beadwork is done on a fine net and then the net is appliqued onto the garment. This has the advantage of being reusable when the garment wears out.

*Special Equipment:* Besides the previously mentioned beading needles, you should also have a rhinestone setter and a sequin foot for your machine. The latter, sometimes called an embroidery foot, is illustrated in Figure 20–23. You will also need an assortment of beads, pearls, and stones. Sequins can be bought by the string and machine sewn. They can also be sewn individually. The technique is to attach them with a bead anchor (see Fig. 20–24).

## Faggoting

Faggoting is a name applied to both a type of embroidery and a type of stitch; it is used to join together two pieces of fabric, leaving an open area be-

tween them. You will find the stitch illustrated in the glossary of stitches in the next chapter. Figure 20–25 illustrates the joining technique.

## Drawn Work

Drawn work is a procedure by which either the warp or woof threads are removed at certain intervals and the remaining threads are pulled together or apart by any of a number of different stitches. This creates a pattern. In very lace-like patterns both warp and woof threads are removed. The name is derived from the fact that the threads are "drawn out." Figure 20–26 is an example of this technique.

## Cut-Out Work

Eyelet is the best example of cutwork. It is done commercially better than is possible by hand. It can be bought pre-ruffled for edgings or by the yard for dresses, petticoats, and lingerie.

You may wish to try the same technique on a larger scale. Figure 20–27 shows the hem of a late Victorian skirt that was done this way. The design

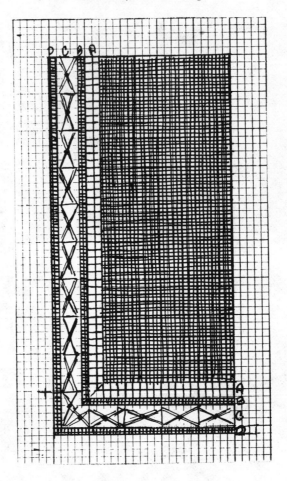

A. EVERY OTHER THREAD WAS DRAWN OUT BOTH
   VERTICALLY AND HORIZONTALLY
B & D. FABRIC AS IS
C. 9 VERTICAL THREADS REMOVED (FROM CORNER
   TO RIGHT) AND 9 HORIZONTAL (TOP TO CORNER);
   THE REMAIN THREADS WERE PULLED TOGETHER
   AND KNOTTED TO FORM A DESIGN

**Figure 20–25.** *The Technique of Faggoting*

was marked on the navy blue outer fabric. Each gore was flat lined in a pale blue. The cuts were made leaving a quarter-inch to be clipped and turned under. This was then basted down. A blue braid was used as an edging as well as further detailing. It was zigzagged around the cuts and elsewhere as necessary. This one step secured the cutwork edges. Then the bastings were removed.

## Bobbin Techniques

Bobbin techniques are usually associated with lace making. Lace is a fine netting of linen, cotton, or silk woven in an ornamental design. How lace making started is a subject for great conjecture. Some of the oldest types are in display in the Vatican Museum in Rome, Italy. Some historians believe it was

The three basic parts of most lace are the netting, called a "ground"; the pattern, called the "flower" (whether it is really a flower design or not); and the "brides," which join together the patterned areas. Brides are sometimes called webs. An example of this woven lace can be seen in Figure 20–28.

*Hand-Made Laces*

Hand-made laces include crocheted lace, tatting, point lace (sometimes called needle or nail lace), bobbin lace, appliqued lace, and embroidered lace. There is no doubt that all of these techniques would be far too time consuming, but you should know them if only to be able to repair them, restore them, or fake them.

*Tatting* Tatting is a lace edging made by a bobbin instrument called a shuttle and very fine cotton or linen yarn. It is a series of half hitch knots done in an alternating under and over pattern combined with ornamental loops called picots.

*Crocheted Lace* Figure 20–29 shows an Irish lace collar made of very fine linen yarn. It is really

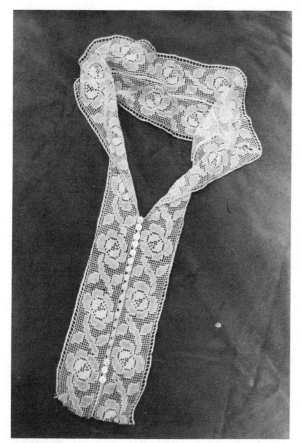

**Figure 20–26.** *Pattern Created by Drawn Work*

**Figure 20–27.** *Cut-Out Work on Victorian Skirt Hem*

**Figure 20–28.** *Woven Lace*

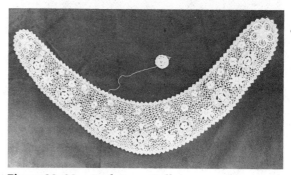

**Figure 20–29.** *Irish Lace Collar*

originally started by cloistered nuns for glorification of the Church. We will never be absolutely sure.

There are as many techniques of lace making as there are places that make it, but whether it is hand-made by a little old woman sitting by the steps of Chartes Cathedral, in a factory in Venice, or by a Campfire Girl with an empty spool into which six nails have been pounded and around which string is woven, the process is endlessly fascinatng.

a crochet technique that starts with a simple rosette like the one pictured between the collar ends. You will find patterns for this in any number of needlecraft magazines. The dress pictured in Figure 20–30 shows Irish lace insertion work.

*Insertion*    Insertion can be done with either lace or ribbon panels. The lace is appliqued onto a garment and then the fabric is cut away from the reverse side. Use small very sharp scissors and cut very carefully. Figure 20–30 shows this in an actual period dress from 1912.

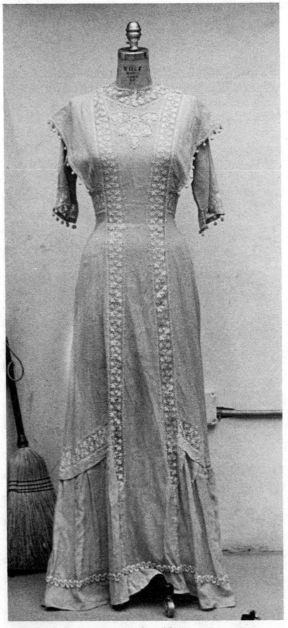

**Figure 20–30.**    *Dress with Irish Lace Insertion Work*

*Point Lace*    Point lace is made from a pattern designed on a piece of paper. This is then tacked to a flat surface into which nails or pins are arranged outlining the design. Fine linen threads, held on wooden bobbins, are knotted around the pins forming the design. This process is illustrated in Figure 20–31.

*Bobbin Lace*    Bobbin lace is sometimes called pillow lace because of the convex leather pad over which it is made. Like its cousin, point lace, a paper pattern is centered on the pad and pins are placed so that the bobbin held threads can be wound around them. That is where the similarity ends.

Usually there are two weights of threads, a very fine one for the ground and a heavier thread for the flowers. Both ground and flowers are worked simultaneously. Figure 20–32 shows a piece of bobbin lace that was saved from an old dress. Save all such items. They are reusable on another outfit.

*Appliqued Lace*    This is a bobbin web gound onto which other items have been "brided" (tied on with the brides). This may include ribbons, beads, and even more lace pieces giving a three-dimensional look.

*Embroidered Lace*    This is usually bobbin net onto which satin stitch embroidery has been done either by hand or machine. The machine-made Mexican embroidered dress in Figure 20–13 has an edging of this type lace, also machine-made.

This is one of the easiest laces to fake. Use very fine tulle for your ground. Regular mercerized thread will work for two needle machine embroidery. DMC will work for hand embroidery.

Draw your design on one side of wax paper with a crayon or grease pencil. Stay stitch your tulle to the other side. Insert carefully into your embroidery hoop. The wax side should be on top if you are doing machine embroidery. When you invert and guide the movement by the frame, you can see your pattern through the tulle. The tulle side must be on top of the hoop if you are doing it by hand.

You can fake more than the lace. Many fabric stores sell a wide variety of either sew-on or iron-on appliques usually done in satin stitch. These range from anchors and sailor's stars, through pink elephants, to some lovely flowers. One such fake "embroidery" is pictured in Figure 20–33.

**Needlecraft Techniques in Combination**

You may never use some of these techniques; others you may use quite frequently. Some may be used in combination with one another. Figures 20–34 and 20–35 show the bodice to Thea's dress built for Flor-

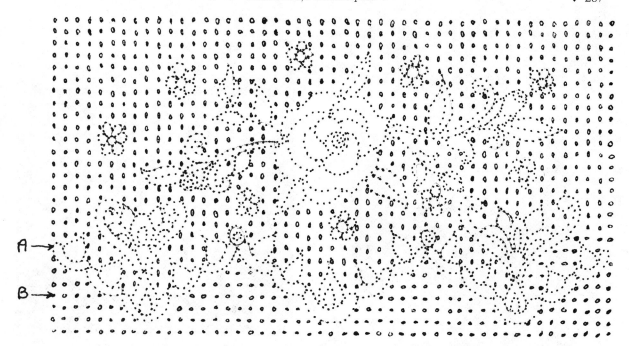

A. FOR EACH TINY DOT A SMALL PIN IS INSERTED, AROUND WHICH THE DESIGN IS KNOTTED.

B. EACH CIRCLE INDICATES THE INSERTION OF A LARGER PIN (OR SMALL NAIL) FOR THE BRIDES.

**Figure 20–31.** *Illustration of a Pattern for Point (Nail) Lace in Actual Size*

**Figure 20–32.** *Bobbin Lace from an Old Dress*

**Figure 20–33.** *Fake Embroidery Applique*

ida Atlantic University's production of *Hedda Gabler*, which was set in the mid 1880s.

You may wish to compare this with one of Hedda's dresses pictured in Figure 4–12. Whereas Hedda's character demanded the height of fashion and luxury, including velvet with fur, black jet trim, and hand knotted fringe, Thea's character would require much simpler "homecraft" detailing.

In Fig. 20–35 you will see a closeup of the detail—simple hand-done embroidery on the collar and cuffs

**Figure 20–34.** *Needlecraft Techniques in Combination*

**Figure 20–35.** *Detail of Figure 20–34*

including French knots, running stitches, lazy daisies, and satin stitches. The eyelet ruffling was bought pre-ruffled. The blanket stitching was done by machine.

Admittedly, I enjoy handwork. My childhood years were during the last great days of radio, which provided a feast for the ears but left the hands free to do other things. I developed the handwork habit. It took one evening of television listening to do that collar and both cuffs of Figure 20–34.

If you don't enjoy needlework, perhaps you can find someone who does and is willing to earn a little pin money or even donate their time to help out your theater organization. I have a delightful character actress friend who does magnificent handwork and enjoys doing it at rehearsals to fill in what she terms her "waiting time." I can usually make sure that these hours are never idle.

# 21

# An Illustrated Glossary of Stitches

In this chapter there are twenty-seven illustrated handwork stitches and the three basic machine stitches. These are the ones most frequently used in everyday costume construction[1] and simple embroidery.[2] There are many more embroidery stitches but they are difficult and time consuming. You probably would not use them, but you should have a good book of crewel in your library for quick reference.

Each stitch is listed alphabetically, its uses and an illustration are given. Also listed is the direction in which it is worked by a right-handed person. Left-handed people must compensate as necessary. The key to the illustrations is as follows: The letter A is always the spot where the thread comes up from the previous stitch. The letter B is the point of re-entry, and C signifies the place for the beginning of the next stitch.

There is always a question about when one should use a double or single thread for handwork stitches. A general rule of thumb is to sew all facings and hems, bastings and tailor tackings with a single thread unless the fabric is so heavy that it must have a double one. Sew all buttons and fasteners with a double thread (see Chapter 25). In embroidery work, choose the type and thickness of thread or yarn by the effect you wish to achieve.

[1]Vogue Patterns, *The Vogue Sewing Book* (New York: Butterick Publishing Co., 1975), pp. 209–211, 362.
[2]Jo Springer, *The Pleasures of Crewel* (New York: Western Publishing Co., 1972), pp. 29–73.

**Table 21–1.** Thirty Basic Stitches

| Name | Description | Illustration |
|---|---|---|
| The Arrowhead Stitch | This stitch is worked from left to right. It is the handworked version of the zigzag stitch and works well for knits and stretch fabrics. In embroidery it is most commonly used for smocking, or in consecutive rows as fill-in work. | |
| The Back Stitch | This stitch is worked from right to left. If you were to build a garment entirely by hand, this would be the stitch used on the seams as its two spaces forward, one back locks each stitch and it looks very neat on both sides of the fabric. In embroidery it is one of the outline stitches. | |

**Table 21–1.** (Cont.)

| Name | Description | Illustration |
|------|-------------|--------------|
| The Blanket Stitch | This stitch is worked from left to right. It is used as a decorative edging. For embroidery purposes it is used as an outline stitch or in a circle it makes a type of flower. | |
| The Blind Stitch | This stitch is worked from right to left but it is essentially the same stitch as the arrowhead. It is worked between two layers of fabric such as hems or facings and its zigzag nature allows ease of movement. | |
| The Bullion Stitch | This stitch is worked from right to left. This is essentially an embroidery stitch but can also be used as a quick bar eye. It is worked in two steps. | |
| The Buttonhole Stitch | This stitch is worked from left to right. It is exactly the same as the blanket stitch, but the stitches are much closer together. Its name describes its primary use. | |

**Table 21–1.** (Cont.)

| Name | Description | Illustration |
|------|-------------|--------------|
| The Cable Stitch | This stitch can be worked in any direction. It is essentially a chain stitch that has been linked with an overcast stitch in the center of each chain. It is used in embroidery. | |
| The Catch Stitch (This stitch when used in embroidery is called the Herringbone Stitch.) | This stitch is handworked from left to right and is used for flexibility, as was the arrowhead stitch. It provides even more stretch because of its ''backwards'' nature. Excellent for dress hems of knitted fabrics. | |
| The Chain Stitch | This is an embroidery stitch, worked in any direction, and used for outline or fill-in work. | |
| The Chevron Stitch (also called the locked catch stitch) | This stitch is worked from left to right and is technically an embroidery stitch. It can be adapted for the same purposes as the catch stitch on the exterior of a garment. Its extra stitch locks each diagonal so that if one breaks, you do not lose the whole row. This stitch is worked in two steps. | STEP 1. STEP 2 |
| The Couching Stitch | This stitch is worked right to left. It is the overlay of a basic whip stitch over another thread and can be done at regular intervals as illustrated or unevenly, in which case it is termed random couching. Both are used for embroidery. | |

**Table 21–1.** (Cont.)

| Name | Description | Illustration |
|------|-------------|--------------|
| The Cross Stitch | This stitch is worked in two steps, each going in the opposite direction. It does not matter which way is first as long as the crossing is from the same direction. This is strictly an embroidery stitch. For more on this, see Chapter 20. | |
| The Feather Stitch | This stitch is worked vertically from top to bottom. It is an embroidery stitch used for thorny stems, borders, and lacy leafed effects. It has also been adapted to the handwork required of four-way stretch fabrics because of its own four-way flexibility. | |
| The Fern Stitch | This embroidery stitch is also worked from top to bottom but you may also work it from the bottom to the top. It too is used for a lacy effect. | |
| The French Knot | This embroidery stitch may be used randomly to create dots in a line or as fill-in. It is particularly effective for flower centers. It is a single stitch and therefore has no direction. | |

**Table 21–1.** (Cont.)

| Name | Description | Illustration |
|------|-------------|--------------|
| The Lazy Daisy Stitch | This embroidery stitch is essentially the same as the cable stitch but worked in a circle. | |
| The Locked Running Stitch | This is a handwork stitch and is worked from right to left and used for the same general purposes as the regular running stitch. At the end of each needle full one takes one back stitch. | |
| The Locked Whip Stitch | This is a handwork stitch that may be worked either right to left or left to right. It is used for hems and its main advantage is that if one stitch is ripped, the rest of them will still hold. | |
| The Long and Short Stitch | This embroidery stitch may be worked in any direction. It is a version of the oaten stitch. Its use is for the shadowing of one color or tint into another. This stitch must be done in two steps. | |
| The Machine Straight Stitch | This is an all-purpose stitch done by the sewing machine in a straight line. | |

**Table 21–1.** (Cont.)

| Name | Description | Illustration |
|---|---|---|
| The Machine Stretch Stitch | This stitch is not on all mchines but it has become standard for most machines built in the 1970s. It is nothing more than a feather stitch in microcosm and is used for four-way stretch fabrics such as lycra or spandex. | |
| The Machine Zigzag Stitch (three styles are pictured. A is very fine; B, a very loose one; and C, a medium stitch) | This is a machine stitch used for applique, overcasting, buttonholing, and for seams of moderate flexibility. | A<br>B<br>C |
| The Outline Stitch | This is an embroidery stitch worked from left to right and used for the purpose stated in its name. | |
| The Running Stitch | This is a handwork stitch used for basting. It can be used as an outline stitch in embroidery. | |
| The Satin Stitch | This is an embroidery stitch that may be worked in any direction. It is the laying of one stitch beside another until a whole area is covered. If one layer of satin stitch is done on top of another, it is called a padded satin stitch. This same stitch technique can be used in darning. | |
| The Slip Stitch (also called the hidden stitch) | This is a handwork stitch used on hems so that only a prick is seen on both the interior and the exterior because the needle travels through the pocket of the turned up fabric edge of the interior hem. | |

**Table 21–1.**  (Cont.)

| Name | Description | Illustration |
|---|---|---|
| The Stem Stitch | This is an embroidery stitch worked from left to right and used for outlining. Essentially it is the same as the outline stitch, but the thread is held under, not above. | |
| The Straight Stitch | This is an embroidery term for an individual stitch. If it is done in a line it would look like a running stitch. The circular straight stitch is illustrated. | |
| Tailor Tacking | This is a herringbone-like stitch worked in rows going from top to bottom in one row and bottom to top in the next. It is used to hold layers of padding or interfacing to a garment until finishing work is completed. It can also be used to tack open seams. | |
| The Whip Stitch | The whip stitch is used for hemming and tacking down facings. It is a handworked stitch and may go either from left to right or right to left. | |

# FIVE

# Miscellaneous Tricks of the Trade

In those questionnaires that seem to be so much a part of today's computer society, there is always a little box marked "all" or "none of the above." This section is devoted to just that—costume problems that are unique to this business and do not fit elsewhere. This includes a variety of odds and ends from "how to" techniques of sewing fur, to aging clothes, to fast changes.

I have always found most theater people warm hearted and willing to share ideas freely for the benefit of "Theater" with a capital T. Many of these next how-to's have been gleaned from notes at theater conferences or the mutual sharing of problems. I don't even remember who first told me about FEV or bird seed padding, or making stage blood out of liquid detergent and food coloring. The list is endless. The best way to thank them all is to pass it on.

FEV can be included in painting techniques. Bird seed padding is classified as padding. Where does one classify stage blood? (Under miscellaneous tricks of the trade?)

# 22

# Aging Costumes

In theater terminology a show that requires aged, ragged looking costumes is often called "a rag show." A list of rag shows would include *The Beggar's Opera, Oliver, Waiting For Godot, Mother Courage,* and *Fiddler On The Roof.* The best rags are made from pure silk. It frays nicely, floats, and dyes beautifully. It looks wonderful when layered. It has only one disadvantage—its expense. The easiest way to get aged clothes is to wear them out. Theatrically speaking this means using those stock items that are on their last legs. If that does not suffice, try to buy what you need from thrift shops and second-hand clothing stores.

There is no substitute for the actual wear and tear look of old clothes, but that is only one consideration. The other is that if you age newly constructed garments, you have ruined their life expectancy as costume equity. You might just as well throw them out at the end of the run.

There are many times when a character requires a costume that does not look brand spanking new, but does not look completely worn out either. Chekhovian plays are wonderful examples of this. In *The Cherry Orchard,* Lyubov Ranevsky, her daughter Anya, her brother Gaev, and her daughter's governess Charlotta all come from the big city and should be examples of studied sophisticated elegance. It is actually the need for this elegant way of life that causes the downfall of the orchard. Lyubov, Anya, and Gaev would be the height of fashion. Charlotta would be the height of cast-off fashion, perhaps her dress is several years old and although in perfectly respectable condition, requires a "lived-in" look.

Trofimov, Pishtchik, and Epihodov are part of the middle- to upper-class gentry. They would dress correctly but simply and neatly. Varya is essentially of this group as well, but as the adoptive daughter of Lyubov Ranevsky, she might have a touch of discarded elegance, a hand-me-down from her mother.

Lopahin is the epitome of the nouveau riche. His dress might be fashionable in its parts but put together in a gauche manner. On the other hand, Yasha, Gaev's valet, is a climber. What money he earns would be spent on himself to better his station. He would probably be almost as elegantly dressed as his master, but in a manner befitting his occupation.

Dunyasha the maid is a flirt, young and pert. She would be dressed as attractively as possible but in country or "nationalistic" mode. Her clothes would be neat, clean, but not new. Firs represents the cherry orchard itself, old and forgotten. His clothes would be ragged and patched and probably too big, as if he had shrunk in old age. The play even includes a vagrant in complete rags.

Because this drawing of class distinction is not unique to this play but is evident in all of Chekov's works, one is led to believe that he is using this as a means of definite social comment on Mother Russia herself. For this one play alone, your aging techniques would run the entire spectrum.

**Elements of an Aged Look**

An aged look is achieved in four ways: by wear, by texture, by color, and by accident. There is one general rule of thumb. Clothes age fastest in places that get the most use. This use is determined by the individual characteristics as defined by the playwright.

*Wear*

In this chapter, the word "wear" does not mean "to put on the body," but "to consume by constant use," as in the expression "wear and tear."

Let us ask ourselves how a garment loses its new-ness. It is washed or dry cleaned. It loses its sizing or "finish" and softens. It becomes limp. If it is cut on the bias, or of certain loosely woven fabrics, it begins to sag in the seat if the character sits a lot. It may wrinkle more if the character is not particular about his or her appearance.

These things need a technique for achieving that "lived-in" look. Wash the garment several times; do not iron it. Steam a wool suit while it has sand bags in its pockets or pants seat and let it dry. The sag will remain. Remove all starch and the garment will be limp.

### Texture

Aged texture is acquired through frequent contact with an abrasive surface, through frequent contact with a hard surface, and through applied texture.

*Abrasive Surfaces*   A man's shirt collar frays in the front because of frequent contact with his chin and neck whiskers. Cuffs fray because of contact with various rough surfaces. Depending on a character's occupation other areas fray.

To get a frayed look, use a nail file, a rasp, or sand paper. You may preweaken the fibers chemically. The best way to do this is to do all the things you were told *not* to do in Part Four. Once again, you should sample test, but this time you are looking for the opposite results.

*Hard Surfaces*   People who have office jobs in which they spend 75 percent of their time sitting down on hard chairs wear a shiny spot into their elbows, pants seat, etc. This shiny look can be achieved by ironing a plush fabric flat. For wool, cotton, or linen, iron as flat as possible and paint with a coat or two of lacquer. Another trick that works extremely well on wool is to place a piece of waxed paper on top and then a piece of brown paper on top of that and iron. The wax paper gives the wool its shine while the brown paper prevents the wax from getting on the iron.

Fabric fades in repeated washing. Fading can be quickened by an overall dunking in a bleach solution or dye remover. Fabrics also collect dirt on the job. This look can be achieved by a fine spray of dye, acrylic, or enamel paint.

*Applied*   Applied texture is that which is added on. Patches are an example of this technique. The addition of glue, sawdust, grit, or dirt is also applied. White glue can be mixed with these. This is then painted on with an old brush.

### Accidents

All of us have daily accidents that ruin our clothes. You cut something in your lap and cut your dress along with it. A taxi driver burns a cigarette hole in your good coat. Some spill glue all over themselves, and many of us never learned how to eat a taco or hamburger neatly. These things happen to characters as well.

Cigarette burns are best achieved by just that. But be careful to singe only the fibers; don't set the place

**Figure 22–1.**   *Distressed Costume*

on fire. Acetone will bubble certain synthetic fibers; mineral spirits will bubble other synthetics. Undiluted bleach will also eat holes. You can cut your fabric into holes and shreds with scissors, but for a frayed edge use a razor blade.

There seems to be a move toward the viewing of more blood onstage these days and as every armchair detective knows, blood stains are hard to get out, even when the blood is synthetic. Try using a blue colored liquid detergent to which a few drops of red food coloring are added. It gives it that bluish-red color of well oxidized blood, maintains the consistency of blood, and even bubbles if air is added, *but* . . . it washes right out in the washing machine and you don't have to use extra soap. Items that receive this should be washed as soon as possible so that the soap doesn't harden into the fiber.

Food stains are accomplished by the judicious use of dyes and paints. If this must be done to an otherwise usable garment, you will want to have it wash out. The detergent trick for stage blood has variations. Mix a little green and yellow food coloring into the detergent and paint it on knees and elbows with a stiff brush for grass stains. Mix a little red and a lot of blue for a red wine stain, and so forth.

For the proverbial pie in the face, don't use whipped cream which leaves a permanent shiny stain. Top your pie with shaving cream. This washes right out. Keep the whipped cream idea for a shiny seat look. Coffee and tea give a marvelous "yellow with age" look to white. They can also be painted on as stains, but they are permanent.

In theatrical lingo the process is sometimes called "distressing." Figure 22–1 shows one garment so distressed. This was a "suppliant" costume for the futuristic production of *Blood Wedding* previously mentioned in Chapters 12 and 15. It was cut, frayed, and splash dyed.

Splash dyeing is the art of literally throwing the dye at the fabric, a little at a time. If the garment is upright, the dye will run down in interesting patterns. If the garment is laid out, the splash will make uneven rings. Spattering techniques from your scene painting class will also work.

# 23

# The Technique of Sewing
# Feathers and Fur

There is nothing quite as rich, luxurious, and tactual as fur. It is sensual, barbaric, and elegant all at the same time. I deplore killing any animal purely for one part of its body; it only seems natural to consume the whole animal for survival—the hide for warmth and the meat for food. We have gone beyond that and therefore I am just as gratified by good fake furs.

From the theatrical point of view fake furs are often more convenient and economical than real ones. In this chapter we shall discuss both real and fake furs; where to buy them and how to sew them. We will also discuss the buying and sewing of feathers. Feathers cannot be faked.

### Sources of Supply

Fake fur can be purchased in most fabric stores during the late summer and fall season, in preparation for winter. Window display supply houses carry it year round as do some upholstery fabric shops. Theatrical fabric suppliers also carry it year round.

Real furs can be bought from a furrier by the skin. In large cities there are wholesale dealers in fur; in small cities there may not be. The Tandy Leather Company sells some fur skins. They have stores from coast to coast. Consult your telephone book.

Some less expensive fur pelts can simulate very expensive ones from the stage but you may not wish to contend with the following ideas or procedures.

Domestic dog and cat can look like a lot of different things depending on the breed. Thousands of these animals are killed daily, thanks to the human population's lack of responsible breeding care. Contact your local animal shelter and pick up what you

need. (They charge nothing.) Take it to a taxidermist. He will skin the animal and tan the hide for a reasonable fee.

You can buy horsehide directly from the slaughter house, and they will send it to the taxidermist for you. Your friendly taxidermist can also supply you with all sorts of skins as hunters often bring in a whole animal but only want the head stuffed. He can also supply you with rare feathers, all sizes of glass eyes, and all sorts of bleached bones, horns, etc. I don't deny that this is a bit ghoulish and takes a strong stomach. It all depends on how far you are willing to go to achieve your specific design.

Most feathers can be bought in a wide variety of places. Peacock feathers are very popular at this time for oriental floral arrangements and can be purchased in florist shops, variety stores, and hobby markets. You will occasionally find ostrich plumes there, as well as packages of dyed chicken feathers. Costume and dance supply houses carry dyed quill feathers. Feather boas can sometimes be found in fabric stores. Hardware stores always have feather dusters, usually either turkey feathers or natural colored ostrich plumes. If you live in an area of the country where people hunt quail and pheasant, the skins can usually be purchased at flea or farmer's markets. You may have to pluck them out of the skin.

Thrift shops may have fur pieces or old fur coats at a reasonable price, as well as old feathered hats.

### Fur

Furs can be divided into five main categories: long haired, medium haired, plush haired, short haired, and woolly. Long haired furs include lynx, fox, coyote, raccoon, llama, wolf, angora goat, and monkey fur. Medium haired furs include squirrels, ermine, mink, muskrat, ferret, miniver, sable, martin, mongoose, and rabbit. Plush furs include chinchilla, beaver, otter, and seal. Short haired furs include the cats, deer, and pony skin. Woolly furs include Persian lamb, sheepskin, caracul, astrakhan, and camel.

Regardless of type, all real furs have two things in common, a "right" and a "wrong" direction to the pelt and a hide. The pelt gives a light and a dark look, much like velvet, depending upon the direction in which it is sewn. The "right" direction is achieved by sewing it the way the hair grows. The "wrong" direction is achieved by sewing the pelt in the opposite direction from the hair growth. The hide requires hand sewing when attaching pelts because machine stitching would damage the fur and weaken the hide.

*Matching the Pelt*   As with fabric dye lots, fur pelts must match in color, but they must also match in luster and depth of plush or length of hair.

*Cutting Pelts*   To cut fur, you have to use a razor blade and cut only the hide. The hair will part. Some hides are more delicate than others. For these delicate ones that cannot take much strain, a narrow twill tape is used as reinforcement when seaming

together the pelts. Some pelts cut better if the hide side has been dampened slightly with a sponge. Pelts are laid side by side and connected with a feather stitch as illustrated in Figure 23–1.

*Cutting the Pattern*   Once the pelts are sewn together in a big enough area to cover your pattern piece, you may draw around the pattern with a felt-tip pen onto the hide side. Add seam allowance where necessary. This must also be cut with a razor and the main seams stitched by hand in the manner previously described.

*Sewing the Fur Garment*   After you have sewn your darts, then you must cut away the excess with your razor blade. The neck, closure, and bottom edges should be turned back a half-inch and a bit of glue used to hold it. Then cover this edge with a narrow bias tape. Make your fabric lining and turn under its neck, closure, and button edges five-eighths of an inch. Align the lining into the fur exterior so that there is an eighth-inch of the fur extending beyond the lining on all sides. With a double thread, slip-stitch the lining to the fur exterior from the lining side.

The lining fabrics should be fairly sturdy. For small fur pieces, such as collars, cuffs, muffs, or hats, a silk faille is excellent.

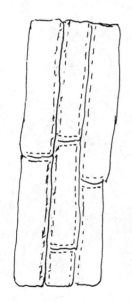  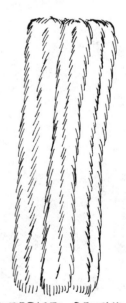

THE CONNECTION OF THE PELTS     FEATHER STITCH     THE EXTERIOR OF THE FUR

NOTE: THE DOTTED LINES INDI-
        CATE TWILL TAPE

**Figure 23–1.**   *The Technique of Sewing Fur*

*Fake Fur*

Real fur coats cost what they do not only because of the cost of the pelt but also because of the handwork involved in their construction. Fake fur is cheaper on both counts, even at $50.00 and $60.00 a yard for the better quality fur fabrics. It is usually sold in pieces 54 to 60 inches wide by two to four yards long. You must also match up these pieces if more than one is required.

Fake fur too must be cut in one direction, but it can be cut with scissors and sewn on the machine. The outer edges may also be glued and the lining should be attached in the same manner as the real fur.

*Sewing Tails*   The only animal tails that are sewn separately are ermine tails, and even that is only done occasionally. Most of the time, if the tail is worn, it is left attached to its skin. If you are sewing ermine pelts, lift the tail before adding on another pelt. Ermine tails can be simulated out of white rabbit pelts or fake fur as shown in Figure 23–2. Once they have been made, dip the ends in a little black paint.

**Feathers**

For the observant ornithologist, feathers come in four basic types—long, short, quill, and curled. There is also down and marabou but technically these are not feathers. A feather must have a central shaft. A diagram of a feather is illustrated in Figure 23–3. As you can see from the diagram, the down is the fine soft fluff at the base of the barbs. Marabou is that same section stripped from the feathers of a Marabou stork of South Africa.

Long feathers, often called plumes, include the tail feathers of the ostrich, peacock, pheasant, and turkey. Short feathers are the body feathers of most birds and include chicken, goose, and ducks. Quills are the medium wing and tail feathers and include crow and egret feathers. Curled feathers are usually the tail feathers of a cock. Ostrich plume barbs can be curled artificially. Most white feathers can be dyed through the process of osmosis. I have not tried this because it is no more expensive to buy dyed ones than natural.

*Feather Boas*   Boas are nothing more than many feathers strung together on cords approximately 72

**Figure 23–2.**   *Pattern for Ermine Tails*

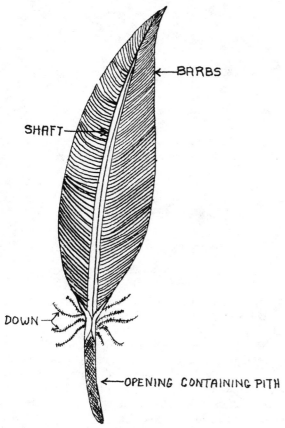

**Figure 23–3.** *Diagram of a Feather*

scissors and put a tiny drop of glue to secure the end. Then sew as desired.

*Sewing the Feathers* Feathers must be hand sewn. When attaching a feather boa, I pin it in place and sew it from the reverse side with a locked whip stitch (see Chapter 21).

When sewing single feathers, a whip stitch can be used, but the shaft should be pierced as little as possible. One hole can be entered several times, as when sewing a button. Too many piercings and the shaft will split.

If you need to sew short feathers on so that they overlap, making a coat of feathers, you must once again copy Mother Nature. Start at the bottom and work up, overlapping the shaft tip with the next layer. If you are making a showgirl headdress, start at the top and work down to the head.

If you wish to make a brush of feathers, gather some netting or tulle to the desired size, and attach it to your hat or garment. Dip the shaft end of each feather in glue and insert it into the net. This principle is illustrated in Figure 23–4.

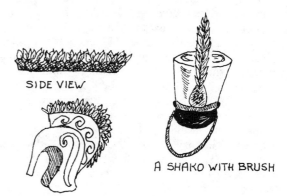

SIDE VIEW

A GRECIAN HELMET WITH BRUSH

A SHAKO WITH BRUSH

**Figure 23–4.** *A Feather Brush and Its Decorative Uses*

inches in length. These can be bought ready made. You may wish to use them as trim for the hem of an evening gown a la Ginger Rogers, or for a collar and cuffs. Each end of the boa has a tail of the cord. This can be knotted to another 72-inch piece (and so on) until you have the desired length. If you need to cut the boa short, give yourself an extra inch. Remove any feathers that have been damaged by the

# 24

# Fast Changes

Whether the playwright is Sophocles, Shakespeare, Sheridan, or Shaw, they all seem to have a complete disregard for how long it takes an actor to change his clothing. Sophocles and Shakespeare did not have union wages to worry about and could hire numerous actors if they so desired. Today the problem of "a cast of thousands" on stage is handled by what is theatrically termed "doubling." One actor plays several parts, each in a separate costume. This may save the producer salary money, but it does not save a thing on the costume budget.

Sheridan was sensible in that his characters play out their follies in a consecutive time span, but being a male, he did not realize how long it took the women of his day to cope with panniers, patches, and wigs. Shaw has no such excuse. His characters wax and wane through years of time, revolution, battle, heaven and hell in the space of two and a half hours.

But the fault is not always with the playwright. Sometimes casting restrictions bring about these problems. I designed one production of Rodgers and Hammerstein's *Oklahoma* in which there were exactly six chorus female dancers. In the middle of the dream ballet three of these had to become the shady dancehall ladies, a complete costume change in 24 measures of music at 4/4 time, or 96 beats. A beat is roughly equivalent to one second. This casting restriction was necessitated by the lack of available bodies who could dance at a certain level of proficiency. This often happens in community and educational theater situations which depend upon the quality of talent available at a given time.

Sometimes the size of the stage demands casting restrictions. Small arena productions must of necessity use smaller casts. Even the amount of dressing room space can affect the size of the cast. I recently read a newspaper account of a particular production

being closed down halfway into its rehearsal period because of fire laws prohibiting so many people in such a confined backstage area.

Whatever the cause of using one actor to play several parts within one production, you can be sure a fast change will be needed. Sometimes fast changes are written into a part for comic effect. One such change is done by Finch in the Frank Loesser, Abe Burrows production of *How To Succeed in Business Without Really Trying*. He makes his entrance as a window washer wearing coveralls. Before your very eyes, he rips these off to reveal a young executive attire underneath. In one step this action illustrates two costume effects, break-away clothing and underdressing.

## Break-Away Clothing

Break-away clothing are garments that are meant to fall apart *on cue*. My favorite solution to this problem is Velcro, a fastener product that has two strips which lie one on top of the other. One strip is heavy plush, the other side has stiff looped "teeth." When placed together, the teeth grip into the plush. It comes in black and white and can be purchased in any fabric store by the yard. When pulled apart, velcro also has a wonderful ripping sound. This is fine for clothes that need to be "torn" on stage, as Stanley's shirt needs to be torn by Blanche in Tennessee Williams' *A Streetcar Named Desire*.

Velcro has another advantage in that it can be used for long lengths that ordinary zippers will not cover, but it also has one distinct disadvantage. It cannot take stress very well. If a costume is very tight, purposely made to reshape a section of the lady, or intended for a lot of action, I don't recommend it.

Break-away techniques can be used for unseen changes as well, but to the Velcro you should add the use of elastic and upholstery zippers.

The elasticized waist saves a lot of time in trousers, petticoats, and skirts. It also works well under shoe buckles for fast changes in that department. You can now buy upholstery zippers in a continuous line by the yard. The metal teeth are inserted in strong twill tape and you receive an accompanying bag of zipper tabs and instructions on how to work them onto the zipper.

### Underdressing and Overdressing

Underdressing is simply wearing one costume under another. This often helps in fast changes. The underdressing does not have to be an entire outfit. Often just a shirt and one pair of trousers worn under another can help. Underdressing can facilitate speedy changes off stage as well as on it. This scheme is the only solution for He and She in John Van Druten's play *The Fourposter* or its musical stepchild, *I Do, I Do.*

Its opposite is overdressing—putting one costume on top of another. This is done by the cellmates of Cervantes in the musical *The Man Of La Mancha*, by Dale Wasserman and Albert Marre with music and lyrics by Mitch Leigh and Joe Darion.

### Preparation for Fast Changes

Break-away clothing and under or overdressing should be planned by the designer well in advance. This is simply proper preparation work. The wardrobe mistress in commercial theater or the head of the costume crew in the non-commercial situation also must make careful preparation for fast changes. (If you are in an educational situation, you may find yourself in both positions.)

The wardrobe mistress must consult the designer for what he or she may have done to ease the change. She must familiarize herself with the script enough to know when these changes are required, and she must consult the stage manager as to where these changes must take place. The easiest way to do this is to watch several rehearsals and take notes, with a stopwatch if necessary. If she is involved in a musical production, she may wish to consult the score (if she reads music) or the conductor.

### Timing the Change

Creating the tempo is a form of timing. Running the lines with the stopwatch is another. If you are the wardrobe mistress, you must now walk the stage. Don't walk the set. You must walk behind the scenery from exits and entrances. You should also walk from the exit to the dressing room and back to the place of the character's next entrance. This alone can be prohibitive to a fast change. In that case, the place of changing will have to be given some thought. A screen and a rack can be placed on the side stage, in a connecting scene shop, or in the wings and used for changes.

The physical changing must be timed. Dress a dummy and see how long it takes one person to change it. If that takes too much time, use two or three people.

### Placing the Change

Sight lines may also require special precautions. I once saw a production of Arthur Miller's *Death of a Salesman* in which Willy Loman's house was centered against a cyclorama skyline drop. Biff and Happy have very fast changes from pajamas to suits and back to pajamas in the middle of a scene. In this case there was no way of getting offstage without being seen. Conversely there was no way for a wardrobe person to get to them either. This was solved by having the wardrobe person get behind the scenery at the act break and staying there until the act was over.

### Controlling the Actors' Nerves

Actors can sometimes be your best help or your worst hindrance in fast changes. The ones that are your best help are those that do what you tell them to do when they are told, and trust you enough not to need a mirror. Preening wastes valuable seconds. They understand that you will not let them go onstage unzipped or with their headdress on crooked. The best way to assure this confidence is to get together and rehearse the actual changes. At that time come to an agreement as to who does what, where, and when. Rehearse it until the pattern has been established.

At the beginning of this chapter, I mentioned the fast change of the dancehall girls in *Oklahoma*. As girls at the picnic they had on gingham and calico dresses, sunbonnets, petticoats, bloomers, white tights, and black character shoes. As dancehall girls, they were to wear the same black shoes, fishnet tights, black dance briefs, a black ruffled skirt, a corselet, a dog collar, spats, and wigs with ostrich plume decorations. They had no time to run to the dressing room, so a dressing area was blocked off in the scene shop. The director helped by having them exit and enter from the same side. It took two dressers per performer.

As designer, I sewed elastic to the shoe buckles so that they could be slipped on and off without actually being buckled. I also used zippers everywhere but the back of the corselets, which of necessity needed hooks. Their sunbonnets were sewn to one set of wigs and the ostrich plumes were sewn to a second set. The performers underdressed, wearing their fishnets and dance briefs under their white tights and bloomers. They then just stood with their arms extended while the dressers did the rest. One dresser was assigned to the bottom half; the second took charge of the top half.

First the shoes were removed. The sunbonnet and its wig were removed at the same time. Then the bloomers and tights were stripped down while the dress and petticoat was pulled over the head. The dancehall skirt was stepped into, pulled up, and fastened at the same time as the choker was snapped into place. The shoes were put on again simultaneously with the corselet. Then the spats were snapped on the feet as the wig was put on the head and adjusted. All of this took 66 seconds. That left 30 seconds for an addition of dark eye-shadow and rouge and a quick breath before their next entrance. I have detailed this example to enable you to think through your own fast change problems.

The way to a speedy "fast change" is careful preparation and cooperation on everyone's part.

# 25

# Built to Last

◆ ◆ ◆

In the introduction to this volume we discussed the figurative difference between dressmaking and costume construction. We discussed the fact that a costume must be fortified against hard wear and tear. In this chapter we shall delve into the "how to" techniques used to accomplish this. We will scrutinize some hand sewing and machine sewing techniques and how they specifically apply to costume construction. It is important to review fasteners with this same format in mind, and perhaps take a look at a few tailoring short cuts. We shall also discuss a few real time wasters.

### Construction Lining

The construction lining has been defined and discussed in several places throughout this book (Chapters 4, 8, and 9). It is the best device for strengthening the total garment but it must follow a general rule of thumb. It should be used on those garments or parts of garments that conform to the body shape. It is unnecessary in areas that have milfoilious pleats or gathers that are intended to flow freely from the body.

### Fasteners

Fasteners include hooks and eyes, snaps, buttons, zippers, grippers, lacings, and fastener tapes. We have used them all many times but there are a few techniques and problems peculiar to the costume business.

*Costume Uses of Hooks and Eyes*  Hooks and eyes come in all sizes, two shapes, and either black or silver. There is the common garden variety hook and two eyes, the round eye and the bar eye. There are also the ones designed for pants and skirt waistbands. These two basic varieties are illustrated in

**Figure 25–1.** *Basic Varieties of Hook and Eyes*

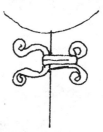

**Figure 25–2.** *Hook and Eye Use to Have Closure Meet (but not Overlap)*

Figure 25–1. The costume business probably uses hooks and eyes far more than regular dressmaking. The modern zipper has replaced them for a good bit of closure work, but for most period detail, zippers are anachronistic.

1. *The round eye has two specific purposes in costuming.*
   a. *The meeting, but not overlapping, of two finished edges, as pictured in Figure 25–2.*
   b. *Their use as "eyelets" for lacings, pictured in Figure 25–3.*
2. *The bar eye is used for almost all other hook and eye purposes.*
3. *There is the large waistband hook and eye that is also good for closures of kneebands, garters, and excellent as a secure closure for "points" when you want your ribbons and lacings to be stationary. Figure 25–4 shows the use of this on*

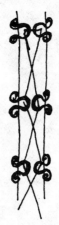

**Figure 25–3.** *Round Eyes Used as Eyelets*

**Figure 25–4.** *Hook and Eye Used for an Overlapping Closure*

an overlapped waistband closure. Putting two on a waistband in opposite directions (on the interior overlap) acts as a double lock against stress.
4. *There is a specific trick to sewing a hook in the costume trade. You will see on the hook illustrated in Figure 25–1 a little bump. Your high school home economics teacher probably instructed you to sew the hook "down" by inserting the needle through this bump and going through the fabric just under it several times for security. This does help to prevent the hook from flipping up, but only a little. For costume purposes we want to prevent the hook from flipping at all. Therefore we must sew it at the end of the hook, as illustrated in Figure 25–5.*

*Costume Uses of Snaps*   Snaps, like hooks and eyes, come in black and silver and in a wide range of diameter sizes, from an eighth-inch to a half-inch.

**Figure 25–5.** *The Costumer's Method for Sewing Down Hooks*

They have either four or six holes and two parts, male and female (see Fig. 25–6). Snaps are far stronger than Velcro but not as secure as hooks and eyes in stressful conditions. For costume work all hooks and eyes, snaps, and buttons should be sewn with a double thread. The four-holed snap should have six stitches per hole and the six-holed snaps, four stitches to achieve security of equal strength.

In dressmaking, a good seamstress always puts the black fastenings on the dark colored outfit and the silver on the pastel.

As we saw in Chapter 24, fast changes are not always made under optimal conditions. It often behooves the costumer to do just the opposite. This enables better "night vision" so to speak.

*Costume Uses for Buttons*   Buttons are either ball, shank, toggle, two-holed, or four-holed, as illustrated in Figure 25–7. Whatever their type, they must be secured as strongly as possible. This is done by winding thread around the underside of the button several times before plunging the needle through the fabric for its final tie off.

When shank buttons are bought, they are usually held onto the card by a little spring-like pin, as illustrated on the shank button in Figure 25–7. This can be used if the shank is fitted into an eyelet.

**Figure 25–6.** *Male and Female Snaps*

←SHANK

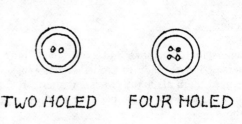

TWO HOLED      FOUR HOLED

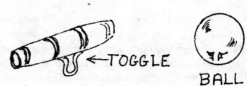

←TOGGLE

BALL

**Figure 25–7.** *Types of Buttons*

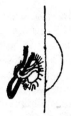

**Figure 25–8.** *Shank Button Held on through an Eyelet*

**Figure 25–9.** *Two Shank Buttons Used as Cufflinks*

Military uniforms often use this technique, which is illustrated in Figure 25–8. Little brass safety pins can also be used for this purpose. This shank and safety pin method can be used as shirt studs. It is particularly effective with small pearls or rhinestone buttons.

Cufflinks can be made by cording two buttons together, as shown in Figure 25–9. Both buttons may be identical, or the exterior may be a handsome jeweled one and the interior, a neutral or unobtrusive one.

*Costume Uses for Zippers* We discussed the use of the continuous upholstery zipper in fast changes. Here I should like to discuss dressmaker zippers. Zippers come in certain lengths and materials. Choosing the right one is too often guesswork when it need not be. Zippers are made with metal teeth, nylon teeth, and polyester teeth. Special zippers are made on a flexible tape especially for knitted garments, and jacket zippers are purposely made to separate completely.

For costume purposes try to avoid nylon zippers. They have a nasty habit of splitting open at all the wrong times. They are not very durable to stress, strain, or heat. Polyester zippers are fine for light to medium weight garments, but for real security I prefer metal.

The length is determined by the use and placement desired on a particular body. Standard lengths are 7, 9, 11, 12, 14, 16, 18, 20, 22, and 24 inches. Once in a while you may find 26-inch zippers in neutral colors such as beige, white, black, and brown, but they are rare. Large-teethed jacket zippers up to 36 inches long can be ordered in most fabric stores.

Upholstery zipper lengths are 18, 22, 24, 32, 36, 48, and 54 inches or the previously mentioned continuous length, but they are almost always on a "natural" or bone colored tape. The following is a comparison of zipper lengths to their possible uses.

1. *The 7-inch zipper: Its standard use is for placket openings in skirts, ladies' slacks, tight sleeves, or pockets.*
2. *The 9-inch zipper: Its uses include the bottom of tight pants legs, ladies' fly-front slacks, or the neck opening of an A line or tent dress when only the head needs to emerge.*
3. *The 11-inch zipper: Fairly standard for the fly openings of men's trousers.*
4. *The 12-inch zipper is best for a side seam opening in ladies' waisted garments because it allows six inches above and six inches below the waist.*
5. *Zippers 14 through 24 inches are used as neckline opening zippers for either the back or front of garments. The way to judge the correct length per garment is to measure the opening from neck to waist and add six inches to it for the opening below the waist. In this case six inches is a standard measure that allows most people enough room to pull a garment up or down their bodies with ease. For a larger person you may wish to allow seven or even eight inches.*

As a hypothetical example, let us consult the measurements of Jane and John Doe. Jane's shoulder-to-waist at center back measurement is 16½ inches. To that we add six inches, which brings the total to 22½ inches. A 22-inch zipper will be fine with the addition of one hook and eye at the top neck.

For John, whose same measurement is 18 inches, we add six inches and buy a 24-inch zipper.

If you are working with an individual who does not exactly fit this formula, you can always buy the next size up and stitch closed the teeth of the bottom of the zipper. Then the excess below that may be cut away, as illustrated in Figure 25–10.

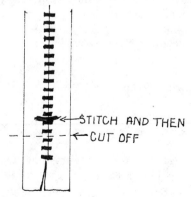

**Figure 25–10.** *How to Shorten a Zipper*

*Costume Use of Grippers* Grippers require a specific instrument for installation. Often the instrument that installs metal eyelets has a gripper installer as well. The gripper is used much the same way as a snap but is now decorative, like a button. However, it is pressed *through* the fabric and cannot be changed or moved without leaving a permanent hole. This is not always advantageous in costume work, as the star's costume in production A will work its way down to the chorus of production Z and will have been worn by 24 other people in between these two shows.

*Costume Use of Lacings* Lacings are the oldest form of fastening garments together. Lacings may be made of everything from leather to rope to any and all kinds of fabric cordings.

For costume work, I make most of my lacings out of double-fold bias tape which I stitch together. It comes in packages of five-yard lengths and can be cut in any length desired. It can also be dipped in a solution of white glue and water to give it added strength when it is completely dry.

Shoe laces can be bought as long as 48 inches and used to lace. Leather thongs can be used as can various ribbons and plastic strips.

For lacing one must have strong eyelets. We discussed the adaptation of round eyes for this. Metal eyelets come in brass, silver, and assorted colors, attainable in any fabric store. Grommets of various sizes can also be used, but they too require special setting instruments.

If the garment to be laced is lightweight or will not encounter too much stress and strain, eyelets may be cut in the fabric and bound with a buttonhole stitch by hand. For added strength a four-ply thread can be used. This is done by doubling a doubled thread.

*Costume Uses of Fastener Tapes* Fastener tapes are either hook and eye tape or snap tape. These can generally be bought in upholstery fabric stores or from a notions jobber or wholesaler. They are a gift from heaven to the costumer who does not have experienced finishers. They eliminate hours of handwork. (Snap tape can also be used as a substitute for Velcro in break-away clothing.)

## Hand Sewing Techniques

The hand sewing techniques that most effect the costumiere are those involving hems and facings.

*Hems* There are garments that need rolled hems, hems for woven fabric, hems for knit fabric, and no hems at all. There are hems that are one inch deep, two inches deep, and sometimes a foot deep.

How do you decide which is the one you need? Hems serve a twofold purpose. They give a finished look that a raw edge at the bottom of the garment might not achieve. They also add weight to a garment to give it an evenly smooth edge even when the body is in motion.

There may be times when you desire just the opposite look, in which case you do not want a hem at all. For a rag show you might want a frayed, uneven look to your garments. In this case cut them off at the desired length and, if a woven fabric has been used, zigzag the edges to prevent fraying. Because knitted fabrics often do not fray, they may not need this step.

If you are designing a dancer's costume for which you desire flowing movement, you would not want weighty hems to interfere. Again, just cut it off at the desired spot. For chiffons and organza, pinking shears are recommended.

You must decide on the depth of the hem in the cutting process. That decision is based on how much weight you feel is necessary to achieve the desired movement in any given piece of fabric. Let us say you are building a Renaissance skirt that is made to look like an overskirt and an underskirt. The overskirt is velvet; the underskirt, silk crepe. You will not need more than a one-inch hem to achieve a good movement in the velvet. You would probably wish to construction line the silk and even then, you might need a six-inch hem to achieve the same stately movement.

For the Victorian dress with its ornate trimming at the hemline, it was often necessary to interface a six- to twelve-inch hem with horsehair, so that the weight of the trimming will not destroy the continuous vertical line of the skirt. Nylon screening makes an excellent substitute for horsehair.

If even more weight is desired than the hem can afford, lead weights can be put in the hem. Lead washers work, but my favorite is a string of lead pellet sinkers obtainble at any fishing tackle shop. Drapery shops carry muslin-covered lead-weighted strings that also work well.

The rolled hem is usually done on the machine in costume work. This hem is generally used for small items, ruffles, sleeves, and blouses. Some knit dresses also benefit from no more than a rolled hem.

Many costumieres do their regular hems on the blind hemstitch of their machines. I do not like this because it is time consuming to remove this the next time the costume is worn by another person. I do my hems by hand. For woven fabrics I use a locked whip stitch (see Chapter 21 for all stitches). The reason is that if one stitch breaks by accident, the whole hem does not come down. For knit fabrics I use the catch stitch, which allows for greater movement without stress, much like the machine zigzag does compared to its straight stitch.

*Facings* I also hand stitch facings. This has a double purpose. Often in quick costume changes, there may not be time to fuss with facings that flip up or flop out. Then too, quite often when a construction lining is used, the facing alone is stitched to it, not the exterior layer. A simple whip stitch is used. Stitch-witchery may be used to bond a facing, but remember that repeated cleanings will loosen this. Whichever method you choose, the desired effect is smooth strength.

## Machine Sewing Techniques for Trimming

In costume construction the more you can do by machine, the better. That includes doing as much trim work as possible. Most trim can be sewn on either with a centered zigzag stitch or a straight stitch down each side. The zigzag stitch works particularly well for multi-curved trims. The straight stitch works well for ribbons or single edging. The stretch stitch is used on elasticized fabrics, such as spandex or lycra, and on such stretchable garments as bathing suits, leotards, tights, and certain undergarments. It should be used not only for the seams but also for the attachment of trims.

Many costumieres rely on glue to attach their trims. I find this only a stop gap measure, used for emergencies. For real strength, trim must be sewn. Glue, acting as a substitute for pins, will work as an intermediate step of holding until the stitching can be accomplished. The advantage to this over pinning is each pin tends to take up the fabric a little. The glue method eliminates this. Remember to let the glue dry completely before sewing.

### Necessary Attachments

Most machines have special features that are fun but not necessarily all that important to the costume business. The drop arm is one. It is nice to have but does not really speed up the sewing time if the adjustment to the machine is difficult. I feel much the same about the buttonhole attachment that automatically measures the button. It does not take that long to draw a line, and buttonholes of the same type can be made with just your zigzag stitch on a "fine" setting.

*Buttonholes* On old straight stitch machines there used to be a wonderful buttonhole attachment which produced a keyhole-shaped buttonhole with a buttonhole stitch around it. It was so easy that you simply marked your garments and at the end of the week did all the buttonholes at once.

*Ruffler* That same machine has a ruffle attachment that automatically gauges ruffles when set for double, triple, or quadruple fullness. Both of these attachments came with a secondhand Singer featherweight portable, manufactured in 1948. That machine runs on AC or DC current and is the greatest investment I ever made. It has been all over the world with me. My local Singer dealer tells me that these machines were made between 1943 and 1953 with all steel parts. If you can find one, grab it. The attachments are often standard to brand and will fit several models. Check into it and you may be pleasantly surprised at how much time you can save.

*Feet Attachments* Most machines have various interchangeable feet for specific purposes. For example, there is a zipper foot and a cording foot. I learned long ago how to put in a zipper without a zipper foot because changing feet wastes time when you have to put in a zipper here and a zipper there. On the other hand, if you organize your work, the zipper foot works very well when doing zippers all at one fell swoop.

The cording foot is useful for attaching bulky trims as well as cording. It is also very useful in hat construction because it allows the needle to get as close as possible to the crown or the brim edge.

## Short Cuts

Thanks to modern invention and ingenuity, there are some handy shortcuts to sewing and tailoring, including stitch-witchery, iron-on interfacing, merrowing, bag lining, and certain clipping techniques.

*Stitch-Witchery* Stitch-witchery has been discussed in several chapters throughout this book. Its greatest boon to tailoring is its use in bonding interfacing to either the exterior or lining of tailored garments. It saves all that tedious tailor tacking.

*Iron-on Interfacing* Iron-on interfacing is an interlining that has the fusible glue already in it. It saves cutting three pieces by only having to cut twice.

*Merrowing* Merrowing is done on a specific industrial machine. There is a small version available called a Baby Lock (see Chapter 1). This stitch seams and overcasts in one step and saves on almost all necessary french seams.

*Clipping and Trimming* In the costume business you should never trim seams. They may have to be let out for the next person. The same holds true for darts. Only slit them open when you absolutely must.

As for clipping around curves, you only have to clip a little bit. You do not need to cut out whole wedges and you certainly need not cut all the way into the seam. Leave at least a quarter-inch. This, too, may need adjusting at a later date.

*Bag Lining* When you bag line a garment, you are essentially making two identical garments and fitting one inside the other. They are sewn together, right side to right side, reversed, pressed, and top stitched about three-eighths of an inch in from the edge. This can often save hours of careful facing and lining work, particularly on men's vests and tailed coats.

### Total Time Wasters

I've tried to show you some ways to save time and build things strongly. There are a lot of couturier touches that are totally unnecessary in the costume business.

*Hand-bound Buttonholes* Hand-bound buttonholes are for the rich who can afford to pay a dressmaker $7.00 for each hole. The ways previously mentioned will suffice for costume work.

*Bound Seams* It is far too time consuming to bind seams in the first place, let alone take them apart when you wish to alter a costume. If you are worried about a piece of fabric fraying, go around its outer edge with an ordinary zigzag stitch.

*Colored Threads* We briefly mentioned in Chapter 1 that colored threads were a waste of time. You should keep black for dark colors, white for pastels, grey for medium colors, and red for red. Red is the one color upon which all neutrals show.

*Covered Fasteners* Many couturiers do lovely corded hooks and eyes or fabric covered snaps. That is totally unnecessary in the costume business. You should only do as much handwork as is necessary.

No one can tell you all there is to know about constructing costumes; it is a neverending process of trial, error, and experiment. That's what makes the job so fascinating.

A good cook is one who follows the recipe faithfully, leveling off every teaspoon and cup. The gourmet cook is one who runs out of vanilla and substitutes almond, discovering a new tickle for the taste buds. I hope that I have given you enough of both flavors to tickle your imagination into its own creative discoveries.

# Bibliography

## General Technical Information

Allison, Alexander W.; Carr, Arthur J.; Eastman, Arthur M. (editors). *Masterpieces of the Drama.* New York: Macmillan Company, 1957.

*American Mail Order Fashion 1880–1900.* Scotia, New York: Americana Review, 1961.

Burris-Meyer, Harold and Cole, Edward C. *Scenery for the Theatre.* Boston: Little, Brown and Company, 1971.

Crisp, Clement and Thorke, Edward. *The Colorful World of Ballet.* New York: Crescent Books, 1978.

Gibbs-Smith, Charles H. *The Fashionable Lady in the 19th Century.* London: Her Majesty's Stationery Office, 1960.

Hanford, Robert Ten Eyck. *The Complete Book of Puppets and Puppeteering.* New York: Drake Publishers, Inc., 1976.

Lord & Taylor 1881. *Clothing and Furnishings.* United States: The Pyne Press, 1971.

Schroeder, Joseph J. (editor). *The Wonderful World of Ladies Fashions.* Northfield, Illinois: Digest Books, Inc., 1971.

Shesgreen, Sean (editor). *Engravings by Hogarth.* New York: Dover Publications, Inc., 1973.

Welker, David. *Theatrical Scene Design.* Boston: Allyn and Bacon, 1979.

## Pattern Drafting

Arnold, Janet. *Patterns of Fashion #1 English Woman's Dresses and Their Construction 1660–1860.* London: Macmillan London Limited, 1972.

———. *Patterns of Fashion #2 English Woman's Dresses and Their Construction 1860–1940.* London: Macmillan London Limited, 1972.

Barton, Lucy and Edson, Doris. *Period Patterns.* Boston: Walter H. Baker Company, 1942.

Croonborg, Frederick T. *The Bluebook of Men's Tailoring.* New York: Van Nostrand Reinhold Company, 1977.

Ewing, Elizabeth. *Dress and Undress.* New York: Drama Book Specialists, 1978.

Harrison, Mary Kent. *How to Dress Dancers.* Kent, England: Midas Books, 1975.

Hill, Margot Hamilton and Bucknell, Peter. *The Evolution of Fashion: Pattern and Cut from 1066–1930.* New York: Reinhold Publishing Company, 1967.

Kunicor, Robert (editor). *Mr. Godey's Ladies.* New York: Bonanza Books, 1921.

Payne, Blanche. *History of Costume.* New York: Harper and Row Publishers, 1965.

Tilke, Max. *Costume Patterns and Designs.* New York: Hastings House Publishers, 1957.

Waugh, Norah. *The Cut of Women's Clothes 1600–1930.* New York: Theater Arts Books, 1968.

———. *The Cut of Men's Clothes 1600–1900.* New York: Theater Arts Books, 1964.

## Construction Techniques

Barton, Lucy. *Historic Costume for the Stage.* Boston: Walter H. Baker Company, 1963.

Ingham, Rosemary and Covey, Elizabeth. *The Costumer's Handbook.* New Jersey: Prentice Hall, 1980.

Johnson, Lillian. *Papier Mache.* New York: David McKay Company, Inc., 1958.

Kraus, Gottfried. *The Saltzburg Marionette Theater.* Saltzburg, Austria: Residenz Verlag, 1966.

Motley. *Theater Props.* London: Studio Vista, 1975.

Paterek, Josephine D. *Costuming for the Theater.* New York: Crown Publishers, 1959.

Prisk, Berneice. *Stage Costume Handbook.* New York: Harper & Row Publishers, 1966.

Vogue Patterns. *The Vogue Sewing Book.* New York: Butterick Publishing, 1975.

Welker, David. *Stagecraft.* Boston: Allyn & Bacon, 1977.

## Jewelry

Flower, Margaret. *Victorian Jewelry.* New York: A. S. Barnes and Company, Inc., 1967.

Gregorietti, Guido. *Jewelry through the Ages.* New York: Crescent Books: 1969.

Rose, Augustus F. and Cirino, Antonio. *Jewelry Making and Design.* New York: Dover Publications, 1967.

## Masks and Makeup

Botham, Mary and Sharrad, L. *The Manual of Wig Making.* London: Heinemann, 1964.

Buchman, Herman. *Film and Television Makeup.* New York: Watson-Guptill Publications, 1973.

Carson, Richard. *Stage Makeup.* New York: Appleton-Century-Crofts, Inc., 1960.

Nicoll, Allardyce. *Masks, Mimes and Miracles.* New York: Harcourt, Brace, 1931.

———. *Stuart Masques and the Renaissance Stage.* London: Harrap, 1938, 1963 edition.

Westmore, Michael. *The Art of Theatrical Makeup for Stage and Screen.* New York: McGraw-Hill, Inc., 1973.

## Fabric Design Techniques

Bemis, Elijah. *The Dyer's Companion.* New York: Dover Press, 1973.

Biegeleisen, J. I. and Cohn, Max Arthur. *Silk Screen Techniques.* New York: Dover Publications, 1942.

Birrell, Veila. *The Textile Arts.* New York: Harper and Brothers, 1959.

Blum, Stella (editor). *Victorian Fashions and Costumes from Harpers Bazaar: 1867–1898.* New York: Dover Publications, Inc. 1974.

Burris-Meyer, Elizabeth. *Color and Design in the Decorative Arts.* Englewood Cliffs, New Jersey: Prentice-Hall, 1935.

Fischer, Pauline and Lasker, Anabel. *Bargello Magic.* New York: Holt, Rinehart & Winston, 1972.

Jake, Joseph (editor). *Great Tapestries.* Switzerland: Edita Lausanne, 1965.

Kafka, Francis J. *The Hand Decoration of Fabric.* New York: Dover Publications, 1959.

Lubell, Cecil (editor). *Textile Collections of the World, Volume 2, United Kingdom and Ireland.* London: Studio Vista, 1976.

Seigler, Susan. *Needlework Patterns from the Metropolitan Museum of Art.* New York: New York Graphic Society, 1976.

Sidney, Sylvia. *Needlepoint Book.* New York: Galahad Books, 1968.

Springer, Jo. *The Pleasures of Crewel.* New York: Golden Press, 1972.

Williams, Elsa. *Heritage Embroidery.* New York: Van Nostrand Reinhold Company, 1967.

## Flowers

*Flower Arrangements* (booklet). Coca Cola Company, 1940.

# Index